Contemporary Perspectives on Politics

Contemporary Perspectives on Politics

RALPH M. GOLDMAN
San Francisco State College

 Van Nostrand Reinhold Company
NEW YORK CINCINNATI TORONTO LONDON MELBOURNE

TO AMERICAN POLITICIANS, *from Far Left to Far Right and all around The Middle, most of whom qualify as the world's most acute "people-watchers," for producing a political system that may prove to be the most adaptive yet invented by man. The genius of American politicians undoubtedly rests upon the behavioral validity of their perceptions and responses.*

Van Nostrand Reinhold Company Regional Offices:
New York   Cincinnati   Chicago   Millbrae   Dallas

Van Nostrand Reinhold Company International Offices:
London   Toronto   Melbourne

Copyright © 1972 by Litton Educational Publishing, Inc.

LIBRARY OF CONGRESS CATALOG CARD NUMBER 70–150727

Manufactured in the United States of America

Published by Van Nostrand Reinhold Company
450 West 33rd Street, New York, N. Y. 10001

Published simultaneously in Canada by
Van Nostrand Reinhold Ltd.

15 14 13 12 11 10 9 8 7 6 5 4 3 2 1

Preface

CONTEMPORARY PERSPECTIVES ON POLITICS is a survey of concepts and theories in the behavioral sciences that in recent years have come to have particular application to the study of politics. The survey is broad in scope and aims to be representative of the behavioral approaches being applied to political phenomena. The student of Political Behavior or General Social Science may use this book as a primary source, and, more generally, it will provide contemporary analytical perspectives upon the behavioral aspects of traditional subject matter in political science and other disciplines. The concepts and theories discussed in this book may be used for the analysis of events and behavior in such subfields as American Government, Comparative Politics, and International Relations.

It has become customary for students of political behavior to focus on such phenomena as (a) groups, (b) human individuals, and (c) political systems. This book is organized to examine in sequence these phenomena and the concepts usually associated with them. Thus, this survey begins with an examination of group and organization theories, leading to such associated behavioral concepts as cooperation, communication, information, linguistics, and the processes of transaction between individual and group (Chapters 1 to 4).

Chapters 5 to 8 deal primarily with the political individual and

v

view him as decision maker, participant in the choices of collectivities, leader, and target of socializing-group efforts.

The survey concludes with an examination of group and individual interactions as they reveal themselves in political conflict (Chapter 9) and as components of political systems (Chapter 10). The discussion of political systems includes consideration of some of the kinds of "practitioners" in systems architecture—planners, futurists, practical politicians, and the like—as they concern themselves with system changes and modifications.

Chapter 11 presents some of the political behaviors preferred by Americans and undertakes to describe them in language consistent with the empirical concepts and theories detailed in this survey. Thus, the preference for free speech is discussed in relation to communication theory. In this way, commonly held American political values are restated briefly in the idiom of behavioral science and examined from the points of view suggested by these behavioral theories. The restatements are the author's, whose hope it is that the intellectual problems of reinterpreting values in the light of empirical knowledge will become matters of classroom discussion and controversy. *Meshing* fact and value is as difficult an intellectual process as *differentiating* between fact and value in the first place.

For those primarily interested in the empirical perspective, this volume suggests how particular conceptual and theoretical approaches may be applied to the analysis of particular areas of political behavior. In the Foreword to Students, three types of intellectual issues—the valuational, the empirical, and the practical—are differentiated in terms of their impact on political analysis. The process of political analysis, both in theory and practice, is then outlined for the benefit of the neophyte. Most chapters are preceded by an introductory overview that highlights the concepts covered, and at the conclusion of Chapters 1 to 9 brief sketches illustrate how particular conceptual or theoretical approaches have been employed in discussion, case analysis, or testing of scientific hypotheses.

Ralph M. Goldman

San Francisco

Foreword to Students

KINDS OF INTELLECTUAL ISSUES

In addition to surveying behavioral concepts and theories, this volume attempts to bring to the student's attention three types of intellectual issues with which he usually must deal in most fields of knowledge: the *valuational*, the *empirical*, and the *practical*. Each type requires that the student ask different kinds of questions and manage his intellectual processes in different ways. (Chapter 3, particularly the sections on political statements, deals with some of the linguistic manifestations of these intellectual processes.)

To make a *value judgment* is different, intellectually speaking, from making an *empirical observation* or a *practical application* of knowledge. A value judgment responds to questions about the relative "worth" of some matter of concern to the actor. Is A worth more than B to me? What priority do I wish to place, given my subjective preferences, upon this or that thing, behavior, or event?

Empirical observations, on the other hand, refer to "things as they are." When a physician observes a particular ailment in his patient or a car owner observes a dented fender, neither may like what he sees, yet he will report and respond to the observed "facts" as he finds them. Identification of the ailment may lead the physician to recommend known remedies. The relationship between the ailment and the remedies is likely to be a consequence of prior empirical tests. Whether the physician actually makes the recommendation may depend, of course, upon his value judgments; if he likes money more than people, he may withhold his advice until compensation is assured. Similarly, the car owner, on the basis of his value judgment, may or may not do something about repairing the dented fender; the empirical fact of the dented fender remains regardless of his behavioral preferences in responding.

The practical application of knowledge, sometimes called applied science, usually calls for the translation of tested knowledge into problem-solving activity in response to existing social and political situations. For example, a candidate for public office now has available to him great amounts of tested knowledge about the voting behavior of American citizens. How he proceeds to employ that knowledge in the planning and conduct of his own election campaigns is in effect the "art" of practical application. He must first ask himself what are the results he wishes to achieve, what are the relevant aspects of reality that he must try to control, what is confirmed knowledge about these aspects of reality, and how he may mesh his attempts to influence these aspects so that chance will favor the outcome he seeks.

No one of these three types of intellectual issues is "more important" than the others. The questions raised by each type simply require that the individual make different types of choices in order to achieve different purposes. A value judgment is a choice among priorities. An empirical judgment is one that identifies degrees of satisfaction or dissatisfaction with the validity and reliability of observations about things and their relationships in the environment. Judgments about practical applications are choices among presumably relevant elements of the problem with the intention of achieving some specific outcome in the immediate future. Each type of judgment requires intellectual procedures that differ from the others, as we shall explain in Chapter 3.

The major concern of this book is the body of concepts and theories developed by behavioral scientists studying political behavior. These concepts and theories are derived from or intended for the production of scientifically tested empirical knowledge. For example, concepts such as communication, transaction, decision making, socialization, etc., become the focus here for discussing the empirical efforts of investigators interested in particular aspects of political behavior.

Of course, empirical facts, when discovered, have consequences for value judgments. People could not learn to like or dislike automobiles until certain empirical discoveries of physicists could be converted by engineers into such practical mechanisms as, say, the internal combustion engine. We now may make any number of value judgments about automobiles, liking them for this reason and disliking them for another. The same may be said about behavioral knowledge. It was once thought that the "independent voter" was a wise and knowledgeable person; empirical research indicates that he is really a disinterested and uninformed person. Given these discoveries, our value judgments about the independent voter are likely to change. Whether these value judgments change or not, we certainly can describe him very differently as a matter of political fact, that is, as an empirically observed phenomenon. We may also need to restate the grounds for our value judgments. In other words, we may still like the independent voter, but, with the new knowledge about him, we may try to educate him rather than merely assume that he is already well educated.

POLITICAL ANALYSIS: WHY AND WITH WHAT TOOLS?

When he has completed reading this survey of behavioral concepts and theories, the student will have familiarized himself with a wide range of *analytical perspectives* from which to view things which interest him in political life. He should be able to analyze his own or a friend's voting preferences. He should be able to analyze a particular decision of the President or the language of a candidate's latest speech. He should be able to analyze an international negotiation or treaty. All too often, however, students are uncertain or awkward about the procedure of analysis. In some cases they have never performed an analysis, nor do they know what it entails. In other cases students may have done innumerable analyses without realizing it.

"Analysis" is the breaking up of a whole into parts in order to examine the parts, the relationships among the parts, the extent to which the parts are present or absent under different conditions, etc. The "whole" may be a drop of water, the human body, the solar system, a political leader, a particular international war, a novel, or any other thing that the human mind wishes to consider as a single entity. As we shall see later in our discussion of language and perception theory, what human beings see and label as "wholes" or "parts" thereof are largely a matter of historical accident in the evolution of human thought. Only after certain men hypothesized and demonstrated that matter can be broken down (analyzed) into elements, and elements into molecular and atomic components, could the "whole" called water be analyzed into the elements hydrogen and oxygen. For the chemist, then, water is analyzable into two parts hydrogen and one part oxygen. When chemists confirmed the composition of H_2O, they were better able to exploit what they already knew about hydrogen and oxygen separately in order to do things (make practical applications) exploiting the presence of these elements in water. In other words, theories suggested ways of analyzing phenomena, and analyses of these phenomena led to new knowledge about their parts, and then the new knowledge could be applied in many practical ways to fulfill objectives desired by men.

Another example of analysis may be drawn from the field of anatomy. Over the centuries anatomists found it convenient and useful to dissect higher animals into components that were "muscular," "circulatory," "neural," etc. The parts of these dissections, or analyses, had been at first suggested by theories about the elements of structure as well as theories about their distinctive functions. In this way a "whole"—for example, a frog—eventually came to have its anatomy analyzed into muscular, circulatory, neural, and other systems. These "parts" were, of course, arbitrarily designated on the basis of theoretical guesses. It would be foolish to think of the whole frog as simply the sum of his muscular, circulatory, neural, and other parts. But the analysis facilitated research on the distinctive functions of the parts, the relationships among the parts, and even the similarities between the same parts of different animals. In the latter instance, for example, the neural activity of frogs was found to be comparable to neural activity of other animals.

All systematic thought and observation of the world around us involves analysis. Arbitrarily designated wholes are constantly being broken down by thinking humans into arbitrarily named parts. Usually a theoretical justification is offered for the way in which the whole is broken down as well as for the designation of the parts. Analysis alone, however, is *not* science; it is only a first step in scientific work. In science, analysis must be followed by observation of the parts that are identified and by a counting of attributes of and relationships among the parts. By observation and quantification, the scientist is able to tell us how likely it is that the attributes and relationships of the parts will occur with some stated frequency. If empirical research supports the usefulness of the analytical scheme by leading us to regularly present attributes and relationships, it continues to be used; otherwise it is discarded. Freud, for example, described the human psyche as a phenomenon made up of a "superego," an "ego," and an "id." Out of these analytical components and their relationships he built an entire theory of psychoanalysis. No one has ever observed a superego, ego, or id, but an entire profession today finds it useful to engage in the analysis of psychological problems on the basis of the theoretical relationships derived from these analytical components.

This book, then, describes many theoretical schemes for analyzing political behavior. Some of these analytical schemes have been tested against reality and found useful; e.g., the importance of reference groups in the voting decisions of citizens. On the other hand, there have been few attempts to test the propositions suggested by the theory of games of strategy, yet the analytical elements of game theory are widely recognized as extremely useful tools of rational thought in situations of conflict. The theory of games of strategy refers to such analytical components as players, prospects, payoffs, rules, strategy, information state, etc., and these lead the analyst to ask questions, derived from the analytical components of game theory, such as: Who are the *players?* What are the *rules* (resources)? What are all the probable *outcomes* of the contest? Which outcome will constitute a *payoff* for the respective players? What is the *state of information* regarding the distribution of resources in the game? These and similar questions, all parts of game theory analysis, help the analyst to "dissect" the whole conflict situation and examine its parts. Thus, in the illustrative case at the end of Chapter 9, the typical behavior of Congress is analyzed as though this behavior were a legislative "game."[1]

Therefore, if the student is asked to apply the concepts and

[1] Good examples of analyses may be found in G. T. Allison, "Conceptual Models and the Cuban Missile Crisis," *American Political Science Review,* 63 (September, 1969), 3, 689–718; and R. C. Snyder and G. D. Paige, "The United States Decision to Resist Aggression in Korea; An Application of an Analytical Scheme," *Administrative Science Quarterly,* 3 (December, 1958), 341–378. Allison, for example, shows how three different analytical schemes—policy as rational choice by a national actor, policy as the output of an organization, and policy as a political outcome—produce different views and evaluations of American action in the Cuban missile crisis.

theories of this survey to the "analysis" of some political phenomenon of interest to himself, he is being asked simply to take apart
the referent that interests him and to do so according to the components suggested by some particular concept or theory. For example, let us assume the student is asked to apply a theoretical
approach to the analysis of a particular case study of the type found
in volumes such as Allan P. Sindler, *American Political Institutions
and Public Policy* (Boston: Little, Brown, 1969), Rocco J. Tresolini
and R. T. Frost, *Cases in American National Government and Politics*
(Englewood Cliffs, N. J.: Prentice-Hall, 1966), Alan F. Westin, *The
Uses of Power* (New York: Harcourt, Brace & World, 1962), Harold
Stein, *Public Administration and Policy* (New York: Harcourt,
Brace, 1952), or the Eagleton Institute, *Cases in Practical Politics*
(New York: McGraw-Hill), and other case collections. If the student
chooses to do a "reference group analysis" of the principal decision
makers in one case, he would turn to the survey of reference group
literature and theories, determine which are the analytical components used by the theorists, and then apply these components, as
defined, and the questions they raise to the facts he finds in the
case study.

Alternately, the student may wish to develop his own case materials and apply one of the analytical schemes in the behavioral
literature to the data of his case. The way he writes up the account
of the case would again depend on the kinds of questions suggested
to him by the theoretical analytical scheme.

Whichever procedure he follows, at first the novice is likely to
prepare an analysis mainly as an intellectual exercise wherein he is
compelled to assign elements from reality to analytical categories
suggested by a theory. As he does this, he will realize a number of
things: that any number of theories may be applicable to the analysis of the same events or behavior; that the identification of the
analytical "parts" may be troublesome because of their poor definition; that the same element in the real world may be classifiable
under two or more parts of the analytical scheme; that the analysis
confuses rather than clarifies, and so on. He will also realize that
hypotheses about some of the analytical parts may be well tested
whereas hypotheses about other parts may never have been subjected
at all to empirical tests. As the novice becomes sensitive to these
analytical problems, he will be on his way to becoming expert as an
analyst, for these are the problems confronted by all theorists and
analysts.

Basically, then, an analysis usually involves the following considerations:

1. Referents of interest to the analyst, such as a political issue, some political event, a case study, a political personality, or some other type of event or behavior. These referents are presumably the "whole" to be broken down by the analysis into component parts.

2. A conceptual or theoretical perspective already available in the literature or invented by the analyst, according to which he raises certain questions about the component parts of the referent. Thus, a decision theory may be applied to the analysis of a choice made by a political leader, a socialization theory may be useful in explaining differences in citizen attitudes in different communities, a transaction theory may be applied to the bargaining process of some international conflict, etc. Each analytical scheme will direct the analyst's attention to different aspects of the referent he is studying.

3. The arrangement of the facts of the case according to the analytical categories required by the conceptual or theoretical perspective. If, for example, game theory requires that the analyst answer questions about such phenomena as players, rules, outcomes, payoffs, information states, etc., the analyst should organize and present his case data under these categoric headings. However, such arranging is more than a simple pigeon-holing process. The analyst must explain and defend his application of the analytical category to the particular phenomenon he is subsuming under it. Why does he consider individuals or groups to be "players" in the particular conflict under study? What are some of the consequences of his classifying particular persons and groups in this way? What are all the possible outcomes of the contest, and where did the analyst learn about them? In short, the arrangement of the real-life facts according to the categories suggested by the analytical scheme is only a beginning of the analytical process. Under each of the analytical categories there may well be other subcategories and further questions to be asked. Or there may be established tested knowledge about the events in some analytical category that should be noted as relevant to a better understanding of the particular case.

The novice to analysis will consider the entire process laborious and unruly. However, as on the tennis court, "practice makes perfect." In other words, analysis is an acquired intellectual skill. Only those who fumble through the first exercises can ever hope to acquire the discipline that comes with experience.

Although there are many examples of analytical work in the be-

havioral sciences that the student could examine in the scholarly
journals and in numerous books on the methodology of the behavioral sciences, this volume attempts to give the student a sense
of the variety of ways that analytical work can be done by including
at the end of each chapter an "illustrative use" of one or another
conceptual perspective discussed in that chapter. These illustrative
applications vary in detail and degree of formality. One is a brief
historical account of the development of the federal judiciary as
described from the point of view of the formalization process. Another describes the political significance of a terminological definition, that of the Korean War as a "police action." In still another
illustration, the findings of research on party leaders are reported
from the perspective of leadership theory. In every illustrative case
the object is to show the student how some familiar phenomena
may be examined and discussed by applying the questions and
gathering data relevant to particular conceptual and theoretical
analytical schemes.[2]

The student must always remember, however, that concepts and
theories are human artifacts, that is, created compositions of language, which may or may not help us perceive, analyze, gather data
about, and possibly control the realities that we call "political." He
should not be discouraged by the large number of untested and
unvalidated theories and paradigms produced by behavioral scientists. Many of these are essentially little more than proposals for
further inquiry. If the student wants to know how behavioral
scientists "talk to each other" on particular theoretical issues, the
student needs to "listen in" and at least recognize the content of
the discussions even though he may not believe or go along with
much that is said. If the student wishes to gain analytical insight
and skill, he needs to struggle with the problems of analysis even
though he may do so with untested and sometimes awkward theoretical schemes. Hopefully, the student will eventually see this analytical activity as an effort to sustain a disciplined communication
process rather than as a game of inventing a facile jargon.

This book takes the position that the idiom of the behavioral
sciences is not a way of creating academic fences between the various
disciplines but rather a tool for building intellectual pathways to

_____

[2] More advanced examples of the application of theoretical models may be found
in Matilda W. Riley, *Sociological Research* (New York: Harcourt, Brace & World,
1963).

previously isolated segments of human experience and knowledge. The President of the United States, for example, is a man like any other, but perhaps one with special experiences, skills, and working situations. To know about the President's behavior under these circumstances is, in the liberal intellectual tradition, to seek knowledge also about one's self. And this, of course, is the purpose of all effort to produce and communicate knowledge.

Acknowledgments

An author's intellectual history is as much autobiographical as conceptual. This, therefore, is the place to acknowledge accumulated personal, professional, and intellectual debts. These include, in order of "autobiographical impact": Theresa Wolfson, Austin Wood, Albert Somit, Avery Leiserson, Charles M. Hardin, the late Quincy Wright, E. M. Kirkpatrick, Paul T. David, Bertram M. Gross, Malcolm Moos, Laurin Henry, Richard C. Bain, Richard Rudner, David Easton, and the late Morton Grodzins. In one way or another each of these colleagues and friends tempered my efforts along the way, for which I am eternally grateful.

This textbook and perhaps the "behavioral approach" in general would not have been possible without the professional statesmanship of that hardy band including, in addition to Easton, David B. Truman, Alexander Heard, Samuel J. Eldersveld, Morris Janowitz, Samuel Huntington, Gabriel Almond, Alfred de Grazia, Robert Dahl, and Heinz Eulau. The more contemporary and perhaps more ardent behaviorists ought not forget the contributions of these midwives of change in the intellectual climate of the political science profession. And even this group had its guiding hand in E. Pendleton Herring, who inspired and nurtured their efforts.

A number of editors have influenced the shape of this book, for which I offer thanks: James U. Rundle, Gardner M. Spungin, and

Jeremy Gowing. Denise Rathbun guided manuscript into print with energy and wisdom.

My colleagues, Mrs. Susan (James) Hobart and Jeff Fishel, have tried out the text in the classroom, with encouraging results.

My wife Joan, son Peter, and daughter Meg have endured listening to the material and the tales of authorship for almost a decade. They seem to believe that it could have been written in one-tenth the time. I admire their judgment, their patience, and them as well. For Peter, Meg, and their generation, I hope this volume may suggest some of the exciting new directions in human self-awareness and self-management now opening in the behavioral sciences.

Ralph M. Goldman

San Francisco

Contents

Introduction to a Behavioral Approach

The last quarter century has seen the acceptance of the *behavioral approach* in the discipline of political science. What is distinctive about this approach? How does the behavioral perspective relate to the long-run concerns of political science? What is there in the content of behavioral science generally that has been brought to bear upon the study of politics?

POLITICAL SCIENCE FROM ANCIENT GREECE TO MODERN AMERICA

People, of course, were acting politically long before scholars and politicians began to analyze, describe, and study the relationships and objects that came to be called "political." About three thousand years ago, the Greek city-states achieved the kind of general affluence that has come to be associated with intellectual and cultural advancement. Thus, some individuals were able to devote their time to the observation of the more enduring features of men's political life. The historian, Herodotus, writing about 450 B.C., reported a remarkable increase in theorizing among the people regarding the governments of the Greek city-states. In order to examine governmental organization more precisely, the Greeks began to categorize governments into three standard types: monarchy, aristocracy, and dem-

1

ocracy. These categories were derived from observations about *"who ran things."* In a *monarchy*, one man above all others made the big decisions. An *aristocracy* existed if a handful of prominent individuals worked openly together to run the community. If large numbers of leaders and citizens came together with some regularity in public meeting places to decide certain issues of widespread concern, the city-state was a *democracy*, or *polity* in Aristotle's term. Thus, a way of classifying something called "government" emerged and has endured in the discussions of political writers across the centuries.

Such focused discussion produces a *discipline*, a deliberate and relatively well-organized examination of particular concepts and questions that preoccupy thoughtful men. Thus the discipline of political science may be said to have begun when Socrates (470–399 B.C.) invited the attention of philosophers, who then concentrated upon studying the natural environment, to the subject of man. What should be of greater concern to men, he argued, than men themselves—alone, in groups, in communities, and in the great variety of their conduct?

In approximately 375 B.C., Plato (428–348 B.C.), an Athenian aristocrat who was a student of Socrates, established The Academy, the first school that engaged in pursuits similar to those of a modern university. Like Socrates, Plato believed that nothing could be more important than each human individual's educating himself to the maximum of his capacity.

While individuals vary in intelligence and potential, it is generally easy, in Plato's opinion, to identify a "good" carpenter, a "good" doctor, etc., on the basis of the degree of excellence in the performance of pertinent functions. A "good" man, in turn, performs such activities as exercising wisdom, displaying courage, acting with temperance, and making decisions with justice. The man who does all of this well is a completely good man. From this functional analysis of the behavior of human individuals, Plato develops his theory of government. Rulers must not only maintain their communities as organizations but must also use every resource of these communities to help each citizen perfect himself to the maximum of his own potential. To rule is to educate, according to Plato; the state is, above all, an educational institution.

Plato's student, Aristotle (384–322 B.C.), also premised his theoretical work upon certain generalizations about human beings. Man is the only animal whom nature has "endowed with the gift of speech." "It is a characteristic of man that he alone has any sense of good and evil, of just and unjust, and the like, and the association of living beings who have this sense makes a family and a state." Thus, "man is by nature an animal intended to live in a *polity*," that is, a political association.

Somewhat more than his mentor, Aristotle was concerned with "methods" of study. He took much more seriously the procedures of comparing similar things. He, in fact, supervised a comparative study of some 158 Greek city-state constitutions. He also looked quite closely at the genetic or developmental features of things in order to try to understand their characteristics better, for example, his well-known reference to the acorn as having within its "nature" the elements and capacity to become an oak tree. Similarly, he saw the household and family as the elementary form of political association, in which the male is to the female and children what the ruler is to the citizens and slaves. The village, as a cluster of families, is the next more complicated form of political association; the *polis*, made up of a number of villages, is the political community at its fullest development.

During the century before the birth of Christ, numerous Roman philosophers carried on Aristotle's interest in constitutions as the source of rules for citizen conduct. Cicero (106–43 B.C.) spoke of "a people," in the political sense, as "an assemblage of people in large numbers associated in an agreement with respect to justice and a partnership for the common good." Along these lines, the Roman Empire developed its greatest contribution to Western civilization: a legal system in which the conceptions of social contract and justice were carefully refined for practical application to human relations.

When dealing with the important question of the origins of laws, the Romans developed a distinction between the universal laws of nature and God and those laws which were the conventions of a corporate body, such as the state. The distinction between natural or "divine" law and conventional law remains with us to this day. It was clearly reinforced when Emperor Constantine (279–337 A.D.) made Christianity the empire's official religion.

Soon the Catholic Church emerged as one of mankind's most active and significant corporate law-making bodies. Writing in 413 A.D., St. Augustine set forth the basic theory of political and social behavior upon which the Church rested its claim to legislative pre-eminence: Without redemption, human individuals do not amount to much; the state, therefore, exists to improve the relationship between each soul and God. Men may attain membership in the City of God only by the gift of grace, and the conferment of grace involves the sacraments of the Church. Thus the Church stands in the position of discoverer, interpreter, and administrator of natural, or divine, law. The medieval discussions of canon and secular law, with all their cosmological and behavioral assumptions, continued over several hundred years, eventually summarized in the works of Thomas Aquinas (1225–1274).

Medieval and Renaissance monarchs could hardly remain enthusiastic about their subordinated status within the framework of Church philosophy, and royal strategists eventually preempted the philosophical and conceptual tools developed by the Church. For example, over the centuries the Church had developed the College of Cardinals as the principal "representative" assembly of mankind as a spiritual constituency. Before long, the monarchs referred to themselves as the representatives of another kind of constituency, the secular nation. The Protestant Reformation, launched by Martin Luther (1483–1546) and John Calvin (1509–1564), by fostering the development of national churches, appreciably aided the kings in their resistance to the political domination of the Catholic Church. It was but a short philosophical leap to a theory of the "divine origin" of kings as defenders of the nation's spiritual life as well as its political order. This leap held the attention of students of politics for two centuries.

As the struggle between popes and kings evolved, a Florentine named Niccolo Machiavelli (1469–1527) began to write his observations about the management of political communities (special kinds of groups), political leaders (individuals with special skills), and political behavior. The latter, in individual men, was based on universal attributes of ingratitude, fickleness, deceitfulness, avidity, and eagerness to avoid danger. According to Machiavelli, these psychological traits, not divine or natural law, were the raw material of government. Men govern men and stand or fall on the basis of their skill in attaining and maintaining power through the management of these raw materials.

Writing from about 1640 to 1651, Thomas Hobbes, secretary to Lord Chancellor Francis Bacon of England and a supporter of King James I, took up the discussion of men's political relations. Hobbes' defense of strong monarchy was in part a reaction to the chaos created by the English civil wars and in part premised upon his psychological assumptions that the lives of human individuals in precivil society are "poor, nasty, brutish, and short," and that men are insatiable in their desires, irrational, and unable to control their own behavior. "The passions that incline men to peace are fear of death, desire of such things as are necessary to commodious living, and hope by their industry to obtain them." Self-preservation, therefore, compels men to enter into contracts with each other to form political communities. Kings are the *product* of these contracts, hence not a party to them. Thus, the nation is essentially a legal body, created by common agreement, and obliged to follow the dictates of the head which may use force and fear, for its purpose according to agreement is to ensure the survival of the collectivity.

For many this was too much prerogative to concede to any human being. The king's authority must be curtailed by the *natural rights* of his subjects, according to John Locke (1632–1704). Human beings are sociable as well as self-interested, he wrote. "Being all equal and independent, no one ought to harm another in his life, health, liberty, or possessions." Governments and laws, including those of kings, exist to preserve the equalities among individual rights; this was the principal reason for entering the social contract described by the Romans and Hobbes. Citizens could easily test the utility of the contract by their observations and judgments about how well their own lives, liberties, and property were protected by it. These arguments set the ground for most modern utilitarian and empirical analyses of politics. Locke also helped shift philosophical attention from *royal* sovereignty to *popular* sovereignty.

Developing this popular perspective were Jean Jacques Rousseau (1712–1778), Jeremy Bentham (1748–1833), and Karl Marx (1818–1883). Rousseau placed the political community—from which emanated the *general will*—on a philosophical pedestal. While human behavior is governed by self-preservation and self-interest, it is, according to Rousseau, tempered by compassion and a feeling of natural good will. This good will becomes, in the larger group, a general will which regulates the conduct of its members. What is good for the collectivity is somehow transformed into more than the total of all individual self-interests, and so a subordination of the members to the general will is required.

Bentham assumed that men are essentially reactors to pleasurable and painful stimuli. Men have been clever in creating institutions that help maximize the attainment of the pleasurable. Political arrangements that help the community discover the greatest good for the greatest number are therefore to be cherished and nurtured. Since the judgment as to what is "pleasurable" or "good" is relative and can be a matter of honorable disagreement among men, the community's judgments should be overt, readily observed empirically, and constantly subject to confirmation.

Marx, on the other hand, carried Rousseauian concern for the collectivity to its extreme. Since a man's personal life and social relationships are, according to Marx, wholly determined by the community's system of production, the evolution, character, and control of that production system must be of primary concern to the student of politics.

Notice that the study of politics over the centuries was carried on mainly in the Greek academies, among the Roman lawyers, in the Church, on the medieval and Renaissance royal staffs, and at the universities. Within the universities, political studies were primarily the concern of philosophers and historians. Toward the end of the nineteenth century, the first distinct academic departments for political knowledge were established. At first, the dominant specialities within the political science field, reflecting its evolution, were constitutional law, political philosophy, and public administration. Today, the well-developed political science department offers such specialized fields as ancient, medieval, and modern political theory; American politics, in its national, state, and local aspects and/or its legislative, administrative, and judicial aspects; comparative politics; and international relations. In the last decade or two, political behavior has become "an approach" incorporated within the above subfields, although in some departments of political science, political behavior is considered a distinct field. Both these tendencies reflect the rapid growth and influence of behavioral literature since the early 1920s.[1]

Paving the way for the behavioral approach were the writings of

---

[1] For excellent reviews of the recent history of the political behavior approach, see Heinz Eulau's treatment in Bert F. Hoselitz, *A Reader's Guide to the Social Sciences* (Glencoe, Ill.: Free Press, 1959), and Robert A. Dahl, "The Behavioral Approach in Political Science," *American Political Science Review* (December 1961), 763–772, E. M. Kirkpatrick, "The Impact of the Behavioral Approach on Traditional Political Science," in Austin Ranney (ed.), *Essays on the Behavioral Study of Politics* (Urbana, Ill.: University of Illinois Press, 1962), pp. 1–29, and David B. Truman, "The Impact of the Behavioral Revolution in Political Science," in Stephen K. Bailey et al., *Research Frontiers in Politics and Government* (Washington, D.C.: Brookings Institution, 1955).

Arthur F. Bentley, Graham Wallas, and Charles Merriam. In a classic work, *The Process of Government,* Bentley, in 1908, urged academicians to observe political groups, large and small, as the best way of discovering the particular characteristics of political processes. Not the written constitutional and legal rules but rather the way in which human beings respond to these rules in their actual life situation is the road to knowledge about politics, according to Bentley. It is simple to read an election law, but more important to find out how a precinct runs.

In the same year, Wallas, an English philosopher, argued for a psychological revival in political studies. Even if we assume, as did the rationalists of the eighteenth and nineteenth centuries, that man is basically a "rational animal," Wallas noted that the irrational appears to be such a predominant part of political events that it certainly merits careful study.

Much of this sociological and psychological advice went unheeded until Charles E. Merriam wrote *New Aspects of Politics* in 1925 and inaugurated the "Chicago School" of political science. This school was characterized by its interdisciplinary interests and its empirical commitments, as typified by Harold D. Lasswell's adaptation of psychoanalytic theories to political behavior and Harold F. Gosnell's field studies of political party organization and voting behavior. Further impetus came from E. Pendleton Herring, who, as president of the Social Science Research Council, influenced the volume and quality of work by political behaviorists.

During the 1930s great advances in research technology stimulated the productivity of the behavioral sciences and promoted the acceptance of their outputs. Improved sampling techniques, new operational conceptions of *attitude,* and confirmation of precisely stated hypotheses led to new knowledge about communication processes and voting decisions. Such reports as *The People's Choice* (1944), *Voting,* (1954), *The Voter Decides* (1954), and other voting studies provided mountains of scientific data about the political individual and his group affiliations as observed in the election situation.

Over these same decades, the conceptual boundaries among the behavioral sciences also tended to change, in fact, crumble. The decision theories of economists and psychologists began to filter into the organization theories of political scientists. The theory of games of strategy, at first a product of mathematical and economic analyses, began to be applied to political phenomena. Social psychology's role theory and reference group theory were drawn into analyses of political behavior. Equilibrium and systems theories of the engineers and conflict theories of the sociologists began to appear in discussions of political processes.

Interdisciplinary communication has also revived the age-old question of the distinctions between "political" phenomena and other things. What is it that we classify as "politics"? Is the election of a pope less "political" than the election of a president? Is war more "political" than a street fight between neighborhood gangs? Professional disagreement about the definition of the term is sharp and as old as the discussions of the classical Greeks. In the last analysis, definition is the prerogative of each of us. From the point of view of the political science profession, definition becomes a matter of recurrent and continued usage. In this latter sense, *politics* is a term that has tended most often to refer to activities associated with legal government, the loci of power in society, or "any persistent pattern of human relationships that involves, to a significant extent, power, rule, or authority" (Robert A. Dahl's definition). David Easton suggests that "what distinguishes political interaction from all other kinds of social interactions is that they are predominantly oriented toward the authoritative allocations of values for a society."[2] Obviously the matter of definition is not one that is likely to be easily or soon resolved, and the political behaviorist is likely to opt for definitions that are more, rather than less, comprehensive.

THE BEHAVIORAL APPROACH TODAY

The *behavioral approach* is relatively new as a separate subfield in the contemporary discipline of political science. However, as we shall see below, certain of the chief characteristics of this approach have roots as ancient as the academies of Greece, a fact that is sometimes overlooked by those political scientists who are eager to be avant-garde and fail to pay due credit to the "primitives" in their discipline.

The principal characteristics of the behavioral approach may be listed as follows:

[2] David Easton, *Framework for Political Analysis* (Englewood Cliffs, N.J.: Prentice-Hall, 1965), p. 50.

1. Empirical procedures of observation
2. Individuals and groups as focal referents
3. An interdisciplinary conceptual language
4. A commitment to scientific explanation and prediction.

As the student reads this book and goes beyond it into the literature of the discipline (some 90 percent of whose producers work in the United States), he should keep these characteristics in mind as he endeavors to distinguish between the behavioral and other approaches.

Empirical Procedures

Political behavior is devoted to direct observation of the environment and how it works. However, empirical procedures did not emerge full-blown with contemporary behaviorism, nor are they technically anywhere near perfect. Primitive forms of empirical procedure may be found in the studies prepared by Aristotle, Machiavelli, and Hobbes. Contemporary forms of the empirical craft are exemplified by the investigations of the Chicago School and the University of Michigan Survey Research Center.

Research technology is constantly in process of development and improvement. To distinguish between "primitive" and "contemporary" in empirical procedures is perhaps an overly simple way of referring to stages of development. From this point of view, however, many political behaviorists have been vulnerable to criticism for the great gap between the *sound* of their methodological aspirations and the primitive *quality* of their achievements. It is not easy to devise techniques for observing the behavior of millions of citizens or of political leaders in the privacy of their conferences. Lone scholars have difficulty in directly observing the activities of entire governments or all aspects of such complex events as war. Yet, since these are some of the phenomena to which political behaviorists apply their relatively modest empirical procedures, large methodological tasks obviously still lie ahead of them.

Empiricism calls for observation conducted under the constraints of preselected focal referents, quantified accounting of elements and relationships, and public reporting of the findings. The empiricist is methodologically committed not only to direct observation by himself or others, he must also proclaim ahead of time what segments of the environment he will examine. If he claims to be looking at one thing but winds up really looking at another, the empiricist must be explicit about this shift or else be penalized for breaking a rule of scientific procedure.

The empiricist is also committed to the achievement, if not immediately then eventually, of some degree of quantification of the objects and relationships he claims to be observing. He counts things so that he can generalize about the degrees of their similarity or difference. He counts so that he can make estimates of the probability of their recurrence under controlled or specified conditions.

Finally, the empiricist is bound to the commitment of publishing his findings. This is the requirement that makes scientific work a public process. The "scientist" who insists upon keeping his procedures and findings secret or who insists that others take *his* word regarding the facts without opportunity to examine the procedures by which he arrived at them is not only suspect, he is entirely out of bounds.

In these ways, empiricism contrasts with introspection, personal and nonreplicable quantifications, intuition, and similar types of intellectual activity. These latter intellectual pursuits are not less legitimate; they are simply different. Empirical procedures are *efficient* if they result in a progressive reduction of error and uncertainty regarding the relationships among observed elements of an event, and it is the intersubjective and public commitment of empiricism that tends to produce the cumulative advances in knowledge.

Let us examine briefly some examples of empiricism in its more primitive forms.

Aristotle collected some 158 Greek city-state constitutions in order to examine them directly and compare them with each other as documents as well as with accounts of their actual operation in practice. The students of his lyceum prepared historical case studies, somewhat like the term research papers students prepare today, incorporating as evidence the direct observations and reports of others. From this large number of cases Aristotle was able to generalize with some confidence about various elements and relationships.

Even though certain evaluative prejudgments were implied by his analytical categories—the ideal or "good" versus the perverted or "bad" types —this did not bias the reporting of events that he and his students carried on. In fact, his intense interest in discovering which were important attributes in the enduring "good" city-states motivated him to be as careful and quantitative about his observations as possible. If certain conditions such as "distributive justice" were found with great consistency in the "good" communities, Aristotle wanted to know and be sure of this so that his findings could be applied to the preservation of "good" and the modification of "bad" cases. Even in Aristotle's day, careful empirical craftsmanship and intense personal preferences were not mutually antithetical so long as the empirical procedures were explicit, careful, and relatively quantitative.

It was Machiavelli who made the first substantial methodological argument for separating out one's empirical efforts from those attending to the good-bad or ethical aspects. Machiavelli warned that one's evaluations of goodness or badness could tend to distort observation, confuse actual political events with hoped-for political goals, and produce biased reporting. While he did not always adhere to the distinction in his own writings, Machiavelli claimed to be concerned with what men do rather than what they ought to do, that is, with empirical observation rather than ethical recommendation. Using a comparative method, he drew upon historical case studies of government and political events in Renaissance Italy and other nations reported in the history books available for study in that day. Thus, Machiavelli tested some of his behavioral generalizations by examining comparable events and regimes.

Hobbes was even more self-consciously committted to a scientific approach. He used the logical and mathematical procedures and style popular among seventeenth-century rational philosophers. Hobbes also turned to the record of human history for data confirming his propositions. For his argument supporting absolute monarchy he drew most heavily from existing cases, that is, the England of James I, Charles I, and the Cromwellian dictatorship. Hobbes failed, however, to exercise as careful an empiricism to test his psychological assumptions about human behavior. His political science was premised upon a view of man as selfish and contentious, of authority as the "child of fear," and of group membership as the only constraining force in the lives of individual men. He never checked out these psychological assumptions.

Contemporary empiricism, perhaps examining narrower segments of the political environment and following more constraining rules of empirical procedure, is no more or less devoted to observation than the primitive empiricists. When Gosnell of the Chicago School wanted to study party and electoral behavior, his empirical procedures included such demanding observational tasks as direct interview of party politicians and examination of election returns. When Lasswell endeavoured to apply psychoanalytic concepts to the examination of politicians, he turned to biography and the psychoanalytic depth interview as his principal empirical procedures.

With the arrival of the attitudinal survey, students of political behavior became more fully aware of the demands of contemporary empirical procedure for observational methods, quantitative reports, and logical inferences. A respondent's answer to an interview question is a small event to observe, a difficult one to quantify, and a risky one from which to draw an inference. Nonetheless, many of the challenges have been met and the volume of well-confirmed knowledge has been impressive. Observe the language and quantitative references in the following statements drawn from a major study of electoral behavior: "In assessing the impact on behavior of the public's cognitive and affective map of politics we will have to describe this map in terms of *individual* attitudes." In other words, the authors are telling us that they are going to observe something called "individual attitudes" in order better to explain how the electorate's knowledge and values produce certain political events.

In another place: "Across the full national electorate the multiple correlation of the six dimensions of attitude [i.e., six variables being observed by the investigators] with the partisan decision [that actually occurred] was greater than 0.7 both in 1952 and 1956, and the magnitude of these coefficients is the more impressive if we keep in mind that they have been depressed by errors of measurements and other factors. . . ." In short, contemporary empiricists not only go out and look for themselves by taking national sample surveys of attitudes but also do so by creating carefully controlled conditions (the careful design of the questionnaire, the training of interviewers, etc.) and by very explicit quantitative reports whose degree of validity the reader may assess exactly.

The studies of voting behavior, we must keep in mind, are only a beginning. Successful procedures have yet to be developed for the observation, quantification, and reporting of many other political phenomena than voting actions. The field is wide open for inventive research technologists.

Focal Referents

The political behaviorist tends to have particular objects in the environment to which he typically directs his attention. Here again, we can better understand the behavioral approach by briefly examining some of the things that have been the center of observational attention in other eras and disciplines.

The scholars of ancient Asia Minor and the Mediterranean communities directed their attention to the physical elements water, air, fire, and earth. Each, some combination, or all of these were the stuff of which all things are made, according to these ancient theorists. In time, they became attentive not only to these structural components but also to the relationships among them, particularly as those relationships remained stable or changed over time.

By the beginning of the fifth century B.C., the focal referents of these ancient observers included, in addition to the structural elements water, air, etc, relationships among such elements as love and strife, and such process consequences as change, motion and reincarnation. Just speculate how influential the selection of these particular focal referents has proved over the centuries, as countless students have accumulated large bodies of evidence concerning them and put the information into fairly well-organized fields of knowledge. Think, for example, how the observation of fire led to the concept of temperature, the development of thermometers as instruments for measuring temperature, and the production of atomic explosions (viewed as "fire-events").

Socrates was, as we have noted, the most influential "caller of attention" to man himself as a referent. Socrates, Plato, and Aristotle sought to identify the psychological, social, and political attributes which, if adequately understood and controlled, might enable man to achieve the purest manifestations of his distinctive attributes. Therefore, they spoke of virtue, knowledge, goodness, causality, and all the other names they gave to referents that came to be the pillars of much of Western civilization's intellectual heritage.

The principal focal referents of medieval political scholars tended to be the few most highly organized manifestations of political life of their day: the Catholic Church and the feudal kingdoms that subsequently became nations. During the seventeenth and eighteenth centuries, scholars gave most of their attention to major political personages such as kings and their prime ministers, as well as to a few large-scale systems of relationship such as war, administration of justice, and management of the economy. To this list were soon added such major political items as constitutions and laws.

In 1908, Bentley urged students of politics to forget about the isolated incidents and the dead documents. His preference was to have scientific attention paid to the activities of human groups. Wallas at this time called for still another focal referent: individual psychology in its irrational and emotional aspects. From the 1920s to the 1940s the group as a focal referent did catch on in American political science as studies of pressure groups, political parties, legislatures, and bureaucracies were produced. The focus on individual psychology came via the psychoanalytic route as part of the rapidly spreading Freudian influence, although elite and leadership studies were an important aspect of this tendency as well.

The data produced by the voting studies of the 1940s and 1950s directed attention to both the individual and the group, and these became the hallmark of the contemporary behavioral approach. The voting act is, after all, an individual decision. Surveys were able to ask questions about the group affiliations of the individual respondent and relate these to his voting tendencies. Given the refinements of probability sampling, investigators were able to draw inferences from the data about both the political personalities of the voters and the nature of the political influence of particular types of groups in society.

In the last decade or so, the attention of political behaviorists has tended to include not only such structural elements as persons and groups, but also abstractly conceptualized relationships among them (role, reference groups, and the like), as well as the process consequences of such relationships (cooperation, conflict, institutional change). This book will pay much heed to the later perspectives, that is, the relational and the developmental.

Conceptual Language

Concepts are linguistic terms (though nonlinguistic symbols are also used, as we shall see later) that help the observer of the environment and his fellow observers identify and look at the same referents. As fields of knowledge develop, they tend to acquire a body of major or central concepts of their own. This happens, presumably, because the members of a discipline are usually interested in "talking the same language" and looking at the same sorts of things in the environment. We can say that certain concepts tend to be "indigenous" to particular disciplines. The following roster represents a sampling of the major concepts *traditionally* indigenous to the study of politics:

absolutism	feudalism	power
anarchy	freedom	property
aristocracy	government	purpose
authority	individualism	rational
autocracy	institution	representation
citizen	justice	republic
collectivism	law	revolution
commonwealth	legislature	right
communism	legitimacy	ruler
compromise	liberty	security
consensus	majority	socialism
conservative	mandate	society
constitution	minority	sovereignty
contract	monarchy	state
democracy	nation	subjects
education	oligarchy	suffrage
elite	order	toleration
empire	patriotic	tyranny
equality	plutocracy	virtue
executive	policy	vote
fascism	politics	war
federalism	polity	will

Each concept has been, in a sense, a candle in the dark casting its light to help in the observation of small segments of the political environment. A concept is a prosthetic device, similar to a pair of binoculars whose quality has a great deal to do with the sharpness and magnification with which an observer sees objects in the world around him. In still another sense, a concept may, as a result of social usage, become value-laden. Conceivably a pair of binoculars could also be called "peeping tube," obviously denigrating the device because of some "bad" use to which it may be put.

Political science concepts have been developed and utilized in ways implied by these various senses. Viscount Henry St. John Bolingbroke, the eighteenth-century English statesman, introduced the concept of *political party* as he observed certain group behavior within Parliament. The term aided the perception of such American political writers as James Madison and his partisan colleagues, who spoke and wrote interchangeably of "parties" and "factions." Interestingly, the Federalist writers tended to deny the existence of parties, calling them by other names and refusing to study them as objects worthy of their attention.

Political science concepts also have quite variable quality. Some are dull tools and others are sharp. Another way of saying this is that some are vague in meaning and obscure in referent while others are well defined and highly specific as to referent; that is, they are *operationalized*. The political scientist who writes about power continues to find it difficult to tell his reader exactly what it is that is being looked at, measured, and generalized about. On the other hand, a political scientist using contemporary definitions of political attitude can identify what he means with sufficient concreteness of referent and measurability of units as to make it clear to his reader what he has in mind; attitude is a well-defined and well-operationalized concept in much the same way that temperature has been operationalized by the development of the thermometer.

One of the more troublesome problems of conceptual development in political science is the prevalence of value-laden terms. Political activity is full of conflict. The key terms of some of the older writings, as a consequence, come to have "good" or "bad" connotations; for example, *power* has been, almost by definition, corrupt and evil; *political parties* and *factions* have been "bad." A "proper" study of politics often meant paying attention to "good" things and turning away from the "bad." We can all agree that fevers are uncomfortable and symptomatic of some unhappy state of illness. However, the more knowledgeable will appreciate that the concept *fever* is itself neither good nor bad, simply a condition of temperature to be observed, interpreted, and perhaps acted upon by the observer. In political science, there is fortunately an increasing tendency to distinguish between value-laden concepts and those that are simply tools; for example, *pressure group* is often used derogatorily, whereas *organized interest* refers to the same phenomenon, but with the observer's evaluational preconceptions set aside.

One final comment concerning contemporary conceptual usage in political behavior studies. Often the members of an academic discipline become quite possessive about the indigenous concepts with which they work. The anthropologist may become a little nervous if a political science colleague refers to "political cultures." A sociologist may take exception to a political scientist working in the field of reference group theory. On the other hand, a political scientist may look askance at a political science colleague who concerns himself with the personality attributes of citizens; that's the concern of psychologists, he would say. Contemporary political behaviorists tend to have little respect for the disciplinary boundaries across which they carry their concepts. They tend to be interdisciplinary. They have even gone to a field as apparently remote as mechanics to pick up the concept *equilibrium*.

Here is a short list of some of the conceptual language drawn from various disciplines that is likely to be found in the political behavior literature:

affect	equilibrium	participation
apathy	expectation	party
attitude	function	perception
behavior	game	personality
belief	goal	pluralism
coalition	gratification	process
cognition	group	propaganda
cohesion	ideology	reinforcement
communication	identification	relation
conflict	indoctrination	reputation
conformity	information	role
cooperation	integrative	sanction
crosspressure	interaction	situation
cybernetics	interests	socialization
decision	loyalty	stability
deference	manipulation	status
deprivation	norm	sample
deterrence	opinion	system
deviancy	organization	valuation

Prediction

There is a great difference between soothsaying and scientific saying. The soothsayer will claim to forecast events, but never tell his listener how he too may arrive at the same forecast, that is, what factors to take into account in making the forecast, or with what probabilities, quantitatively stated, the forecast is likely to occur or not occur. The scientist, on the other hand, predicts in the sense that he forecasts events that may occur under clearly specified conditions and with quantitatively stated probabilities. The scientist will make his prediction in somewhat these terms: "If conditions A and B occur together with X degree of relationship and Y frequency, then, in the future, whenever condition A is found so will B in the degree X and the frequency Y."

Prediction and forecasting are an accepted part of the American scene. There is much interest in the United States in maintaining statistical records, best-guessing, and risk taking. Sports fans and weather fans abound, and they understand the language of previous record and future prospects. Forecasting is popular, and there is even a tendency to place on a pedestal the prognosticator who turns out to be right despite the odds. Few events have done as much to elevate the respectability of the behavioral approach as the successful forecast of the 1936 presidential election by the Gallup Poll, whose sampling of just a couple of thousand American voters proved to be correct whereas the *Literary Digest* Poll of millions of voters turned out to be dramatically wrong.[3]

Few performances are as impressive as the laboratory scientist who combines materials and elements in a prestated way and is able to tell you exactly what is going to happen. The behavioral approach, therefore, rests heavily upon its search for factors and evidence from which to make scientific explantions and predicitions.[4]

Because it involves comments on future events and states of affairs, prediction may be easily misunderstood. Plato, for example, spoke of future states of affairs *aspirationally;* that is, "good" men *should* strive for the ideal state which Plato believed would include, for instance, philosopher kings and polygamy. To aspire to some future condition is, of course, quite different from stating the probabilities of its occurrence. Aristotle, on the other hand, spoke of future states of affairs *developmentally;* that is, as invariant out-

---

[3] That forecasting success was somewhat tarnished by the polls' forecast of a Dewey victory in the 1948 presidential race. President Truman never let the pollsters forget their error. For the polling organizations, on the other hand, the error was a reminder of the limitations of their scientific procedures, and they proceeded to refine those procedures and related methodological safeguards.

[4] In a strict sense, explanation and prediction are logically the same and take the same propositional format. To say that C occurs every time A and B are found together in X degree and Y frequency sounds like explanation, but it is logically the same as the prediction, "If A and B occur together in X degrees and Y frequency, then C will occur."

comes of certain present conditions. In his case, the estimate of probability was somewhat overstated, that is, 100 percent. To this day it is difficult for thoughtful people to grasp fully the distinction between *desired* future states of affairs (goals, purposes, objectives) and *probable* future states of affairs, or outcomes likely to occur given specified antecedent or contingent conditions.

Even more difficult, how does one apply the *desire* for some future condition to the observed *prospects* that the condition may actually occur? An example may be helpful. In the United States, the "independent voter" is highly revered. This conception of voting is reflected in such phrases as "the man above the party" and in the legal arrangements for permitting voters to register as "independents." This independent voter has been glorified in some writings as if he were a philosopher carefully deliberating and deciding on the basis of all the facts available. If that is not the way the voter really behaves, it is suggested, it is the way *he ought to* in the future. Unfortunately, behavioral research has discovered that this much touted "independence" consists of attitudes related to inertia, disinterest, and sheer lack of political information. Conversely, behavioral research shows that the more educated the voter, the more likely he will be strongly affiliated with one or the other political party.

What do those who hold the aspirational conception of the independent voter do with such findings? Their first reaction might be to attack the behaviorists as liars and destroyers of American values. With a little more thought, however, those who cherish voter independence will accept the empirical conditions reported by behavioral scientists, but continue to work toward their valued goal by fighting inertia and distinterest with education, by accepting the political party as a legitimate vehicle of politics, and by creating the conditions within these parties for the exercise of independence and insurgency by the well-educated voters who are party-affiliated. The political behaviorist has given the promoters of independence a more realistic account of existing, contingent circumstances with which they must work to achieve their goal.

The political science profession has been beset in recent years by a nagging—and usually fruitless and boring—controversy between so-called "traditionalists" and "behavioralists" (who prefer to be called "behaviorists"). In their more extreme statements, the former argue that a "science of politics" is improbable, unpromising, and, at worst, untruthful (about its findings). On the other side, the behaviorists, many of them still poorly or entirely untrained in the rigorous procedures of scientific work, reiterate their faith—not their achievement, which remains relatively small—in the scientific route to political progress, at the same time deriding the traditionalists for their intuitiveness and value-laden accounts of political reality.

More recently, still another faction has emerged in the profession to engage the behaviorists, namely, the highly ideological "activists" who insist, for example, that the political science profession *as a profession* (rather than as individual citizens who happen also to be political scientists) take policy stands on race relations, the war in Vietnam, and other highly charged contemporary political issues. The activists argue that most behavioral research tends to produce results so slowly that it lags far behind the practical policy needs of the times, and, further, when such research does produce scientific findings, these tend to be conservative, that is, supportive of the political status quo. In his presidential address to the American Political Science Association in 1969, David Easton described these as "the battle cries of *relevance* and *action*," heralding a "postbehavioral revolution." The new activists, Easton observed, hold that neutrality is impossible. "For the aphorism of science that it is better to be wrong than vague, post-behavioralism would substitute a new dictum, that it is better to be vague than non-relevantly precise."

Much of the debate among the factions may, however, be based on ignorance or uncertainty about the relations among normative theory, scientific work, and practical politics. (These relations are considered at length in Chapter 3 of this book.) The political scientist who conducts research on the problem of war is as much an "activist" as the peace marcher who demands that a particular war be ended. This political scientist's action begins with a personal commitment to study war as a general problem in human affairs. His investigations are carried forward with the hope of discovering reliable information about the attributes of wars which, if made available to working politicians, may enable them to design policies and strategies effective in the prevention or termination of war. Whatever his motivating values, the scientist studying any other political problem is similarly an activist from the day he decides on the problem he will study.[5]

---

[5] For a skillful extension of this view of activism and relevance, see Scott Greer, *The Logic of Social Inquiry* (Chicago: Aldine, 1969).

This same political scientist is a traditionalist-intuitionist-artist every time he invents a theory or a hypothesis that he wishes to test. He becomes a *pure* scientist when, and only when, he carries on the empirical tests of his theory or hypothesis. Having made the decision to play the "science game," he must, as he would in any other organized game, abide by the rules of scientific procedure. Otherwise, he risks losing the game, that is, committing errors by basing decisions upon an inadequately substantiated theory. The scientist once again becomes an activist when he argues that his research findings, which must be general in scope, may be applied to the resolution of a particular political problem. Here he runs the risks of all activists: overeagerness to attempt a cure before the effectiveness and side effects of the proposed solution are well tested; confusion of wishing and reality; neglect of the many elements of the problem that he has not investigated.

In other words, the activities of valuation, science, and application are distinct from each other and equally legitimate in a professional man's life. As at the dinner table, a professional person may take food now from one dish, then from another. Each dish is a distinct part of the menu; together they become a meal. Similarly, normative philosophy, scientific investigation, and practical politics are distinct activities of political scientists; together they make up a discipline and a profession. All members of the discipline cannot engage in one to the exclusion of the others. The profession must engage in all. It must promote the training of specialists in each type of activity. It must encourage its members, as part of their professional experience, to take part in each type of activity at one time or another.

A CONCEPTUAL PREVIEW OF THIS BOOK

Behavioral scientists almost invariably start with or return to the proposition that *people live in groups*. This, too, is the point of departure for most political behaviorists. The *group* concept and its counterpart in *organization* theory, therefore, are the first with which this survey deals. As do all living things, organizations are born, grow, change, and die. Different organized groups have different objectives, structures, and other attributes. The United States of America is itself an organized group made up of tens of thousands of other organized groups, each emerging, developing, and declining in its own unique way.

From contemporary theories of organization, we learn that *cooperation* between two or more individuals occurs only when there is *communication* between them as they pursue some *shared purpose* in *exchange* for which each member is willing to give something of his own to the group's effort. These fundamental observations about organized groups lead us directly into the phenomena dealt with by communication, linguistic, and transactional theories.

Communication theories tend to agree in their use of this basic paradigm: a communicating source encodes signals that may transmit information to a destination that, upon adequate decoding, may respond with some audience effect. Various aspects of communication theory have been extensively employed by political behaviorists, although somewhat less has been done with a related concept, *information*. From communication engineers we learn that information is the reduction of uncertainty and that uncertainty is measurable not simply as an attitude, but also as a matter of probabilities about the outcome of a state of affairs. The "informed" baseball fan, for example, is the one who has best quantified the measurable elements of the game so that he can state odds about the future of any team he may be discussing.

A second aspect of the behavior of people in organized groups relates to the purposes they share. A *purpose*, or goal, is a present conception of some envisioned future state of affairs. Present conceptions are often articulated with language. In fact, one of the main activities of politicians is the articulation of purposes. But *linguistic statements* descriptive of the future can also do other things: predict events within probabilities indicated by empirical observation, or identify priorities on their user's scale of preferences. Thus, purpose and policy, particularly in political behavior, rest heavily upon the content and uses of human language.

The third feature of organized cooperation is the contribution of effort and activity that each member makes in order to help implement the outcomes he seeks through group undertakings. This exchange behavior is an aspect of political *transactions* generally. Of long-standing importance in economics, and more recently in psychology, transaction theory has emerged in recent years as a significant conceptual approach in the study of political behavior. An examination of political transactions leads into the somewhat neglected subjects of *trust*, group *integration*, and political *market-places*.

Transaction requires choice, and *decision making* has a well-established place among the concerns of political behavior. Alone and within the context of his group life, the human individual is distinctive in his reconciliation of *purpose* and *prospects* into *beliefs* with which he makes choices. Some political scientists have argued that decision theory is the paramount concept of this discipline, because "power," the traditional "master concept" of political science, is the other side of the decision-making coin.

The survey of decision theory presented here notes, among other things, that the *utility* theoretical approach of the economists and psychologists has been, in recent years, significantly augmented by the *reference-group* and *role* theoretical approaches proposed by sociologists. Furthermore, analysis of *collective decisions* requires more analytical components and dimensions than the act of decision taken by the lone individual. The creation and maintenance of *group decision rules* are perhaps among the most difficult assignments of political life. The chapter dealing with this problem offers a classification of decision rules into *verbal, violent,* and *numerical* types. It also touches upon the special problems of *situational analysis* on the part of the group as it confronts the necessity of choice.

Within organized groups there are individuals whose specialty may be said to consist primarily of decisional activity. These persons are usually referred to as leaders, the subject of *elite* and *leadership* theories. Contemporary theory tends to support the view that leadership is an aspect of group life and that leaders are "special" mainly because of the prerogatives they assume or receive. Thus, *investiture* in positions of leadership becomes a matter of extreme interest in political controversy and group decision making.

Groups and organizations are, of course, the creations of human beings, but it is also true that human individuals are very much the creatures of the groups to which they may belong. *Politicization*, as a type of *socialization* process, tends to be both an *educational* and a *propaganda* effort by socializing groups. The individual finds that his socialization involves the acceptance of group guidance about what he should see (*perception* theory), what he should know (*cognitive* theory), and how he should feel about these things (*attitudinal* theory).

Differences in perceptions of reality, variations in cognitions held, and disagreement over alternative attitudes suggested by different socializing groups may lead to political conflict. Theories of *conflict* have been expounded since early in recorded history, and many conflict theories are found in contemporary behavioral science. Recently, the theory of *games of strategy* has become one of the most intellectually influential of these. Numerous theorists also view political conflict as a continuing process or series of processes. Among the latter, the present survey notes the *formalization process* associated with conflicts over the tasks and duties of particular offices, the *socialization process* that results from role and other types of personality conflicts, and the *investiture process* related to conflicts over incumbency of particular individuals in particular group offices. These conflict processes have profound consequences for the life histories of organized groups and for the individuals within such groups as they cope with the difficult choices of making cooperative or conflictual responses to the disagreements at hand.

Systems theory, finally, has been that perspective that examines the structure and the function of relationships within and among organized groups over time. Political systems tend to be self-maintaining patterns of relationships among individuals and groups who have, by cooperation and by conflict, pursued both future political goals and the preservation of preferred status quo. Despite controversy among system theorists about the definitions and propositions of their field, systems theory in general attempts the most comprehensive view of political purposes, structures, and processes.

These pictures of total systems serve as the foundations for recommendations for change that originate with various types of political architects—reformers, planners, policy scientists, futurists, as well as practical politicians. While other nations and societies may claim to be better organized for *planning* to control the shape of the present so people may live better in the future, the United States may claim an unusual abundance of systems engineers and political architects, a discussion of whom may be found near the conclusion of this volume. One of the most prominent and influential system designs in human history, in fact, is the Constitution of the United States.

Groups and Organizations

The human individual, a weak and limited creature in isolation, acquires capacity to cope with the environment from membership in groups. Human groups, and their more formal counterparts, organizations, are a pervasive feature of the life of every individual. There are many types of human groups, among the most significant of them political groups such as governments, political parties, organized interests, and mass media of communication. Group and organizational theories, therefore, are indispensable analytical tools for characterizing and explaining the structure, functions, and development of these vital entities.

Organized groups are systems of cooperation arising out of shared attitudes and purposes. In addition to common purpose, every organized group is characterized by communicative activity and the contribution of effort by its members. Sometimes temporary groupings endure and become institutionalized groups, as purposes and the tasks expected to implement them become increasingly formalized with the passage of time. The group gathers its task expectations into positions, and the individual learns roles deemed appropriate for group positions. Much social and political conflict is a consequence of disagreements about task expectations and disparities between task expectations and role performances.

Group and Organization Theories

1

Governments are organized groups. Thus, the Constitution's preamble reported that it was being written "for the United States of America." At the time, the group so named consisted of thirteen states; today it numbers fifty.

Article I organized "a Congress of the United States, to consist of a Senate and House of Representatives." Today, as organizations, the Senate consists of 100 members plus the Vice President; the House of Representatives has 435 members. There are also hundreds of Congressional staff and service personnel who are a significant part of these organizations.

Article II designated "a President of the United States of America," placing him in command of such organizations as the Army and Navy of the United States, the militia of the several states under certain conditions, and the executive departments; today, the estimated number of people in the military services and civil bureaucracy of the national government, one of the largest organized groups of this kind in the world, exceeds five million.

Still another organized group established by the Constitution in Article III was "one Supreme Court, and . . . such inferior courts as the Congress may from time to time ordain and establish." The Federal judicial organization today consists of nearly ninety district courts, eleven circuit courts of appeals, and the one United States Supreme Court.

These, then, are the formal *constitutional* organizations of the United States of America. Note that these particular organizations did not actually exist as such at first. The Constitution created *a* United States of America, *a* Congress, *a* President, and *a* Supreme Court. Even before these organizations existed in fact, the writers of the Constitution gave them names. The Constitution also went into some detail as to which persons or groups of persons would compose the membership of these various formal organizations of the national government. Almost at once, therefore, the Constitution discussed elements that, as we shall see, are theoretically essential attributes of all organized groups, namely, a statement of the general organizational *purposes* in the preamble, a *naming* of the organization ("United States of America") and its suborganizations ("Congress," "President," etc.), and a specification of *membership*. Other aspects of organized group formation—specification of *activities* to be performed, channels of *communication* to be maintained, procedures for *allocating resources*, etc.—are also dealt with in the Constitution. Let us now examine some of the definitions and theories associated with such concepts as groups, organized groups, and organization.

ASPECTS OF SUSTAINED HUMAN COOPERATION

The individual human organism is a severely limited creature. For example, it cannot propagate alone. Sex differentiation requires that the reproductive process be a collaboration between at least two individuals of different types. This is a rather dull way to refer to human mating; Sigmund Freud has described the process and its psychic implications far more interestingly. All that we need to notice here is that a biological limitation on the part of the male or the female human is frequently the occasion for an elemental *shared attitude* (perhaps more glandular than propagatory) and a social *interaction* of a limited cooperative sort. Other human limitations have similar cooperative consequences.

Human Limitations: The Stimulus to Cooperate

Babies are of course one of the consequences of mating. The mother who has carried a child within herself for several months, whether under primitive or modern circumstances, is likely to view the newborn infant with some pleasure, excitement, and pride. The infant, for his part, is not about to wander off into the world. The child's obvious incapacity to care for himself or to overcome the limitations of locomotion, combined with the favorable maternal attitudes just noted, almost invariably set off a second intense human grouping tendency which becomes the parental-filial group. If the father's interest in the infant is also stimulated, as it is in so many human cultures, we have the final ingredient for an enduring human collaboration among mother, child, and father. Whether the events described are given romantic names or are simply classified as social interactions resulting from certain glandular, mating, gestatory, and locomotive *limitations* of the human individual, either way it remains just as true that these factors and human limitations are the *antecedent conditions* of our most ancient form of social grouping, the family.

The developments of human history that reinforced the family grouping process are fairly well known. Families grew to be tribes. Most nomadic tribes eventually settled down to become pastoral tribes. With settlement came intensification and specialization of the social relationships bearing upon the family. As population growth within the family and the tribe continued, an inadequacy of available food supplies and other natural resources became evident. To meet the threat of starvation, men invented procedures of intensive care for domesticated animals and developed the intensive cultivation of products of the soil; in short, they invented animal husbandry and agriculture. Medicine men and priests emerged as specialists dealing with the dramatic and often incomprehensible events surrounding the individual organism from birth to death; before long, historically speaking, human beings would respond to growing knowledge about the complexities of life by organizing themselves into churches, medical professions, life insurance companies, social security and medicare systems, etc.[1]

We need not dwell upon the evolution and proliferation of human groups and organizations. Let us simply notice that the family is a type of group fundamental to most human societies, and similarly, government is the most comprehensive type of human organization, emerging in response to the need for stabilizing the arrangements for the cooperation and conflict which surround the widest variety

[1] For an anthropological view, Max Gluckman, "The Origins of Social Organization," *Rhodes-Livingstone Institute Journal*, 12 (1951): 1–11.

of needs. If we listen carefully to the talk of politicians, we notice that their messages usually relate to "getting together" or "fighting it out" about something.

Groups: Ad Hoc and Institutionalized

The biological and physical compulsions for two or more human beings to interact about some shared objective have been, from earliest times, quite substantial. These and other observable conditions of human behavior are relevant to most social science definitions of the concept group. A human *group* comes into being when two or more persons engage in a minimum frequency of interaction in response to some shared attitude (or shared characteristic about which they have a common attitude) which produces among them specific uniformities of behavior.[2]

For example, two motorists driving in opposite directions along a highway may come upon a fallen tree across the highway at the same time. If both are relatively interested in proceeding in the directions they were going, they may be said to have a *shared attitude* toward the tree, namely, annoyance with its presence. A gesture or a brief conversation may be the *minimal degree of interaction* needed for the two to perceive that they share this attitude. Further communication may carry them to some agreement about the activities that each might contribute, that is, *uniformities of behavior* such as lifting or pushing, in order to remove the fallen tree from the road. If the agreed-upon behaviors are actually performed and prove effective in removing the tree, this tiny ad hoc group will have fulfilled its objective and probably disintegrate as a group. If the uniform behaviors that are actually performed fail to remove the tree, the two motorists may begin to communicate with each other rather intensively about alternative plans and behaviors. The communicative activity may reveal disagreements about what to do next; that is, even while sharing an antitree attitude, their communicative interaction may follow a conflictful course. Behaviorally, this is precisely what political communicators are doing when they argue, for example, about raising or reducing taxes. All parties to the debate may be intensely interested in achieving or maintaining

2 The characteristics of the individuals who compose a group are profoundly related to the member behavior and effectiveness of the group. W. W. Haythorn, "The Composition of Groups: A Review of the Literature," *Acta Psychologica*, 28 (1968): 97–128.

economic prosperity; they differ over what immediate governmental behavior in the taxation field is most likely to produce that prosperity.[3]

A human group becomes *institutionalized* when, to a relatively high degree, its patterns of membership and interaction become stable, uniform, formal, and general. In the writings of social scientists, the notion institutions and institutionalized groups are frequently used interchangeably. Legislatures, bureaucracies, organized churches, and family systems are examples of *types* of institutionalized groups.

The attribute of *stability* usually refers to the tendency of the participating members and components of the group to revert to a prior pattern or equilibrium in their interactions following disturbances of one sort or another. Members of a stable legislature, even after the most heated campaign for reelection, tend after election day has passed to return to the customary task of producing statutes. An "abnormal" election may produce severe instability, as did the presidential election of 1860 which preceded the Civil War, and this may of course destroy an institutionalized group.

The attribute of *uniformity* refers to the similarity in behavioral patterns among groups belonging to the same type of institution. For example, political parties, whatever their nation or particular form of organization, everywhere tend to be uniform in attempting to place their leaders into governmental offices.

The attribute of *formality* refers to the relatively highly organized character of most institutionalized groups. Task expectations, for example, are minutely spelled out and decision-making procedures are carefully detailed. We shall see the implications of this characteristic below when we deal with the concept organization.

Finally, the attribute of *generality* underlines the cross-societal comparability of particular types of institutionalized groups. For example, while the family, as a type of institutionalized group, is not

---

[3] For a survey of the social science literature relating to the "group" concepts, David B. Truman, *The Governmental Process* (New York: Knopf, 1951), Chap. 2. Truman cautions that groups are sometimes "categoric" in nature; that is, categories or classifications or collections of things that some observer believes to have particular characteristics in common. Thus, blondes, teetotalers, or Democrats may be groups according to an observer because of the existence of a common characteristic for each. These *categorical groups* become *social groups* when interaction and shared attitudes (possibly with respect to the shared characteristic) also exist. The interaction, sometimes unconscious and sometimes deliberate, is what makes the group social. "Small group" analysis is surveyed by Robert Golembiewski, *Behavior and Organization* (Chicago: Rand McNally, 1962).

necessarily found in *every* society, neither is it peculiar to any one society.

While much of the literature of social and political science deals with institutions, the term has not been a satisfactory one from an empirical point of view. It is difficult for the scientific observer to measure degrees of stability, uniformity, formality, and generality. The tendency increasingly has been to write and speak of "organizations," because they are more observable and concrete social referents.

Organized Groups

Organization is a major concept of contemporary behavioral science; definitions and theories abound.[4] One of the most influential definitions was offered by Chester A. Barnard and has, in one way or another, been incorporated into most subsequent definitions and theories.[5]

According to Barnard, a *cooperative system* is a complex of physical, biological, personal, and social components which are in a specific systematic relationship by reason of the cooperation of two or more persons for at least one definite end. Here again the underlying premise is that the human individual is a single, unique, independent, isolated, whole thing, embodying innumerable forces and materials past and present which may be classified as physical, biological, and social factors.

To each individual may be attributed certain properties: (a) activities or behavior, arising from (b) combinations of physical, biological, and social influences resulting in psychological factors, to which are added (c) the limited power of choice, which results in (d) purpose. Persons without the power of choice are unfitted for

---

[4] Bertram M. Gross, *The Managing of Organizations* (New York: Free Press, 1964); James G. March and Herbert A. Simon, *Organizations* (New York: Wiley, 1958); James G. March (ed.), *Handbook of Organizations* (Chicago: Rand McNally 1965). Also, Raymond V. Bowers (ed.), *Studies on Behavior in Organizations* (Athens: University of Georgia Press, 1965); Mason Haire (ed.), *Modern Organization Theory* (New York: Wiley, 1959); Peter M. Blau and W. R. Scott, *Formal Organizations* (San Francisco: Chandler, 1962); R. M. Cyert and J. G. March, *A Behavioral Theory of the Firm* (Englewood Cliffs, N.J.: Prentice-Hall, 1963); Amitai Etzioni, *Modern Organizations* (Englewood Cliffs, N.J.: Prentice-Hall, 1964); T. Caplow, *Principles of Organization* (New York: Harcourt, Brace & World, 1964); Chris Argyris, *Organization and Innovation* (Homewood, Ill.: Irwin, 1965); Rensis Likert, *Human Organization* (New York: McGraw-Hill, 1967).

[5] Chester A. Barnard, *The Functions of the Executive* (Cambridge, Mass.: Harvard University Press, 1938).

cooperation and become isolated from other human beings or destroyed. Each human individual chooses whether or not he will enter into a specific cooperative system, a choice which places an aspect of his individual behavior into phase with the cooperative system.

A *formal organization* may be viewed as a system of the consciously coordinated activities or forces of two or more persons. An organization comes into being when (1) there are two or more persons *able to communicate* with each other (2) who are *willing to contribute action* (3) to accomplish a *common purpose*. The essential attributes of an organization are therefore (1) communication; (2) willingness to serve; and (3) common purpose.

Notice that these attributes of organization are not unlike the principal attributes of group:

ORGANIZATION	GROUP
purpose	shared attitude
communication	minimal interaction
contributed effort	uniform behaviors

A *purpose* (read also: goal, end, objective, target, function, etc.) is a *present mental conception* of some *future state of affairs* regarding which two or more persons may have a shared favorable or unfavorable attitude. For example, a pair of newlyweds may, by communication of one sort of another, arrive at the common purpose of wishing to build a house. Each may have a very different mental picture, one of a twenty-room mansion, the other of a two-room bungalow. Whatever their respective mental images, both initially share a favorable attitude toward the idea "house." Further communication about this overtly shared purpose may carry each a substantial distance from his original mental picture toward some more precise and overt conceptualization in the form of a detailed blueprint. The blueprint continues to be little more than a purpose, that is, a present image of some future state of affairs. When the house is constructed, then the purpose is no longer in the future; it has been fulfilled and, by definition, no longer exists.

The purpose "house" is a relatively familiar and specific illustration; "house" is also a purpose that is commonly achieved. On the other hand, the purposes "justice" or "equality among men"—well-known political goals—are obviously far more difficult to blueprint and achieve. The mental imagery involved in sharing *political* goals is far more varied and difficult to describe, let alone realize. Nonetheless, purposes they are, and they continue to be the subject of intensive political communication. A consensus about political purposes is a general sharing of the same attitudes about the present sketchy pictures of some particular but vague future political state of affairs.

The concept group has a second attribute, namely, a characteristic minimal *interaction*. By and large, such interaction is that which, according to organization theory, is communicative in character: a gesture, a word, a series of communication exchanges—usually aimed at clarifying a common purpose, making explicit a shared attitude, describing the recommended behaviors to be performed, or spelling out the system of communication to be followed.

The third pair of attributes of group and organization that appear to have great similarity are *uniform behaviors* and *contributed effort*. Each term refers to actual activity. What each member of an organization does to fulfill his assigned tasks is presumably a contribution of effort intended to help implement the shared goal. The input of effort is presumably rewarded by some output from the organization to the individual, either the achievement of the entire shared purpose or some more immediate reward, such as a monthly salary check. The collective activity of members of the organization constitutes a kind of economic system. The contributed effort is very likely to be a set of uniform behaviors prescribed for any individuals who may in the present or the future become involved in performing the assigned tasks.

If the essential attributes of groups and organizations are so similar, in what way does organization differ from group? Organizations, particularly *formal* organizations, are made up of individuals who are apparently more conscious, deliberate, and overt in their coordinated behaviors as members. Closer to the group in its attributes is the *informal organization* which, according to Barnard, results from those interactions between persons which are based on personal rather than on joint or common purposes. Because of their repetitive character, these interactions establish certain attitudes, understandings, and habits—many of them *unconscious*—which very often create the conditions within which formal organizations arise. Although informal organization is necessarily antecedent to formal organization, often formal organizations generate informal ones as means of communication and attitude development.

One other characteristic that distinguishes formal organizations from groups and informal organizations is the greater concern of formal organization members for the specification of leadership or executive positions. All groups and organizations, almost immediately upon coming into being, have *leaders,* either informal or formal. The necessity for leaders arises from the requirements of orderly communication within the group or organization; leaders, whether they are the most influential persons in the group or not, are invariably in the principal positions of communication. The more formal the organization, the more formal the position of leadership.

PROCESSES OF GROUP FORMALIZATION

Formalization of Purposes and Tasks

The process of specialization within an organization soon places upon the executives the primary responsibility for defining and redefining the purposes of the organization, maintaining and modifying its system of communication, and coordinating the contributed effort of the individual members as each endeavors to fulfill, in one degree or another, his special activities to implement the goal of the organization. As a consequence, executive or leadership positions lie at the center of what we shall call the *formalization process.* Persons who are executives or leaders spend much of their time dealing with the formalization process.

As interactions between persons lead to the discovery of shared purposes, arrangements for continuation of these interactions must also be discovered or invented. This necessity leads to further communication and specification of tasks; what each participant is to contribute to the coordinated effort and what "satisfactions" he is to secure in return are described. Decisions about the allocation of tasks are normally designed to guide immediate actions along lines that are presumed by the group or its leaders to implement the goal. To circumscribe their respective *present* situations of choice, the members of an organization, either together with or through delegation to their leaders, will analyze a goal (*present* image of a *future* state), breaking it down into specific immediate tasks whose accomplishment is delegated to particular individuals. The achievement of the organization's goal presumably becomes contingent upon the achievement of all present tasks by incumbents in different positions.

A *task expectation* may be defined as a description or conception of a behavior or an activity believed by a predominant portion of the membership of a group to be instrumental or contributory to the achievement of a particular shared goal. Task expectations may be found in the job descriptions of positions in governments, businesses, manufacturing establishments, etc. A job description simply states in words those activities that are expected of individuals occupying the named position. A carpenter, for example, is expected to be able to: make or repair a completed structure, usually of wooden materials; select the materials to be used; lay out, shape, frame, and finish the materials; use a variety of tools, such as saws, hammers, and drills, characteristic of his trade; follow the instructions of a blueprint or a scale drawing, etc.

Similar recorded statements of task expectations may be found in the Constitution, the Federal statutes, Federal administrative regulations, and Supreme Court judicial opinions. Article II of the Constitution, which describes the duties of the Presidency, is, according to our present definition, a collection of task expectations, a job description. These basic task expectations have, of course, evolved and expanded through amendments to the Constitution, new congressional enactments assigning additional duties to the President, Supreme Court interpretations of presidential prerogatives, and administrative and personal interpretations made by individual Presidents. The more formal an organization, the greater the likelihood that task expectations within it will be carefully set down in widely available documents.

Even if a task expectation cannot be found in some written description, it may well exist in the minds and memories of the members of a group. These individual mental expectations may vary quite widely in scope and specificity. Thus, a citizen with only an elementary school education may be able to name just two or three duties he expects of the President, whereas a constitutional lawyer may name dozens. Yet, both are part of the total membership of the nation; in an election, for example, both degrees of information and expectation are relevant as, say, each of the two citizens decides which man to support for president.

A *position* in an organization is a set of task expectations consistently linked with each other by group members and usually, although not necessarily, given a position name by the group. Examine, for example, Section VIII of Article I of the Constitution which lists some eighteen powers of Congress. While the powers are prescribed for the Congress as a whole, each member in the House of Representatives and the Senate is expected to perform the tasks of decision making implied by these powers and in accordance with the decision-making procedures of each house, respectively, and the Congress as a whole.

Thus, according to Section VIII, each member is in a position whose task expectations require that he: lay and collect taxes, duties, imposts and excises, to pay the debts and provide for the common defense and general welfare of the United States; borrow money on the credit of the United States; regulate commerce with foreign nations and among the several states; establish uniform rules regarding naturalization and uniform laws concerning bankruptcies; coin money and regulate the value thereof; establish post offices; promote the progress of science and useful arts through copyright and patent procedures; constitute tribunals inferior to the Supreme Court; and so on down the list of specified expectations.

Each member, because of his formal position, shares equally with all the other members the "responsibility" for performing these tasks. In the first few Congresses this was, in fact, exactly the case; every member participated in every discussion and decision. When the workload and the variety of problems became too numerous for every member personally to deal with adequately, the usual process of specialization and delegation of authority and responsibility within the formal organization began to take place. The congressional committee system came into being. Thereafter, each committee dealt with some subset of the total expected tasks.

The Constitution provides some excellent examples of the relationship between a group's stated goals and the task expectations and positions intended to implement these goals. The group was, of course, simply "We, the people of the United States." The goals, in all their political ambiguity, were: "to form a more perfect Union, establish justice, insure domestic tranquility, provide for the common defense, promote the general welfare, and secure the blessings of liberty. . . ." To "establish justice," for example, Article III prescribes tasks and establishes positions. "The judicial power of the

United States shall be vested in one Supreme Court, and in such inferior courts as the Congress may from time to time ordain and establish. . . . The judicial power shall extend to all cases, in law and equity, arising under this Constitution, the laws of the United States, and treaties made, or which shall be made, under their authority. . . ." and so on through the other sections of the Article. The precise activity implied by the term "judicial power . . . in law and equity" may seem ambiguous at first reading. But each of the Founding Fathers believed, since most of them were lawyers, that these phrases represented the long and well-developed tradition of Anglo-Saxon jurisprudence which then prevailed in most of the colonies.

Thus, we have an example of a political goal ("to establish justice") implemented through task expectations (judicial powers) and named positions (one Supreme Court and inferior courts) whose incumbents would be expected to perform these tasks. Presumably, if every judge did his job adequately from day to day, one of the great goals of the nation would be fulfilled, and the nation itself would expect to endure as an organization. Similar relationships may be drawn between the goals of the Preamble and other tasks and positions enumerated in other parts of the Constitution.

Formalization Conflicts

Task expectations are not always clearly held nor wholly agreed upon as contributory to the achievement of an organization's goals. Consequently, men disagree, engage in a process of political conflict, and frequently resolve those conflicts by one or another procedure of collective decision making. If the resolved issue relates to task expectations, we may say that the group has advanced a stage in its formalization process.[6]

Continuing our example from American judicial history, this is exactly what happened in the case of *Marbury* v. *Madison* in 1803. Marbury had been given a last-minute appointment as a justice of the peace in the District of Columbia by the outgoing President Adams. The new Secretary of State, Madison, however, refused to deliver the commission. Marbury asked the Supreme Court for a

---

[6] Cf. discussion in Chapter 9 where formalization, socialization, and investiture are viewed as three related types of conflict process.

writ of mandamus to compel delivery. In the opinion of Chief Justice Marshall speaking for Court's majority, Marbury had a clear right to his commission. However, the Supreme Court, which was presumably authorized to issue writs of mandamus to public officers by Congress in the Judiciary Act of 1789, could not do so constitutionally, according to Marshall. In other words, the Supreme Court believed in this case that an act of Congress had been unconstitutional. Here, for the first time, the Supreme Court not only asserted supremacy but the Court also clearly implied that the power to interpret and maintain this supremacy—for the moment on a matter relating to its own prerogatives only—resided with itself. Although President Jefferson and his fellow partisans objected strenuously, the Marshall view of the Supreme Court's task as supreme interpreter of the Constitution prevailed. The conflict ended with the national government formalized in a way not specifically stated or perhaps anticipated by the writers of the Constitution.

Conflicts about task expectations among members of an organization or between members of different organizations are usually raised by one of the following questions: What particular actions are specified in the task expectations? What is the distribution of task expectations among the named positions? What is the expected consequence of the performance of particular tasks for the goal that the organization members have in mind? In other words, conflicts relating to the formalization process have to do with the activities to be performed, their location in the position structure of the organization, the prospect that such activities will produce anticipated outcomes, and similar considerations.

Conflicts over task expectations may be resolved in one of several ways. The task activities may be described more specifically than previously. In effect, this is what Hamilton, Madison and Jay attempted to do in *The Federalist Papers,* written during the campaign to have the Constitution ratified in the various states. These men endeavored to give practical contemporary illustration to the various task expecations delineated more abstractly in the Constitution itself.

Another kind of formalizing conflict resolution involves transferring one or more task expectations from one position in the organization to another. This is what invariably occurs in governmental "reorganizations," in which established positions may be terminated and their activities transferred to other or new positions. An early case of this kind was the effort of Secretary of State Jefferson to have the postal service (with its opportunities for patronage in every state) transferred from Secretary Hamilton's jurisdiction in Treasury to his own department. Jefferson failed in this conflict, but another politician, President Jackson, saw the point some three decades later. One of Jackson's first acts was to elevate the Postmaster General to Cabinet status, directly responsible to himself.

Still another outcome of the formalization process may produce changes in the task expectations held by the members of a group. For example, since the days of Washington, Presidents have, in one way or another, denied or obscured their activities as political party leaders; a sitting President usually assumed the posture of a statesman standing above party strife. President Wilson made the first declarations to the contrary, acknowledging that a President cannot escape being the de facto leader of his party. Nineteenth-century public expectations frowned upon partisanship in its Presidents, but twentieth-century popular opinion increasingly expects a President to be, among other things, a strong party leader. Even President Eisenhower, who was particularly reluctant to "intervene" in Republican Party affairs, lent himself to party interests from time to time.

THE INDIVIDUAL AMONG HIS GROUPS

Positions and Roles

As a society, a political community, an organization, or a group becomes increasingly formalized, this is evidenced in the growing specificity of task expectations and positions. Even as simple a group as the family has become enormously formalized with the advance of civilization. The relatively casual relationships of lovers and accidental parenthood in the primitive world came, over the millenia, to be formalized as a social organization in which ceremonial weddings marked the beginning of the marriage relationship and such specialized positions as "husband," "wife," "parent," "child," "brother," and "sister." These ranged from primitive expectations that the wife gathers roots while the husband hunts and fishes to the more contemporary expectations that the husband shall provide most of the family income while the wife handles the child rearing as one of her principal tasks. The unwritten customs of the primitives have become elaborately delineated in the family statutes of modern communities. These laws announce the behaviors expected between husband and wife, parent and child, family members and outsiders, and even, in adoption and custody laws, the conditions of family membership itself. Centuries of formalization have transposed the simple and elemental position of, for example, "father" into the volumes of task expectations discussed and elaborated on the bookshelves of modern lawyers.

Clearly the young American male, recently married, who contemplates the activities of fatherhood is not likely to turn to the lawyer's bookshelves for the latest word about the task expectations of this position. If conscientious, he might turn, at his wife's suggestion, to a quick reading of Dr. Benjamin Spock's famous little volume, *Baby and Child Care*. Most likely, he will learn about the task expectations associated with the father position from his observations of the behavior of his own father, his friends in their roles as fathers, from what his church and similar groups say about the duties of fatherhood, etc. In this way he learns, accepts, and performs some or most of the tasks expected of fathers, that is, of the father "role."[7]

We have already noted that the Constitution established a position called "President" at the head of the executive branch of the United States government. The Founding Fathers then described the tasks they expected any man filling the position to perform: exercise the executive power; command the Army, Navy, and on certain occasions the militia of the states; grant reprieves and pardons; make treaties (with advice and consent of the Senate); provide Congress with information on the State of the Union; etc. The position "President" existed in writing and in the expectations of the Founding Fathers before a man was elected to fill it. The position continues to be a

---

[7] The behavioral literature frequently uses the terms *position* and *role* interchangeably. This book will endeavor to distinguish between the two. *Position* refers to the expectations held by most of the members of a group. *Role* refers to those expectations held by an individual who may prospectively or actually be performing the activities of a particular position. The distinction is maintained here in order to facilitate differentiation between what the *group* is thinking and what a *particular individual* may be thinking. For further treatment of *role*, see Chapters 5 and 9.

thing apart—in the Constitution, the statutes of Congress, the interpretations of the Supreme Court, the practices of the executive branch, and the minds of the people—from the men who actually fill it. Any man who wants to be or is President may fully inform himself about the *position* from written sources, the advice of experts, the examples of predecessors, and other means. What *he* learns—and this may be only a fraction of all that there is to learn—then becomes *for him* role information. He performs the presidential *role*—which may differ from everyone's expectations about the position—to the extent that he has learned and actually acts upon his role information. To *know* what a President does is different from *doing* what is expected of a President. A *role*, therefore, is a mental or neural preparation on the part of a person who may or does perform prescribed and standardized patterns of individual activity, usually—but not always—in response to specific positions and situations in group life.

In the actual event, a person's *role performance* is matched by the group against its criteria for a job "well done," or its *position expectations*. In a subsequent chapter we shall deal in greater detail with individual socialization as a role-learning process. At this point, we wish to notice how the position structure of a group or organization may influence the role information acquired by the individual.

The eminent sociologist Georg Simmel took the role-learning process as the point of departure for his comments regarding the growth of individualism and psychic freedom in contemporary societies. The medieval man had very few groups with which he could affiliate: his parental family, his marital family, his occupational group, his church, and perhaps the household of his lord's manor. The positions in these few groups were few in number and fairly stable in expectations throughout his lifetime. By contrast, the modern individual living in societies with a vast range of groups may affiliate, either by accident or by choice, with a very large number of groups whose position expecations he may adopt as learned roles. If it is true that the modern adult may know and perform as many as thirty or forty learned roles, he clearly has a wider choice in his conduct than the medieval individual with only four or five learned roles. As a result, according to Simmel, the modern individual, although living in a world with large-scale organizations that appear to constrain him with highly formalized expectations, may nonetheless be freer than his medieval ancestor to pursue his personal development because of the larger number and variety of groups with which he may affiliate and whose many roles he may learn.[8]

Some Types of Groups to Which People Belong

There are of course any number of categories by which different types of groups and organizations may be classified. The following is a list of several *types* frequently found in the behavioral science literature. At a later point in this book we shall discuss at greater length the political consequences of many of the role-instructional and socializing efforts of particular groups within these types. They are mentioned here to elaborate upon Simmel's view that the group affiliations of individuals in contemporary life are numerous and complex.

Kinship groups, among the first and most pervasive with which an individual remains affiliated, usually consist of the parental and marital families, although a variety of family associations for special purposes are common in American society.

Locality groups are those commonly referred to as "neighbors" or residents of one's community whether it be a town, city, state, or nation.

Age groups are well known and quite self-conscious in this country of long-lived citizens: children (who frequently distinguish between "kids" and "people"), subteens, teenagers, young adults, senior citizens, etc.

Faith groups are those associations of persons who are affiliated with a church, unaffiliated, or antichurch. Most political ideologies have a substantial faith-oriented idiom.

Sex groups are an ancient and obvious focus of affiliation, perhaps in recent years complicated by the aggressive civil rights demands of organized homosexuals.

In a society as devoted to formal education as the American, countless *educational groups* and organizations may be readily identified, from preschool nurseries to postgraduate and alumni associations.

There are also *ethnic, occupational, friendship*, and *political groups* and organizations. While we are interested in the political consequences of socialization processes in all types of groups, we are most

---

8 Georg Simmel, *The Web of Group-Affiliations*, trans, by Reinhard Bendix (Glencoe, Ill.: The Free Press, 1955). Role conflict is discussed further in Chapter 5.

concerned in this book with those that we commonly refer to as *political.*

An Illustrative Use of the Conceptual Perspective[9]

FORMALIZATION OF THE FEDERAL JUDICIARY

By the seventeenth and eighteenth centuries the English judicial system, with its many special organizational forms, became the principal model for the Founding Fathers. In England there were local justices of the peace and judges who traveled "the circuit." English lay juries assisted in the determination of evidence. Depending upon the subject at issue or the type of case, there were different systems of English courts through which appeals could be made. The ultimate court was the "king in Parliament," or more specifically, the King's Bench. English common law was also administered in the Court of Exchequer and the Court of Common Pleas. The Court of Chancery emerged for cases meriting equity—relief petitioned as an act of grace—when the King's courts could find no adequate remedy within the common law. In the pre-Revolutionary period, the King's Bench established substantial independence from the king as well as from Parliament, which led Montesquieu to comment favorably upon judicial independence in the English system.

The Founding Fathers came to judicial organization with several dissatisfactions. Because of distance and the special character of colonial charters, the English court system was never adequately extended to the colonies. Colonial cases were often handled by the maritime courts rather than the regular courts of common law and equity. In private as well as government conflicts with royal officers and agencies, the colonists found it unusually difficult to get their cases into the relatively advanced judicial process of the mother country. As a consequence, the colonists developed many of their

---

[9] Theoretical concepts may be "applied" to the description and analysis of real things and events in a number of ways. Concepts may be strictly defined variables in formal hypotheses. They may be aids to perception, helping the observer select some things and events rather than others for examination. Concepts, particularly when they are somewhat ambiguous or poorly defined, may also serve as simple tools for orienting or organizing a discussion about real things and events. The present case illustration is of the latter type. We urge instructors and students to delve more thoroughly into the implications of group and organizational concepts for the example presented.

own indigenous courts patterned after both English and Continental systems.

The colonies failed to develop a conception of a central court system and, in fact, provided for no judiciary under the Articles of Confederation. Hamilton summarized the problem in *Federalist Paper* Number 22:

> If there is in each state a court of final jurisdiction, there may be as many different final determinations on the same point, as there are courts. . . . To avoid the confusion which would unavoidably result from the contradictory decisions of a number of independent judicatories, all nations have found it necessary to establish one tribunal paramount to the rest, possessing a general superintendence, and authorized to settle and declare in the last resort an uniform rule of civil justice.

The Constitution, therefore, vested the "judicial power of the United States" in "one Supreme Court, and in such inferior Courts as the Congress may from time to time ordain and establish." Article III delineates the task expectations for the Federal judiciary agreed upon by the Founding Fathers. These expectations referred mainly to certain types of cases—those involving the Constitution, the laws of the United States, and the treaties of the nation—as well as to special parties to such cases—the Federal government, the States, ambassadors, ministers, consuls, and citizens engaged in controversy with any of these.

The Judiciary Act of 1789 spelled out the initial organizational structure of the Federal system. Below the Supreme Court, then consisting of six justices, were established three circuit courts each encompassing several states and district courts in every state. In the ancient English manner, the Supreme Court justices were required to "ride circuit" at specified times. By 1801, another Judiciary Act ended the circuit riding of the justices, reduced the court to five members, created six circuit and additional district courts. Needless to say, the business of the Federal judicial increased with each passing year, and so did its task expectations and position structure.

Today, the Supreme Court consists of nine justices, a clerk, a marshall, a reporter, a librarian, and the lawyers authorized to practice before the Supreme Court. Over 2,000 cases are handled by the Court annually.

At the next judicial level below are eleven circuit courts of appeals, each encompassing three or more states. These circuit courts are made up of from three to nine judges, depending upon the circuit work load. The eleven circuit courts of appeals process nearly 4,000 cases annually.

Below the intermediate appellate courts and within states are the United States district courts. Some states have up to four districts; more than ninety district courts are distributed among all the states and possessions. From one to eighteen judges may sit in each district, there being approximately two hundred and fifty district judges. The total district court case load is impressively large: over one hundred thousand bankruptcy cases, fifty-eight thousand civil cases, and twenty-nine thousand criminal cases annually.

Also within the Federal court system are three special courts: the United States Court of Claims, which hears suits on claims against the United States: the United States Court of Customs and Patent Appeals; and the Customs Court, which deals with the classification and valuation of imported merchandise.

The Federal judiciary, it must be remembered, is but a small part of the total judicial organization of the United States. Each of the fifty states has its own court structure, ranging from justices of the peace, municipal courts, county courts, intermediate courts of appeals, to the state supreme courts.

Formalization of judicial positions and court organization goes on continuously in the Federal system. An illustration is the development of expectations regarding the use of juries. Criminal trials by jury were *not* a well-established legal procedure either in England or the colonies at the time the Constitution was written. In Article III the requirement was simply that "the trial of all crimes, except in cases of impeachment, shall be by jury; and such trial shall be held in the State where the said crime shall have been committed; but when not committed within any State, the trial shall be at such place or places as the Congress may by law have directed." After some controversy over the ambiguities of the language, in 1791 the Sixth and Seventh Amendments added assurances of "speedy and public trial, by an impartial jury" with the right "to be informed of the nature and cause of the accusation; to be confronted with the witnesses against him; to have compulsory process for obtaining witnesses in his favor, and to have the assistance of counsel for his defense." In addition, in civil suits where the value in controversy exceeds twenty dollars, the defendent was to be assured opportunity for trial by jury.

As late as 1930, expectations were further formalized in *Patton* v.

United States, wherein it was ruled that loss of one member of a jury was the same as losing the entire jury, that no modification of the unanimous verdict requirement was allowable, and that the same judge had to be present throughout the trial. Then, expectations regarding the right to counsel were changed. Congress, in 1790, had required the courts to assign counsel in cases of capital crimes, leaving the impression that no such obligation existed in other kinds of cases. In *Johnson* v. *Zerbst* (1938), the obligation of the court was extended to all criminal cases except those in which the defendent waived the assistance of counsel, and even on this point the court has to rule regarding the knowledgeability of the defendent in making the waiver. Innumerable other aspects of the trial-by-jury expectation have been similarly formalized.

Substantive as well as procedural aspects of judicial organization have evolved in formality and specificity. There has been a seemingly endless restatement of the scope of subjects and situations that the courts have been expected to adjudicate. Could the Supreme Court comment on the nature of the Federal union? Indeed; in the words of Chief Justice Marshall in *McCulloch* v. *Maryland* in 1819, the court declared the national government "supreme within its sphere of action." Could state legislatures, executives, or courts re-examine orders of Federal courts? They definitely could not, according to *United States* v. *Peters* (1809). Did the Congress have power to regulate *all commerce?* In *Gibbons* v. *Ogden* (1824) and *The Passenger Cases* (1849) a negative response emerged as separate courts began to draw the distinction between "interstate" and "intrastate" commerce, leaving the latter entirely within the jurisdiction of the states themselves.

The examples of formalization of judicial activities not only fill many volumes, they take up whole libraries. Supreme Court decisions are published as *The United States Reports,* of which more than 350 volumes have been issued thus far. Federal district court rulings appear as *The Federal Supplement,* and intermediate appellate decisions are published as *The Federal Reporter.* So voluminous has "the law" become that the legal profession has begun to turn to the electronic computer for help in keeping track of civic task expectations embodied in statutes and court decisions. The American Bar Association has had several committees on electronic data retrieval and the Association of American Law Schools has, during the past decade, encouraged developments in this type of automation.

Communication and Information

Communication is an essential aspect of group and organizational life. Some theorists consider communication as an activity and others as a process. One influential approach analyzes communication in its most elemental form as a single act, that is, a Communicator A transmitting information to Audience B about something X, using *discriminative stimuli* (language, gesture, etc.) to help convey the information. This simple act is far more complex than it appears and has numerous pitfalls leading to error, misunderstanding, and conflict. The problems inherent in the transmission of information are better grasped by a study of information theory. This body of theory, derived mainly from the concerns of communication engineers, defines *information* as any phenomenon that reduces uncertainty about the outcome of events, choices, or relationships. Information theorists have developed a logic which enables them to quantify and measure amounts of uncertainty, that is, information needed to predict exactly. Some of the problems of information transmission and management that become evident from the perspective of information theory are information costs, information storage capacity, redundancy, and channel capacity.

2

The Communication of Political Information

Communication is an indispensable part of group and organization life. Aristotle thought man's uniqueness among the animals arose from his "gift of speech." We have since learned, however, that systematic communicative activity is common to all social animals. Furthermore, in an era when talking was the principal form of human communicative activity, Aristotle could have had no way of knowing the extent to which printing and electronic media would produce other significant human communication techniques.

The writing of the Constitution was itself an act of communication, not only among the states of the Confederation but also between "we, the People of the United States" (as of 1787–1790) and "our Posterity" for whom the great goals of the Preamble were being sought. In addition, throughout the Constitution various communication procedures are identified or prescribed for Federal governing organizations. A few may be mentioned as illustrations.

The Congress is called upon to *assemble* regularly. Each state legislature is required to *prescribe* the times, places, and manner of holding elections for senators and representatives. Each house is to keep and *publish a journal* of its proceedings. Documents called *bills* become *laws* after certain acts of acceptance by both houses and the President. Under certain circumstances, the President is to seek the *advice* of the Senate. From time to time the President is to

49

give information to the Congress regarding the state of the Union and *recommend* to them such measures as he shall judge necessary and expedient. From the principal officer of each of the executive departments, the President may require *opinion in writing*. Amendment VI calls for speedy and public *trial* of the accused in all criminal prosecutions. Perhaps the most important communication prescription of all is in the First Amendment, prohibiting the Congress from making any law abridging the freedom of *speech* or of the *press* or of the right of the people peaceably to *assemble* and to *petition* the Government for a redress of grievances. The Founding Fathers were keenly aware of communication processes.

In contemporary political life, communication often seems to be the major activity of American society. Presidential messages seem to flow constantly from the White House to the Congress, the press, the people, and other nations. Congress is involved in interminable discussion and debate. The Supreme Court constantly conducts hearings or renders opinions. Interest groups make demands or mobilize support without letup. Political parties seem forever to be preparing or conducting election campaigns. The electorate's mandates seem daily to be reiterated or polled. Press, radio, television, publishers, and other mass media regularly bathe the populace in an ocean of words and images.

One prominent theory of nationalism goes so far as to equate a nation with its communication system. A nation consists of people, but they are a people only as an extension of their community of communication. To the extent that a people's communication processes are efficient in information transmission, nationalism prevails. A nation's communication habits are in large part a consequence of learning that occurs during the assimilation of minorities. Efficient communication habits lead to national integration and mobilization.[1]

What is all this communicative activity? Much of it is intended to describe some situation or condition that the communicator wishes to call to the attention of some audience. Much may be motivated by the communicator's interest in informing some audience about *his* perception of a situation, *his* suggestions regarding an appropriate audience response to the situation, and, inferentially, news about *himself*. The communicator may also wish to share or

[1] Karl W. Deutsch, *Nationalism and Social Communication* (Cambridge, Mass.: M.I.T. Press, 1953).

reveal information about particular relationships between himself and the situation or between himself and his audience, as does the politician who boasts that he and his constituents are in close agreement with each other.

PERSPECTIVES ON COMMUNICATION

Although Greek writers appreciated the important place of communication in human affairs, substantial theoretical work in this field began only as recently as the 1930s. Since then, the concept and its behavioral ramifications have fascinated theorists and investigators in a number of fields ranging from electronic engineering to poetry. Communication has been examined as an element in the regular interactions between human beings, as a process, and as a particular type of behavioral activity. Most theoretical formulations view the transfer of information as an integral aspect of communication. In the last decade or two, the behavioral sciences have learned from communication engineering and the computer sciences that the concept information, too, may have special meanings.[2]

Systematic Activity as Communication

Not all communication takes linguistic form. A gesture, such as the wink of an eye, may carry meaning and information from a communicator to an audience. A situation, unaccompanied by language of any sort, may carry significant messages to an audience; imagine that a cache of weapons was discovered in the headquarters of a political party on the eve of an election. Often the term *communication* is applied to any *regularized or systematic interaction* that involves the transfer of information, whether or not so intended, by a communicator. For example, biologists have, in recent years, discovered how RNA (ribonucleic acid) molecules in the genes transfer information from the parent animals into DNA (deoxyribonucleic acid) molecules which control the protein synthesis and development of the new living organisms; this information transfer is regularly referred to as a type of cellular communication.

On the other hand, other types of systematic activity have been

---

2 Colin Cherry, *On Human Communication* (Cambridge, Mass.: M.I.T. Press, 1957); Claude E. Shannon and Warren Weaver, *The Mathematical Theory of Communication* (Urbana: University of Illinois Press, 1949).

called communication because the organisms involved also have other attributes of a social species. A moot question in some of these cases is whether or not the communicator organism is acting so intentionally. Investigators have found, for example, that bees communicate with each other about the location and availability of nectar by using a complex system of visual signals, mainly consisting of ritual "dances." If a source of nectar is about two hundred to three hundred feet away from the hive, bees will communicate this to their fellow workers by a circling dance. If the distance is greater the dance changes from circling to wagging. If more than three thousand yards away, the dance takes the form of long turns, whose frequency provides additional distance information. One part of each dance includes a head-up or head-down position, which is the signal that the nectar is to be found in the direction of the sun or away from it. Evidence that the bees are intentionally communicating with each other is the chirping beep that other bees make to indicate "message understood." There is substantial evidence that all types of lower animals have fairly explicit communication systems, utilizing visual, auditory, olfactory, and other sensory transmission devices. Animals that tend to develop organs of visual reception also tend to engage in gestural communicative activity; animals with organs that tend to produce sound also tend to develop specialized auditory organs.

In order for two or more humans to form a social group, some minimum degree of interaction among them must produce uniformities of behavior. The production of behavioral uniformities presumably requires a recurrence and regularity of interaction. Even in cases where the interaction involves no intentionally systematic language, gesture, or other sign, the "audience" members of the group may interpret the actions of a "communicator" member as a meaningful "transfer of information," that is, communication would be entirely by inference. In this minimal sense, a regularity in human interaction may have a communicative aspect.

Human interactions rarely remain devoid of explicit communicative activity for very long. Even the grunt of primitive man was sufficiently explicit to promote group formation processes. With the rapid development of linguistic tools, human beings have become so accustomed to communication that they tend to find messages even when there is silence or nonactivity. (Is the expressionless visage of an adversary evidence of hostility? Is his silence the ominous sign of the calm before a storm?)

Communication as a Process

Communication has also been studied as a social process since it requires two or more individuals interacting for at least some minimum period of time. The time may be short, perhaps no longer than it takes to smile meaningfully. The time may be long, as in the centuries-old academic discourses regarding particular fields of knowledge. Viewed as a process, one may analyze communication as a series of stages or phases.

The rule-of-thumb formulation of the basic components of the communication process has been as follows: a *communicator* transmits *content* through *channels* (or media) to an *audience* to produce an *effect*. Sometimes this is put in the form of a question: *Who* tells *what* through what *means* to *whom* and with what *success?*

The first component is the *communicator*, the one who initiates or emits the message. This may be an advertiser who calls attention to his product, a politician soliciting votes for himself or for a particular solution to a public problem, or a scientist reporting a discovery.

Content refers to the messages and their intended meanings. Content may take a number of signal forms. An obvious way of classifying some of these forms is according to sensory characteristics. Visible signals include printed language, pictorialization, and gesture. Audible signals include speech, music, and coded sounds of the Morse code type. Tactile signals include the hand codes of the deaf-blind and the touch skills of braille readers. Olfactory signals are a familiar product of perfume manufacturers and skilled chefs around the world. Content may be classified in many other ways. The terms *sign, signal, symbol,* and *sufficient cue* refer to certain characteristics of the messages, as we shall see. An investigator using the technique known as *content analysis* may be interested in such categories as words, symbols, sentences, paragraphs, articles, themes, etc. Subject matter, or the referents of the message, is another common basis for categorizing content.

Channels are the devices or agencies for carrying the messages from communicator to audience. They are sometimes classified as *unmediated* and *mediated*. Unmediated channels are usually those in which there is direct observability between communicator and audience, as in face-to-face conversation, round-table discussions, and classroom lectures. A mediated channel is one in which equipment or message handlers intervene between communicator and audience. Among the mechanical mediated channels are the telephone and the telegraph. The postal service is an agency type, as are the mediated channels normally subsumed under the term mass media: newspapers, magazines, books, films, radio, and television. Mediated channels are a consequence of man's ingenuity in developing remarkable technologies for carrying his messages to widely dispersed and remote audiences.

The *audience* is the target or destination of the communication, the readers, the listeners, and the viewers of the messages coming through the channels. Often enough the intended audience may not be the receiving audience; a candidate may make a last-minute television appeal to his constituency, but most of it may fail to tune in. Unintended audiences are also common, as evidenced by such pastimes as eavesdropping and wiretapping. The composition or characteristics of an audience may vary with different mass media: magazine audiences, for example, tend to consist of people different from those in radio audiences. Politicians and advertisers are particularly aware that audiences may have different background information, interests, attitudes, and personalities, and that this may have significant consequences for the effects of their messages.

Effect refers to any change in the audience's behavior as a consequence of the communication exposure. Such behavior may be overt, such as voting, writing, buying, making a communicative response, or it may be a subjective change, such as modification of an attitude or learning of information.

Somewhat more rigorous theorists refer to communication as an attempt to establish a *commonness* with another individual, that is, to share an attitude, a concept, or information with the latter. To complete the communication process at least three basic elements are necessary: the source, the message signal, and the destination. A *source* may be any individual or organization omitting message signals. The *message signal* may be in any one of several familiar physical forms: ink on paper, sound waves in the air, impulses in an electric current, a gesture of the body, a wave of a flag, or any other signal capable of being meaningfully interpreted. The destination may be any individual or organization engaged in such receiving activities as listening, watching or reading.

Encoding and *decoding* are two other aspects of the communication process. The source, in his attempt to establish commonness with an intended destination, converts the information or feeling that he wishes to share into a form that may be transmitted. This conversion is the encoding part of the process. If the source wishes to make his commentary accessible to a receiver, he must get it out of his own head, onto paper as written words, onto canvas as a painting, into a speech as a sequence of sound signals, and so on. Encoding may sometimes involve several mechanical conversions, e.g. the vocal vibrations that become sound waves converted into electrical impulses by the telephone and transmitted along wires to a receiving telephone. Decoding reverses the process, from electrical impulse to sound wave to vibrations within the auditory organ. Even the most perfect mechanical encoding and decoding is pointless, however, if the meaning of the message signals is not shared by both source and destination; an insurmountable decoding gap occurs if flawless French emitted by the source is heard by a receiver who understands only Japanese.

The full communication process, as just described, may be pictured as follows:[3]

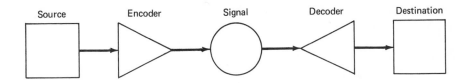

| Source | Encoder | Signal | Decoder | Destination |

Meaning is perhaps the most important element to be shared by source and destination if communication is to be successful. For shared meaning to occur, the physical *signs* making up the message must serve as a signal for or a representation of something in the experience of both the sender and the receiver. The signs must provide a *sufficient cue* to enable the receiver to identify the information being transferred to him by the source. To illustrate, the ink marks on this page are a type of physical sign. When we put these signs together to form the word "jury," we have produced a potential *signal*. This linguistic signal stands for something in the experience of *some* individuals, that is, it stands for a group of official persons

[3] From Wilbur Schramm, *The Process and Effects of Mass Communication* (Urbana: University of Illinois Press, 1955), p. 4. Diagrams used with permission of the University of Illinois Press.

in a court who hear evidence in a trial. To those who have never seen or heard about such groups, the signal is meaningless. For others who have, the printed term "jury" is signal enough, that is, a *sufficient cue* to enable them to make an identification with a degree of confidence.[4]

Unless both the source and the destination have shared the same or similar life experiences represented by a particular signal, communication about these experiences breaks down. For example, the words "vote" and "platform" are signals that represent aspects of the political experience of certain people. In the United States, large numbers of people have heard about or observed the referents of "vote" and "platform," and, to the extent that they have, share a sufficient degree of experience to be able to communicate by these signals. On the other hand, the primitive tribesman, in some removed corner of the world where elections and party organizations are unheard of, will have no familiarity with the terms themselves or with the objects to which they refer. Since the source can encode and the destination can decode only in terms of the experience each has had, only those signals that represent some overlapping or shared field of experience by both can be instrumental as a sufficient cue in transferring information between them. The following illustrates this point.

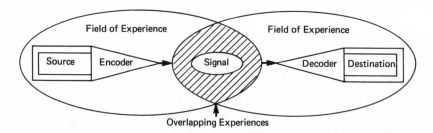

Overlapping Experiences

The communication process, as presented here, is unidirectional, that is, going from the source to the destination. When the destination emits its own signals in response to the source or in transferring the received information to others, the destination in turn becomes a source. Thus, in a normal conversation, the original sender may alternately be sender and receiver during the entire process.

Once a source has emitted signals, he may wonder with what suc-

[4] The concept *sufficient cue* is Alfred Kuhn's; *The Study of Society* (Homewood, Ill.: Dorsey Press, 1963), p. 105.

cess his intended meanings have been received and decoded. He looks for *feedback*, that is, evidence from which he may infer the degree of successful decoding of his message. The feedback may consist of a quizzical look, suggesting to the sender that his message is not comprehended. As a result, he may repeat the original message in some other formulation. Or, the feedback may be inferred from the appropriateness of a return message; an invitation to lunch ought to draw a "yes" or "no" reply rather than a "what?" One of the principal characteristics of mediated communication is the long delayed and somewhat sparse feedback. This may explain why many "old-fashioned" politicians prefer ringing doorbells and attending rallies during a campaign to sending their appeals over mediated channels such as television; the unmediated communication affords instant feedback, which is essential to the adaptiveness of campaign strategy and tactics.

Communication as an Act

Communication may also be studied as a particular type of act, distinguishable from other human acts such as eating, sleeping, building, etc. Newcomb has constructed an efficient model of communicative acts. An important feature of the Newcomb approach is that it enables us to infer from the character of a communicative act consequences leading to group formation. It also helps explain some of the particular properties that different groups acquire. To a great extent, group properties are predetermined by the conditions and consequences of communicative acts, according to Newcomb.[5]

The theory starts from the notion (noted above) that many social interactions may be better understood if we think of them as communicative acts. The useful consequences of communicative acts among human beings are essentially these: two or more individuals are enabled to achieve *simultaneous orientation* (1) toward one another as communicators and (2) towards the objects or referents of communication. *Orientation*, as used here, refers to an individual's *information about* and *attitude toward* some referent (real or not). When two individuals, A and B, have exactly the same information and attitude toward a referent X, their orientation to X may be called *symmetrical*. To the extent that A and B approach

[5] Theodore M. Newcomb, "An Approach of the Study of Communicative Acts," *Psychological Review*, 60 (November 1953): 393–404. Diagram reproduced by permission of the American Psychological Association, Inc.

a symmetrical orientation to X *and* also have comparably identical information and favorable attitudes toward each other, A and B may be said to have arrived at simultaneous orientation, or *co-orientation*. If A and B have orientations toward X and toward each other that are different or negative, they may undertake to improve their co-orientation by *straining toward symmetry*, that is, expending communicative effort. The strain toward symmetry is facilitated by the growth of favorable attitudes toward each other (*attraction*) as persons and by each of them toward X. These are the communicative antecedents of cooperation and group formation, which are viewed as consequences of strain toward symmetry.

Basically, every communicative act may be viewed as a transmission of information, consisting of discriminative stimuli, from a source to a recipient. *Discriminative stimulus* is a concept similar to "sufficient cue," used earlier, that is, some stimulus that is arbitrarily, symbolically, associated with some thing, state, event, or property, and which enables the stimulated organism to discriminate or distinguish this thing from others. Thus, by prior arrangement, Paul Revere was able to signal friends in Charlestown whether the British detachment would be going to Concord by water (two lanterns) or by land (one lantern). The number of lanterns provided the discriminative stimulus (or sufficient cue) by which information was transferred.

Thus, the simplest communicative act is described as one person A transmitting information to another person B about something X. The usual discriminative stimulus used by human beings tends to be representational, that is, a conceptual substitute, e.g., the word "cow" for the real cow, the symbol "X" which we put in quotation marks here to distinguish it from some referent X in the environment. The communicative act proper is the A-B-X relationship, that is, a complete behavioral event. As indicated earlier, the more A and B are attracted to each other and the more they share the same favorable attitude toward X, the more simultaneously oriented or co-oriented are A and B. The relationships may be illustrated as follows:

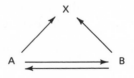

In the realm of actual behavior, this extremely simple model may quickly become complicated. The facts of A's orientation, that is, information and attitude, toward X must be matched against B's orientation toward X. These may vary in content and degree over a wide spectrum. Then, A's and B's orientations toward each other, also widely variable, must be ascertained. The odds against this four-way match being perfectly symmetrical are so great that the initiation of straining toward symmetry is highly probable. Of course, if the topic X is of little interest to one or both of the individuals, or if the attraction between A and B personally is minimal or negative, not much strain will be undertaken. Neighbors avoid discussing religious or political differences with each other when these topics seem less important than, say, remaining good neighbors. Under other circumstances, two warring nations are not likely to expend much effort straining towards symmetry with each other, particularly if interest in communicative activity itself could be interpreted as evidence of weakness.

The A-to-B-re-X model becomes even more complicated when we realize that A, B, or both may have *perceptions* about the degree of symmetry between themselves that may be quite different from the objective facts. One of the skills of a political leader is to listen to a petitioner so well and so acceptingly that he gives the latter the impression that he is in substantial agreement. Subsequent events may demonstrate the contrary, but the petitioner will have come away with a *perceived consensus* that lasts long enough, perhaps through election day, to serve the purposes of the political leader. Conversely, if one nation perceives another as more hostile than it actually is, the prospect increases that accidental events may lead to war between them. Perceived consensus, therefore, may have important consequences for the strain towards symmetry which leads to cooperation or, failing, to conflict.

Why do human beings strain toward symmetry at all? As Newcomb puts it: "It is an almost constant human necessity to orient oneself toward objects in the environment and also toward other persons oriented toward those same objects." Since each of us, in a short lifetime, cannot obtain information and develop attitudes about everything we encounter, we are compelled to rely heavily on the observations, information, and evaluations of others. Human beings have developed various procedures of social confirmation and a *social reality* consisting of information and attitudinal recommendations. Was there a Ho Chi Minh? We believe so because, for example, (1) we read about him in the news media and (2) we know that a President of the United States had written a letter to North Vietnam addressed to "President Ho Chi Minh." In both instances, however, belief is based upon our acceptance of the sources—the press and the President. The more complex our environment, the greater our reliance upon such sources of social reality. What we are willing to expend to gain such information depends a great deal upon the significance of the uses to which we wish to put it.

Straining toward symmetry may be rewarding for other reasons best explained by the A-to-B-re-X model. A likes to have his present information and attitudes about X validated. To the extent that straining toward symmetry about X produces greater attraction between A and B, the more confident each will be about the other as a source of information about social reality and the more likely the state of information and attitudes of each will be reinforced. We talk to people we like because they are likely to tell us what we want to hear. Members of the same political groups tend to make each other happy by confirming each other's information and attitudes about political issues and personalities. After bolstering each other's confidence, they are braver about making forays into the political arena with their demands and recommendations. We sometimes hear of organizations—the National Association of Manufacturers, the American Farm Bureau Federation, the AFL-CIO, the John Birch Society—inviting "outsiders" or "the opposition" to address them. However, these exposures to challenging orientations tend to be quite brief and are usually taken as an occasion for reaffirming the organization's own information and attitudes. The more extremely ideological the group, the more fervent the reaffirmation. Similarly, recent voting studies find that political party members tend to talk mainly to other members of the same party, providing each other with information on current issues, the candidates, and political events generally. Very rarely do members of one party seriously attempt to convert members of the other.[6]

A second rewarding aspect of straining toward symmetry is the reduction of one's uncertainty about the probable behavior of others. When A and B communicate with each other about X, each is also,

[6] Bernard Berelson, Paul Lazarsfeld, and William McPhee, *Voting* (Chicago: University of Chicago Press, 1954), pp. 109 ff.

coincidentally, acquiring information about the other's information and attitudes. Informed leaders of the NAM have a fairly good idea what AFL-CIO leaders believe, and vice versa. Each knows from previous communication and behavior to what degree his own and the opposition's orientations toward some X (e.g. labor-management contracts) are symmetrical. Despite all the shooting at each other, the predictability of each other's behavior, inferred from previous communicative activity, is an element of importance in the reduction of political tension and the elimination of political miscalculation.

Sources of Error and Conflict in Communication

There are circumstances under which communicative activity produces errors, asymmetry, cessation of efforts to communicate, and social conflict. There are many pitfalls associated with discriminative stimuli or signals. In the first place, overlapping fields of experience associated with the signal may not exist for both the source and destination; "minimum wage" is a fairly well-defined term for most Americans but unheard of in, say, Yemen, and so could hardly be a meaningful signal in a political discussion between an American and a Yemenite.

Secondly, the same signal may represent very dissimilar experiences. In the Soviet Union "party membership" represents a major political involvement and achievement; in the United States, it is a casual, almost fickle, relationship.

A third pitfall arises from the fact that the source and the destination may share only a limited part of their respective fields of experience. While many informed Americans of all generations know about the Great Depression of the early 1930s, the youngest and the oldest inevitably attach very different meanings to descriptions of that traumatic national period.

A fourth pitfall is the possibility that different signals may represent the same shared experience, a familiar hurdle compounded by the variety of languages in the world. The signal "love" in English means the same as "amor" in Spanish, "an airplane" is "un avion" in French, and "wasser" in German is "aqua" in Latin.

The elements of Newcomb's A-to-B-re-X enable us to identify other sources of difficulty arising out of communicative activity. For example, if A and B dislike each other as persons, they are not likely to strain toward symmetry. Or, if A likes but B dislikes X, they may strain toward symmetry only to the extent that their mutual personal attraction makes it worthwhile; at some point, such communicative activity may cease because the degree of personal attraction between A and B has declined or the topic X just does not seem worth the risk of personal enmity. In the latter case, individuals who are attracted toward each other may "agree to disagree" in silence about some matters because the topic X is of less interest than the maintenance of co-orientation toward each other as persons.

The list of possible sources of error and conflict in communicative activity can be long. Such a list leads us to wonder how human beings manage at all to comprehend, co-orient, strain toward symmetry, or cooperate. Even feedback, the means by which the communicator checks out the success of his communicative effort, may be a source of difficulty. The long incumbent politician who is enthusiastically supported by old political friends for his conduct in office may misread this as support from his entire constituency; the feedback on election day may, and frequently is, filled with surprisingly different evidence.

There is next the problem of noise. *Noise* refers to any phenomenon that distorts or interferes with the signal emitted by the communicator. Traffic sounds become noise when they interfere with the sounds of a concert. Heckling is noise to a speaker trying to deliver an address. Because of noise, an audience may receive incomplete and distorted signals and may have great difficulty in decoding the intended meanings of the communicator.

Men have institutionalized some types of communicative activity precisely to identify and pursue conflicts among themselves. Debates and propaganda efforts are of this type. Conflicts over the meanings of words as discriminative stimuli, as is so common in court litigation, are another. Verbal bluffing and misinformation are still other sources of error and conflict. Clearly, communicative activity may be productive of disorientation as well as co-orientation.

INFORMATION THEORY

Information as Certainty about Outcomes

If communication is essentially a transmission of information, what then are the principal attributes of *information?* In recent years communication engineers, psychologists, and other specialists have produced a professional literature often referred to as information theory. In it, we learn that not every statement about or observation of the world provides information. A statement or an observation is informative (1) if it tells us something about the world that we did not already know, and (2) if it helps us predict outcomes of choices or events. We gain information only about matters concerning which we are to some degree ignorant or uncertain. Information has therefore been defined as that which reduces uncertainty. If we are able to measure uncertainty, we are also able to measure amounts of information.

Information may help us organize our responses in coping with the environment. Organizing our capacity to cope with the environment introduces predictability into our relationship with that environment. The *amount* of predictability—hence the *amount* of information—depends on whether the information permits us to guess accurately regarding which of several possible outcomes will be the one that actually occurs.

Uncertainty regarding the outcome of an event increases with the number of possible outcomes it may have. Assuming that the different outcomes may occur with equal probability, a good coin, when tossed, can fall only one of *two* ways; a die may fall any one of *six* ways. The outcome of a toss of a die is more uncertain that the outcome of a toss of a coin. More uncertain than these is the draw of a card from a deck in which there are *fifty-two* equally possible outcomes.

What does it take to reduce uncertainty? Imagine that you have before you a checkerboard like the one below. Think of a particular square on it. Invite a friend to find out which square it is by asking you questions. Your friend starts out by being totally uncertain or uninformed. He could point randomly at *each* square of the sixty-four on the board, ask you "Is this it?" and, with exceptionally poor luck, eventually point to the correct square after you have answered his *sixty-third* question. This would certainly be an inefficient and costly way for him to gather the necessary information.

If he pursues a more efficient line of questioning, he can reach the exact answer in *six* inquiries, as follows: "Is it one of the 32 on the left half of the board?" (Let us say your answer is "Yes"). "Is it one of the 16 in the upper half of the 32 remaining?" ("No.") "Is it one of the 8 in the left hand of the 16 remaining?" ("No.") "Is it one of the 4 in the upper half of the 8 remaining?" ("No.") "Is it one of the 2 in the left half of the 4 remaining?" ("Yes.") "Is it the upper one of the 2 remaining?" ("Yes.")

In other words, his quest for information was conducted in such a way that each response in a series of possible binary responses (yes-no) enabled him each time to *reduce by half* the number of possible locations of the square you had in mind. Each reduction by half of the possible answers or outcomes constitutes, in information theory, a *bit* (*bi*nary un*it*). In our checkerboard illustration, there could be no ambiguity about your responses; each had to be either "yes" or "no," never "maybe." Furthermore, as far as your friend was concerned, there was an *equal probability* that each response could be either "yes" or "no."

In order to go from total uncertainty or lack of information to complete certainty or total information, your friend had to put *six well-designed questions* to you. These were well-designed because two equally probable alternatives (yes-no) compelled the production of information a "bit" at a time (that is, providing a basis for dismissing half of the available alternatives at a time). It required six such questions to arrive at certainty. Theoretically, therefore, the *amount* of uncertainty in the original question ("Which square on this checkerboard am I thinking of?") was *two* equally probable alternatives multiplied by each other six times, that is, raised to the *sixth* power ($2 \times 2 \times 2 \times 2 \times 2 \times 2$), or *six* bits. Another way of saying this is that the number of *messages* producing the exact correct answer carried six bits of information.

Because information theory undertakes to be rigorously quantitative, it is interesting, although not necessary for the purposes of this introductory survey, to note how its theorists proceed with their

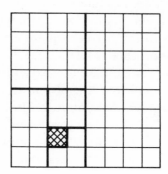

quantification work. For example, to simplify the mathematical operations involved in information theory, experts in this field have resorted to using logarithms to represent the amounts of information carried by a series of messages. The basic formula is: $H = \log_2 m$. The amount of uncertainty is represented by H, the number of alternative outcomes or answers for the question at hand is represented by m, and 2 (used as the "base" number) represents the binary, equiprobable messages carrying information in response to each question. In our checkerboard illustration, m is 64. Therefore, $\log_2 64 = 6$. In other words, if 2 is raised to its sixth power, we have the total number of possible alternatives or answers to the original problem. Six, then, equals H, or the amount of information needed, that is, six bits.[7]

What is the amount of uncertainty, or H, about which side of a die will turn up upon a throw? A die has six sides, which puts m equal to 6. $H = \log_2 6$ (read, "log six to the base two"), or 2.58 bits. This means that from two to three bits of information, presumably in response to two or three well-designed questions, would be needed to identify the face of the die likely to turn up. The questions might go something like this: "Is the up-turned side an odd number?" ("No.") "Is the upturned face larger than 4?" ("No.") "Is the upturned face the larger number?" ("No.") This, of course, leads us to the conclusion that the upturned face of the die in this throw is 2. The halving of possible outcomes proceeded as follows:

Possible Outcomes	First Query	Second Query	Third Query
1			
2	2		
3		2	
4	4		2
5		4	
6	6		

How many bits of information would we need to be certain which of a deck of fifty-two cards had just been drawn in some hypothetical

---

[7] Logarithms are a mathematical shortcut for handling complex computational procedures. An ordinary number such as 100 may be broken down into a *base*, customarily 10 (but 2 for the convenience of information theorists dealing with binary units), and *exponent*, that is, the number of times 10 would have to be multiplied by itself to produce the original number. In this case, $\log_{10} 100 = 2$; that is, 10 multiplied by itself twice produces 100. Using logarithms, the multiplication of, say, 64 × 4096 becomes a simple addition problem. Reach for the nearest mathematics book and look for the logarithm table in one of its appendices. Log 64 turns out to be 1.806 and log 4096 is 3.612. Adding the two figures produces a total 5.418, which, again using the table, converts back to 262,144, our answer.

card trick? $H = \log_2 52$, or 5.70 bits; in other words, between five or six bits of information. Notice how precisely this formula quantifies what we might have known intuitively, namely, that more information is needed to guess the card drawn than the face of the die thrown. In this case, 2.58 (for the die) is exactly 3.12 bits less information than 5.70 (for the card).

Of course, most of our situations of uncertainty, or *informational need*, in real life do not have the precise and explicit character of our checkerboard illustration, with an exact number of possible answers. Nor, in real life, do most of us have the insight or perception to put well-designed questions in order to elicit information efficiently. Worst of all, most of our answers are not "yes" or "no" with equal probability of being one or the other, but read more like "maybe."

For information theorists, these difficulties are merely complications of their basic theoretical approach. In order to deal with the "maybe" kinds of information they have simply added a probability dimension to the formula $H = \log_2 m$. This was done by converting m—which refers to an exact number of equally possible outcomes— to $1/p$—which states that any one outcome has only the probability p of occurring.

Ordinarily a sound coin, if tossed, has only two equally probable outcomes: "heads" with .50 probability, and "tails," with .50 probability. A bent or biased coin, however, may have different outcomes. For example, heads may come up nine-tenths of the time and tails only one-tenth. The probability p of seeing a heads is .90 and tails .10. In the information theory formula the amount of uncertainty about the fall of the particular alternative heads (with its .90 probability) is:

$$H = \log_2 1/.90 = \log_2 1.11 = .15 \text{ bits}$$

The amount of uncertainty about the fall of tails (with its .10 probability) is:

$$H = \log_2 1/.10 = \log_2 10 = 3.32 \text{ bits}$$

Intuitively, in this example, we are more confident or more certain about the turning up of heads, which seems bound to turn up more often, than we are about the turning up of tails. By the information theory formula, this intuition is confirmed mathematically, since .15 bits represents less uncertainty and 3.32 bits more uncertainty.[8]

[8] For further material on the technical aspects of information theory, George A. Miller, "What is Information Measurement," *American Psychologist* (January 1953):

This brief introduction to the mathematical side of information theory is given here simply to be explicit about what is involved in the prediction of particular future events from information gathered about past events. Two examples of forecasting (which, as we shall see in a later chapter, is a more accurate term under these circumstances than predicting) may be built upon the findings of voter behavior studies of recent years; the first, a personal illustration; the second, the Simulmatics Project in the 1960 presidential election campaign. Both examples involve forecasts about how voters will behave under certain circumstances.

In the first illustration let us assume that you are interested in guessing how a Catholic friend is likely to vote in the next election. Or the bases of previous studies of voting we may safely guess (hypothesize) that religious affiliation has something to do with party preference. By asking well-designed questions in careful surveys of party preferences among a sample of voters, political behaviorists have discovered that Protestants vote Democratic in slightly less than five out of every ten cases, Catholics vote Democratic about six to seven cases out of ten, and Jews do so eight times out of ten. Repeated observations have confirmed that this is *usually* the case, hence we have good information in probabilistic form from which to make some shrewd guesses about the party preferences of particular individuals we may encounter. Thus, odds are about six in ten that a Catholic we meet probably votes for the Democratic party whenever he goes to the polls. A well-designed second question about this Catholic, say, about his income, may enable us to make an even more accurate guess; e.g., *upper income* Catholics tend to vote Republican. If our friend is a low-income Catholic, the odds that he is a Democrat increase.

Many behavioral scientists are optimistic that large amounts of information about human behavior will eventually be produced, enabling us to cope with some of our more serious psychological and social problems: war, crime, mental health, etc. One impressive demonstration of the use of substantial amounts of accumulated behavioral information was the Simulmatics Project developed during the 1960 presidential race. Since 1936, public opinion survey organizations have been sampling national voter opinion. A group of

---

1-11; Fred Attneave, *Applications of Information Theory to Psychology* (New York: Holt-Dryden, 1959); F. M. Reza, *An Introduction to Information Theory* (New York: McGraw-Hill, 1961); Henry Quastler (ed.) *Information Theory in Psychology* (New York: Free Press, 1955), esp. pp. 8–12.

M.I.T. and Columbia University social scientists collected the findings of sixty-six of these nationwide opinion surveys made since 1952 and stored the information bits into an electronic computer in the format of a mathematical model of the United States electorate. The information represented interviews with 100,000 eligible voters, whose social characteristics (religious affiliation, income category, rural-urban residence, regional location, sex, and many other attributes) and opinions on as many as fifty issues (civil rights, labor legislation, McCarthyism, the H-bomb, etc.) were, in effect, "well-designed questions" whose answers constituted the specific bits of information stored in the memory of an IBM 704 computer. In all, some six to seven million bits of information were mobilized to tell which of several possible ways the 100,000,000 eligible voters of 1960 might react to particular issues introduced into the 1960 presidential campaign.

One question asked of the computer was: "What will be the (presidential) voting consequences of an embitterment of the religious issue raised by Kennedy's Catholic church affiliation?" The computer and its programmers had enough information to make the predictions in the first column of the table below, that is, about social attributes of voters, their attitudes on particular issues, and the various degrees of correlation among these and other factors. The "embitterment" actually did occur during mid-August, 1960. By coincidence, an opinion polling organization conducted a national survey at just this same time, revealing the distributions in the second column below. The Simulmatics predictions, based on information about behaviors that had taken place between 1952 and 1959, came remarkably close to the actual behaviors of August, 1960.

VOTER PREFERENCE FOR KENNEDY, 1960, AT TIME OF
"EMBITTERMENT" OF RELIGIOUS ISSUE
(Regional percentages favoring Kennedy)

Region	Simulmatics Forecast	August Survey Findings	Difference
East	51%	54%	3%
Border	49	42	7
South	47	47	none
Midwest	45	48	3
West	46	44	2

The Simulmatics report to Robert F. Kennedy observed:

Kennedy today has lost the bulk of the votes he would lose if the election campaign were to be embittered by the issue of anti-Catholicism. The net worst has been done. If the campaign becomes embittered he will lose a few more reluctant Protestant votes to Nixon, but will gain Catholic and minority group votes. Bitter anti-Catholicism in the campaign would bring about a reaction against prejudice and for Kennedy from Catholics and others who would resent overt prejudice. It is in Kennedy's hands to handle the religious issue during the campaign in a way that maximizes Kennedy votes.[9]

The Simulmatics Project demonstrates that even for as complex a political phenomenon as the collective behavior of 100,000,000 American voters relatively well-confirmed bits of information, such as produced in the recent studies of American voting, may reduce uncertainty to a predictable outcome. The laboratory scientist has, of course, appreciated this fact for a long time in fields other than the study of political behavior.

Information Management Problems

Social animals, as we have seen, give each other information and mutual aid through signaling systems, that is, through communicative activity. Such information helps the individual animal overcome uncertainty about its adjustment to environmental conditions, such as location of food, shelter, mate, other members of the species, etc. The communicating animal often emits signals in a variety of forms, depending upon the sensory specialization of the species. In the case of the human species, language is perhaps its most remarkable invention for conveying large amounts of information. For example, there are about one thousand commonly used monosyllables in the English language; the *amount* of information conveyed by a single monosyllabic word selected at random therefore is about ten bits.

Human communication is a difficult and costly process to organize and manage. Skill in communication and information management is nonetheless essential for successful adjustment to environmental conditions. *Lack* of skill may be costly in terms of survival itself. For example, the first nuclear chain reaction produced at the University of Chicago was an event never before produced by man. Unskilled information management could have produced a grievous error, conceivably the destruction of the planet or all life on it. The

9 Thomas B. Morgan, "The People-Machine," *Harper's*, January, 1961, pp. 53–57.

amount of confirmed information relevant to the production of such chain reactions was obviously sufficient to enable the atomic scientists to predict with confidence the probable outcome of their experiments.

Consider some of the elements with which a communicator must deal:

1. He must design and deliver the message in a way that will gain and hold the attention of the intended audience. It is a commonplace among experienced politicians that the key to most election victories is simply getting enough voters to remember his candidate's name.
2. The signals must adequately refer to experiences and phenomena known in common by both the communicator and the audience. The concept "equality," for example, is experienced differently in a caste society and in a classless society.
3. The meaning of the message must somehow relate to the audience's expectations, goals, and personality needs if an effect is to follow from the communicative activity. Thus, a sex-and-beauty-conscious populace makes an excellent audience for cosmetics advertising.
4. The communicator, either by words or example, must explicitly suggest behaviors that could implement the audience's expectations, goals and needs. "You may be assured of peace and prosperity, fellow citizens, *if you cast your vote for me.*"
5. The communicator must accurately "read" and interpret audience response as either feedback or as a performance of the intended behavior. A well-applauded speech may not necessarily mean support for a candidacy at the ballot box.

COSTS   These communication problems demand skill, effort, and expenditure of costly resources. The communicator must concern himself with clarity of his own intention, signal design, media construction, audience analysis, and facilitation of audience response. As he expends his own resources, the communicator must at the same time endeavor to reduce to a minimum the cost of information acquisition to the audience. Some citizens, for example, feel that politics is "not worth" much attention, so they are willing to leave the important decisions to others, rely on party labels in their choice of leaders, and decline to vote on difficult referenda propositions. For some, even the small effort required to register for voting is too high a cost compared with the small reward they see themselves receiving.

STORAGE CAPACITY   Information may be emitted, received, applied to a decision, and dissipated. A telephone line, for example, receives and transmits information; it has no "memory." A brief description of electronic computers, which are often compared to the human nervous system, may help demonstrate what is involved in information storage.

There are well over three hundred types of electronic computers, each with different operating characteristics and storage capacities. In general, information goes into the computer system by way of holes on punched cards or paper tape, magnetized spots on magnetic tape, letters and numbers printed on paper in magnetic ink, or the signals of an electric typewriter connected directly to the computer. This information may consist of *data observations* about the world (e.g., sets of numbers reporting population information, information about checks clearing through a bank on a particular day, observations made during a laboratory test, etc.) or *program instructions* concerning the desired machine manipulations of the data (e.g., add the data, list the checks according to bank of origin, correlate information about certain variables observed in the laboratory, etc.) The human operator encodes the original information as ordinary decimal system numbers or as English language sentences. These must be further encoded into the binary form manipulable by the computer. The electrical circuitry of the computer can only deal with the fact that an electrical impulse is present or absent, on or off, yes or no, zero or one. Decimal numbers must be converted to binary numbers, and letters of the alphabet must be converted into binary code.

A computer receives information, flashed along wires as electrical impulses, not unlike those of the nerve fiber, and stores the information in *memory* or storage devices. Computer memories are, in effect, electronic file cabinets set up according to a prearranged index scheme. Several types of storage "bins" have been invented, including the magnetic core (a tiny ring of ferrous material that may be magnetized in one direction or the other to represent zero or one in the binary digit system) and cathode ray tubes (wherein zero or one are represented by the presence or absence of an electrical charge).

DIAGRAM OF ELEMENTS IN ELECTRONIC COMPUTER INFORMATION FLOW

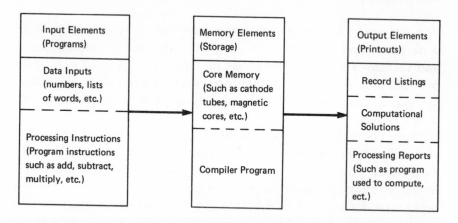

Information may consist of data observations, program instructions, results of different stages of the computations, and reference tables. Input information is stored on one set of *addresses* or storage units and manipulated according to instructions or *programs* stored at other bins or addresses. There are just a few basic ways in which the data may be processed—addition, subtraction, multiplication, division and a limited number of logical operations such as determining if one number is larger than another—but the many combinations of these basic operations permit a substantial range of data manipulation. Since everything inside a computer is in binary code, programming also encompasses an elaborate set of encoding and decoding instructions. Once the instructions are carefully laid out, however, large volumes of information may be received, processed, and retrieved in seconds and milliseconds.

There is a growing body of psychological theory which views the human memory equipment as strikingly analogous to that of the computer. Distinguished scientists have speculated about whether or not the operation of the nervous system can be imitated on computers and have even written computer programs to do so. This field is called "computer simulation of cognitive processes." Computer programs have also been developed for performing logical analyses, chess playing, musical composition, and solving human decision-making problems.

A very important limitation in the use of computers is storage capacity. Computers are currently able to store as many as several hundred thousand bits of information, and that capacity may be augmented by pooling several storage units. Some manufacturers are able to produce machines capable of storing *several million* bits. Like the computer, the brain is able to store bits of data observation and programs of instructions for manipulating these data. The human brain, however, is composed of some *ten billion* nerve cells, each capable of the binary alternatives of firing or not firing electrical impulses.

If the brain has greater storage capacity than the electronic computer, it also has far more to store. Several guesses have been made as to how many items are accumulated in human memory over a lifetime. Some tests suggest that each tenth of a second is a single "frame" (in the camera sense) of experience for the human brain. In that tenth of a second the brain can receive perhaps as many as a thousand bits of information. In seventy years, assuming no reception during sleep, some *fifteen trillion bits* may come into the brain for storage. This number is over a thousand times larger than the total number of nerve cells in the brain; a problem of storage capacity obviously exists for each of us. This lack of storage space may in part be what the "forgetting" process is about.

Returning, however, to the "remembering" process, it is the information that is adequately stored that we use to organize our beliefs and make decisions, as will be described in Chapter 5. Recent scientific investigations provide dramatic new insights into the biochemistry of memory, reinforcing speculation that the nervous system and the computer may indeed be analogous in important ways. Experiments reveal a number of events that take place in the synapse between neurons in the nervous system whenever electrical impulses carrying information bits are received. As the electrical impulses leap across the synapse from one neuron to another, chemical substances regularly located at the synapse are altered in molecular structure. The restructuring of these molecular arrangements is theoretically analogous to magnetizing cathode ray tubes or other storage devices in computers; the same binary coding system operates. For this reason, any chemical or physical damage to selected synapse areas, in the brain particularly, may destroy memory by destroying the chemical storage units and their contents.

The limited storage capacity of the human neural structure is a problem. How does the nervous system handle it? Many theorizers believe that the answer lies in the way the synapse "dismisses" or "absorbs" redundancy and reinforcement information. Somehow, redundant information makes little "impression." Information that reinforces what is already known is somehow "laid over" previous information like a new coat of paint.

REDUNDANCY   Information managers must deal not only with the acquisition and storage of information, they must also look into the presence of redundancy. *Redundancy* refers to the efficiency of the message signal. In linguistics, for example, how much can one reduce the signals used in a message and still communicate the full meaning of that message? The part we can eliminate is "redundancy" of the message. FR EXMPLE WENTYIVE PRCET OF HE LTTERS I TIS SENTENCE HVE BEN DLETED AT RANM (For example, twenty-five percent of the letters in this sentence have been deleted at random). Even a random removal of letters leaves a message that is relatively intelligible.

The redundancy found in the English language is said to be over 50 percent. Eliminating redundancy is important to a stenographer, who must abbreviate to the extreme without introducing confusion. In cryptography, redundancy may lead to the breaking of a code. Mathematical and symbolic logic are basically attempts to avoid redundancy; note the absence of redundancy in Einstein's formulation: $e = mc^2$. Compare this earth-shaking equation with the kinds of messages encountered in political science. How many books have been written about the nature of the state, and still we remain uncertain about that nature! Can the relationships among liberty, equality, and fraternity be reduced to the trim simplicity of an Einsteinian equation? Perhaps, some day.

Redundancy in the messages of many of the sciences may simply be a reflection of lack of information. Redundancy is the attempt of the message sender to reduce error and misunderstanding that could result from his message. The large amount of redundancy humans seem to need in their normal communication reflects the basic inefficiency of language and other human information-handling systems. It has been argued that if we used our alphabet more efficiently we could reduce most of our books and other communications to one-fourth of their present size.

Linguistic redundancy is also a consequence of the fact that we use words *in sequences* when communicating. Each word in a sequence influences the probability that some other particular word will follow. "I hope to see you again very . . . ." The word you might choose to complete the sentence is "soon," "often," or perhaps "much." You would hardly choose "boat" or "fountain pen." As a result of customary linguistic usage, the context (or previous information) provided by the words that went before reduces the range of word alternatives. When the final word ("soon") does occur, some of the information it conveys is identical with information we already have received from the context. This repeated information in the sequence is redundancy.

CHANNEL CAPACITY   How much information can the human neural channels handle at one time? How do we organize information in memory and program its manipulation and recall?

In a good communication system there must be some systematic relationship between what messages go *in* and what comes *out*. The sound wave inputs into a telephone are expected to produce the same sound wave outputs at the receiving end. If the telephone lines are "overloaded" because more sound impulses have been put in than the equipment is able to carry as electrical impulses, the sound outputs may be systematically reduced. The level at which such signals begin to fail to pass through regularly is called *channel capacity*. The variance between input and output establishes the limit within which the channel handles information. "Noise" along the wires may, by using up some of the capacity, have a further channel-limiting effect.

In human channels, the amount of information that a communicator emits may be easy to measure by counting the number of bits put into the communication channel. It is another matter, however, to determine how much of the emitted information is actually received by the audience. Any instructor who has tried to gauge the amount of information he has transmitted by submitting his students to examination knows, sometimes sadly, how much has been lost en route, perhaps because of limited channel capacity.

In a number of psychological experiments, channel capacity is inferred from measures of the subject's ability to discriminate visually or otherwise among given stimuli. The findings suggest that human visual and auditory channels have relatively low capacity. Try the following experiment. Grasp and throw a handful of beans onto a table. Look, and report instantly your estimate of the number thrown. With each throw vary the number of beans. If the number is from one to about five, you will notice that you rarely make a mistake in your estimate. When the number of beans reaches six or seven, you will notice that you begin to make errors in the estimates. At ten beans, your estimates will probably be wrong half the time; at fifteen, you will almost always estimate incorrectly.

Experiments of this type have also been performed with variations in pitches of sound. It was found that listeners can distinguish fairly accurately up to about six or seven different pitches. Beyond this, the rate of confusion rises rapidly. These experiments suggest that something happens to the normal individual's capacity for transmitting and processing information whenever the number of discrete items or alternatives becomes greater than six or seven. Seven seems to be the normal information channel capacity for people.[10]

Consider the relevance of the concept of channel capacity for a President who may suddenly need thousands of bits of information about some international or domestic crisis. Are the missiles placed by the Soviet Union in Cuba of the "offensive" or "defensive" type? Have the North Vietnamese communicated a willingness to negotiate or simply restated old and untenable conditions? Which side fired the first shot in the Middle East? What were the circumstances of the latest civil rights demonstration?

The President, and for that matter each of us, faces the managerial problem of *cognitive integration* of information. How do we classify, package, and label information received from the environment? As we saw in the checkerboard illustration, well-designed questions (hypotheses) may help reduce uncertainty about the environment in an economical way. Similarly, well-packaged messages may permit an economical use of channel capacity and an effortless integration of information into the cognitive organization of the individual. If information bits can be well organized into a manageable number of units (presumably, seven for people), then, psychologically speaking, storage and retrieval may be vastly facilitated. If a President needs a large bureaucracy to help him handle information this efficiently, think what the poor average citizen faces when he tries to incorporate and work with the daily outpourings of the newspaper he reads.

One old strategy of learning, or information storage, is to associate new information with something already known. A simple illustra-

---

[10] George A. Miller, "The Magical Number Seven, Plus or Minus Two," *Psychological Review*, 63 (March 1956): 81–97. Also, Harold W. Hake, "A Note on the Concept of 'Channel Capacity' in Psychology," in Henry Quastler (ed.), *Information Theory in Psychology* (New York: Free Press, 1955).

tion of how information may be organized efficiently follows. First, think of a 25-word *sentence*. Then, think of a sequence of 25 unrelated words. Which seems shorter? The sentence, of course. Whereas each of the series of 25 unrelated words is a separate information unit, the sentence is not 25 words, six or so phrases, or 100 or so letters, but rather *one* proposition. Another example is as follows. A normal person can repeat nine binary digits (made up of zero or one) without great strain. The informational value of nine binary digits is nine bits. The same person can usually repeat five monosyllables with as much effort as the nine digits. However, the informational value of the five monosyllables, as we saw earlier, is 10 bits per monosyllable, or about 50 bits.

This same process of cognitive organization goes on in academic disciplines. The major concepts and theories of a field of knowledge are, in effect, devices for integrating a broad range of information economically. Learning-by-association assumes that individuals can acquire competencies as information managers. Learning-by-rote, on the other hand, implies that the individual is a blank blackboard, not an organizer of knowledge.

The philosopher Schopenhauer commented on cognitive organization in an essay entitled "On Thinking for Oneself." The illustration he provided will undoubtedly be relevant as long as students and scholars pursue learning and knowledge.

> A library may be very large; but if it is in disorder, it is not as useful as one that is smaller but well-arranged. In the same way, a man may have a great mass of knowledge, but if he has not worked it up thinking it over for himself, it has much less value than a far smaller amount which he has thoroughly pondered. . . . It is only when he has turned it over that he can be said to know it.[11]

In more contemporary and behavioral terms, Boulding calls attention to the fact that each individual has his own image of the world, society, himself, etc. Such distinct images are essentially systems of data organized by the individual, an information-organizing activity unique to man. A vital part of this human data bank is made up of feedback from the environment.

Psychic order within the individual depends upon the person's ability to maintain an open information system into which feedback data may be readily incorporated. In Boulding's opinion, communi-

---

[11] Arthur Schopenhaeur, *The Art of Literature* (Ann Arbor: University of Michigan Press, 1960), p. 43.

cation and feedback are the essential sources of orderly growth in both the individual and society.[2]

Group organization in society has a counterpart to the psychological organization of the individual, in that both types of organizational activity depend a great deal upon the goal or purpose of individuals. A common purpose is an essential component of organized group life. An individual's goal or purpose is an essential element for cognitive organization and information management. How much cost the individual is willing to expend in acquiring, storing, and organizing for systematic retrieval the information that is being constantly transmitted to him is contingent upon the *anticipated utilization* or *purpose* of the information for him. The student who wants to earn a scholarship judges high grades to be important, and he is willing to study hard to obtain information instrumental in receiving high grades. The nation whose physical security is in possible jeopardy at the hands of a powerful adversary is willing to pay for expensive intelligence networks. In both examples, the existence of highly valued goals makes high information costs seem well worthwhile. Political philosophers and practicing politicians will of course agree that the statement and restatement of goals are perhaps the most important as well as most difficult tasks of the political executives of a society. The need to communicate information about these goals will perhaps help explain the apparent verbosity of political leaders, particularly in a complex, multigoal society like that of the United States.

An Illustrative Use of the
Conceptual Perspective

PHILOSOPHY AND FACT ABOUT INFORMATION IN A DEMOCRACY

The American political culture is hostile to secrecy in public affairs, claims to infallibility, and aristocratic monopolies of information. Put more positively, ready access to and widespread sharing of in-

---

[12] Kenneth Boulding, *The Image* (Ann Arbor: University of Michigan Press, 1956). In contrast, see Norman Maier, *Frustration: The Study of Behavior Without a Goal* (Ann Arbor: University of Michigan Press, 1956).

formation is a fundamental good in the view of most Americans (although this view differs markedly from the fact that Americans tend to have very little political information personally). The consequences of these preferences are manifest in many places in the political system.

Secret societies are either discouraged or outlawed. Secret political deals, either in domestic politics or in the international field, are suspect. Supersecret agencies, such as the Central Intelligence Agency and the Federal Bureau of Investigation, are invariably the objects of mixed feelings; Americans have yet to be convinced that spying (TV heroes notwithstanding) is an essential part of national security activity. Even at the peak of wartime secrecy, government scientists and their colleagues outside of government have been reluctant in their acceptance of "secret" classification of the reporting of their work, insisting that science and discovery suffer from such censorship.

Another widely held view in the American culture is that people are fallible, particularly "the other fellow." Rare is the individual whose information, assumptions, and evidence are not subject to challenge. Not only the judicial process but also popular literature and entertainment sustain the view that "reasonable doubts" may and do exist regarding most human situations. Furthermore, it is part of the authentic style of many political leaders that they approach with "modest wisdom" all public issues and that they earnestly solicit advice and information from whatever source.

Nor does any select group or aristocracy possess a monopoly of information and knowledge. The omniscience attributed to central committees in some societies and elites in others is rarely imputed to any group in the United States. Even the Founding Fathers, whose aristocratic views are well known, felt that the privilege of education, while enjoyed by the few could, in the long run, be possessed by the many. To educate and inform as many citizens as possible, is, in the American view, not simply a gesture in the direction of the great merit and worth of the individual but rather a capital investment in the human resources of the nation. The more educated the populace, the easier for the nation to develop and maintain an advanced technological society. A knowledgeable working force can better deal with the sophisticated tools of modern industry. A knowledgeable consuming public can better earn the funds to buy and read the instructions for use of modern industrial products. In politics and social life, the more educated the individual, the greater is the informational bank on which he may draw for his day-to-day judgments. The better educated produce better goods, consume more goods, earn more money, and pay more taxes. From this point of view, the free and widespread distribution of information through free public education is perhaps the best technique any society can develop for reducing the general cost of information. In the United States, with the largest per capita allocation of resources for free education, this technique has consistently been used.

A community's stream of free information may be perceived and decoded differently by different citizens. Certain specialists tend to sharpen this differentiation by trying to reduce information costs relevant to *their own* particular purposes. Since every community must cope with uncertainty and accept divisions of labor, it is impossible for all men to be equally well informed politically, no matter how equal they may be in any or all other respects. A conception of democracy that is based upon the notion that every member of the electorate should be equally well informed denies the facts of uncertainty, specialization, and inequality in the distribution of information. As Anthony Downs points out, it would be irrational for citizens to try to become equally well informed since this effort would waste for most of them the cost-saving advantages of specialization.[13]

What do we know about the distribution of political information in the United States? A great deal of well-confirmed data has been gathered over the past two decades. A sample of the findings is as follows. At least one-third of the eligible voters of the United States have practically no political information upon which to base their decisions. This lack of information is closely associated with feelings of political ineffectiveness and disinterest in politics.[14] It is consistently found that, at the height of presidential election campaigns when free political information is probably at its most abundant, fully 10 percent of the eligible voters cannot name either candidate for President, and only about 50 percent can name either vice-presidential nominee.[15] In 1954, when highly publicized investigations into communism conducted by Senator Joseph McCarthy were at

[13] Anthony Downs, *An Economic Theory of Democracy* (New York: Harper, 1957).
[14] Angus Campbell et al., *The Voter Decides* (Evanston, Ill.: Row, Peterson, 1954).
[15] Herbert H. Hyman and Paul B. Sheatsley, "The Current Status of American Public Opinion," in Daniel Katz et al (eds.), *Public Opinion and Propaganda* (New York: Dryden Press, 1954), pp. 40–41, based on Gallup Polls.

their peak, 30 percent of the adult population could not name a single political leader—not even Senator McCarthy—taking a major part in such investigations.[16]

If we accept formal education as a rough yardstick of information about the political and social context of one's life, it is consistently found that college-educated persons are five times as likely to be very active politically and very well informed about politics as persons of grade school education.[17] Yet, even among the 10 percent rated "very active," there apparently exists a substantial degree of "political illiteracy." One-third of these "actives" could name no United States senator whose actions they disapproved. Ten per cent of those who did name a senator named someone not in the Senate.

In its 1956 presidential election survey, the Survey Research Center at the University of Michigan developed an "index of issue familiarity." The index ranked persons according to their willingness to express an opinion on the sixteen issues presented them by the interviewer. Those with the greatest degree of issue familiarity were also those who participated most in politics by talking to other people, giving money, attending political meetings, working for one of the parties or candidates, belonging to political clubs, and similar activities.[18]

All this in the United States, with only 5 percent illiteracy, one of the lowest in the world. What levels of political information may be expected in one of the emergent new nations with 90 percent or more illiteracy and with only a handful of leaders possessing any advanced formal education?

16 Samuel A. Stouffer, *Communism, Conformity, and Civil Liberties* (Garden City, N.Y.: Doubleday, 1954).

17 J. L. Woodward and Elmo Roper, "Political Activity in American Citizens," *American Political Science Review*, 44 (1950): 872–885.

18 V. O. Key, Jr., *Public Opinion and American Democracy* (New York: Knopf, 1961), p. 185.

Political Terms and Statements

Language is a principal means by which human beings communicate information to each other. Language is also a uniquely human artifact whose design features, production procedures, and practical use carry important implications for the conduct of politics. A term may acquire a definitional history of its own, and much of politics is concerned with the defining of terms. A symbol is a term that has become a sign valued by human beings. Statements, which may be empirical, valuational, or future-descriptive, are also information-transmitting human creations. One profoundly important use of language is as an aid in the perception and communication of time, particularly as this relates to purposes in the form of statements about the future. Much of the content of political traditions, philosophies, and ideologies consists of statements about the past and the future.

3

The Linguistic Aspects of Purpose, Policy, and Practice

Without language a group's members would have to communicate goals, task expectations, and other purpose and policy information by gesture and other nonlinguistic signs. This is how prelinguistic man had to do it. As a result, only the most immediately observable goals could be shared and only the most limited task expectations could be held by members of small and transitory groupings. Imagine trying to communicate the substance of the Constitution by means other than language or linguistic codes. From this we may sense how much the government of men must rely on linguistic tools.

LANGUAGE AS A POLITICAL TOOL

Organized groups of all kinds depend greatly upon language for communication of purposes, policies about task assignments and resource allocations, and descriptions of situations and behaviors experienced by members. Although there are other communication signs available to human beings, language provides for the most discriminative stimuli for human transmission of information.

Recall that a purpose or a goal is essentially a presently envisaged future state of affairs. To communicate the present mental image about the future, an individual or members of a group ordinarily resort to language; for example: "We need to invent techniques of human conflict that do not require violence." "Our cities must be rebuilt." "Every citizen should have a guaranteed annual income." Words such as these permit one individual to transmit to others what he *now* has in mind about the *future*.

Once the members of a group have identified a goal for themselves, their next problem is to specify and coordinate member behaviors and available resources in ways that may move the group as a whole toward its shared goal. Policies—public and private—are essentially choices among alternative behaviors and resources, made with the intention of implementing the group goal. The guidelines for conduct consonant with task expectations and the directives that allocate group resources are, for the most part, linguistic statements, perhaps in constitutional, statutory, or regulatory form, whose main audience consists of the group's members. "All residents will pay income taxes on April 15 according to specifications of current tax law." "All males 18 years of age and over shall register with their local Selective Service Board." "The 65-miles-per-hour speed limit on this highway will be strictly enforced." These are familiar public policy statements, in which specific members of the community are informed what they are expected to do under indicated circumstances.

Not only does language facilitate the description of goals and policies, it also aids in the reporting of past behavior and events, that is, communicate information about "practice." Newspaper reports and history books, for example, are usually accounts of what people did, their practices and actions, in the past. There are those who believe that a practice can be begun or ended by declaring a policy about it, but all too frequently it does not work out that way. The Eighteenth Amendment, with its proponents' goal of sobering up and protecting the health and morals of the American people, stated a policy that prohibited "the manufacture, sale, or transportation of intoxicating liquors within, the importation thereof into, or the exportation thereof from the United States . . . for beverage purposes." As every written account of American history shows, the practice was quite different from the policy or its goal; the Prohibition Era was a time of gross lawlessness and intensified liquor consumption.[1]

---

[1] Generations of political scientists and lawyers have analyzed constitutions, statutes, and public policy statements *as though* these political prescriptions described political practice. Confusion between what *ought* to be and what *is* is easy because both look alike in language.

Political language may consist of political *terms* and political *statements*. The rules of definition and of statement have been developed over the centuries by logicians and philosophers of science, and are still being developed by them. In the most significant way, politics concerns itself with the definition of its terms and the construction of its statements. When political terms and statements are woven together in any substantial length, we find ourselves dealing with ideologies, philosophies, propaganda, and empirical theories.[2]

EVOLUTION OF LANGUAGE

Archaeological research variously dates the emergence of early man from among the nonhuman primates between 25,000 and 250,000 years ago. Whatever the date, there is little doubt that early man was a communicator very much in the manner of the higher primates, using bodily gestures and relatively undifferentiated vocal sounds as his signaling system.[3] As vocal and auditory organs became more specialized, so did the intricacy of the human sound-making signal system. Successions of noises, tones, pauses, transitions, and other feature of *nonlinguistic speech* became *spoken language:* consistent, ordered, and traditional. Today's primitive communities in remote corners of the world continue to furnish evidence regarding the characteristics of early spoken languages. For example, the number of terms in these primitive language is few. The rules for combining or relating terms with each other are simple. The terms usually refer to very specific and concrete objects and situations in the immediate environment. Abstract terms or concepts are almost entirely absent.

Written Language

Some 50,000 to 100,000 years ago in the early years of the Old Stone Age, primitive men began to develop tools and weapons. Some exhumed incised tools, ivory carvings, and animal paintings date back

---

2 There are numerous ways of classifying the signs that serve as discriminative stimuli transmitting information. For example, signs may be classified according to the particular sensory organs serving as their channels: audible signs would include the music of national anthems; visual signs, paintings of national heroes, gestures such as the salute, as well as written language; tactile signs range from the hand-clasp to the punch; olfactory signs may include smells characterizing a community or an event. In such a classification, language would be a type of audible and visual sign.

3 Richard J. Andrew, "The Origins of Facial Expressions," *Scientific American* October, 1965, pp. 88–94.

about 20,000 years to the latter part of the Old Stone Age. Invariably, objects in the "artist's" immediate environment were depicted; usually people, animals, and objects of particular interest to him. As objects came to be represented by relatively standardized pictorial shapes chiseled or painted on stone or wood surfaces, these same objects were also being referred to with specific spoken sounds.

The attempt to relate standardized pictures with standardized sounds was a small connection that nonetheless took a long time to complete. The Egyptians and the Sumerians of Babylonia accomplished this connection, at the same time moving from pictography to script (4000–3000 B.C.). Both cultures conventionalized their pictures, marking them into soft clay tablets with blunt reed styli. As these styli marks grew increasingly wedge-shaped, they ceased to bear any resemblance to the objects they originally represented.

In time, the two cultures analyzed their *spoken* language into syllables and adopted a conventionalized written symbol for each syllable. This enabled them to denote in writing any spoken word without ambiguity. The Egyptians eventually coded the sounds of their spoken language to the point of producing written symbols for twenty-four consonants; the vowels were supplied by the reader, as is done today in shorthand writing. The Egyptians came close to producing a complete alphabet. Not quite trusting the understandability of a phonetic rendering, however, they retained the practice of adding a picture after spelling the consonants of a word. Redundancy is still motivated by this kind of distrust of language.

About 1000 B.C. the Phoenicians learned the Egyptians' writing technique, but, before long, discarded pictography completely and used only consonant sounds. Borrowing from the Phoenicians, the Greeks added vowel signs and produced the first complete modern alphabet. Greek interest went beyond the production of an alphabet, however, into problems that led them to produce rules of definition and logic for the management of language. The Greeks also were the first to record extensively systematic written observation about the world around them.

Today, only 3,000 years later, some 3,000 languages exist in the world. The more advanced language communities have vocabularies that include tens of thousands of terms. Libraries are filled with dictionaries that purport to compile the terms employed by each language community, and it is not uncommon for the average dictionary to report four or five different "meanings" or "definitions" per term. The mass production of language is a human industry whose rate of output seems to multiply with each passing decade.

Design Features of Language

Students of linguistics and communication have discovered that language has thirteen characteristics or *design features*. Certain of these features are lacking in nonlinguistic human systems and in the communication systems of other animals. Language is the only system that possesses all thirteen characteristics, confirming language to be a truly unique human tool.

Vocal-auditory channel is the first of the design features. This is the vocal-cords-to-ear-drums relationship, which has the advantage for primates of leaving the rest of their bodies free for other activities at the same time that communication takes place. When a linguistic signal can be heard by any auditory system within earshot and the source can be localized by binaural direction finding, a second feature is present: *broadcast transmission and directional reception*. *Rapid fading* is the disappearance of the sound signal after it is sent which allows the emission of a series of signals in quick succession.

Interchangeability enables a speaker to produce any linguistic message he can understand. (In nonlinguistic communication, the message receiver is not able to reproduce the sender's communicative activity; e.g., the characteristic courtship motions of the male and female stickleback are different, and neither can act out those appropriate to the other). The "total feedback" feature is the capacity of the speaker to hear everything of linguistic relevance in what *he* himself says. This is important to the internalization of communicative behavior, which is a substantial factor in human thinking processes.

Other features include:

> *specialization*, that is, the bodily operations for spreading the sound waves of speech serve no other function than signaling;
> *semanticity*, referring to the relatively fixed associations between message elements (words) and recurrent objects and situations in the world around the communicator;
> *arbitrariness*, the arbitrarily assigned meanings to particular

message elements, e.g., "salt" is neither salty nor granular but is arbitrarily the term assigned to an object with these characteristics;

discreteness, in which the available variety of sounds may be broken up into absolutely differentiated units, e.g., "bin" sounds different to the ear from "pin" at one specific point in the two sound sequences;

displacement, or the ability to talk about things that are remote in space or time or both from the location in which the talking goes on (unique to man, with the exception of bee-dancing);

productivity, the capacity to say things that have never been said or heard before and yet be understood by other speakers of the language;

traditional transmission, or the communication of language conventions by teaching and learning;

duality of patterning, the ability to take the same basic meaningless sounds and combine them into different permutations ("team" and "meat").[4]

Human language has all thirteen of these features, the most distinctive of which are: traditional transmission; productivity; duality of patterning; and displacement. Without traditional transmission, there could be no enduring grammatical usages or systems of logic, nor could there be an accumulation of definitions of terms that affords men a common starting place in communication between generations. Without productivity and duality of patterning, the invention of new sound combinations and concept formation with which to label the ever-increasing number of objects and relationships noticed in the human environment would be gravely inhibited, if not impossible. Without displacement, there could be no mass-distributed ideologies, philosophies, theories, or similar collections of statements about the universe and recommended conduct for dealing with it.

Arbitrariness, although not unique to language, has nonetheless been another influential feature. Arbitrariness refers to the dependence of the meaning of every message signal upon the message sender's and *only the message sender's* intention regarding its meaning. The audience may discover but it *never* bestows meanings (although it often tries) upon the message signals, except upon

[4] Charles D. Hockett, "The Origin of Speech" *Scientific American*, September, 1960.

agreement with the sender. Such agreements and conventions may facilitate the audience's task of discovery or make it easier to share meanings. But, in the first place, the sender can never be "wrong" about his choice of message signals, although he may be unwise, clumsy, or disinterested in making the audience's task less difficult.

If each message sender has the prerogative of arbitrariness, that is, using whatever terms he wishes and bestowing upon them whatever meanings he wishes, we can readily see how misunderstandings and disagreements may arise and how the problems of definitions of terms may become a significant element of politics. For example, the term "war" may be assigned arbitarily to events with violent or explosive characteristics. If a national leader declares that actions by another nation constitute "war," the latter, as an audience of the message signal, cannot change the former's meaning although he may challenge the *use* of the term "war" as arbitrary or refer to the indicated actions as a "police action" or "an act of self-defense."

Studying the Sign Process

The study of language systems has become the concern of several highly specialized academic disciplines. One of these is *semiotics*, or the study of signs and sign processes. A *sign process* is a mediated taking-account-of something. The three aspects of the process are the interpreter (usually the human source or recipient of messages), the sign as an object (sound waves in the air, markings on paper, etc.), and the thing signified or represented, that is, the referent. There are *natural* signs, such as clouds that signify for some the possibility of rain, and *conventional* signs, such as the idiom developed by a language community.

The three subfields of semiotic are concerned with distinct aspects of relationship among the three elements of semiosis or sign process. *Syntactics* studies the relationships that hold among sets of signs, as in grammatical relationships, formal logic, and pure mathematics. *Semantics* concerns itself with signification, that is, the relationship between a sign and the thing signified; problems of operational definition discussed below are essentially semantic issues. *Pragmatics* studies the relationship between the sign and the interpreter, that is, the psychological and social aspects of semiosis—whether the communicators know "the language" and can share the meanings of its terms. After all, knowing the language of the political science profession is what makes a political scientist.

Those who have studied mathematics and logic will appreciate that it is possible to produce a language system as a purely syntactical procedure without taking into account semantic and pragmatic issues. A logical syllogism or a mathematical formula can represent fictions entirely in the mind of their creator, without concern for actual referents or communicated meanings. Such artificial or constructed language systems may be found in formal logic, where the systems have a basic *vocabulary* (terms, or elements) and a *grammar* (a set of rules, or syntax). The syntactical rules (also called *formation rules* in logic) indicate the conditions under which the language's elements may be combined with each other into *well-formed formulations* (*wffs*), that is, *sentences* or *statements*. Rules for the definition of terms are among the syntactical rules of a language system.

The special work of students of language interests us because it provides insights into certain aspects of political life. A political battle over the meaning of a term may be better understood if we know some of the considerations behind the logician's rules of definition.

THE PRODUCTION AND DEFINITION OF POLITICAL TERMS

In examining the world around us and within us, we slice that world into many parts. We then assign names to the parts and to the relationships among them. The terms and their definitions, most of which we receive from our forebears, are influential intellectual "binoculars" through which we perceive our environment. Although we have the option of inventing new terms and definitions, if we wish to remain members of a particular language community and be understood in our communicative activity, we are likely to work with the available terms and language rules, deriving new terms and new rules from the old. Language, then, becomes an important part of the shared field of experience requisite in a communication process.

The individual who adopts the language agreements of his community also discovers that he is confined to certain established ways of interpreting his environment as a consequence of the language employed by his predecessors to analyze that environment. Thus it is difficult for him to describe that environment with impartiality. "All observers are not led by the same physical evidence to the same picture of the universe, unless their linguistic backgrounds are similar, or can in some way be calibrated."[5]

Calibration is a matching of degrees of meaning assigned to a term. A "warm day" to one man may be a "chilly day" to another, subjectively. By sharing a particular language and technological background, the temperature experiences of both men could be calibrated by showing each that the thermometer reading is 70 degrees. Their subjective experience would probably remain the same, but they will know more about their individual differences for having the thermometer reading. Similarly, a "capitalist" in the meaning of the Chinese or Soviet Communists would be difficult to calibrate with an American conception of the term.

Defining Terms

The definitions of a *natural* language community arise out of the meanings that members of that community become willing to share as a result of historical—often accidental—usage. A dictionary is a compendium of such historical usages. If they report accurately the extant terms and their meanings, dictionaries are historically sound.

Definitions developed according to the rules of logic are something else again. The rules of logic, which are always under discussion and revision among philosophers, attempt to keep the definitional process a public activity subject to open conclusions openly arrived at. The goal of workers in the field of logic has been precision of terminology when words are related to other words in some specific manner (as in the syllogism) or when terms are to be applied to very specific objects or conditions in the environment with consistency (as in the operational concepts of empirical science).

According to the theory of terms, a linguistic term is "any expression-type that may be treated for logical purposes as a single unit, insofar as its tokens may be thought of as purporting to refer or apply to an object or objects in the world at large."[6] *Tokens* are those specific things—noises, bits of writing, or gestures—with de-

---

[5] Benjamin Lee Whorf, "Science and Linguistics," *Technology Review*, 44 (1940):229 ff.
[6] Henry S. Leonard, *An Introduction to Principles of Right Reason* (New York: Holt, 1957), p. 184. Much of the discussion of definition that follows is based upon Leonard.

finite locations in space and time. The particular bits of writing that you observe on this page are tokens combined into letter-types, word-types, and phrase-types, all of which add up to *expression-types*. These shaped letters of the alphabet, then, are a conventionalized set of things abstracted from reality and composed into expression-types by this writer. If the reader understands the tokens as expression-types representing some referent in the world at large, the tokens may be called a *sufficient cue*[7] for achieving shared meaning between the sender and receiver of the communication.

A *term* may consist of one or several words. What is important is that the word or words contribute only one logical item to a proposition. For example, "Bob is taller than Sam" contains the phrase "taller than," two words which contribute only one logical item to the proposition.

Logicians have classifications for the process of definition. The two basic types that will concern us are *extensional definition* and *intensional definition*. These two types may be different perspectives upon the same term, just as one may examine a house from inside or outside.

Extensions of Terms

The *extension* of a term defines it according to the group or class of all those actual objects in the world at large to each of which the term refers or applies. The term may refer to attributes; e.g., "held the office of President of the United States during the 1960s." The objects are all actual things to each of which the term refers: Dwight D. Eisenhower, John F. Kennedy, Lyndon B. Johnson, and Richard M. Nixon comprise the extension of the term "President of the United States in the 1960s." The objects may be nonexistent, as in the case of "took office as President of the United States in 1962." Since no man took office in 1962, this term has a *null extension*, that is, it consists of a set with nothing in it.

The extension of a term may include all things that ever were, are, or will be actual things referred to by the term. An extension is, in effect, a listing of all the elements or members of a set alluded to by the term being defined. There *have been* many Presidents of the United States, there *is* a President of the United States, and there *will be* many others in the future (most probably) who will be Presidents of the United States. Thus, an extensional definition

[7] See Chapter 2.

depends a great deal on the facts of history. Were the objects "pointed to" by the term *actual things,* or are they likely to be *actual things* with the passage of time? Further, an extensional definition may be either complete (listing all the objects that were, are, and ever will be included in it) or *incomplete* (listing many or most of the objects to which it refers, but without giving assurance that all have been covered). It is more common for extensionally defined terms to be incomplete.

What would constitute an extensional definition of the term "democracy"? The question is obviously a politically significant one. An American might point to the following as the incomplete extension of the term: United States, Great Britain, France, and Sweden. A Soviet citizen would probably insist that the Soviet Union and the "people's democracies" of Eastern Europe be included as part of the extension and would probably raise some questions about the appropriateness of including the United States. Each of these individuals, as communicators, has the prerogative of defining the term arbitrarily *in any way he wishes.* Problems arise when acceptance is sought from an audience. Sometimes, particularly in political propaganda, acceptance by a hostile audience is never expected, the term being used primarily for its emotional effect upon a favorable audience and for including certain favored referents and excluding others. If the particular term generates favorable attitudes, as in the case of "democracy" or "peace loving," political adversaries may simply compete for possession of the term by arguing about its extension, that is, who ought to be "in" and "out." The audience decides for itself which extensional definition it wishes to accept.

DEFINING A TERM

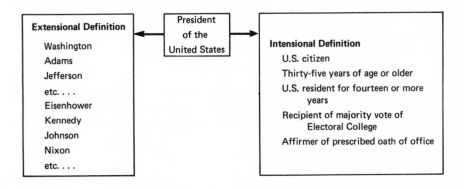

Intensions of Terms

The communicator may also wish to raise questions about the *intensions* of the term "democracy." This is the aspect of a term's meaning which, once clarified, will enable us to decide, with respect to objects newly brought to our attention, whether they do or do not belong to the extension of the term. An *intension* is an agreed-upon rule by which it can be determined whether or not a given object is a member of the set referred to by the term being defined. In our example, what criterion must the analyst use for including some of the countries listed as democracies and excluding others? One writer, for example, defines a democracy as "a political system which supplies regular constitutional opportunities for changing the governing officials."[8] The criterion or intension here is "regular constitutional opportunities for changing the governing officials." Notice that a number of factors are included in this intensional definition: the changing of governing officials; opportunities that are constitutional; opportunities that are regular. If our hypothetical American and Soviet citizens were to agree upon these intensions (although not likely), they would then proceed to argue whether to include or exclude one or another of the countries listed. New difficulties would probably then arise, e.g., the precise referent for "regular."

Characteristics that are *common* and *jointly peculiar* to the extension of a term, then, are, as a set, called the intension of the term. We could, for example, list thirty-six names (Washington, Adams, etc., to Nixon) and call them the extensions of the term "President of the United States." The intensions of the term "President of the United States," that is, the characteristics common and jointly peculiar to *all* of them would undoubtedly include: (a) citizen of the United States; (b) age of thirty-five years or older; (c) residency of at least fourteen years within the United States; (d) recipient of a majority of the votes of the whole membership of the Electoral College; (e) affirmation of the oath of office prescribed in Article II, Section I, of the Constitution. Substitute characteristics would be, in lieu of (d), election of the President by the House of Representatives, that is, a lack of an absolute majority

---

[8] Seymour M. Lipset, "Some Social Requisites of Democracy," *American Political Science Review*, 53 (March 1959): 69–105.

of the Electoral College plus achievement of a majority of the House of Representatives, each state delegation casting one vote or, in lieu of a President, elevation of the Vice President to the Presidency if the President is removed, dies, resigns, or is unable to discharge the office. All of these characteristics (or their substitutes) are *common* to the thirty-six men named as the extensions of the term "President of the United States." These characteristics are also jointly peculiar; together and only together, by prescribed definition in the Constitution, do the characteristics give meaning to the term.

The intension of a term, therefore, is that aspect of the term's meaning which, once established, will enable us to decide with respect to objects new to our attention whether they do or do not belong to the extension of the given term. This decision would rest upon certain explicit criteria. One criterion, since every object may have many characteristics, requires that *every characteristic* of the set of characteristics included in the intension of the term be possessed *in common* by the group of objects under examination. *Every* President of the United States is (a) a citizen, (b) aged thirty-five or more, and (c) a fourteen-year-old resident of the United States. This set of characteristics is *common* to all Presidents, but not peculiar to them. There are other Americans who have the same characteristics, yet are not Presidents.

A second explicit criterion is the *peculiarity* of the set of characteristics to the objects in the extension. A characteristic is peculiar to a certain set of objects if nothing except those objects have that characteristic. For example, no one but Presidents of the United States are designated by a majority of the votes of the whole membership of the Electoral College; the election procedure is peculiar to this set of objects. To say that a certain set of characteristics is *jointly peculiar* to a certain set of objects means that nothing except objects in that set of objects have all the characteristics in the set of characteristics. Thus, every President of the United States has all five of the characteristics listed above (common), and only Presidents have all five (jointly peculiar).

The set of all characteristics common to the extension of any term —and the set can be so large as to be infinite—is called the *total contingent intension* of that term. The characteristics in the total contingent intension may be further classified as two types: first, those ("taking the Presidential oath") that are common to the extension of the term because of the defined meaning of the term, and second, those ("nomination by a national political party convention") that are common to the extension of the term because of the facts of history.

Any characteristic belonging to the *first* of these types is called a *necessary member* of the term's total contingent intension. These members are necessary in the sense that objects *must* have them in order to be granted admission to the extension of the term. For example, no one can be counted as a President of the United States without having taken the presidential oath. The intension of a term which consists of all and only the necessary members of its total contingent intension is called the *total strict intension* of a term. Any characteristic belonging to the *second* of these types is a *merely contingent element* of the total contingent intension of that term. These merely contingent elements are usually of special interest to empirical scientists.

In general, an extensional definition is an effort to indicate the things that the definer wishes to have belong in the extension of the term *without* going so far as to indicate essential characteristics from a total strict intension which would guarantee inclusion in the extension. In contrast, a strict intensional definition indicates characteristics belonging to referents whose possession is a logical guarantee of inclusion in the extension of the defined term.

Once an investigator knows the strict intension of a term, he can proceed to an examination of the world around him in order to discover what objects do in fact belong to that term's extension. All he needs to find out about objects, by observation or by other means, is whether or not they have the characteristics listed in the strict intension. If they do have them, they are included in the extension; if not, they are kept out. Thus, knowing the strict intension (e.g., the first five Presidential characteristics mentioned above) provides a starting point from which to gain a knowledge of the members of the extension. On the other hand, knowing the extension (e.g., the names of all the Presidents) does *not* provide a sufficient starting point from which to gain a knowledge of the characteristics of the strict intension. In this way intensional definitions are "stronger," or more explicit, than extensional ones.

Students of logic and mathematics concern themselves primarily with the total strict intension of terms. They are interested in identifying the necessary characteristics of objects they wish to include in their terms. Similarly, lawyers and legislators are concerned with clarification of the total strict intension of such terms as "voter," that is, the specification of necessary characteristics which shall serve as "tickets of admission" for persons seeking to vote, such as having reached twenty-first birthday, some specified length of residence in the community, and so on.

The laboratory scientist, on the other hand, is mainly interested in the *merely contingent* characteristics of the total contingent intension of the terms he uses; that is, he is most concerned with the facts of history and human experience as they actually occur. In defining the term "voter," for example, an empirical scientist would look for evidence that a person *actually* voted, not whether he is eligible to do so under the law. The distinction between "voter" and "nonvoter" would thus rest upon discovered rather than prescribed characteristics. This concern with facts of history and observable events motivates the empirical scientist to create definitions that are *operational*.

Operational Definitions

Both extensional and intensional definitions may be operational. What distinguishes an *operational definition* is its conditional form ("if . . . then . . .") and its provision for an experimental test by which an object may be included in the extension of a term. The "if" clause of the definition describes a performable experiment involving the object under examination; the "then" clause describes an observable outcome of the experiment which either admits that object into or excludes it from the set of objects referred to by the term. For example, a substance X found in a field may be described by the term "gold" if it meets the conditions of the following operational definition of gold:

X is gold = if X were placed in aqua regia, then X would dissolve.

The definition of "democracy" noted earlier, namely "regular constitutional opportunity for changing the governing officials," is *not* an operational definition until agreed upon and observable tests of each of the required characteristics are indicated. These characteristics included regularity; constitutionality; opportunity; governing officials; and the changing of them. But these were the intensions of one definer. There are more than 300 definitions of the term "democracy," and very few even attempt to establish a set of operational conditions to serve as an empirical test of the term.[9] The difficulties of any such attempt are easily understood. What small set of behaviors or events is there to observe which would distinguish a "democracy" from any other form of government with the precision, certainty, and consistency of the operational definition of gold above? With over 300 definitions on tap, no "small set" of test variables is likely to emerge.

A term such as "voter" may be less difficult to operationalize. To test whether Mr. Smith is a voter, we could simply ask him: "Are you a voter?" The question is an operational definition in that it is *the* test. A "yes" reply is prima facie evidence that Mr. Smith should be classified among things called voters; a "no" reply excludes him. Of course, the possibility that Smith may be a liar or a lazy, non-voting-but-eligible voter is large enough to make us wary of placing too much confidence on this mode of definition and classification. A check of the voter registration lists would add further information and, if added to the operational test ("if he says 'yes, I'm a voter' and also appears on registration lists, then he's a 'voter.' "), would increase our confidence in the definition. Yet, there is a risk of error here, too, for 20 to 60 percent of registered voters fail to go to the polls. In other words, eligible voters are not always actual voters. The most direct observational test would be to watch Smith actually cast his ballot, but this is not possible under our system of secret ballot.

Notice that our construction of an operational definition of "voter" involved us in problems of direct observation and confidence (or reliability). The greater our assurance that we really are observing a voter, the greater is the predictability of any findings about relationships between voters and other things. A "poor" operational definition is one that leads the observer into error in his tests of hypotheses.

In the tests of "voter" noted thus far we have had specific things to observe: a "yes" answer; a registration list; a casting of a ballot or pulling of a lever. If the definition were of the type that is based on attitudinal information, the directness of our observations would recede and the reliability of the definition would probably be re-

[9] Arne Naess, *Democracy, Ideology, and Objectivity* (Oslo: Oslo University Press, 1956).

duced. Such a definition, and there are some, might ask such questions as: Do you think you will vote in the next election? Do you think your vote makes a difference? Do you enjoy voting? Should all citizens vote whether they like to or not? And so on. These data may be easier to collect but are likely to be too removed from the referent we are trying to define.

The "Natural History" of a Term

The historical evolution of definitions is a matter of particular interest in the study of politics. We have already mentioned how the centuries-long discussions of specific terms and concepts comprise a major activity of entire academic disciplines. This is also true of key terms in political life.

There seems to be a "natural history" in the evolution of definitions. At first, objects are grouped into sets by an observer and given a common label, that is, a term that is extensionally defined. Next, the observer looks more closely for shared characteristics of the observed objects, endeavoring to meet some of the requirements of intensional definition. As the political significance of the term increases, so, usually, does the need for precision and predictability in matters relating to that term. At this point, the politicians concern themselves with operational characteristics, that is, those attributes of the objects that are observable and precisely measurable. In Congress, for example, when one leader wants to conduct an "experimental test" of the influence of another leader in connection with a particular piece of legislation, he will press for a vote on some minor parliamentary issue such as postponement of debate. If the opposing leader can "deliver votes" to defeat this motion, he is, by a kind of operational definition, "influential."

There are other aspects of the natural evolution of definitions. One involves three general stages in the development of typologies of concepts: the ideal-type stage, the polarity stage, and the scalar stage.[10]

Ideal types are objects with general properties whose operational definitions remains to be developed. In physics, one example is "perfect gas." In economics, there is the concept "profit." An ideal-type

[10] This discussion is based upon Carl G. Hempel, "Typological Methods in the Social Sciences," in Maurice Natanson (ed.), *Philosophy of the Social Sciences* (New York: Random House, 1963), pp. 210–230.

political term, first used by Aristotle, is "revolution," referring to a cycle-like sequence of changes in government structures. In the ideal-type stage of its definition, a term is quite susceptible to evaluation as "good" or "bad" depending upon any number of accidental conditions of usage, e.g. most Americans today would consider the American Revolution "good" but any contemporary attempt at a revolution in the United States "bad."

Ideal-type terms may be reformulated into *polar types*. In psychology, for example, the reward-punishment polarity is a familiar one. In economics, the notion of "profit" soon acquired a polar companion in the concept "loss." "Revolution" has come to be contrasted with political "equilibrium." Polar typologies present problems of measurement. It is usually impossible to identify a precise point of demarcation where one polar extreme (revolution) becomes the other (equilibrium). It is also difficult to determine the "purity" of the polar attributes. In the physical sciences, for example, at what point does "hot" become "cold"? What point indicates the end of "depression" and the beginning of "prosperity"?

Both empirical science and practical politics have need for operational definitions. In the evolution of concepts this is usually achieved with the development of *scalable properties*, that is, units for measuring degrees of particular attributes. The thermometer is an example of a scalar device for measuring degrees of "temperature," an ideal-type concept whose later polar categories were "hot" and "cold." "Love" and "hate" make up a polarity as old as Zarathustra, which, in the last four decades, has been operationalized by "attitude" scales.[11] In American politics, scales exist in the form of statistical measures such as the cost-of-living index, the Gross National Product, etc. Furthermore, practical politicians are notoriously inquisitive about "how much" a public policy will cost or "how many" votes it will win or lose.

SIGNS AND SYMBOLS

Nonlinguistic Signs

While language as a tool of information transmission holds most attention among students of human communication, the nonlinguistic sign processes are also of fundamental significance. Gesture,

[11] See Chapter 8.

pictorialization, nonlinguistic sounds, odors, and recognizable nonlinguistic characteristics of a social situation may also serve to transmit political and other information from a source to a receiver.[12]

Over the last decade or so a science of gestural and body behavioral communication has developed. Called *kinesics*, the field devotes itself to the observation and measurement of paralinguistic phenomena on the assumption that it is possible to code body motions such as facial expression, gesture, and posture in ways analogous to the coding of written and spoken language. Basic coding units are called *kine* and *kineme*. A kine is a least perceptible unit of body motion such as an eyebrow lift and return. A kineme is a set of body motions providing the least possible communication cue, such as a raised and clenched fist. About thirty-four American kinemes have been isolated thus far. Important practical applications of the growing body of knowledge in this field are becoming increasingly evident, e.g., the diagnosis of various types of mental illness from evidence provided by characteristic patterns of body movement, and the amelioration of communication difficulties between allied soldiers of different nationalities, languages, and nonverbal communication habits.[13]

Gesture in politics may run the gamut of human nonlinguistic behaviors. The salute is one of the most familiar political gestures, usually part of a ritual of respect for a nation's emblems or officers. Differences in salute gestures distinguish one nation from others and thereby reinforce the sense of national identity. Imaginative politicians may adopt a personal gesture as a kind of trademark, as in the case of Winston Churchill's V-for-victory sign during World War II. When Soviet Premier Kosygin read a condemnation of Israel during the Middle East Crisis of 1967 before a special meeting of the United Nations Assembly, observers noted that he was almost expressionless and immobile, as though reading a telephone directory. Comparisons were made with former Premier Khrushchev's earlier performance under similar circumstances, which included

---

12 The sign language of the deaf is, of course, a notable body of nonlinguistic signals. One manual contains over 3,000 entries. Edna S. Levine (ed.), *Peet Dictionary of the Language of Signs* (New York: Harper & Row, 1965).

13 The ground-breaking scientific work in this field is Ray L. Birdwhistell, *Introduction to Kinesics* (Louisville, Ky.: University of Louisville Press, 1952). Other important references include: Jurgen Ruesch and Weldon Kees, *Nonverbal Communication* (Berkeley: University of California Press, 1956); Edward T. Hall, *The Silent Language* (Garden City, N.Y.: Doubleday, 1959); and Erving Goffman, *Behavior in Public Places* (New York: Free Press, 1963).

banging his shoe on his desk. Significant political inferences were drawn from the difference, for the anger in one case was real and in the other not apparent. A political gesture of a much larger scale was the movement of the Seventh Fleet into the Straits of Formosa during the Quemoy-Matsu crisis of 1955.[14]

Pictorial signs abound in the political art of election campaign posters, political emblems, portraits of national heroes, and political propaganda of all types. A news photograph or televised film may, as do many pictorial signs, carry more meaning than thousands of words; consider a photo of police turning dogs loose among civil rights marchers. The antiwar propaganda of Picasso's *Guernica* is as significant as its cubist painting technique.

Nonlinguistic sounds carrying political information may be heard in national anthems, campaign music, the distinctive laughter of a political leader, or the roar of gunfire. The odors of a ghetto, a battlefield, or a political convention may convey more information than a lengthy newspaper story. The special characteristics of certain situations also may have communicative consequences; the presence of Senator Everett Dirksen, Republican Minority Leader, as guest in President John F. Kennedy's box at a baseball game at the height of the former's campaign for reelection was a situation generally interpreted at the time as a tacit endorsement of a powerful Republican leader by a Democratic President.

Information transmitted by nonlinguistic signs runs particular risk of producing ambiguous messages or errors in decoding. When is a fleet on "exercises" and when is it an explicit threat? Was President Kennedy's hospitality really a political endorsement of Senator Dirksen? The cost of ambiguity and error may be substantial, inviting, as it may, redundancy. The terrible atomic "message" delivered upon Hiroshima on August 6, 1945, provoked no clear response from the Japanese Supreme War Council, which apparently tried to contact U.S. officials. The nuclear message—nonlinguistic in the extreme—was repeated three days later at Nagasaki.

Symbols and Behavior

A major difference between man and other living creatures is his use of signs as symbols. No other creature does this. "An organism has

---

[14] Numerous examples of the use of military gestures in international politics may be found in Thomas C. Schelling, *The Strategy of Conflict* (Cambridge, Mass.: Harvard University Press, 1960).

the ability to symbol or it does not; there are no intermediate stages."[15] A horse, a bird, or an ape cannot understand the symbolic meaning of the sign of the cross to a Christian, the difference between holy water and distilled water, the distinction between a cousin and an uncle, or the difference between the American flag and a bed sheet.

A *symbol* may be defined as a thing the value or meaning of which is bestowed upon it by those who use it. All symbols must have a physical form, otherwise they could not enter our experience. A symbol may have the form of a material object, a color, a sound, an odor, a motion, a taste. The meaning, or value, of a symbol is in no instance derived from or determined by properties intrinsic to its physical form; the cloth and color of a flag when in special relation to each other have little intrinsic meaning except to the extent that they symbolize for us some other object, e.g. the United States of America.

In the initial use of *any* symbol, the user assigns, arbitrarily, a meaning or value to it. This is the same kind of arbitrariness noted as a design feature of language and manifest in the defining of terms. A conventional symbolism, like a conventional definition, is simply the acceptance of an initial user's meaning or value for the symbol by subsequent users.

A physical thing may be a *sign* in one context and a *symbol* in another. This has caused some confusion in establishing the differences between the terms sign and symbol. In a sign context the meaning of a word can be grasped with the senses. In a symbol context the meaning of a word cannot be perceived with the senses but rather is created and bestowed arbitrarily by the observer. This capacity for assigning arbitrary signification and evaluation is man's special skill. The cry "Halt!" is a vocal stimulus which may mean nothing beyond the sound waves created. Both a man and a dog can be taught to cease movement upon hearing the sound of "Halt!" The difference between the dog and the man is that the former does not and cannot play an active role in determining what the value of the vocal stimulus may be, whereas man can and does play such a role. Only the man will wonder if he heard correctly, if he had wandered onto a military reservation, if the sound was associated with a threat to his physical safety, if the source was friendly or not, and so on.

---

15 Leslie A. White, *The Science of Culture* (New York: Farrar, Straus and Cudahy, 1959), Chap. 2.

With the evolution of symbolism and symbolic processes came the growth of human civilization.

> It was the exercise of the symbolic faculty that brought culture into existence and it is the use of symbols that makes the perpetuaion of the culture possible. Without the symbol there would be no culture, and man would be merely an animal, not a human being.
>
> Articulate speech is the most important form of symbolic expression. Remove speech from culture and what would remain? Let us see.
>
> Without articulate speech we would have no *human* social organization. Families we might have, but this form of organization is not peculiar to man; it is not *per se, human*. But we would have no prohibitions of incest, no rules proscribing exogamy and endogamy, polygamy, or monogamy. How could marriage with a cross-cousin be prescribed, marriage with a parallel cousin proscribed, without articulate speech? How could rules which prohibit plural mates possessed simultaneously but permit them if possessed one at a time, exist without speech?
>
> Without speech we would have no political, economic, ecclesiastic, or military organization; no codes of etiquette or ethics; no laws; no science, theology, or literature; no games or music, except on an ape level. Rituals and ceremonial paraphernalia would be meaningless without articulate speech. Indeed, without articulate speech we would be all but toolless: we would have only the occasional and insignificant use of the tools such as we find today among the higher apes, for it was articulate speech that transformed the non-progressive tool-using of the ape into the progressive, cumulative tool-using of man, the human being.[16]

THE CONSTRUCTION AND TYPES OF POLITICAL STATEMENTS

Linguistic terms, however, are only a small part of the technology of language. To communicate to a young child that some objects in his environment are called "pebbles" and others "candies" gives him only a limited amount of information. The characteristics of relationships among, and relevance for himself of these objects are a few of the other informational elements that require more language than the simple denotative terms. Which of the two—pebbles or candies

[16] White, *op. cit.*, pp. 33–34. Copyright Leslie A. White; quoted with permission of the publisher.

—is "edible," a prospective relationship between the objects and the child? In what situations should the child like or dislike pebbles and candies? What happens if the child eats candies? Pebbles?

If term is a basic logical unit of language, *statement* (variously called *sentence, proposition, thought*) is the next more comprehensive linguistic unit. In logic as in grammar, statements are intended to describe some condition of a term or some relationship among terms, for example, the relationship between a subject and a predicate, between one variable and another, or between an attribute and an object.

One familiar way of differentiating among statements is to call certain ones *factual* and others *valuational*. To say that "water boils at 212 degrees Fahrenheit" is to report a consistently observed state of affairs, or fact. On the other hand, it is a value statement to say, "I prefer water that has been boiled." One of the skills presumably provided by a liberal education is the capacity to distinguish between a fact and a value.

For the present discussion, we shall distinguish among three types of statements:

empirical statements
valuational statements
future-descriptive statements

Consider, out of context, the simple statement: "All men are created equal." Is this an empirical statement, reporting the results of systematic observation and describing a consistent state of affairs? Or, is this a valuational statement, indicating that we prefer to think of men as equal to each other rather than, by implication, unequal? Or is it a future-descriptive statement, anticipating a future in which the conditions of human life are more equitable? Any one or all of these meanings may be decoded from this particular message. In fact, a substantial part of American political activity is devoted to the decoding of this particular statement. The statement is an excellent example why even the most liberally educated person, because of the pitfalls of linguistic formulations, may have insurmountable difficulty distinguishing fact from value and both from a statement about the future.

At the risk of destroying the poetic simplicity of the statement "All men are created equal," how would this statment have to be rephrased in order to make it more recognizably empirical, valuational, or future-descriptive?

As an *empirical statement* it would have to look like this:

All of the attributes of all human beings *tend to have a normal distribution*, with no significant deviations.

As a *valuation statement,* it would have to appear as follows:

Their equality is the *most important* aspect of men's creation and existence.

As a *future-descriptive statement,* it would appear as:

Whatever their differences, men are created to *become* equal.

These somewhat awkward revisions of "All men are created equal" are intended to emphasize the major differences among the three types of statement. The differences, in brief, are these. The *empirical statement* alludes to observable attributes and to quantifiable relationships among them. The *valuational statement* refers to preferential priority and, either implicitly or explicitly, indicates a rank order of preference among the factors being considered; in this case, equality as the "most important." The *future-descriptive statement* tells in language of varying clarity about some future state of affairs, sometimes implying or declaring that such a future state is desirable (adding thereby a valuation).

These differences are confounded somewhat if taken out of context. A future-descriptive statement, for example, may have valuational implications. A *goal* is a desired future state of affairs. When several prospective futures are placed before a decision maker, he must come up with a valuational statement, that is, which of all the desirable goals he desires the *most.*

A similar confusion arises between the predictive aspect of an empirical statement and the future aspect of a future-descriptive statement. In an empirical statement, the "if . . . , then . . ." formulation indicates what is likely to happen in the future if certain elements are brought together in the present. "If a match is struck against a rough surface, then a flame is likely to burst forth." Such an empirical statement is different from one that describes a possible future state of affairs: "Get some matches so that we may soon start a fire." These examples recommend caution in decoding statements out of context and precision in ascertaining the rules by which they were formulated. Empirical, valuational, and future-descriptive statements, when produced deliberately, are constructed according to distinct rules and practices.

Empirical Statements

The rules of empirical statements are highly developed as a consequence of generations of work by logicians and philosophers of science. The most important characteristic of an empirical statement is that its referents *may be* or *have been* accessible to human observation and amenable to quantitative measurement. If observation and quantification have yet to take place, then the empirical statement is called a *hypothesis* or, if part of a series of statements, a *theory*.

A *hypothesis* is basically a question, a conjectural statement. It speculates about the extent to which two or more fairly specific elements or variables in the environment are related to each other. A hypothesis is usually stated in such a way that its readers can readily identify which variables the communicator has in mind and to which measurement procedure the communicator is committed. For example: "The greater the formal education of the American citizen, the higher his rate of political participation." This hypothesis is a special way of asking the question: "Are educated Americans more politically active than other types?" The elements or variables, under examination are two attributes of American citizens: (1) the degree of their education, and (2) the rate of their political participation. What the observer is asked to look for are: American citizens; a measure of educational variation; a measure of variation in political participation; and a measure summarizing the quantitative relationship between education and participation data. The hypothesis is empirical in its commitment to an intersubjective test (more than one person doing the observing and counting) of the quantitative relationship between two explicit variables. Observation and counting (research) must be completed before this statement becomes a *fact*, that is, a confirmed hypothesis.

Confirmation or testing of a hypothesis requires that an observer develop (a) operational definitions for the variables to be observed and (b) specific quantitative procedures for carrying on the test. Further, the test must be intersubjective, that is, of such a character that any two or more human observers could conduct it and find the same data.

Let us see how an investigator might proceed with the hypothesis about education and participation. His operational definition of "American citizen" might simply be a "yes" response to the question: "Are you an American citizen?" Assuming that most people would tell the truth about this status, the investigator may feel that this is a reliable enough operational definition, thus eliminating the necessity of other tests such as checking birth certificates and citizenship papers.

An operational definition of "education" may be more difficult, especially if the investigator undertook to measure how much general knowledge each person has. A test of an individual's general knowledge could be a very elaborate questionnaire indeed. In the interest of economy, the investigator might decide simply to ask how many years of formal schooling the individual has had or what level—elementary, secondary school, college, etc.—of education the individual has completed. The amount of precision would depend upon the extent to which the investigator wants to break down his scale of degrees of education, that is, by number of years, level, or some other basis.

The third factor, degree of political participation, may also be quite complicated to define operationally. When is a citizen "participating politically" in a way that is measurable in different degrees? When he votes? When he contributes money to the party of his choice? When he holds party or pressure group office? When he talks to his friends about politics? Or some combination of these and other observable activities? Any one or some index of several of these may be used, arbitrarily, in the measurement of political participation. Some investigators have, in fact, used information about number of group memberships held by individuals, whether the respondent had ever written a letter to some government official, etc. Whatever the operational definition, it must be explicit, measurable, and replicable, that is, capable of repeated testing.

Having identified and defined the variables to be examined, the hypothesis next requires a test procedure by which observations may be made and counted. Should every American citizen be interviewed? The expense would be prohibitive. Therefore, the investigator must turn to the problem of drawing a good sample of all American citizens, that is, a sampling procedure based upon probability theory. Next, a questionnaire must be designed so that the responses allow quantification in terms of (a) years of attendance in formal schooling and (b) evidences of political participation.

After the sample of citizens has been questioned and the data summarized, various statistical analyses must be made indicating the relationships and tendencies discovered. If the findings support to an impressive degree the original hypothesis, the investigator may claim that the hypothesis is confirmed. Otherwise, the hypothesis is discarded or rewritten so that it describes the actual empirical findings more closely. At this point it is a fact, that is, a validated empirical statement. Presumably anybody can go out and check it. It is this willingness to consider *no* hypothesis exempt from falsification or modification that makes empirical science a constantly self-correcting linguistic and observational enterprise.

A number of investigations are available which illustrate how validated hypotheses look as statements. One such study is based upon a sample of 525 registered voters of the city of New Haven, Connecticut.[17] This study found that participation in local political decisions tends to be greater (a) among citizens with high than among citizens with low incomes, (b) among citizens with high than among citizens with low social standing, (c) among citizens with considerable formal education than among citizens with little, (d) among citizens with professional, business, and white-collar occupations than among citizens with working-class occupations, and (e) among citizens from better residential areas than among citizens from poorer areas. The precise statistical presentations are too lengthy to include here, but among them were an "index of local action," a scale of income with gradations of $3000, a scale of standard occupational categories used by the Census Bureau, and educational categories that set twelfth grade schooling as a dividing point. These particular findings were summarized in a single general proposition: "Political participation tends to increase with the amount of resources at one's disposal." This latter statement followed logically from the validated hyotheses and in turn became the basis for more general theoretical statements and speculations.[18]

17 Robert A. Dahl, *Who Governs?* (New Haven: Yale University Press, 1961).
18 The statistical issues dealing with the adequacy of a sample, acceptable levels of confirmation, tests of significance, etc., need not detain us. The very explicit standards of sound craftsmanship and confidence in one's findings are given careful atten-

Valuational Statements

The concept *value* has been no less troublesome than fact. Three basic usages may be distilled from the enormous literature.[19] Common to all usages is a pro-and-con element.

The first usage of the concept *value* refers to objects or properties of objects. One may possess a "valued" thing, such as a house, health, or a friendship. A property (attribute) may be a "valuable" one, such as the oratorical skill of a politician. The notion of economic "goods" is associated with this use of the term "value," for an economic good is usually some *thing* that is valued enough to be exchanged in transactions, involving positive or negative reaction from a decision-making transactor.

A second usage views values as a kind of behavior: *preferential behavior.* This is sometimes called "valuing," to distinguish the acting or behaving from the object valued. Preference may be manifest in the attraction or rejection of each particular available alternative or it may involve a ranking of the available alternatives in a kind of priority arrangement. The individual's value or preference may be inferred from the selection act or it may be indicated by signs such as words or statements.

A third usage deals with values as ends, goals, purposes, fulfillments, and the like. Since these are usually identified as being sought after, the assumption is that the decision maker considers them valuable. Values of this kind almost invariably require communication by signs or symbols since, as we have seen earlier, they involve a future state of affairs presently envisaged. Since two or more distinct goals, both desired, may be mutually exclusive as possibilities, the two or more descriptions of the future states of affairs (the future descriptions) require some indication of priority.

A summary of the characteristics of valuational statements should include the following:

---

tion in any number of research and statistical theory books: Fred N. Kerlinger, *Foundations of Behavioral Research* (New York: Holt, Rinehart & Winston, 1966), William L. Hays, *Statistics for Psychologists* (New York: Holt, Rinehart & Winston, 1963), Hubert M. Blalock, Jr., *Social Statistics* (New York: McGraw-Hill, 1960).

[19] Excellent surveys, with extensive bibliography, are: Philip E. Jacob and James J. Flink, "Values and Their Function in Decision-Making," *American Behavioral Scientist*, 5 (Supplement, May, 1962); William J. Wilson and F. Ivan Nye, "Some Methodological Problems in the Empirical Study of Values," Washington Agricultural Experiment Station, Washington State University, Bulletin 672, July, 1966. See also, P. Fishburn, *Decision and Value Theory* (New York: Wiley and Sons, 1964).

1. A ranking or ordering of available alternatives. Sometimes the ranking is implied. For example, to say that "taxes is the *most important* issue of this election" without listing any of the other issues is to imply that, whatever the other issues, taxes should have first priority.
2. A decisional property. To state priorities among alternatives is to attribute decision-making capacity among persons for whom the ranking may be influential.
3. Group differences in valuation. Values vary not only among individuals but also among groups and cultures. Social and cultural values are *norms* in the statistical sense, that is, a central tendency among numerous individuals.
4. Durability of values. While preferences may persist through time from generation to generation through social learning, it is also possible that the objects, goals and rankings may change for individuals and groups. When values are stable and enduring, we have the substance of culture, national character, or individual personality.
5. Self value. As in symboling, valuation requires the presence of a conception of the self and its relationship to the available alternatives. In order to decide among alternatives according to his own system of values, the individual must be able to relate the alternatives to standards that he has learned to apply to himself. He must have the ability to be self-constraining if his preferred alternative is not available. It is in this sense that the distinction is made between rational and irrational behavior. The latter is the decision makers's selection of an alternative that *he* himself considers less desirable than some other alternative on *his* own scale of values.[20]

From the point of view of statement construction, several straightforward clues may help identify valuational statements. The terms "ought" or "should" are usually part of rationalizations for actions and imply a ranking of preference. If a statement associates actions or situations with guilt, shame, indignation, approbation, or similar good-bad estimations, it is highly likely that it is a valuational statement. In the utility theory of the economist or the decision theory of philosophers, substantial attention is given to the ranking of preferences or priorities. Whether the alternatives are two or a

20 Based upon Jacob and Flink, *op. cit.*, pp. 15–16.

hundred in number, rankings or scales are the most common feature of valuational statements.

Future-descriptive Statements

The critical attribute of this type of statement is its reference to some *future* state of affairs. As we shall see below, the concept of futurity is not a necessary or universal one. Historically, it may in fact be more important in the evolution of Western than any other civilization. Concern with temporal considerations and future states seems to be one of the salient characteristics of the West.

We have already noticed that statements about the future may be *derived* in at least two ways. There is the empirical derivation, in which an event is predicted as likely to occur in the future if certain present conditions exist or are made to exist. In empirical derivation, statements about the future are based upon past occurrences and the probabilities for their recurrence inferred from a count of past occurrences under the stated conditions. "If the atmospheric pressure is X and the humidity Y and the temperature Z, then rain will probably fall." In this statement, "the falling of rain" is the future state of affairs being described and predicted as "likely." As all followers of weather forecasting know, the likelihood can be stated as fairly precise quantitative odds derived from past data counts.

A second derivation of future-descriptive statements is, as we have seen, preferential or valuational. An end or goal is desired or ranked in preference above other possible alternative states of affairs. "Give me liberty or give me death." This famous patriotic cry stated a preference between two possible future states of affairs—with all of the economy of revolutionary sloganeering; given a choice between the state of affairs called "liberty" or the state of affairs called "death," the preferred future state was life-with-liberty over life-without-liberty.

Unfortunately, human writings are replete with confusions about future-descriptive statements. These confusions may be traced to the problem of derivation, that is, whether the statement is a probability estimate derived from empirically examining past events or whether it is a valuation reporting the subjectively ranked preference of the communicator. And sometimes it may be both! A Madisonian statement about the historical conditions for successful creation of republican governments may be as much a mixture of past fact and present preference as a Marxian statement about the historical tendencies leading to the disappearance of the state. Logicians and linguists have yet to work out rules of communication that could assist an audience in its comprehension of future-descriptive statements.

The problem of future-descriptive statement appeared in the very first works of political science. The nature of human government was discussed in Plato's inquiries. He described the state as an association of individuals to achieve the many needs of mankind through specialization. The particular concern of government is "justice," which is a virtue for both the state and the individual. The most just state is also the one that is most self-sufficient; all its internal dealings result in justice for all its citizens as well as in fulfillment of all their needs. The creation of justice is the function of government, which in turn is essential to the existence of a state. The function of government requires the identification and training of a special class of individuals—the guardians—capable of guarding the public good, administering justice, and thereby preserving the conditions of virtue that make a state.

As the student explores Platonic statements about the state, he is bound to wonder whether Plato was describing political reality or developing a picture of an ideal. The inescapable conclusion is that he, along with his many successors in political writing, undertook to do both, that is, select elements of human behavior that seem to him common to all people and then recommend the management of these patterns of behavior to produce his conception of a desirable future state of political affairs. In Plato's case, the ideal state was the one that achieves virtue through the full achievement of justice. Because justice requires just men, such men need to be especially trained in a state-controlled system of compulsory education and then removed from all of the temptations of private interest by sharing all property and family relationships in common, including wives, children, and other family interests. The ideal of Plato's *Republic* gave way to his writings on *Laws* in which he describes a future second-best state.

The future-descriptive statements of Plato were similar in linguistic construction to all those that followed. Aristotle, for example, was a careful student of constitutional systems as he and his students found them in the Greek world. While his statements could claim stronger empirical derivation than those of Plato, Aristotle nonetheless inferred from his data that some communities were "true" or constitutional states (monarchies, aristocracies, and polities) and others were perverted or despotic states (tyrannies, oligarchies, and democracies). Having made this evaluative classification, he devoted his analyses to the identification of characteristics promotive of constitutional states and preventive of perverted ones. The search continues in political writings to this day, particularly as new nations emerge across the world and as constitutional and authoritarian governments offer themselves as models to their new brethren.[21]

Theories and the Future

Marschak has argued that the measurement of preferences (involving valuational statements) and the measurement of probabilities (involving empirical statements) are inescapably tied together in every choice. A preference scale is the set of priorities among the alternatives under consideration by the decision maker. A scale of probabilities is made up of the empirically derived prospects that one or another alternative, if chosen, will result in the future state of affairs envisaged. Uncertainties about future outcomes (empirically derived) must be taken into account as much as preferences among the outcomes (valuational derivation). Thus, the certainty of a moderately pleasant outcome may be preferred by a decision maker to the very slim chance for an extremely pleasant outcome. Marschak's argument leads to the conclusion that future-descriptive statements are meaningless as guides to choice if unaccompanied by valuational statements indicating preferences and empirical statements indicating probabilities.[22]

[21] An excellent example, from the democratic point of view, is Herbert J. Spiro, *Government by Constitution* (New York: Random House, 1959). For an interpretation of three well-known American political novels that are filled with future-descriptive statements inferred from selected premises about human behavior, Alex Gottfried and Sue Davidson, "Utopia's Children," *Western Political Quarterly* (March 1962): 17–32. The novels are Nathaniel Hawthorne's *The Blithedale Romance*, the story of Brook Farm; Mary McCarthy's *The Oasis*, the story of a group's flight to Utopia; and Harvey Swados' *False Coin*, about the trials and tribulations of Harmony Farm. For a survey of utopian propositions as a form of social thinking, Frank E. Manuel (ed.) *Utopias and Utopian Thought* (Boston: Beacon Press, 1967). Mark Holloway, *Heavens on Earth* (2nd ed., New York: Dover, 1966) describes utopian communities in America from 1680 to 1880.

[22] Jacob Marschak, "Toward a Preference Scale for Decision-Making," in Martin Shubik (ed.), *Readings in Game Theory and Political Behavior* (Garden City, N.Y.: Doubleday, 1954), pp. 22–32.

Rudner puts the problem somewhat differently. Even though the scientist may test his hypothesis with extreme care and report his observations with the highest accuracy, he, in his functions as a scientist, must also make value judgments. He must decide at what level of confirmation he would be willing to take chances with his findings. Such a decision is invariably steeped in value considerations.[23] For example, during the mid-1950s, American scientists began to express concern over the prospective genetic damage that could result from unchecked pollution of the atmosphere during thermonuclear weapon testing. There was some difference among scientists regarding the danger level in atmospheric pollution. Some preferred to place the danger level very low because there was evidence that several hundred thousand persons in future generations would be malformed as a consequence of even limited testing. The preference of these scientists was to avoid entirely genetic damage to any future human being. Other scientists preferred to mark the danger level high in order to permit some nuclear testing of military devices. These scientists preferred to risk several hundred thousand lives in order to develop weapons that could protect several hundred million lives, particularly after Chairman Mao's remark that even if nuclear war killed 300 million Chinese there would still be 300 million left to build the Communist world of the future. Thus, scientists differed about the danger level of nuclear testing because of their value differences regarding the priority to be given genetic health vis-à-vis military safety.

Still another formulation of the problem is Rapoport's. Four meanings of the concept *theory* are identified. "Scientific theory" consists of a collection of derived theorems tested in the process of predicting events from the observed conditions. "Understanding (*verstehen*) theory" is concerned with the identification and definition of elements in the environment as a stage in the "understanding" of them; classification rather than prediction is the primary interest of these theorists. "Hortatory theory" consists of those theoretical statements that seek to impart the communicator's intuitive understandings about political and other behaviors and events, and uses the argument that perception varies with individuals, the perceptions of some individuals having more merit than others for the development of knowledge. Finally, there is "norma-

23 Richard S. Rudner, "The Scientist *Qua* Scientist Makes Value Judgments," *Philosophy of Science*, 20 (January 1953).

tive theory" which concerns itself with establishing priorities among present behaviors and among conceptions of the future, e.g., theories about the "best form of government" or statements of hypothetical laws that "ought to be" true under ideal conditions. Each of these types of theory may be found in the literature of political science. Each needs to be recognized for the particular kind of statements it offers the body of political knowledge.[24]

Some of the implications of these different forms of linguistic statement for political policy making may now be evident. The policy maker, as he is confronted by events in the immediate political environment, must make choices in the *present*. Even inaction constitutes a kind of choice. Whose "word," that is, whose statement of the realities and the prospects, is he to believe as the basis for his decision? Whose preferences in the body politic is he to give greatest consideration? How may he combine and explain these, especially in a constitutional system that provides for recurrent electoral accountings by policy makers.

TIME PERCEPTION AS A CONSEQUENCE OF LANGUAGE

Language is not only an instrument of politics but also a shaper of political life. One aspect of language that may have greater impact on political life than hitherto recognized is its temporal formulations. A language that has past, present, and future tenses permits its users to communicate about the historical past, the decision-making present, and purposes for the future. A language, such as the Hopi, that has no concept of dimensional time or linguistic tenses, is likely to deal with linguistic meanings in a very different way from English language treatment. In the case of the Hopi, gesture, in the sense of pointing to some empirical referent or indicating by gesture that the referent is something in the communicator's memory, is a significant adjunct of language. "What are to English differences of time are to Hopi differences in kind of validity."[25]

The cultural consequences are perhaps somewhat more evident in Chinese, which has no future tense. Significantly, the Chinese culture is heavily concerned with ancestral and traditional considerations. Contrast this with the future-oriented cultures of the West

[24] Anatol Rapoport, "Various Meanings of 'Theory'," *American Political Science Review*, 52 (December 1958): 972–988.
[25] Benjamin Lee Whorf, "Science and Linguistics," *Technology Review*, 44 (1940): 229ff.

whose future tenses permit easy references to life in the hereafter, religious and national goals that are millennial in character, and conceptions of evolution and progress whose implications reach into every walk of Western life. In the broadest philosophical sense, the West has embedded the concept and measurement of time into every aspect of the ordinary Western individual's life, from his basic relationship to the cosmos to his demand for watches in order to help coordinate his own activities with those of others in highly technological and synchronized societies. From the East, on the other hand, have come the philosophies of irrationality in which nothing is predictable about a future that cannot grammatically be said to exist.[26]

Linguistic Aspects of Time

Scientific speculation regarding origins of the human time sense are as fascinating as those dealing with the distinctive development of human language. Time perception and the concept of time, as in the case of language, have features that help distinguish man from other animals. While all animals exist in time and store sense data about past and present experiences, only man is *aware* of time to the extent that he has *conceptualized* it and has developed operational definitions for it.

It has been argued that what makes man human is his capacity to employ both the past and the future as guides to present action. In this formulation, memory and foresightedness are the most rel-

---

[26] The literature about the time concept and the behavioral consequences of time perception seems to be rapidly growing. Review of most human conceptions of time seems imminent with the new temporal management demanded by space travel. We have already seen how Einstein revolutionized physics by showing, among other things, how time changes with motion. Contemporary psychological inquiries have noticed and begun to study the relationship between time orientation and psychological disturbances, e.g. the compression of time relations by the paranoid schizophrenic. Deterioration of the frontal lobe of the brain, in which time data is stored, under conditions of Pick's Disease is followed by marked disruptions in time perception; the patient has great difficulty in perceiving sequence. Some recent studies: Stephen Toulmin and June Goodfield, *The Discovery of Time* (New York: Harper & Row, 1965); Wilbert E. Moore, *Time and Society* (New York: Wiley, 1963); John B. Priestley, *Man and Time* (Garden City, N.Y.: Doubleday, 1964); Nathan Israeli et al., *Abnormal Personality and Time* (New York: Social Science Research Council, 1936); M. F. Cleugh, *Time and Its Importance in Modern Thought* (London: Methuen, 1937); John M. Stroud, "The Fine Structure of Psychological Time," in Henry Quastler (ed.), *Information Theory in Psychology* (New York: Free Press, 1955); Gardner Lindzey (ed.), *Handbook of Social Psychology* (Cambridge, Mass.: Addison-Wesley, 1954), Vol. II, pp. 633–636; Edward T. Hall, *The Silent Language* (Garden City, N.Y.: Doubleday, 1963); Roland Fischer and Arne Sollberger (eds.) "Interdisciplinary Perspectives of Time," *Annals of the New York Academy of Sciences*, 138 (Feb. 6, 1967).

evant elements of human intelligence. Many animals have been trained to react to time cues; a rat can learn to press a lever every twenty-five seconds in order to be rewarded with food. The animal closest to man in time perceiving capacity, particularly as it relates to foresight, is the chimpanzee. Chimpanzees can learn to stack boxes in order to produce a platform for reaching a banana. They have also been observed making tools, such as stripping a twig of its leaves to make a probe for driving termites from their hole. Tool making is one of man's most characteristic ways of preparing for future contingencies. However, significantly, a chimpanzee probing for termites never makes this tool *before* setting out on a termite hunt, but does so only when the insects are actually seen. For the chimpanzee, the "future" and his tool-making response are immediate to the situation.

Some two million years ago ape-man also began to make tools, but not for any immediately visible purpose. When ape-men began to carry tools about, this was evidence of the beginning of human foresight. Foresight seemed to increase as brains grew larger. As noted above, the frontal lobe, where human brain enlargement has been the most distinctive, is also the locus of the time sense. The tool that truly revolutionized man's relationship to time, however, was language. Words enabled men to record the past and write goals for the future. The combination of language and time concept, particularly in the articulation of human purposes, facilitated human grouping processes and the rapid development of modern social organization.[27]

Man's awareness of duration and the passage of time led to the linguistic categories *past, present,* and *future.* As in so many other fields, the Greeks made the first attempts to define time and its categories. Aristotle stated the time-motion paradox: "We apprehend time only when we have marked motion. [Yet] not only do we measure the movement by the time, but also the time by the movement, because they define each other." Aristotle's was also the first major attempt at *genetic* analysis, that is, the identification of relationships between past, present, and future events, tracing the development of the household, the village, and the polis as different phases in the growth of human associations.

Philosophical concern with the relationships between past and

[27] Samuel A. Goudsmit et al., *Time* (New York: Life Science Library, 1966), pp. 10–11.

present led to (a) the concept *causality* and (b) reverence for tradition. Concern with the relation between present and future led to the concept *prediction* and the search for utopias and millennia. In more primitive settings, temporal considerations became significant aspects of the work of medicine men, priests, and sage elders as they recorded and analyzed past events, issued interpretations of present events and directives for present choices, and prescribed or forecast future developments and actions.

As time-perceiver, man has become a purpose-creator. As purpose-creator, man is a distinctively "teleological animal" capable of identifying goals around which have emerged systems of social and political cooperation and conflict.

Time As a Political Resource

Time is a scarce resource in politics as in other areas of human life. This probably first became evident as early chairmen of deliberative bodies contemplated their dilemmas in allocating time for such bodies. In Athens, when the popular assembly was the principal decision-making body of the community, approximately five thousand of the forty thousand citizens responded to calls to convene on the most important occasions. Meeting from sunrise to sundown, that is, approximately twelve hours, it was common for leading orators to take at least one hour each. Thus, only twelve speakers in a body of five thousand exercised a right that presumably belonged equally to all participants. If the presiding officer were to award equal time to each of the five thousand, each would have about eight or nine seconds to state his case. Obviously, the presiding officer had to apply principles of recognition other than that of formal equality. He had to choose those who would, when called upon to speak, exercise that right with maximum economy, retain the greatest amount of attention, and represent the widest distribution of opinion.[28]

The "Chairman's Problem" continues to be a difficult one, just as time continues to be one of the scarce resources of politics. Thus, in American politics, the time of the President is carefully allocated by his appointment secretary. Congress manages itself with agendas, calendars, and debating schedules, the Senate being particularly

[28] Bertrand de Jouvenal, "The Chairman's Problem," *American Political Science Review*, 55 (June 1961): 368–372.

concerned about time-limiting cloture procedures. Legislative sessions, terms of office, and time limits on budgets and war powers of the President are among the many other time concerns of Congress. The courts, too, maintain careful schedules of calendars and proceedings, and penal judgments are usually meted out in units of time.

In the strategies of organized interests and political parties, timing is frequently a major consideration. Will the opposition be worn down by dilatory tactics? Can pressure for a decision be created by enunciating a deadline? What part of a long-run goal should be compromised in the short run? Will the prolongation of a political battle give public opinion an opportunity to develop and make itself felt, as happened in the Supreme Court "packing" struggle of 1937 when delay by Congressional Democrats helped them outmaneuver President Roosevelt?[29]

Policies about Time

The utilization of time has become a subject of growing concern for policy makers. The shortening of the workday, for example, has been a long-time objective of American organized labor and industrial management. This has been accomplished in part by legislation and by automation. One consequence has been "the new leisure." The eighty-hour work week in agriculture and certain industries has given way to the forty-hour work week. This reduction has been accompanied by technological advances that have lightened the physical strain of many occupations, leaving human energy and attention free for significant activities during non-income-producing hours of the week.

The availability of nonwork time during a week has made it possible for individuals to devote significantly more time to personal care, household-related activities, schooling, and recreation, with major economic consequences for industries and services related to each of these.[30] In the half century since 1900, leisure time for vacations has doubled, with a commensurate rise in the travel, resort, and other aspects of the vacation "industry." The entire concept of

[29]F. V. Cantwell, "Public Opinion and the Legislative Process," *American Political Science Review*, 40 (1946); 924–935.
[30] That nonwork time may not necessarily mean an increase in time usable for leisure is demonstrated in a study by Edwin Blakelock, "A New Look at the New Leisure," *Administrative Science Quarterly*, 4 (March 1960): 446–467.

retirement as a use of time after the ages sixty to sixty-five may soon undergo reconsideration because an increasing proportion of the population lives longer and is healthier during the post-sixty-five period. Furthermore, the concept of two or three "retirements" at the end of two or three different careers in a person's lifetime is gaining currency.

Public policy problems arising from the many twentieth-century adjustments and trends in time utilization will easily come to mind: the workweek demands of labor; the risks of unemployment arising from automation; social security and retirement arrangements; availability of adult and continuing education facilities; public control of the more exploitive and criminal aspects of the recreation-enter-tainment-vacation-personal services industries; the more directly visible issues of traffic congestion, television aerials, and other contemporary blights on "good living."

As entry into the labor market is postponed for younger people and as older people retrain themselves for new careers, the demand upon the American educational system is likely to grow accordingly. At least one form of time use has been "outlawed," that is, unemployment. According to the Full Employment Act of 1946, it is the responsibility of the Federal Government to keep unemployment at a minimum.

Awareness of the impact of time as a factor in contemporary public policy has led a number of behavioral scientists to such inquiries as the International Comparative Time-Budget Project begun in 1964. The citizens in some thirteen communities in about ten nations were studied in connection with their use of time during different parts of the workweek and year. A number of the findings were fascinating, others amusing; e.g., television viewing increases as a leisure-time activity of married persons in all countries except the United States, where viewing is always considerable whether the person is married or not.[31]

Many philosophers refer to time as man's scarcest resource. How each individual employs his time is thus in large part a function of his personal goals or the goals of the groups to which he belongs. If a lifetime is perceived, philosophically, as meaningless, the individual and the culture of which he is a part will exhibit little concern

[31] Alexander Szlai, *American Behavioral Scientist*, 10 (December, 1966). See also, James C. Charlesworth, "Leisure in America: Blessing or Curse?" American Academy of Political and Social Science, Monograph 4, 1964.

about the purposes for which his time is spent. Thus, numerous Eastern cultures place little value on the life of the individual and do little on behalf of its preservation. In contrast, Western cultures are devoted at one and the same time to the prolongation of life as well as to the preparation for an afterlife.

The goal-mindedness of Western cultures has probably been one of the greatest stimuli to its linguistic activity as men clarify purposes, maintain practices, and discuss policies most likely to maximize the achievement of such purposes. In many ways, the communication of purpose and of guidelines to the implementation of purpose has become a highly specialized activity. The propagandist, in order to attract support for his proposals, will describe his purposes and goals in language selected for its emotional and affective meaning to his public. The politician, crosspressured by interests with conflicting goals, will take refuge in skillfully stated ambiguities. The legislative or diplomatic negotiator will argue long and hard for inclusion, exclusion, or modification of specific language in a bill or a draft treaty, depending upon the purposes he wishes to see served.

The skillful political leader, more than most persons, appreciates that the broad human goals of organized groups are distant in time and uncertain of attainment. Political goals such as "freedom," "equality," and "justice" are meaningless references to vague future states of affairs unless implemented by more immediately stated goals such as "freedom to speak and associate," "equality of political opportunity to vote," or "just treatment in the protection of the individual in any court."

Even these more immediate future-descriptive statements are general and vague, requiring greater specification and operationalization of key terms. The long-run goal of building something vaguely called a "house" may be brought closer to short-run implementation if one approves an architect's plans and signs a contract with a builder. Of course, the "house" is no more real and no less a future state of affairs after the architect's plans and the builder's contract are made. However, *in order to get to* the "house" in the long run, other antecedent future states of affairs must be achieved in the short run: architect's plans, contract with a builder, etc. Even before these short-run goals are accomplished, others even more immediate must be accomplished: agreement with one's spouse regarding the desirability of building a house; agreement about the approximate location of the house; location and purchase of a parcel of land on which to build; consultation with an architect regarding style and probable cost; arrangement with bank regarding financing; identification of a prospective builder, etc. If one's purpose is to build a "house," a time sequence of interrelated goals must be planned.

Of course, the "ultimate" purpose may have little to do with the building of a "house" but rather with making a sound investment (for which there are alternate possibilities other than home building), impressing friends (for which there are other expensive choices), or constructing a "retirement community" for one's in-laws and parents (for which, happily, there are also other alternatives). What, then, are the *ultimate* and what are the *instrumental* purposes in this chain?

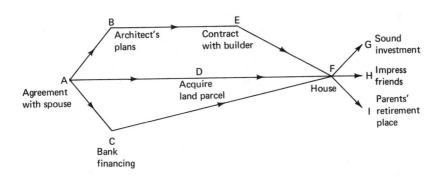

Notice how the valuation of each of the purposes could vary at different moments of decision making. After a severe conflict with his wife, a man may decide to invest in assets that are more readily negotiable than a house or in a small house rather than a large one. Basic shifts of this type in the long-run purpose will have all kinds of consequences for the short-run purposes.

Now, consider a familiar long-run *political* purpose: "the advancement of democracy and peace in the world." How do a nation's leaders program today's policy decisions in order to produce this kind of long-run goal? Library shelves are filled with future-descriptive statements about how such a world might look and how we could get to it by (a) exploiting human tendencies revealed in certain empirical statements and (b) maintaining priorities suggested in certain valuational statements. The more skeptical reader may wish to dismiss all this as mere words, but first let him suggest a better instrument than language for the identification of human purposes, transmission of information and attitudes, and achievement of co-orientation of the behaviors that seem most likely to produce these goals.

An Illustrative Use of the Conceptual Perspective

THE TACTICS OF TERMINOLOGY IN INTERNATIONAL POLITICS

Much of the activity of politics consists of battles over the definitions of terms. Was a military action by Nation X "aggression"? Is a current rise in prices and wages an "inflationary" trend? Was a remark by Mr. Y "slanderous"? Each of these questions must be answered. Is there general agreement regarding the extensions and the intensions of the key terms? Is there a consensus regarding the behaviors or events in question? May these behaviors and events be subsumed within the defined meaning of the terms? Is there some previously agreed-upon procedure for fixing the definition of the terms and for reviewing the empirical conditions to which they allegedly apply?

The President, without question, uses the heaviest verbal artillery available to the executive branch. As the principal elective official of the nation, his every word and innuendo is subjected to widespread speculation and interpretation. As Chief of State, for example, language is one of his principal tools in international affairs. Great political import rested upon President Truman's reference to the American military operations in Korea as a "police action" rather than a "war."

Korea was under Japanese rule from 1910 to 1945. As World War II ended with the defeat of Japan, military forces of the United States moved north to the 38th parallel. The Soviet Union's units moved down to the same point, which cut the country approximately in half.

The General Assembly of the United Nations agreed in 1946 to supervise elections throughout all parts of Korea in order to establish a national government. The Soviet Union refused to permit this in the northern part of the country. In South Korea, elections were held May 10, 1948, under the surveillance of the United Nations, resulting in the formation of the Republic of Korea. North of the 38th parallel, the Communists proclaimed a "People's Democratic Republic of Korea." Both South Koreans and North Koreans took the position that their respective governments had jurisdiction over all Korea.

Meanwhile, at the end of World War II, a civil war had begun between Nationalist and Communist elements in China. By 1949, the Nationalist government, led by Chiang Kai-shek, retreated to Formosa, and the Communists established a new mainland government under Mao Tse-tung. This put both Soviet and Chinese troops at the northern border of North Korea.

Even as the Soviet Union and the new Chinese Communist government were sending aid to North Korea, the American Secretary of State, Dean Acheson, was explaining a new American conception of its Far Eastern defense perimeter. This perimeter, he said in January 1950, would run from the Aleutians to Japan, to Okinawa, and to the Philippines. The line so drawn did not include Korea and Formosa, where, Acheson said, ". . . the initial reliance must be on the people attacked to resist it and then upon the commitments of the entire civilized world under the Charter of the United Nations which so far has not proved a weak reed to lean on by any people who are determined to protect their independence against outside aggression." Thus, the United States shifted responsibility to the United Nations for the ultimate defense of South Korea and Formosa. This was perceived by the Communists as an abdication of American military commitments in two vulnerable areas of the Pacific. The Communists apparently did not take seriously the prospective role of the United Nations. On Saturday June 24, 1950, the North Korean Communists attacked South Korea.

President Truman, to provide effective assistance to the Republic of Korea until such time as the United Nations Security Council could meet in emergency session at the request of the United States, directed American naval and air units into combat support of the ROK army *on behalf of the United Nations.* American policy continued on the premise that defense of South Korea was "a United Nations matter," although, in practical terms, most of the United

Nations forces were likely to be American. A fortuitous boycott of the Security Council by the Soviet Union enabled that body to pass a resolution on June 27, declaring the North Korean attack as an "act of aggression" and calling upon all members to give military aid to South Korea.

According to the American and United Nations view, all nations were now part of a new world government, which made inapplicable any concept of "war" between a nation and the U.N. In this sense, international military activity was no longer "international" but "domestic." The Korean War, therefore, was not a "war" as traditionally defined, but rather a "police action," as Truman put it.

Truman was condemned by political opponents at home and abroad for a "play on words." The use of the term "police action," however, was part of a determined American effort to press the new world organization into situations of major responsibility. The sovereignty of each nation could no longer, within the framework of the United Nations, be considered unlimited, just as the sovereignty of the states within the American union had been constrained by the Constitution. The term "police action" was a tactical use of language challenged by those unwilling to see U.S. sovereignty in any way subordinated to the U.N.

Transaction and Political Currencies

When persons contribute effort and action to an organized group, they are giving something in the expectation of receiving something else— a salary, a share of the goal when achieved, psychic payoffs, etc. This exchange is also typical of political transactions generally. Although transaction theory has developed mainly in the field of economics, it has great antiquity among political theorists. A transaction requires at least two parties, each possessing something desired by the other yet also valuable to himself, who negotiate an exchange of these things; tangible or nontangible, all are labeled *currencies* here. Political currencies may be classified as shares (decisional elements), incumbencies (positional elements), and commodities (materiel elements). A satisfactory transaction is one in which both parties consider that they have profited. A significant side effect of successful transactions between parties is the development of attitudes of trust toward each other. Exchanges do not continue if either or both parties fail to profit (by whatever subjective yardstick each employs). Successful transaction and trust may have important consequences for broadening cooperation between parties, reducing conflict, and contributing to political integration. Politics also has its marketplaces in which the business of exchanging political currencies is carried on, but usually without the overtness and legitimacy enjoyed by commercial transactions.

4

Effort and Activity as Political Transactions

In Book Two of *The Republic*, Plato relates the following dialogue:

> A state, I said, arises, as I conceive, out of the needs of mankind; no one is self-sufficing, but all of us have many wants. Can any other origin of a state be imagined?
>
> There can be no other.
>
> Then, as we have many wants, and many persons are needed to supply them, one takes a helper for one purpose and another for another; and when these partners and helpers are gathered together in one habitation the body of inhabitants is termed a state.
>
> True, he said.
>
> And they exchange with one another, and one gives and another receives, each under the idea that the exchange will be for his own good.
>
> Very true.

Similarly, Chester Barnard stated in his theory of organization that an organized group comes into being when (1) there are two or more persons *able to communicate* with each other, (2) who are *willing to contribute action*, (3) to accomplish a *common purpose.*

129

The essential attributes of an organized group: (1) communication; (2) willingness to serve; and (3) common purpose.[1]

Barnard explains "willingness to contribute action" as a surrender of control of personal conduct, or the "depersonalization of personal action."

> Activities cannot be coordinated unless there is first the disposition to make a personal act a contribution to an impersonal system of acts, one in which the individual gives up personal control of what he does.

> The outstanding fact regarding willingness to contribute to a given specific formal organization is the indefinitely large range of variation in its intensity among individuals. If all those who may be considered potential contributors to an organization are arranged in order of willingness to serve it, the scale gradually descends from possibly intense willingness through neutral or zero willingness to intense unwillingness or opposition or hatred. The *preponderance of persons in a modern society always lies on the negative side* with reference to any particular existing or potential organization. Thus, of the possible contributors only a small minority actually have a positive willingness. . . .

> Willingness to cooperate, positive or negative, is the expression of the net satisfactions or dissatisfactions experienced or anticipated by each individual in comparison with those experienced or anticipated through alternative opportunities. . . . Willingness to cooperate is the net effect, first of the inducements to do so in conjunction with the sacrifices involved, and then in comparison with the practically available net satisfactions offered by alternatives. . . . Thus, from the viewpoint of the individual, willingness is the joint effect of personal desires and reluctances; from the viewpoint of the organization it is the joint effect of objective inducements offered and burdens imposed. The measure of this net result, however, is entirely individual, personal, and subjective.[2]

In the behavioral sciences, the study of "inducements" and "burdens," more often called "needs" and "costs," has been primarily the concern of economists. Before political science became a distinct academic discipline, political economy was an established subfield of nineteenth-century economics. In recent decades, economists have become increasingly interested in the psychological dimensions of

---

[1] See Chapter 1, *The Functions of the Executive, op. cit.*
[2] *Ibid.*, pp. 84–86. Quoted with permission of the Harvard University Press.

transactions, whereas the social psychologists have begun to describe behavior as a form of social exchange.

Of course, all along, skilled practical politicans have always known a good "deal" when they are offered one and seem to have a sixth sense about locating the appropriate "marketplace" in which to find the "best deal."

THEORIES OF EXCHANGE AND TRANSACTION

Together with production and consumption, exchange of goods is at the heart of the study of economics. Exchange has been defined as "a situation in which each of two parties provides some good(s) to the other." In the traditional sense, the giving up of goods by one party is contingent upon receipt of goods from the other. A *transaction*, then, is an exchange, along with the attendant bargaining or negotiations. There may be two or more parties involved in a transaction, and the parties may be either individuals or organizations.[3]

According to economists, transactions take place during the marketing process or in marketplaces. In a primitive society, the marketplace may be simply an open area to which the producers themselves bring the whole range of goods customarily exchanged by barter or sale: domesticated animals, foodstuffs, cloth, pottery and similar artifacts, slaves, etc. Modern marketplaces, with their large company of middlemen, are infinitely more organized and specialized. There are buildings, such as stockyards, grain markets, and clothing exchanges, in which distinct products are processed through various stages of marketing.

However, not all economic transactions need take place in a physically distinct marketplace. In some cases the "market" may simply be a term summarizing all of the transactions for a particular product, e.g. the housing market. We are less accustomed to the notion of a *political marketplace*, but these too exist, sometimes in specific locations such as party conventions and sometimes as general political processes such as diplomacy.

Marketing usually consists of a number of distinct activities, according to economic analysts. The central activity is the exchange of

3 Alfred Kuhn, *The Study of Society* (Homewood, Illinois: Irvin-Dorsey Press, 1963), p. 269. Most of the explanation of economic transaction is based upon Kuhn's excellent formulations.

goods, which involves selling and buying. Next is the physical supply and removal of goods, which includes such activities as transportation and storage. A third activity relates to market information, particularly if goods are complex or trading is *in absentia;* market information is critical for matching buyer needs with product characteristics. Finally, in modern money economies, the financial and risk-taking functions have been separated out for management by middlemen, insurance brokers, and others.

The Transaction

A transaction is a social event in that it requires at least two parties. It also involves communicative activity since, by definition, transactions are accompanied by negotiations. A successful negotiation culminates in a cooperative act in which the respective individual wants of the separate transactors become the shared goal; for example, two fellow legislators may share a goal if they both seek passage of the *same* piece of legislation. However, if the goal is the mutual facilitation of *different* objectives, then we have the makings of a transaction. If Legislator A wants to have Bill X enacted, if Legislator B wants Bill Y to be passed, and if they need each other's vote to accomplish their respective objectives, they may enter a negotiation in which they trade votes even though neither man may be interested in the other's bill per se. The transaction consists of an exchange of voting support which enables each man to have his legislation passed, even though his bill was not the same goal as the other's. This transaction is more familiarly known as *logrolling.*

Although many Americans tend to decry "deals," transactions such as this require fairly sophisticated behavior. Each party must cooperate in fulfilling the other's goal in order to advance the cause of his own objective. The happiest transaction is the one in which each party feels that he has gotten the best deal possible for himself.

The behavior of each party to a transaction must be further analyzed in order to understand the combined behaviors of the two parties. Kuhn's approach does this by examining *Effective Preference* (EP). "Effective Preference" is, according to Kuhn, "the degree of capacity to get some desired thing plus the will to get it rather than to satisfy conflicting desires."[4] EP, then, consists of three considerations: (1) the specification of a desired thing from a set

4 *Ibid.,* p. 319.

of conflicting desires; (2) the will, or decision, to exercise an available opportunity to get the desired thing; and (3) the capacity, or negotiable resources, to get it.

Person A, let us assume, is a student with a set of conflicting desires: enrollment at college, requiring payment of tuition fees; retention of his automobile, requiring a payment to the car loan company; or replacement of worn clothing, requiring purchases at a local department store sale. Student A has $100 worth of "capacity," or cash on hand. Let his set of conflicting desires be called Y_1, Y_2, and Y_3, respectively. Let the negotiable resources or capacity that he must forego to get his desired good be called X, in this case, $100. Although X would be sufficient capacity to obtain any one of the three Ys, he must first decide which one is the most desired at this moment. It turns out that Y_1, payment of tuition for enrollment at college, is his greatest preference. The *objective* cost of Y_1 to him will be X, the $100. However, the *subjective* cost will be something else again; obviously he held enrollment at college in greater value than $100 in cash, since he was willing to give up the latter in exchange for the former.

Student A's choice depends, therefore, on his valuation of X and Y. The value of X in A's preference system may be designated as AX, and the value of Y as AY. When A prefers Y to X, we may say that AY exceeds AX. A's Effective Preference for Y is AY-AX. In such a case, A's choice would be "rational" only if he chooses to obtain Y rather than retain X. (When an individual makes a choice contrary to *his own* preference system, he is said to be acting "irrationally.") If AY were equal to AX, A would have an Effective Preference of zero, that is, he would be indifferent in a choice between X and Y. If his Effective Preference were AX-AY, he would retain X, that is, not incur the cost of exchanging it for Y.

Effective Preference, according to Kuhn, depends on objective opportunities as well as subjective desires. Student A can have all the desire in the world to spend his $100 on tuition but, if he has just been expelled for failing grades, he does not have the objective opportunity to do so. His only real alternatives are to make a car payment or purchase clothes.

Person A will, in a completed transaction, exchange goods with person B. B possesses Y, which is the good that A seeks. B, of course, has his own Effective Preference with respect to X and Y. The values he places on X and Y can be designated as BX and BY. To follow the transaction, the preference ordering of two persons must now be examined simultaneously. A transaction requires two decision: A's decision to give up X for Y, and B's decision to give up Y for X.

A transaction will usually require opposite preference orderings on the part of A and B. If A and B both prefer Y to X, then A will be willing to offer X for Y, but B will refuse. If both prefer X to Y, B will be willing to give Y for X, but A will refuse. But if A prefers Y to X, and B prefers X to Y, then exchange is possible, and both parties will judge the transaction as profitable.

However, if A and B have the same preference orderings of X and Y, a difference in their relative valuations of X and Y may also be sufficient to permit a transaction. Jim and Joe, for example, both prefer Jim's rebuilt Ford car to Joe's motorcycle. Joe, however, emphatically wants the rebuilt Ford. Jim knows he can always rebuild another, and he also happens to be quite interested in having a motorcycle. Despite his preference for his own Ford, Jim decides to make the trade.

For each person to perceive a prospective exchange as profitable (a necessary condition for completing the transaction), each must attach some value to the same things or currencies being negotiated. Each person's valuation of the currency may be different in degree, but each must to *some degree* value it if there is to be any negotiable overlap of Effective Preferences. In other words, each transactor must be willing to *keep* what he is offering as well as to *exchange* it.

Some Typical Effective-Preference Situations

In a bargaining transaction, each party's power to acquire what he desires depends not only on his own but also on the other's Effective Preference. A number of combinations of Effective Preference may result. Examples of these will be discussed below as EP Situations 1 to 5.[5]

Each EP Situation is accompanied by a diagram in which A's EP for Y is represented by the double bar at the left and B's EP for X is represented by the single line at the right. The scale below the bar indicates units of value that each party places upon the resources he has available for an exchange. A has X, and B has Y. A presumably

[5] Based upon Kuhn, *ibid.*, pp. 236–37, who in turn has adapted and extended the discussion of Kenneth E. Boulding, *Economic Analysis* (3rd ed.; New York: Harper, 1955). Diagrams adapted by permission of Harper & Row.

wants Y, and B wants X. The "No" and "Yes" indications just below the scale tell whether a transaction is possible. The exclamation mark indicates that each party's EP is satisfied precisely, which means that each goes away from the transaction feeling that he has gotten exactly what he wants for exactly as much as he wanted to give for it. The question mark indicates that there is enough overlapping of EPs to leave the exact point of transaction in doubt; these are bargaining situations.

A *unit* is any unit of value *revelant to each particular transactor.* There are six units indicated on each side of the center line in the diagrams, but these are for visual convenience only. The remarkable thing about the human mind is that it can create subjective gradations of value that cannot be quantified objectively. This human capacity has been a major source of frustration for economists interested in designing utility scales by which they may observe and predict transactional behavior. But how does anyone create a value scale for a transaction in which Johnny gives Bill a pack of bubble gum and a sling shot in exchange for a pocket knife? Or, as Professors George C. Homans and Peter Blau suggest, what units apply when one executive in an organization gives deference to another in exchange for professional advice?

In money economies, units of value have been assigned to various currencies and their denominations. These have served as great intellectual and practical conveniences by, in effect, operationalizing the valuational units for particular marketplaces. Money and similar currencies have permitted the depersonalization of the marketplace and mass volume in transactional activity. If Smith in Boston tells Jones in Iowa how many dollars he is willing to pay for a bushel of corn, and if Jones in Iowa can tell Gomez in Mexico City in dollars-converted-to-pesos how much he is willing to pay for Mexican artifacts, transactional activity is facilitated to the advantage of all.

Theoretically speaking, it would be useful if we could extend currency measures to exchangeable things not so readily quantifiable as money: bubble gum, sling shot, pocket knife, deference, advice, affection, or even "political curencies." If Legislator A can deliver eleven votes for a bill that is important to Legislator B, would B's endorsement in A's next election campaign be sufficient "political currency" to permit them to consummate the transaction?

Turning to the EP Situations: In Situation 1, A is willing to give only four units of his own double-bar currency for Y, but Y is not

EP Situation 1

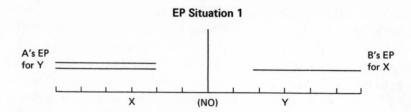

available to A unless the double-bar reaches B's single-line demands. Conversely, B is willing to exchange four units of single-line currency for X but runs into A's demand that exchange currencies (eight units) reach the double bar. In Situation 1, therefore, no transaction can take place. Each party prefers to keep what he has.

In EP Situation 2, A's EP for Y has risen or extended to the center line, whereas B's remains the same as in Situation 1. A apparently now wants Y more than previously and so is willing to demand less for X. Nevertheless, no transaction is possible in this case either.

EP Situation 2

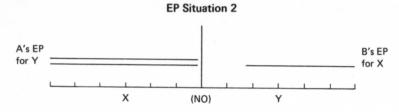

In Situation 3, A has extended his EP to the point that it meets B's. A transaction can take place under these circumstances. A is willing to give all that is necessary (X) for Y, and B is willing to give all that is necessary (Y) for X. There is no room for bargaining in this situation. Each side is incurring a cost that is acceptable and receiving a good that is satisfying.

EP Situation 3

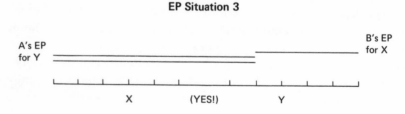

This is a "good deal." Incidentally, an observer might say, from looking at the currency scales alone, that B made the better bargain because he exchanged what appears to be fewer units of value. Such an observation completely overlooks the subjective character of the units in the minds of B and A, respectively. It is in these two minds that the ultimate yardsticks are located.

Situation 4 shows A willing to go two units of his own currency beyond what B requires for Y. As Kuhn puts it, each party has passed the other's minimum terms, or threshold. A transaction can take place, but at what point of the scale will the price be fixed? If A and B are skillful bargainers, they will find and split the difference, which could mean nine double-bar units from A in exchange for three single-line units from B. In such a bargaining situation, it is obvious that each party needs much information not only about the respective goods to be exchanged but also about the other's skill as a bargainer. As we learned from communication theory, if the trans-actors like each other (attraction), they will probably engage in much communicative activity in order to acquire information for successful completion of the transaction. In international affairs, this is what two friendly nations will do as they attempt to con-summate a treaty in some difficult area of their relations. On the other hand, hatred between parties, as occurs in war situations, will disrupt communicative activity and make negotiations impossible.

EP Situation 4

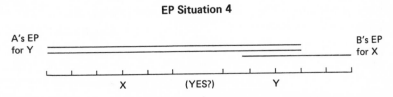

EP Situation 5 is similar to Situation 4, but with B now ready to extend his price over to A's side of the scale. Here again is a bargain-ing situation with a range of four scale units within which to nego-tiate, as compared to two units in Situation 4. Here, too, a trans-action is likely to result at the end of negotiations.

EP Situation 5

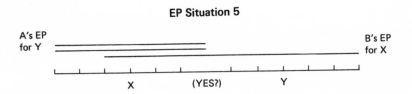

The charts for the five illustrative transactional situations make it simple to identify the issue of *overlap*. Only if there is *some minimum overlap* of transactors' EPs can a transaction take place. This means that the parties must know about each other, want each other's goods, have information about the respective goods, and be willing to enter negotiations to determine their respective EPs. With all this to accomplish, very few social interactions are likely to end up as successful transactions. On the other hand, the need for overlap of EPs makes clear the importance of marketplaces in bringing potential transactors together in some convenient and rational manner. If a prospective transactor wants to trade in wheat or bonds, he knows exactly where to find appropriate marketplaces in the United States.

A second problem related to overlap is its *amount*. The greater the overlap, according to Kuhn, the greater the uncertainty about where the terms will fall, but, at the same time, the likelihood that the transaction will take place is greater. Thus, the greatest likelihood of a transaction is found in EP situation 5, while the minimal prospect is in Situation 3 where any small difficulty may cause the transaction to fail.

When political commentators write about the "great areas of consensus" that make the Democratic and Republican parties attractive to most Americans, they are in effect describing the existence of many transactable policy differences between the parties for which the amount of EP overlap is great enough to assure negotiability. For example, in the civil rights policy field, the apparently different approaches of the Democratic and Republican parties are in fact basically similar and fall well within a large area of EP overlap. The likelihood that the two parties could arrive at some civil rights transaction in a legislative situation is great, although the exact point of agreement within the area of overlap will depend a great deal upon the bargaining power of the parties at the time of the legislative vote. A very different transactional situation would exist if, as in EP Situation 3, Democrats and Republicans barely had a meeting of the minds regarding civil rights.

The *position* of overlap is still another consideration in the transaction. This refers to the general location of the overlap area—on A's side, B's side, or in the middle. From the subjective view of either A or B, any overlap that leads to a transaction will, by definition, produce net satisfactions for both parties. If this did not happen, the transaction could not take place. Each party must *himself* believe that he is getting a "fair deal" if he is to be willing to consummate the transaction.

On the other hand, society provides on-the-average views regarding the "fairness" of transactions. As others watch the transaction between A and B, each observer will use his own value scale to make his own subjective judgments. These judgments may have no immediate consequence for the actual transaction between A and B, but if the observers outside the transaction are able to affect the value scales of the participating parties, this may produce important consequences regarding the *position* of overlap. For most Americans accustomed to "free" water supply, for example, payment of a dollar a gallon for home-delivered distilled water will seem exorbitant and "unfair." They would view the price as favorable to the water supplier in the same way that they might view B's demands in EP Situation 4 as favorable to B because the *average observer's* scale of values "sees" the consummated transaction as falling over *on B's side*. A, of course, does not see it this way in Situation 4. But if A were the average American accustomed to "free" water, he would probably feel uncomfortable about paying a dollar a gallon for distilled water, if he purchased it at all. In other words, the *social consensus* about paying that price for water would influence the individual's acceptance of different amounts and positions of overlap. We may see the position of overlap influenced by daily and monthly fluctuations in average prices for particular commodities in different marketplaces. When farmers introduced the concept "parity," they were in effect saying to the rest of the nation that the position of overlap between the prices of farm goods and the prices of nonfarm goods was "unfair."

Once the fact of overlap between transactor EPs is established, the parties will proceed to the settlement of the transaction within the overlap. Kuhn describes these proceedings as the *tactics of settlement*.

Tactical considerations are almost nonexistent for most Americans who, living in a standard-price marketplace, simply pay the price on the tag. This is very much in contrast to the bargaining activity of an American tourist purchasing goods in, say, a Mexican marketplace. The tourist who fails to bargain vigorously, to feign disinterest in the goods, or to make at least two or three gestures at walking away from the negotiations is considered by the Mexican vendor as an "easy mark" or "sucker." The tactics of settlement in such situations requires skill, patience, and an amount of bargaining effort that most Americans would consider excessive.

In American political transactions, the tactics of settlement may be in many ways similar to the Mexican marketplace, requiring skill, patience, and effort. The factional leader who fails to bargain vigorously and believably may find himself receiving not only the poorer end of the bargain but also being perceived by other politicians as lacking in skill. The ways many American politicians go about making their respective bargaining positions believably tough would produce a large inventory of tactical maneuvers: threatened defection, threatened violence, "tough talk," unwillingness to contribute activity in a campaign or a civic enterprise, public demonstrations, petitions showing large-scale support, aggressive bargaining style, etc.[6]

The preceding models of transactional behavior are, of course, a magnification of the theoretical elements in one particular transaction. In real life, particular transactors may be carrying on bargaining negotiations with several transactors simultaneously, with the progress of one set of negotiations influencing progress in negotiations elsewhere. In other words, overall transactional activity can be voluminous and complex despite the fact that the basic theoretical model for a single transaction may be reduced to the few elements just discussed.

Behavioral Exchanges

Classical economics has been incorporated into behavioral psychology by the work of Professor George C. Homans, who views social behavior as a form of exchange or transaction. Homans' theory examines face-to-face contacts between individuals as "an exchange of activity, tangible or intangible, and more or less rewarding or costly" to each individual.

"Activity," according to Homans, is a comprehensively descriptive term referring not only to the transfer of materials and objects from one individual to another but also the emission of sentiments by one to the other. A friend gives advice to another in exchange for senti-

---

[6] In the discussion of political conflict in Chapter 9, these considerations about transactions and bargaining will have relevance for coalition formation as an aspect of the strategy of games.

ments of affection or deference from the other. Neighbors exchange attentions and favors. Members of a seminar exchange ideas. The fundamental behavioral transaction to which Homans directs our attention occurs when an "activity" emitted by one person is rewarded or punished by an "activity" emitted by another person regardless of the kinds of activity each emits.[7]

As in economic theory, Homans views a "cost" as a value foregone. The person who emits an activity must, in so doing, have foregone a rewarding alternative activity before the emitted one may be counted as a "cost." The friend who responds to a request for advice and sets aside an enjoyable evening at the theater to provide it has incurred a cost. If the advice is received with displeasure or disdain, the evening is costly for him: missing the theater. Further exchanges with the disdainful transactor are likely to be few because of their "unprofitability." In Homans' terms, the more costly an activity is to a person, the less often he will emit it. Psychic profit, therefore, is reward less cost. No behavioral exchange continues unless *both* parties are making a profit. This axiom is consistent with economic transactional theory.

Homans illustrates his theory by drawing upon the findings of a study of interpersonal behavior in a bureaucracy.[8] The study describes the behavior of sixteen agents of a Federal law-enforcement agency. These men held the same job title, but they varied in competence; consequently, the more skilled received more requests for assistance from their co-workers. While the participants in such consultations benefited, they still incurred costs in their exchange. That is, the agent requesting help usually was rewarded by being enabled to do a better job. However, he paid the price of implicitly admitting his inferiority to a colleague who, by title, supposedly was his equal. The consultant, on the other hand, gained prestige; nevertheless, he incurred the cost of time taken from his own work. Both investigators netted a social profit if their reward from the interaction exceeded the personal costs. Social justice was realized in this situation if the rewards of both participants were proportional to their costs. The criterion of proportionality was *each participant's own* normative expectation, derived though it was from his social

---

7 *Social Behavior: Its Elementary Forms* (New York: Harcourt, Brace and World, 1961). An earlier exposition by Homans appears in "Social Behavior as Exchange," *American Journal of Sociology*, 47 (May 1958): 597–606.

8 Peter M. Blau, *The Dynamics of Bureaucracy* (Chicago: University of Chicago Press, 1955).

environment, regarding what constitutes "justice" or "fairness" in the distribution of rewards and costs between persons.

Thus, a behavioral exchange exists where the activity of each of at least two individuals reinforces (or punishes) the activity of the other, and where, accordingly, each influences the other. Men engage in activities when they are transferring objects and materials from themselves to others, and they are also engaging in activities when they emit sentiments of approval in response to the behavior of another. An interaction occurs when an activity (or sentiment) emitted by one man is rewarded (or punished) by an activity emitted by another man, regardless of the kinds of activity each emits.

What units exist for the measurement of the exchange value of emitted activities? Homans asserts that a person's past is where we must look for information regarding the things *he* values, for each individual is the ultimate judge of what *he* considers valuable. With the person's biographical data in hand, an observer may further determine a man's values by the amount of activity he has emitted to get those values.

No man can have all his values at once. In real life, choice is simplified by the usual circumstance that only two or three alternatives are perceived by the transactor as being available. Choice is usually made predictable by the fact that each man has values that are more or less constant over the long run, although he may prefer particular values more at some times than he does at others. The more of a particular value the person has gotten in the recent past, the less valuable he holds it. In general, however, his overall "value structure," as it is sometimes called, is invariably a factor in his subjective cost-estimating procedures, even though components in that structure may vary somewhat for situation, time, or particular juxtaposition against each other in particular circumstances.

TRUST AND ORGANIZATION INTEGRATION

Promises and Trust

Time is an important aspect of transactions. The simplest transactions are those in which two parties transfer goods between themselves simultaneously. When the transfers take place at different times, anticipation and trust become significant elements in the situation. The local grocer will extend noninterest credit to a customer until pay day; he will exhibit an attitude of trust toward the customer in anticipation of completion of the transaction at some normal time such as pay day. A more complicated economic transaction is the purchase of a house in which the buyer signs a mortgage contract to pay, say, $30,000 plus interest in specified amounts over a period of years. The mortgage company extends trust at a socially acceptable price (the going interest rate) if investigation establishes the trustworthiness (credit standing) of the buyer.

According to Blau, social exchanges are somewhat different in that they entail unspecified obligations. Bankers can bargain over price and interest rate, but friends can hardly bargain over the expectation that an invitation to dinner will be reciprocated at some future time.[9] Another difference is the ambiguity of the currency units involved in social exchanges. A dinner invitation from a friend who is a good cook is "worth more" than an invitation from a poor cook. How are the units of value to be measured in such an exchange? In the aforementioned study of Federal investigators, what units of value can be applied to the advice given and what units to the deference extended? Possibly the only measure in such social exchanges is the inference that may be drawn from the consummated transaction, namely, that a pair of Effective Preferences involved must overlap, or else the transaction could not be completed.

Social exchange, therefore, involves transfers that create diffuse rather than precisely specified future obligations and a return that cannot be bargained about but must be left to the discretion of the one who makes it. Since there is no way to assure an appropriate return for a social favor, social exchange requires trusting others to discharge their obligations. Typically, according to Blau, exchange relations evolve slowly, usually starting with minor transactions in which little trust is required, but neither is there much risk. By discharging obligations for goods received, individuals demonstrate their trustworthiness, leading to gradual expansion of exchanges accompanied by growth of mutual trust. Examples are familiar: the individual who repays a small loan promptly in order to establish his credit for a larger one; the nations that engage in business and cultural exchanges with the prospect that the trust needed for political exchanges will eventually come into being.

Why are promises kept? Why will an individual keep a trust? Kuhn offers three general conditions under which promises are

9 *Ibid.*, pp. 93–94.

made and accepted. First, a promiser is likely to fulfill a promise when he has a greater stake in fulfilling it than in not fulfilling it. A second condition is the *giver's* conviction that the promiser has a greater stake in fulfilling the promise than in not fulfilling it; the giver perceives the promiser as making such an evaluation. Finally, if a person wishes to acquire something valuable on the basis of a promise, he must be able to demonstrate convincingly that he has an adequate stake in its fulfillment, that is, he must help the other transactor in the latter's evaluation of his (the receiver's) attitude toward the worth of the stake.

It has been the absence of these conditions, for example, in the Vietnam war that has led each side to discount the offers of the other. Prior to the 1967 American bombing pause, the North Vietnamese expressed a willingness to negotiate in exchange for a termination in the bombing of their terrain, but under the significant proviso that the termination be "permanent." The Americans, on the other hand, offered to terminate the bombing if the North Vietnamese indicate "when" and "for how long" the negotiations would take place. In such a situation of distrust, neither side could demonstrate convincingly that he had an adequate stake in the fulfillment of his promise.

In a sequence of exchanges between two parties, an initial attitude of trust is likely to increase with the number of successful transactions, and trust is likely to engender mutual personal attraction which, in turn, is so important to communicative activity and the process of straining toward symmetry. We have already seen how personal attraction and strain toward symmetry may advance cooperation and group formation. This series of events—transaction, trust, attraction, cooperation, strain toward symmetry, group organization—lies at the heart of the relationship between an organization and its members' willingness to contribute effort to it.

Transactional Trust within Organizations

The organizations may, in the first place, induce the member to contribute effort simply by engaging in a purely *economic* transaction with him. If he works regularly at specified hours in the performance of specified tasks, the organization may promise to deliver to him a certain salary on the first day of each month. In this way, the machinist on the assembly line may be more interested in his monthly salary check than in whether he is helping produce General Motors automobiles or B-52 bombers.

But *social* exchanges involve currencies other than money. A machinist who is an auto buff will probably take pride even in the limited craftsmanship afforded by the General Motors assembly line, and this may induce him to remain at the auto assembly line despite the possibility that he could earn more money elsewhere. On the other hand, the machinist who is a pacifist will find it difficult to remain on the assembly line of a bomber manufacturer and is likely to leave the job at the earliest opportunity. In both illustrations, the overall production goal of the manufacturing organization may or may not be a significant nonmonetary inducement in the contributed activity of the machinist.

The nonmonetary currencies tend to assume larger significance in other types of organizations. For example, in revolutionary movements, the major inducement for intense contributed activity may be the promise of recognition by a beloved leader or the satisfaction in seeing a hated regime overthrown. Summarizing empirical research in the field of group cohesion, Cartwright and Zander found that an individual's attraction to a group will depend upon two sets of conditions: (1) certain properties of the group, such as its goals, programs, size, type of organization, typical characteristics of members, etc., and (2) the particular needs of the individual for affiliation, recognition, security, and other goods which may be acquired through the group. In the language of transactional theory, the individual member will *give* to the group according to the capacity of various group properties to be *rewarding* to him. In this sense, cohesiveness and morale are concepts describing the EPs of individual members as they contribute activity and effort to the group. For example, if the group's goal is especially important to a member and if significant steps toward the accomplishment of that goal are being taken successfully by the group, the morale of the member will be high, and his willingness to expend effort will be great. Conversely, if the goals are important to the member, but the group's achievements few, something akin to EP Situations 1 and 2 will exist, and the member's morale and contributed effort will drop accordingly.[10]

Every group and organization is a four-sided economy, according

[10] Dorwin Cartwright and Alvin Zander (eds.), *Group Dynamics: Research and Theory* (Evanston, Ill.: Row, Peterson, 1953), Chap. 7.

to Barnard. One side consists of the *physical energies and materials* contributed by members and derived by the group from its work upon the environment; these materials in turn are expended on the environment and given to the group's members. A second side is the *individual's economy*—what is it that he gets out of his personal performance and contribution. A third side are the *social utilities* derived from the social environment, for example, the great pleasure that people of like characteristics get from working well together. The fourth side is the complex and comprehensive *economy of the whole organization* within which both material services and social services are contributed by members and material and social things are secured from the environment, and material is given to the environment along with material and social satisfactions to the members. The only measure of this whole economy is the survival of the organization. If the organization grows, it obviously has been effective in its transactions. If it contracts, its effectiveness may be questioned. Of course, an organization may contract for precisely the reason that it has accomplished its goals.

Underlying this quadruple economy is the problem that it is impossible to balance output and input in detail. In the nature of cooperative systems, they are as a whole different from the sum of their constituent parts or contributions. Each incoming contribution goes into a pool, and each outgoing contribution comes out of a pool, but the two cannot be identified as equivalents.[11]

The "balance of payments" in the whole organizational economy may be significantly influenced by the other three economies. The individual's willingness to contribute effort, for example, may be greatly heightened by his trust in a charismatic leader, his intense faith in the group's goal, or his sheer joy in "belonging." These are obviously behavioral currencies that are quite different from the material and monetary currencies that may pass between the group and the member.

If such transactions intensify trust, attraction, and cooperation, what of the transactional promises not kept and the anticipated exchanges that are unfulfilled? In the usual mortgage transaction, foreclosure, forfeiture of the house at some auction price and the payments previously made on it, is a familiar procedure. In social exchanges, unkept promises and unreturned obligations may lead to the loss of such stakes as reputation, friendship, honor, credibility,

11 Barnard, *op. cit.,* pp. 251–54.

and opportunities for group membership. In other words, the transactional relationships shift away from trust, attraction, and cooperation toward distrust, alienation, and conflict. Unless the amount of transactional overlap is great and the opportunities for other transactions numerous, the shift toward conflict may lead to the kind of breakdown in communication and refusal to negotiate that are common features in war situations.

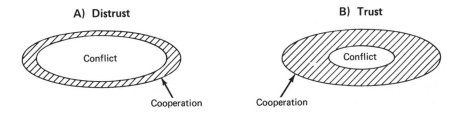

The conflict-cooperation consequences of distrust and trust within multitransactional organizational or societal economies are suggested in the accompanying diagrams. Both diagrams represent conflictful human relations as an area within an encircling framework of human association and cooperation. In Diagram A, the conflict area nearly fills the cooperative circle when transactors tend to be distrustful of each other. In other words, the area of cooperation is thin and narrow; the grounds and opportunities for communicative activity, negotiation, attraction, and successful transaction are few. In the situation of trust of Diagram B, the conflict area is compressed by an expanded area of cooperation perhaps resulting from a long series of successful transactions.

The history of many representative assemblies might well be explained by their transformation from the conditions of Diagram A to those of Diagram B. The early history of numerous legislatures, bringing together a sampling of the whole political community, is usually a tale of great hostility and distrust among the representatives who become members. In time, and as the result of innumerable successful small transactions, these members develop an ingroup etiquette and camaraderie; the honor of all members comes to be affected by the honor of each, and the area of cooperation is ever-increasing. Thus, it was not unusual for members of Congress, in the early years of the Republic, to engage in personal vituperation, threats, and duels. Today, the daily transactions of Congress are serious, numerous, and usually successfully conducted. Despite political differences, the Senate, for example, is often referred to as the most powerful "club" in the world.

Irreversible Transactions and Group Integration

When the members of a group share its goals, contribute effort to implement the goals, remain in communication with other members, and participate in the group's decisions, that group may be described as *integrated*.[12] Conversely, *disintegration* consists of defection or departure of members from the group. As a group evolves from informal relationships among its members to a high degree of organization among them, it is probable that the group is well integrated. Usually, high morale among the members and high cohesion among the parts of a group constitute evidence of integration.

In transactional terms, a group is integrated when each of its members and parts considers it more costly to contribute effort and activity elsewhere than to the group. When the ninth state ratified the Constitution, undecided voters and leaders in the remaining four undoubtedly realized that the Confederation had become a Federal Union and that it would be costly to be isolated from the Union. The Union was a more integrated version of the Confederation, with each member state more intensely committed by function and participation than previously.

A group or organization is integrated if there is a disappearing probability that members' costs of participation will lead to defection. Since we are dealing here with probabilities and with possible changes in cost estimates, it is obvious that group integration can never be counted on to remain a permanent condition. On the other hand, group development may be such that cost continues to decline and intraorganizational transactions become increasingly irreversible.

The "clearance sale" is a familiar event among American merchants. The merchant sets an especially low price on his goods and declares all sales "final." He is interested in disposing of an inventory of goods at the same time covering all costs to himself. To improve

---

[12] For significant attempts to develop a theory of integration, Claude Ake, *A Theory of Political Integration* (Homewood, Ill.: Dorsey Press, 1967) and Johan Galtung, "A Structural Theory of Integration," *Journal of Peace Research*, (1968): 375–395. On members' commitment to an organization as a whole as distinguished from commitment to its values, policies, etc., Helen P. Gouldner, "Dimensions of Organizational Commitment," *Administrative Science Quarterly*, 4 (March 1960): 468–490.

the prospect that this will happen, he reduces prices below normal in order to attract buyers. However, with prices at a minimum, he leaves himself no margin for the kinds of overhead costs usually associated with returns of goods. To avoid this risk, he classifies each sale as "final." On the other hand, buyers are just as interested in minimizing expenditures as well as the risk of purchasing unsatisfactory goods and will therefore take special care in examining goods prior to purchase. If the irreversibility of the transaction is maintained, each party will, as in EP Situation 3, emerge with a minimum but satisfactory profit. Any attempt to reverse the process, that is, take back or return the goods, would involve both transactors in unwanted costs. The degree of integration of an organized group will increase as the irreversible transactions among its members increase. From this point of view, an irreversible transaction may change the behavioral environment of each individual in a permanent way.[13]

POLITICAL CURRENCIES AND MARKETPLACES

Political Transactions

The social exchanges identified by Homans and Blau and the economic exchanges described by economists are not far removed from the kinds of transactions dealt with in certain theories of politics. Following the Platonic line of analysis noted earlier, Aristotle produced a conception of *distributive justice* according to which the offices of the state and the rights adhering to these offices are to be

---

[13] The conception of *transaction* employed here should be distinguished from another usage found in psychology and social psychology. The latter is employed by theorists in the field of perception, learning, and cognition. The basic postulate is that the organism cannot be separated either from the environment or from the things it observes in the environment. *Transacting* refers to the alterations that the organism experiences in the process of perceiving, knowing, and interacting with its environment. The emphasis is on *trans*-action and *inter*-action. For example, once the student has read this page, he can never be the same as before. The perceptual and cognitive experience, according to the transactionalist, has modified him forever as an organism (although this writer hopes the damage is not too severe).

Further statements of this conception of transaction may be found in: John Dewey and Arthur F. Bentley, *Knowing and the Known* (reprinted, Boston: Beacon Press, 1949), pp. 517–22; Franklin T. Kilpatrick (ed.) *Explorations in Transactional Psychology* (New York: New York University Press, 1961).

Transaction has also been introduced into the field of general systems theory in referring to the exchanges that go on between the system and its environment. Charles A. McClelland, "General Systems and the Social Sciences," *ETC.: A Review of General Semantics*, 18 (1962): 449–68.

distributed to each citizen in proportion to his contribution to the ends of the state, that is, to the good quality of life sought by the state. Aristotle acknowledged the difficulties arising from different criteria for judging a meritorious contribution; each social class, he observed, tries to give priority to its particular criterion (wealth, noble birth, personal virtue, greater numbers, etc.), and this leads to different forms of state and to revolutions that change states from one form to another.[14]

Edmund Burke makes his reference to the transactional character of politics in his *Speech on the Conciliation of the Colonies:*

> All government, indeed, every human benefit and enjoyment, every virtue, and every prudent act, is founded on compromise and barter. We balance inconveniences; we give and take; we remit some rights, that we may enjoy others. . . . In every arduous enterprise we consider what we are to lose, as well as what we are to gain. . . . Man acts from adequate motives relative to his interest and not on metaphysical speculation.

Sir Henry Maine described the leader in democracies as "the Wirepuller" who is skilled in "cutting up political power into petty fragments" and trading upon these fragments. A. Lawrence Lowell wrote of politics as "a species of brokerage," noting that "one of the functions of politicians is that of brokers" among the group interests in the community. Innumerable other writers on government and politics—Bentley, Herring, Lasswell, Downs, Kuhn, Mitchell, and others—have reiterated the transactional character of political activity.[15]

If politicians are viewed as transactors operating within political systems, what, then, are the things they exchange? The economists deal with exchanges of goods and services, usually with man-made monetary units serving as common denominators for values assigned to the goods or service by each transactor that he brings to the transaction. Homans refers to activities, behaviors, and sentiments as the currencies of social exchange. What, if any, are the distinctive

---

[14] Ernest Barker, *The Politics of Aristotle* (Oxford: Oxford University Press, 1946), pp. 116–37.

[15] Edmund Burke, *Speech on the Conciliation of the Colonies* (1886); Henry Maine, *Popular Government* (1886); A. Lawrence Lowell, *Public Opinion and Popular Government* (1913); Arthur F. Bentley, *The Process of Government* (reprinted edition, Evanston, Ill.: Principia Press, 1949); E. Pendleton Herring, *The Politics of Democracy* (New York: Norton, 1940); Harold D. Lasswell, *Politics; Who Gets What, When, How* (New York: McGraw-Hill, 1936); Anthony Downs, *An Economic Theory of Democracy* (New York: Harper, 1957); Alfred Kuhn, *op. cit.;* William C. Mitchell, "The New Political Economy," *Social Research,* 35 (Spring 1968), 76–110.

currencies of political exchanges? Such currencies, of course, need not necessarily be amenable to quantification or operationalization.

A few familiar examples of currencies exchanged in political transactions may help prepare the reader for a more general classification. There are, for example, the currencies typically exchanged during American election campaigns: support for a candidate in the forms of financial contributions, contributed services, endorsement, or commitment of a bloc of votes, in exchange for appointments to public offices or preferential treatment in public policy decisions.

Congress and political party conventions are the marketplaces of well-known transactions, commonly referred to as logrolling or "wheeling and dealing." Congressional statutes are, in fact, a public record of the currencies exchanged in particular transactions. The balanced tickets and platforms of party conventions are the consequence of political transactions among party factions.

A further illustration may be drawn from exchanges in the international political system. When some fifty nations conferred with each other in 1945 regarding the creation of a United Nations Organization, only five were militarily powerful enough at the close of World War II to lend any substantial future military support to such an organization: the United States, the Union of Soviet Socialist Republics, Great Britain, France, and the Republic of China (prior to withdrawal of the Chiang Kai-shek government to Formosa). These five were recognizedly very special transactors whose participation could command a special price from the other nations interested in a world organization. The special price was the veto. Each was permitted to exercise a veto over adoption of the Charter and certain collective decisions of the Security Council, particularly in matters involving economic and military sanctions. Without unanimity among the Big Five, it hardly seemed likely that the United Nations' decisions could be implemented. Any attempt to ignore the objection, expressed by its veto, of one of these five major powers, would carry with it the risk that the vetoer might resort to the very violence that the United Nations was created to prevent.

General Behavioral Currencies

As employed here, then a *currency* is any empirically observable object, action, or condition perceived as valuable by a particular person or set of interacting persons and capable of being transmitted by one to the other of them.[16] This conception of currency is similar to Homans' "activity," which he applies to "kinds of behavior." One of the activities that men engage in, according to Homans, is the transfer of physical objects and materials, that is, "goods." Non-physical goods, such as the advice of a lawyer, are called "services." Homans adds a third class of activities: "sentiments," that is, the observable attitudes and feelings one person has toward another person or persons. Each type of activity has the properties *value* and *frequency*. These properties vary in amount and ease of measurement. All are reinforcers or punishers.

Is it possible to create other general typologies of behavioral currencies? Three are suggested here: *positional* currencies, *decisional* currencies, and *materiel* currencies.

POSITIONAL CURRENCIES   All social transactions are a concomitant of group life. Shared values, we have seen in Chapter 1, are an essential element in the formation of human cooperative systems. Groups come into being when two or more persons hold in common at least one attitude about some goal. Each member of the group contributes effort toward the implementation of the goal in direct ratio to the worth he attaches to the goal. The more valuable it is to him, the more effort he will be willing to put into group activities designed to achieve the goal.

To help in their immediate choices, the members of a group or their leaders will analyze the goal into specific tasks whose accomplishment is then delegated to particular individuals. These are the *task expectations* described in an earlier chapter. Sets of task expectations comprise the *positions* in an organized group. The more a group believes that a particular set of tasks or skills will be instrumental in moving it to its goal, the more will that group esteem the position and reward its incumbents. A group position or incumbency therein, therefore, may be a valuable good or currency amenable to exchange in social transactions. The job patronage distributed by party leaders in exchange for party service is a well known example of positional currency.

The position of justice of the Supreme Court of the United States, to cite another example, is one of the most highly esteemed in this

---

[16] See also this author's "A Transactional Theory of Political Integration and Arms Control," *American Political Science Review*, Vol. 62 (September, 1969): 719–733.

nation, which should not be surprising in a society that places the highest import upon the rule of law in achieving its goals and survival.

As further evidence that the American people are willing to exchange valuable things for positional currencies, notice the quadrennial outlays of hard cash for nominating and electing public officials throughout the nation in, say, a presidential election year: between $175 and $200 millions. But this is cheap. Elsewhere, revolutions and civil wars are often the EP situations in which political currencies are transacted to decide who shall hold the key public offices.

DECISIONAL CURRENCIES   Groups, like individuals, must make choices. A group may delegate, by fiat or silent acquiescence, all of its decisional activity to a single individual, a familiar arrangement in dictatorships. At the opposite pole, a group may require the explicit and unanimous consent of all its members before proceeding with an action alternative. Between these extremes are the countless other collective decision-making procedures invented by mankind, including such familiar types as the Quaker sense of the meeting indicated by the termination of communicative activity and the majority-rule voting arrangements of major representative bodies around the world.[17]

Whether the group consists of only two persons, e.g. husband and wife, or millions of persons, e.g. the American presidential electorate, its decision making is normally a matter of selecting one or two or more perceived and available alternatives of action. What is decided, if behavior is rational, is the action alternative most likely, in the opinion of group members, to be instrumental in moving the group toward its goal. The greater an individual's weight or *share* in the collective decision process, the more likely will *his* valuation of group goals and *his* interpretation of the best means for achieving these goals prevail. *Power*, a major concept in political analysis, may thus be viewed as a matter of *sharing in collective decisions*.

It follows, then, that shares in collective decision may be another valuable currency. Of course, position and prerogative often go hand in hand, but it is also possible for a position to be without prerogative, as in the case of honorary presidencies. On the other hand, prerogative may exist without position, e.g., "powers behind the throne" and "bosses" who govern without holding public office.

17 See Chapter 6 on "Theoretical Aspects of Group Choice."

Invariably, decision making is an individual act or event. Group or collective decision making, therefore, requires some method for summarizing relevant individual decisions in order to discover and act upon the group's choice of alternatives. As a consequence, any system of distributing or sharing collective decision making prerogative is a system of participation that responds to the following problem: *Who* takes *what part* in deciding *what kinds of matters* and on *what occasions?* Each of the underscored components of the question may be a subcurrency or denomination of decisional currency, as described below.

MATERIEL CURRENCIES   This is perhaps the most familiar of the types of transactional currencies. In the language of economics, these are goods, merchandise, wares, and commodities. The term *materiel* is employed to emphasize that this type of currency pertains to things of physical matter: iron ore, houses, foodstuff, bombs, clothing, typewriters, etc. In ordinary commercial practice, most materiel currencies are assigned a price in monetary units, so that an automobile may be worth $2,000, or a typewriter $200, or a loaf of bread 20 cents. Money itself, however, is also a materiel commodity with fluctuating value. As every loan company knows, money is worth much more just before pay day than just after.

A substantial portion of human activity is devoted to the acquisition, conversion, and utilization of the materiel resources of the environment. H. G. Wells spoke of economics as a "branch of biology" because what the economist studies is the human being gathering, modifying, and consuming environmental matter such as food to satisfy hunger, clothes to provide warmth, housing to give protection from the elements, vehicles to help move them about, and so on.

Civilization has embellished these basic activities with advanced technologies, such as steps in the conversion processes, market superstructures for information processing, and elaborate aesthetic variations associated with otherwise similar products. Materiel currencies, like other currencies, are valued to the extent that they are perceived as instruments for the achievement of desired goals. Cultural influences are often crucial in establishing the valuableness of materiel; the aborigine is hardly an audience for televised toothpaste commercials.

A special subtype or denomination of materiel currency are

weapons and armaments. The dictionary definition of "armament" is convenient: "equipment for hostile action." A hammer is a piece of materiel used as equipment in construction—until it happens to be used as a piece of equipment for committing murder. In the latter situation, a "constructional tool" is identified as a "murder weapon." Obviously, classification as *weapon* is a consequence of purposive and situational factors: the intention of the user; the weapon design; the moral category into which the purpose is placed by society; perhaps just the name assigned in conversation: "This hammer would make quite a murder weapon," or "This hunting rifle can be used as a revolutionary weapon."

A weapon, therefore, is a materiel device designed to destroy, damage, or otherwise disrupt the normal operations of life and property. Such devices become weapons only among persons who recognize the destructive potentiality of the device under circumstances of conflict and place value upon given "normal operations of life and property." The aborigine who has never seen a gun can hardly be threatened with it until its effects are demonstrated to him. Materiel devices are not perceived as weapons by persons who place little value on living (martyrs, suicides); such devices may even be perceived by such persons as instruments of salvation.

Political Currencies

The specific observable, valuable, and transferable political things suggested by the three general behavioral currencies (positional, decisional, and materiel) may be called *incumbencies, shares* and *commodities.*

INCUMBENCIES When organizations, including governments, are created, positions are also brought into being. Such positions are usually given (a) names, (b) sets of tasks to perform, (c) conditions of investiture according to which the group places into incumbency some particular persons, and (d) conditions of divestiture according to which the group may remove an incumbent from a position. Each of these four aspects of incumbency may become negotiable currency in political transactions.

(a) *Position name.* A position name alone gives no assurance that a group exists or that any person will ever be chosen to fill the indicated position. A political adventurer may call himself "king," but he is not likely to be able to trade on the title until a group accepts it as the locus of specific group activities. On the other hand, a group may agree to set up a position called "king" but be unable to find or agree upon any particular person to make the incumbent of the position.

If a position is created and named by a group, the naming may be part of a significant transaction. Should the executive head of the new Federal Union (in 1787) be called "king" or "president"? Should the chief executive office of the United Nations be called "president" or "secretary-general"? These kinds of questions about the naming of positions may carry implications for the political symbolisms of interested parties. For example, "president" implies a republican governing organization; "king" implies a monarchy; and "chairman" suggests a committee form of executive leadership.

Honorific titles are, in some societies, a common form of social recognition. A distinguished scientist, for his great contributions to the community's knowledge, may be given the position of "knight" and be expected to do nothing more than use the title as part of his signature.

(b) *Task specification*. The creation, assignment, and withdrawal of duties or task expectations associated with an office is another subtype of incumbency currency. The analysis of goals into specialized tasks, which are then gathered together as group positions, is one of the great skills of organizational architecture and leadership.

Task specification requires information and judgments about the following kinds of issues: What are the odds that particular tasks will produce particular events leading to the goal? What personal talent is available among the members that is most relevant to an adequate performance of the tasks expected? How are conflicting conceptions of instrumental activities—the fight over means—to be reconciled in the design of job descriptions? How may the group compensate for inadequate performance by irremovable incumbents? For each question, the specification and allocation of tasks may become negotiable currency.

Politics offers many illustrations: "If you let my group (because it knows so much about farming) determine the policies that tell the Secretary of Agriculture what he should be doing, we'll agree that your group (because it knows so much about business) determine what the Secretary of Commerce should be doing."

(c) *Legitimizing conditions.* The relationship between a person and a position, when the former "fills" the latter, is called an *incumbency.* When a group designs the legitimizing conditions that are to signal a conclusive choice of incumbent for a position, the elements of that design may become negotiable incumbency currency.

In a nation led by noble families, for example, royal birth is likely to be a principal condition for vesting kings with royal office. In a nation with popular suffrage, some kind of electoral majority is likely to be among the legitimizing conditions for attaining office. Warrior nations tend to choose leaders from among men with demonstrated military prowess. In establishing any of these types of legitimizing conditions, groups in the community must negotiate valuable currency, such as the status of royal families, the arrangements for popular sovereignty, and the demonstration of military prowess.

Some typical legitimizing conditions are:

1. Election by lot, which assumes equality of individual talent and avoids the cost of factional strife by leaving the decision to chance
2. Heredity, which assumes that leadership is a family talent, sometimes a capacity divinely transmitted, in which selection is prescribed by the laws of primogeniture
3. Demonstrated skill—military, oratorical, financial, managerial, or other—which places great value on the personal record of individuals and is used particularly in societies that place great value upon individuality and past success as evidence of prospective leadership achievements
4. Election by special groups or special numbers, considered useful in heterogeneous societies wherein a multiplicity of changing group interests must be accommodated from time to time
5. Appointment by an authorized official, a practice usually found in large-scale bureaucratic systems, intended to facilitate the work of major officials by allowing them to have personal or partisan friends in key positions

(d) *Divesting conditions.* To create a vacancy in a position is, in effect, to increase the number of available incumbencies for political transaction. For example, in the heyday of Federal post office patronage (1850–1890), tens of thousands of postmasters customarily resigned or failed to have their appointments renewed each time a different political party captured the presidency. This made way for appointment of the loyal rank and file of the winning party.

To recall or impeach an elected official is to make room for the selection of another. To limit the length of a term of office is to make possible a high turnover of incumbencies. A retirement procedure establishes a divesting condition, creating political currency by creating vacancies.

Sometimes divesting conditions are not specified or readily operable, and the creation of a vacancy may become costly—as in the case of wars and revolutions aimed at removing dictators and tyrants from long-held offices.

SHARES Politicians are often conspicuously concerned about the distribution of shares of prerogative in the collective decisions of the community. To distribute shares of participation in collective decision making is to structure a system of power dispersion. This leads politicians to consider the question indicated earlier: *Who* takes *what part* in deciding *what kinds of matters* and on *what occasions?* Political inventors over the centuries have produced a variety of arrangements dealing with each of the components of this question: (a) the attributes that identify *who;* (b) the units of participation that prescribe *what part;* (c) the substantive topics that tell *what kinds of matter;* and (d) the situational conditions that identify *occasions.*

(a) *Personal attributes.* Who shall participate is a major denomination of shares currency. Historically, participation in collective decision making was first extended to groups per se rather than to individuals. The House of Lords and House of Commons, as organized groups in the early English Parliament, came to share the king's prerogatives in certain public decisions. Similar kinds of group participation emerged in the Estates General of the *ancien regime* in France. Upper houses of legislatures still represent previously sovereign political groups; e.g., the representation of states in the U.S. Senate, and the representation of cantons in Switzerland. Today, this type of group representation is often seen in international congresses and organizations in which nations participate as group entities.

Still another kind of group participation arises from distinct branches of a particular government. This is found in separation-of-powers arrangements, as in the American system. The branches of government operate as suborganizations with explicit shares in collective decisions. In Federal statute making, for example, the shares are: a majority in the House of Representatives, a majority in the Senate, presidential approval, and at least tacit acceptance by the Supreme Court.

In designating different classes of participants, many political communities, either explicitly or implicitly, as often will indicate who shall be *excluded* from participation. Even a partial list of the criteria of eligibility for candidacies or for voting privileges shows the range of categories that has developed: citizen status; a minimum age; residence or other geographical restrictions, registered party membership; nomination by a party; educational achievement and literacy skill; real or personal property ownership; sex membership; payment of taxes or special fees; religious qualifications; mental or penal disqualifications; race, nationality, or belief requirements; and oaths of loyalty.

Another way of classifying participants follows from certain delegations of authority. When particular public officers are granted authority to make decisions on behalf of the entire community, this delegation is a way of classifying who shall participate. The President, for example, is constitutionally the key decision maker on matters of national military security but certain of his military responsibilities have been delegated to the Secretary of Defense. Thus through the process of delegation this public officer shares with the President participation in national military policy making.

(b) *Units of participation.* The part a participant shall have in decision making usually refers to his share of voting units. Shall the vote of each participant weigh equally with that of every other? Shall the "say" of certain participants weigh more heavily than others? These questions run through the history of voting and apportionment systems. Every plan of apportionment is controversial because some are necessarily given an advantage over others; one standard of equality among voting units may create a bias under some other standard, e.g., the equal representation of small and large states in the U.S. Senate. Apportionment is also affected by vote-counting procedures. Should there be one ballot or run-off elections on each candidate or issue? What kind of majority or plurality shall determine the final choice? A remarkable variety of apportionment and vote-counting plans have been invented.

(c) *Substantive topics.* Types of issues are another basis for parceling out participation, wherein only certain topics or issues may be included within the prerogative of certain types of participants. The Constitution has many such specifications: only Congress may declare war; only the House of Representatives may initiate tax measures; only the President may grant pardons.

Sometimes certain issues are *excluded* entirely from the prerogative of the collectivity, to be left entirely to individuals. Bills of rights are the most common place for such specifications. Religious affiliation, right of association, right of petition to public officers, freedom of communication, freedom to bear arms, possession of property, and other matters are specified as subject only to individual, never collective, decision.

(d) *Situational conditions.* Kinds of occasions are a fourth denomination in the shares currency. These are types of situations, frequently identified in law or by some procedure, that may trigger the exercise of shares. Specification of such situations may place important limits upon power dispersion. For example, in a parliamentary system, a legislative vote of "no confidence" in the incumbent ministry may trigger a general election, where voter participation becomes operative. In war or national emergency situations, usually carefully described in law, the President is allowed to become a "constitutional dictator," with unusual prerogatives for deciding certain matters. In assemblies and conferences, decisions to vote are ordinarily decisions about creating an occasion for the exercise of shares; for example, when Congressional committees refer bills to the floor, when petitions are signed for the conduct of a referendum, or when courts decide to accept or reject review of a case.

A political system's *opportunities for dissent* are related to situational currency. An opportunity for dissent is a legitimate, legal, generally acceptable occasion for soliciting and mobilizing shares of participation in order to demonstrate the existing ratio of dissent to consensus. Organized groups that leave *all* collective choices in the hands of one man or require unanimity of all members on every decision provide no opportunity for manifestations of dissent or for measurements of dissent-consensus ratios. On the other hand, groups whose collective decisions are made by plurality or majority rule do provide such opportunity.

Human disagreement is a constant concomitant of social life. Men are bound to find themselves in conflict because they invariably must deal with each other on the basis of imperfect knowledge, varying perceptions of reality, and uncertainty regarding human goals and the means for reaching them. Total agreement and total cooperation among human beings are neither possible nor desirable. Opportunities for dissent may be associated with three general methods of collective decision making, which we shall discuss at greater length in Chapter 6. These are verbal, numerical, and violent opportunities. *Verbal* opportunities are those in which communication is allowed to take place under nearly all conditions, as when constitutional provisions for free speech exist. *Numerical* opportunities are usually those in which voting may take place, and the various adversaries in the community produce a "quantitative performance" demonstrating the current ratio between dissent and consensus. *Violent* or destructive opportunities may gather and use weapons for the destruction of persons or property.

COMMODITIES   A substantial portion of government decision making is concerned with the allocation of materiel resources among the members of the political community. An overwhelming proportion of what may be called public business is conducted with commodity currencies; so much so, that Karl Marx and other political economists came to believe that economic considerations determine *all* operations of government. Even less ideological documents, such as party platforms, are largely discussions of demands for and allocations of government funds, services, goods, armaments, and credit. An astute visiting politician from Mars, seeking an immediate sense of American public policy, could, from this point of view, obtain such an overview by examining the published U.S. Federal budgets and reports of tax receipts of several recent years.

(a) *Government funds.* Government funds are those monies collected into the public treasury through tax receipts and other revenue sources and reallocated by public officials whose discretion is, to one degree or another, circumscribed by statutes and other policy guides. The degree of discretion may also be crucial to the manner in which the funds are expended. A legislature may appropriate public funds for highway construction, but the political party in power may determine which "friendly" communities shall benefit from the highway or which "friendly" contractors shall receive the construction work.

(b) *Government services.* Government services rendered by personnel under the direction of public officers are frequently used as money substitutes; e.g., the use of the services of military personnel in a disaster area to help rebuild a community. A Federal agency, the Coast Guard, renders valuable but unofficial service to port communities by providing emergency aid to private crafts sailing in these areas for pleasure or business; for port communities this service is as good as money. What is an efficient traffic control agency worth to a community in exchange for the physical safety maintained, the hours in transit saved, and the orderly flow of daily business that results from such efficiency?

(c) *Government goods.* Many public agencies are producers of economic goods. These are government goods because of some special circumstance under which they are produced, processed, or sold. Government operated or controlled dams produce electricity. Government agencies purchase surplus agricultural products for resale or gift to foreign nations or disadvantaged American citizens. Prisons are public agencies whose inmates produce saleable goods.

(d) *Government credit.* A fourth denomination of commodity currencies is government credit. This has become increasingly prominent in the political transactions of recent decades. Low-interest loans to farmers or homeowners are now a well-established form of aid to these important contributors to the nation's prosperity. Government credit is extended in the granting of veteran loans and small business loans.

(e) *Armaments.* As indicated earlier, a weapon is a physical device designed and intended to destroy, damage, or otherwise disrupt the normal operations of life and property. The distinctive characteristics of armaments are that they may be highly significant even though never used, and, if used, may *deny* rather than *give* the other transactor things of value (life, property). To "trade shots" is the essence of a transaction involving armament currency. Some may prefer to call armaments a "negative commodity," but this is not entirely accurate. A tax dollar spent on guns is a tax dollar less for schools, but a railroad built for military transport may be converted into civilian transport. A pilot trained to fly bombers may also be employed by civilian airlines. In this sense, armaments are government commodities, sometimes totally expendable, sometimes convertible to nondestructive uses. It is the latter that sometimes produces the surprising affluence associated with wartime economies.[18]

[18] *Deterrence* is a term frequently associated with armaments. The American nuclear arsenal, for example, is viewed in military and diplomatic discussions as a

Political Marketplaces

A marketplace is often less a physical structure than a process, and this is more often the case in politics than in other areas of human transaction. Yet, politics does have its highly visible and structured marketplaces, witness the Capitol in which the Congress of the United States meets, the convention halls of party nominating conventions, and the White House and other offices of the executive branch. Less visible and less formal are the private conferences of political leaders. On the other hand, the well-publicized statements of international adversaries have tended to make a marketplace of the world press.

As in the case of all marketplaces, political marketplaces are centers for the communication of relevant market information, particularly if such information identifies prospective transactors, reports their respective Effective Preferences, and provides negotiating opportunities. Political marketplaces are also centers for transport and storage of political currencies, the former usually relating to the movement of policy proposals through the "political mill" and the latter having to do with the preservation of proposals in the public record until an appropriate time for transaction arrives.

Other market activites may be observed. Political currencies bought and sold are often made explicit in the declarations, statutes, treaties, and other public documents that represent exchange contracts. Risk-taking services may be rendered, as in the case of the Congressman from a "safe" district who agrees to handle a highly controversial piece of legislation on behalf of his party. He is, of course, better able to absorb the electoral risks involved and expects some return for his service.

The more structured and concrete the marketplace, the greater the ease with which interested prospective transactors may find each other. In facilitating political business in this way, marketplaces may be highly economical of politicians' effort. Explicit political marketplaces also afford regular opportunities for judging a political col-

---

deterrent to Soviet or Red Chinese aggression. In this usage, the deterrent is *presumed*, sometimes erroneously, to deter an adversary from choosing action alternatives that involve the use of armaments and violence. The adversary is expected to view the deterrent as too threatening and costly to try to counter. He is also *presumed* to have other action alternatives than violence from which to choose.

league's negotiating skills; or, if he is found wanting, the marketplace may afford him opportunities to learn.

One of the most significant contributions of a well-organized political marketplace is in its promotion of the conditions of trust. A marketplace permits politicians to demonstrate trustworthiness or to test the trustworthiness of others. The continuity of negotiating communications and the multiplicity of political transactions tend to produce respect and trust even among constant adversaries.

An Illustrative Use of the Conceptual Perspective

TRANSACTING A PARTY PLATFORM

Political parties are perhaps second only to legislatures as dealmaking marketplaces—at least, so this seems to the layman. Contrary to popular belief, however, most party deals are likely to be highly visible to the public rather than secrets of "smoke-filled rooms." The reasons for such visibility are compelling; the transactions worked out by party leaders are necessarily subject to subsequent approval by factional followers and by the general public, usually on Election Day.

In addition to the composition of the ticket, the traders in the partisan marketplace do business with each other while building the platform. Party platforms are often viewed, even by professional observers, as scrolls of ambiguity read by few and believed by none. Such a view is a grave misreading of the significance of platform writing. The platform is, in many respects, a public record of the outcome of significant political trading. David Truman describes it as follows:

> From the standpoint of the party as a vote-getting mechanism, writing a platform is part of the process of forging a coalition of leaders and actions that can nominate a candidate and carry on a nation-wide election campaign. . . . The platform is thus an outward sign, visible to those who can see below its manifest ambiguities, of the elements constituting the faction dominating that stage of the nomination process. . . .

From the standpoint of the political interest groups, the significance of preparing a platform lies primarily in the evidence that the negotiations provide concerning what groups will have access to the developing national party organization. Interest groups ordinarily will seek the insertion of planks that are as explicit as possible. The well-known ambiguity of such documents, however, is not in itself a matter of concern to them. Only if ambiguity or silence indicates reduction or denial of access to the coalition and its nominees will a group become alarmed.[19]

Contrast, for example, the writing of a civil rights plank into the Republican and the Democratic platforms of 1952. The issue had its immediate origin in the large-scale migration of Negroes from the South following World War II. The Democratic Party was most pressured to deal with the issue, because the Negro newcomers were being incorporated into the Democratic Party machines of the large Northern urban centers. Furthermore, new postwar civil rights organizations were pressing hard for removal of voting obstacles in the South, particularly those barring participation by Negroes in Democratic party primaries.

In the 1948 Democratic national convention, the civil rights plank became a test of the dwindling intraparty strength of the South, which previously had been capable of exercising a veto on most convention actions. The 1948 Democratic platform committtee attempted to write a compromise plank that could be supported by the entire convention. However, a Southern amending proposal was offered and defeated, 925 to 309. A strongly worded pro-civil-rights Northern substitute, offered by the then mayor of Minneapolis, Hubert H. Humphrey, was next approved, 651½ to 582½. The adoption of the Humphrey plank led to a Southern bolt of the convention and to a Southern third-party candidate for the presidency.

In 1952, the issue was still primarily a Democratic one, although the Republicans, wishing to attract Negro support but constrained by a desire for the votes of "presidential Republicans" in the South (those Southern Democrats who tend, from time to time, to split their ticket in presidential races), were also beginning to feel cross-pressure within the party. In 1952, in fact, the civil rights issue was the only difficult one faced in the platform writing of either party. The Republican platform committee compromised by rejecting pro-

[19] David B. Truman, *The Governmental Process* (New York: Knopf, 1955), pp. 284–285. Copyright David B. Truman. Quoted with permission of the publisher.

posals for a Federal fair employment practices act and by advancing a plank that was "probably too weak to please the liberal elements of the party and too strong to please all Southern Republicans or Southern Democrats who might be 'presidential Republicans.' "[20]

The Democrats, on the other hand, had to contend with three well-organized interests with distinct planks, each eager to do battle: the strong-plank civil rights group, the weak-plank Southern forces, and the Truman Administration moderates. The strong-plank people wanted a plank calling specifically for a Federal fair employment practices commission as well as for a new cloture rule in the Senate to end the filibuster as a roadblock to civil rights legislation. The weak-plank faction, unwilling to bolt the party again but also sensitive to the demands of its Southern constituencies, sought, in Senator Richard Russell's words, "a plank which will state the Democratic party's objectives on civil rights, without spelling them out in the form of specific legislation." In a convention with 1230 votes, the strong-plank faction claimed 650 and the weak-plank group about 300.

The principal negotiators in the Democratic platform committee were Senator Herbert H. Lehman of New York for the strong-plank side and Governor Robert F. Kennon of Louisiana for the Southern side. The moderates were represented by Senator John Sparkman of Alabama, who later became the nominee for Vice President, and Representative Brooks Hays of Arkansas. During the preconvention negotiations, Sparkman and Hays made it clear to the strong-plank groups, some 54 of which shared a single headquarters, that they could not go along with such strong language as "compulsory FEPC," "enforceable by federal authority," or "repeal of the Senate Rule 22 relating to cloture."

During the convention, the same factions, more or less, were engaged in struggles over credentials and rules, particularly with respect to the liberals' demand for a "loyalty pledge" binding all delegates to support the ticket when they return home. Compromises were negotiated by the convention leadership on the loyalty pledge and the seating of contested delegations. The Southern leaders, "perhaps sensing the retreat of the Northern liberals on other fronts throughout the day," appeared increasingly reluctant to accept even the moderate proposals regarding the civil rights plank.

[20] Paul T. David, Malcolm Moos, and Ralph M. Goldman, *Presidential Nominating Politics in 1952* (Baltimore: Johns Hopkins Press, 1954), Vol. I, p. 90.

The platform subcommittee handling the plank remained dead-locked throughout the last night prior to the full platform committee's report to the convention. At 5:30 a.m., a modified plank was agreed upon, with Senator Lehman reserving the right to introduce a strong plank from the floor if the South undertook any further maneuvers. Clearly, the negotiation was less a matter of specific language than it was a test of the Effective Preferences of the factions. Were the Northern liberals, the Administration moderates, and the Southerners able to hold out sufficiently to make a public display of their respective influence and access to the leadership of the Democratic party at this time?[21]

21 *Ibid.*, Chap. 4.

Choice, Roles, and Reference Groups

Decision making is a central theoretical concern of several disciplines. In political science it is often equated with *power;* that person is "powerful" who not only may make his own choice among alternatives, but also is able to make others decide on an alternative he prefers. Before an individual is capable of making a decision, however, he must hold beliefs, that is, be favorably disposed to act as though something, usually a proposition, were true. For centuries people believed the proposition: "The earth is flat"; hence, many decided against exploring it "too far" for fear of falling off.

Decision theorists, in their analytical formulations, usually identify the following as elements of every decision: the actor(s); the situation in which choice is to be made; the objective set of alternatives; the subset of alternatives actually perceived by the actor; the scale of outcomes as they relate to his scale of preferences; the instrumental information that indicates for the actor which alternative leads to which outcome and with what probability. The "rational" person will always choose that particular alternative that *he perceives* as most probably leading to his most preferred outcome.

In addition to utility theories of decision making, other approaches are suggested by role theory and reference group theory. Role theories analyze behavior as individual responses to social roles that have been learned or as actions expected of persons occupying particular social positions. The person's decision process would thus depend upon the elements in his particular role structure. Reference group theory, on the other hand, views the individual as making choices after taking into account the expectations of groups he values.

5

The Decision Making Process

The individual person is invariably the center of choice. His choice may be made in the company of other members of a group, as part of a group decision making process. His choice may be that of one of the parties in a transaction. His choice may be influenced by a variety of social factors and situations. But any choice is, in the first instance, individual and personal.

This does not alter the fact that groups and organizations also make decisions as collectivities of individual persons. Nor do these comments deny that social and political constraints upon an individual's alternatives and choices may be overriding. Nor do they overlook the fact that the ordinary member of an organized group is likely to function somewhat differently from a leader as decision maker. Such distinctions are recognized here by devoting a chapter to the individual decision maker, a second chapter to decision making as a group process, and a third to leaders as distinctive decision making types.

HUMAN CHOICE: ANCIENT AND MODERN APPROACHES

Intellectual interest in the human capacity for decision making goes back more than 2,500 years. The Iranian philosopher-poet Zarathustra (*ca.* 660–583 B.C.) alluded to the notions of conflict and choice

169

in human affairs in his references to "powers of Light" and "powers of Darkness" that struggle within and around each human individual. Zarathustra was one of the first to conceptualize the individual person as a unit capable of separation from others and also capable of experiencing division within himself; in fact, a unit perennially confronted by alternatives. "Decision has to be made, man by man," he wrote.

Reemphasized by Plato and Aristotle two centuries later, this Iranian view of human struggle, purposiveness, and necessity for human ethical choice became a pervasive influence in Western thought. The dualism made explicit in the Light-and-Darkness distinction was carried forward by Greek philosophy and Christian doctrine in such terms as Good versus Evil, Heaven versus Hell, etc. In contrast, Eastern philosophies and religions have tended to be monistic, that is, premised upon theories of the unity of all reality, with the human mind an integral part of that unity. As a consequence, Eastern monism tends to be deterministic and fatalistic about human action; the capacity and scope of human individual choice is, from such perspectives, limited and inconsequential, and not fit for serious philosophical concern.

In the West, Christian dualism kept decision theory alive by devoting much thought to man's *capacity* for choice. The central concept was *will*, God's and man's. At first, Church philosophers argued that God foreordained all events and behaviors, leaving it to each person to accept or deny God's will as it became known to him. Descartes, on the other hand, took the position that God was "indifferent" and the human mind too unique an endowment to serve any other function but the fullest exercise of individual free will. Descartes, Spinoza, and other seventeenth century rationalists in effect restated Plutarch's (48–125 A.D.) earlier formulation of the free-will concept. Plutarch, accepting Greek notions of good and evil deities, insisted that individual man is completely responsible for any suffering that he experiences as the wages of sin, for it lies within his personal choice to withstand the promptings that emerge from his lower nature and the more evil deities.

Seventeenth-century rationalists viewed suffering as a failure in the use of human reason, that is, as an error in knowledge or an emotional departure from the dictates of reason, Scientific philosophy, as the heir of rationalism, led the swing away from free will. This culminated in the extreme behaviorism found in the more vigorous statements of conditioned-reflex theory in psychology, that is, that all human decision making is determined by discoverable factors from which the individual has little, if any, power to depart.

Modern economics owes much of its interest in decision theory to the British Utilitarians. Jeremy Bentham (1748–1832) postulated that pleasure and pain are the mainsprings of human action. Both the individual and the community must judge the worth of alternative courses of action according to their respective capacities to provide "the greatest happiness for the greatest number." In other words, the moral value of behavior, private or public, is to be measured in terms of its usefulness. Bentham, James Mill, and the latter's son John Stuart Mill developed the economic implications of utilitarianism in their writings throughout the nineteenth century. Modern references to the utility function in theories of economic choice are derived in large part from these writings.

Today's theoretical discussions of economic decision making focus upon such issues as cardinal utility function (the ranking of alternatives according to the decision maker's preferences), management decisions in business firms (managerial motivation with respect to profit maximization), theory of games (choice in situations of competition and uncertain outcomes), risky choices (decision making under conditions of imperfect information), and subjective utility (identification of the particular value judgments of individuals).[1]

In some behavioral disciplines, decision theory has been to a large extent a subsidiary aspect of other conceptual concerns. In psychology, behaviorism devoted attention to immediate responses, learning, and conditioned reflexes; learning and cognitive theories

---

[1] Excellent surveys of decision theory in economics may be found in: J. von Neumann and O. Morgenstern, *Theory of Games and Economic Behavior* (Princeton: Princeton University Press, 1947); Ward Edwards, "The Theory of Decisionmaking," *Psychological Bulletin*, 51 (September 1954): 380–417; R. D. Luce and H. Raiffa, *Games and Decisions* (New York: Wiley, 1957); Herbert A. Simon, "A Behavioral Model of Rational Choice," in *Models of Man* (New York: Wiley, 1957); "Special Issue on Decisionmaking," *Administrative Science Quarterly* (December 1958); Herbert A. Simon, "Theories of Decision-Making in Economics and Behavioral Science," *American Economic Review*, 49 (June 1959): 253–83; Ernest W. Adams, "Survey of Bernoullian Utility Theory," in Herbert Solomon (ed.), *Mathematical Thinking in the Measurement of Behavior* (Glencoe, Ill.: Free Press, 1960), pp. 151–268; C. West Churchman, *Prediction and Optimal Decision* (Englewood Cliffs, N.J.; Prentice-Hall, 1961); Ward Edwards, "Behavioral Decision Theory," in Paul R. Farnsworth et al., *Annual Review of Psychology* (Palo Alto: Annual Reviews, Inc., 1961), pp. 473–98; Rollo Handy and Paul Kurtz, "Decision Making Theory," *American Behavioral Scientist*, Supplement to Vol. 7 (March 1964); James A. Robinson and Richard C. Snyder, "Decision-Making in International Politics," in Herbert C. Kelman (ed.), *International Behavior: A Social-Psychological Analysis* (New York: Holt, Rinehart and Winston, 1965), pp. 435–463.

continue to present a somewhat deterministic approach to human decision making. In psychoanalysis and social psychology, great contributions were made in identifying the ego and the self within settings provided by such primary groups as the family. Social psychology and sociology have shared an interest in field theory and reference group theory, but with a somewhat less immediate concern for particular situations of choice. In political science, the pre-twentieth-century conceptions of sovereignty and authority were substantially concerns about human decision processes. In more recent decades, the concepts *power* and *influence* have been reformulated to focus upon factors that have consequence for the particular selection of decision alternatives.

In general, rational philosophy has probably been the field most concerned with decision theory during the past several centuries, usually stating theoretical problems as matters of choice between good and evil, right and wrong, or optimal behaviors calculated to achieve some desired effect. Radical advances in decision theory developed in the present century, particularly with the emergence of utility theory and statistical theory. The work of von Neumann in game theory and Wald in statistical decision theory became widely known during World War II and led to a "basic reorientation concerning decisional problems." The "modern look in decision theory" emerged in the mid-1950s.[2] Harold D. Lasswell found "a remarkable convergence of interest on the study of choice . . . in political science and in the behavior sciences generally." On the other hand, Snyder, in the late 1950s, noted "pages and pages . . . *on the substance* of decisions and *on the formal structure within which decision-making takes place,* but very few pages on *how to analyze decisions* and decision-making."[3]

BELIEFS AS PREREQUISITES OF CHOICE

All living creatures spend their lives adjusting and readjusting to the environment that operates within and around them. Some pur-

---

[2] R. M. Thrall, C. H. Coombs, and R. L. Davis (eds.), *Decision Processes* (New York: Wiley, 1954).

[3] Harold D. Lasswell, "Current Studies of the Decision Process," *Western Political Quarterly,* 8 (1955): 381–99; Richard C. Snyder, "A Decision-Making Approach to the Study of Political Phenomena," in Roland Young (ed.), *Approaches to the Study of Politics* (Evanston, Ill.: Northwestern University Press, 1958), pp. 3–37.

sue adjustment more intensively and skillfully than others; the pursuit, in general, has been called *learning*. Among the skills most often required are a capacity for observing the environment carefully, asking questions about the predicaments and problems found in the environment, and successfully solving these problems. Failures in observation, hypothesis formulation, information gathering, and problem solving may leave the creature frustrated, threatened, and possibly dead. The decision situation, whether it presents a problem in food acquisition or candidate selection, must first be perceived as such, then analyzed, and finally responded to with decisional behaviors. What the individual already believes, in the broadest sense of this term, is prerequisite to his perceptions, analyses, and choices.

The environment, then, prompts the individual to speculate about appropriate responses and adjustments. In formal philosophy, speculative thought is presumed to be less disciplined than any other form of thinking. Yet, speculative thought is not mere random daydreaming. *Speculative thought*, like other forms of human thinking, attempts to explain, to unify, and to order experience. It never departs entirely from experience, although it often transcends experience as it attempts to order it. Speculative thought employs hypotheses, although these hypotheses have little of the formal structure found in scientific propositions. Like most human hypotheses about the environment, both primitive and modern ones can usually be reduced to some kind of linguistic statement.

Probably the major difference between ancient and modern belief systems in general is the view taken by the ancients regarding the natural phenomena they observed. The ancients invariably saw man as part of society, and society as imbedded in nature and dependent upon cosmic forces. While modern, scientific man views the cosmic world as essentially made up of nonliving events and elements, ancient man saw in the natural phenomena about him a live presence with all of the personal and unpredictable characteristics that could be found among human beings.

This ancient view rested on projective and linguistic factors. Ancient man, after all, had only his own psychic experience from which to formulate explanations about natural phenomena; therefore, he projected that personal experience onto cosmic events. Furthermore, he had only personal modes of expression in which he spoke of himself and others as persons, and this mode easily applied to the elements of the environment that he identified and dealt with in making his ordinary adjustments.[4]

With the Greeks and the Romans came rational philosophy and a systematic concern for the grounds of human belief and thought. *Rational philosophy* has identified three general approaches in human responses to environmental predicaments: *trial and error, imitation,* and *systematic thought.* Each of these approaches may have quite different consequences for the safety of the individual decision maker, the economy of his efforts, and the goal productivity of his choice of alternatives.

Grounds for Belief

TRIAL-AND-ERROR METHOD   This is the toss-of-a-coin approach. Confronted by an environmental predicament, the individual makes a random, unpremeditated response. Behaviorists in psychology base their studies upon this formulation of the response problem. How, then, does the individual move from a completely chance selection among available alternatives to a considered, premeditated selection?

In trial-and-error response, a successful outcome is entirely a matter of guesswork and probabilities. The gladiator who must choose between two doors, one leading to a fair lady and the other to a starved tiger, may have to proceed on a trial-and-error basis. The choice may be a 50-50 toss-up; the riskiness of the choice and the cost of error are obvious. However, given less deadly possible outcomes, trial and error may sometimes be productive of information and learning. Animal A may be poking around his environment in search of food, activated by an internal disequilibrium called "hunger." As he "tries out" various objects in his path, A may notice that objects X and Y seem available for consumption. Animal A, encountering object X first by chance, may notice its shape, color, or other characteristics, chew it up, and experience partial satisfaction of his hunger. Still hungry, however, A proceeds to object Y, again by chance, perhaps noticing its distinctive shape, color, etc., but, upon attempting to eat Y, finds that Y bites back. The trial-and-error shopping tour may produce some learning in A if A noticed the difference between X and Y. In the future, if an X-appearing

4 Based upon Henri Frankfort et al., *Before Philosophy* (Baltimore: Penguin Books, 1949).

object is encountered, A is likely to eat it; if a Y-appearing object is encountered, A is likely to avoid it. Very few bits of information may be needed to reduce the element of chance in problem solving. Animal A need only survive his unpleasant experience with Y in order to have another opportunity to choose. The politician's choice between war and nonwar often seems to be a trial-and-error procedure.

METHOD OF IMITATION   By watching others with more experience and more information as they deal with environmental predicaments, an individual may learn how to deal with similar predicaments. The method of imitation is operative when a young intern watches the procedures of older physicians, when an apprentice watches skilled master craftsmen, or when an inexperienced observer undertakes to learn about a group through participant-observation. The assumption of this method is that prior success by persons with attributed experience is prima facie evidence of sound response. Imitation is assumed to be safer, more economical, and usually more productive of desired goals than the trial-and-error method.

Imitation works for problem situations that are recurrent in character but about which information is poorly generalized. If some novel feature is introduced into an otherwise familiar problem situation, the imitator may unwittingly and habitually make standard responses that, in the particular case, may be utterly inappropriate. From this point of view, imitation may be risky, costly, and unproductive of desired effects.

METHOD OF THOUGHT   In this approach, the most important part of a search for the best response to the environment is carried on within the neural system of the decision maker. It involves a program of thinking, that is, recollection and application of stored information.

Thinking requires a series of regularized steps. The decision maker analyzes his predicament or problem by breaking it down (mentally, of course) into component elements. He then tries to recall relevant information that he may have stored away in memory regarding the particular elements and their relationships to each other. For most of us, this involves stimulating memory, searching files or books, or calling upon a consultant such as the family doctor or lawyer. Presumably, the more educated the decision maker, the more information he will have stored in memory regarding a wider variety of possible environmental predicaments.

Very often, the stored information will take the form of a proposition about the elements of the problem. Pulling together this information and related beliefs, the decision maker will next proceed to develop *in his imagination* various possible solutions to the problem before him, possibly testing out the alternative *in his mind* by endeavoring to relate each alternative against a range of other information in his store of knowledge. In this way, he may estimate the costs of different alternatives, the risks of failure, and the prospects of producing the desired outcome. By "thinking it out," the decision maker has saved himself physical risk, time, and effort. Also, he may accomplish something that is not possible in the other methods, namely, the application of available knowledge to completely novel situations of choice.

Beliefs

The philosophy of science and the field of logic are particularly devoted to working out efficient and successful rules of procedure for the method of thought. To improve the method of thought is to improve the grounds for *belief*.[5]

> To hold a belief is to be prepared to act in a certain manner under given circumstances. . . . Belief involves a readiness to act as though something were true. As long as the readiness so to act persists, the belief persists; when the readiness so to act has disappeared, the belief has disappeared. This "readiness" to act persists even when we are not acting on it, that is, when we are not utilizing it.
>
> Whether beliefs are conscious or unconscious, they always involve two major components: an "attitude" (conscious or not) and a "content."[6]

If the attitude is one of acceptance of the content of the belief, it constitutes a readiness to act. The content of a belief may be called a *proposition*. Hence, a belief is the holding of an attitude of acceptance toward a proposition. In this context, a proposition refers to

---

[5] The following quotations and analysis are based primarily on Henry S. Leonard, *An Introduction to the Principles of Right Reason* (New York: Holt, 1957).
[6] *Ibid.*, pp. 8, 44–5.

any situation or state of affairs whatsoever, whether actual or not and whether any person has conceived of it or not. In this sense, a proposition is *not* any declarative sentence; rather, it is that situation which a declarative sentence may indicate or express. The declarative sentence itself may be called a *statement*. Thus, the following statements indicate certain propositions: "The earth is flat." "There are going to be a billion inhabitants in China before the end of this century." "Catholics have tended to vote Democratic."[7]

Propositions, or states of affairs, are usually spoken of as either *true* or *false*. When a proposition is classified as "true" by a decision maker, it is also commonly said to be a "fact" *for that individual*. As such, it constitutes a belief for him, since he may act upon it "as though true." On the other hand, "false" propositions are said to be either "fictional" or "unfactual."

> We have beliefs about history, beliefs about the structure of material aggregates, beliefs about the future, beliefs about God, beliefs about what is beautiful or what we ought to do. Most of these beliefs we state categorically. . . . Each of these statements, similar to thousands we make every day, is elliptical in that the preliminary statement is omitted. We might reasonably preface each of these propositions by the words "I believe" or "There seems to be good evidence that." Every proposition becomes in fact a judgment, and man is a creature greatly concerned with his own judgments. We take our judgments seriously and, foolish as we are, we are deeply interested in the correctness of our judgments.[8]

As in communication theory, the meaning conveyed by a statement lies in the proposition about which it communicates. A statement usually *purports* to refer to one and only one proposition. If the proposition, that is, state of affairs referred to, exists, the statement's referent is *actual*. If the proposition does not exist, the referent is a *purported referent*. "The United States is a major nation" is a statement referring to an *actual* proposition; there is substantial evidence that the United States exists and that it is classified

[7] In the idiom of communication theory, a *statement* consists of linguistic signs that may allude to some referent in the environment of the communicator. The referent, whatever it may be, is the *proposition* of the present discussion. Lewis A. Froman, Jr., in *People and Politics* (Englewood Cliffs, N.J.: Prentice-Hall, 1962), pp. 19–28, provides a definition of *belief* as statements which people use to describe the environment. Beliefs, according to Froman, are of two kinds: beliefs *in something*, which are matters of faith, not subject to empirical proof; and beliefs *about something* which are subject to empirical proof. Froman's discussion of belief is based upon Milton Rokeach, *The Open and Closed Mind* (New York: Basic Books, 1960).

[8] D. E. Trueblood, *The Logic of Belief* (New York: Harper, 1942), p. 24.

by most people as a major nation. On the other hand, "Valhalla is a land of peace and plenty" is a statement whose proposition is *not actual*, that is, one with a *purported referent*. A statement with a purported referent has no "meaning" in the sense used by scientists; no such place exists, therefore it may be said to have a null extension. Yet, the *statement* itself may be believed, that is, have psychological meaning for a particular person. In such a case it is the statement itself rather than the purported referent that is *actual* and *meaningful*.

This somewhat compressed discussion of belief will suggest the large importance of language as the vehicle of beliefs and as an instrument for the method of thought. As suggested in the chapter on language, entire bodies of belief may be brought together more or less systematically in linguistic productions that we describe by various names: utopian doctrines, philosophies, ideologies, empirical theories, and bodies of knowledge. These systems of statements make different claims to logical consistency and empirical validity. Nevertheless, each offers a way of looking at the environment, suggests procedures for dealing with it, and claims to reduce the disorientation of the individual.

When the purported referents of a particular system of belief statements turn out *not* to exist or to exist differently from the manner stated, the individual may be confronted with the necessity for modifying his belief. If an ideology expresses the belief that capitalism will destroy itself, the survival and growth of certain capitalist nations presents a challenge to the believed proposition, leading to ideological controversy such as the one between Chinese Communist orthodoxy and Soviet revisionism. In empirical theories, on the other hand, a falsified statement (hypothesis) may simply be discarded or rewritten.

The accompanying chart summarizes some of the conceptual relationships with which we are dealing. The individual makes *decisions* on the basis of *beliefs* that he holds to be true. A belief rests upon an *attitude* of acceptance regarding a proposition. It also rests upon a particular *content* of that proposition. The content of a proposition may consist of an *unverbalized observation* or, more commonly, one of the several types of *linguistic statement*—empirical, valuational, or future descriptive.

In a later discussion of socialization, we shall note that the principal source of these belief statements are the many socializing

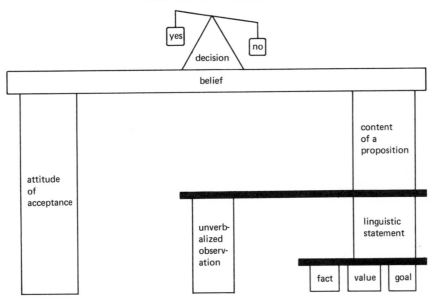

LINGUISTIC SUPPORTS FOR THE
"EDIFICE" OF A DECISION

groups emitting communications of one sort or another to the particular individual. We also need to appreciate that the belief structure of any particular individual consists of literally tens of thousands of observations and statements. Further, each of us holds beliefs about false as well as true propositions and beliefs about purported as well as actual propositions. Add the human propensity for accepting illusion and imperfection in knowledge. A person's belief structure may easily be a hazardous basis for decision making.

ANALYSIS OF DECISION ACTS

The concepts *decision* or *choice* are often used interchangeably. They are defined in a number of ways in the theoretical literature. Quotation of several definitions reveals certain common analytical components.

Lasswell describes *choice* as a term usually applied to situations in which the individual or the group (or organization) has at least a minimum degree of freedom in selecting or interpreting goals (or purposes, ends) and strategies (or means, behaviors, actions). His emphasis on "minimum degree of freedom" indicates that at least two or more goals and two or more alternatives (strategies) must be available to the decision maker.[9]

According to Bates, a decision-making process involves a decision maker, an environment in which the decision maker must operate, a set of actions available, and a set of goals to be accomplished. An *optimal decision* is one that follows from a procedure which chooses one of a set of actions consistent with the indicated importance of the goals. Any model of decision making must include some measure of the efficiency of an action for a goal, a measure of the value or importance for the goal, and a measure of the adequacy or effectiveness of the selection procedure.[10]

Snyder defines decision making as a process which results in the selection from a socially defined, limited number of problematical, alternative *projects* (that is, courses of action) of one project to bring about the particular state of affairs envisaged by the decision maker. Notice that Snyder broadens the notion of "minimum degree of freedom" to include a "limited number" from which one course of action is selected. That decision making requires at least two alternatives is further evident from Edwards' statement of the basic issue of decision theory; namely, given two states A and B, into either one of which an individual may put himself, the individual chooses A in preference to B (or vice versa); what factors make it possible to predict the choice?[11]

In his succinct behavioral model of rational choice, Simon endeavors to examine the properties of the choosing organism. In so doing, he provides a relatively complete summary of the elements suggested in the foregoing definitions as well as in other theoretical literature dealing with the decision process.[12]

The Actors

What decision theorists study is that analytical class of creatures called *decision makers*. A decision maker is an organism capable of the various activities identified below. Since one of these activities involves "envisaging some future state of affairs," man, we have

[9] Harold D. Lasswell, "Current Studies of the Decision Process," *op. cit.*

[10] James Bates, "A Model for the Science of Decision," *Philosophy of Science*, 21 (October 1954): 326–339.

[11] Snyder, *op, cit.*; Edwards, "The Theory of Decision Making," *op. cit.*

[12] Simon, *op. cit.*, in *Models of Man*, pp. 241–240. Much of the following discussion is adapted from Simon's presentation.

noted, is the only creature with this capacity. In brief, when we speak of decision makers, we are examining human beings. Further, we are examining a facet of human behavior that involves some or all of the activities of choice making. In other words, we are *not* examining human beings as food-processing mechanisms, baseball players, or home builders.

Within the category of actors called "decision makers" it is possible to identify two general types: the individual person as a decision maker, and the group as decision maker. Our interest in this chapter is the person.

Situation

Choices occur within an infinitive variety of situations or contexts. However, a situation of choice never exists unless the actor perceives the situation as such. We may see a person surrounded by fire and in danger of his life, but if *he* does not perceive his situation, he will not respond as a decision maker.

A *situation of choice* exists if a selectively perceived pattern of relationships among events, objects, conditions, and other actors is organized around a focus which is the center of interest for the decision maker. The homemaker who notices a bare cupboard *may* perceive the absence of food as a problem. If she does, and if the bare cupboard is related to the imminence of a mealtime, a situation of choice will occur for the actor.[13]

Much of the "noise" of American politics consists of the "calling of attention" to some problem so identified by a person or a group. For example, the economic plight of elderly citizens was completely overlooked by public and politicians alike until a retired city health official, Dr. Francis E. Townsend, launched the Townsend movement in 1933, demanding a pension of $200 a month for every person over sixty who agreed to stop work and spend the money within thirty days. A thousand Townsend clubs were organized within the first year, and another thousand during the next two years. Congress was

13 How an unexpectedly high degree of obedience may be the consequence of the situation in which an experiment occurs is described in Stanley Milgram, "Behavioral Study of Obedience," *Journal of Abnormal and Social Psychology,* 67 (1963): 371–378. Of 40 student subjects, 26 administered what appeared to be dangerous high voltage shocks to other persons on instruction from the experimenter. Since the American culture admonishes against physical harm to others, this large degree of obedience may have been induced by the fact that Yale University (where this experiment was conducted) is a reputable institution, the research was for a "worthy cause," the victims were volunteers, etc.

much shaken up by the activities of the movement, and President Roosevelt drew from it some of the political energy he needed to compel public study of the question of social security legislation. In other words, legislators saw themselves in a situation of choice which they had not previously perceived.

Nearly every field of public policy has had its early moments of intense excitement and "calls to action" which have thrust political decision makers into situations of choice. Sputnik in 1957 suddenly made American politicians aware that the Russians were not a "peasant people" and that American educational policy needed drastic attention. Activists in the field of race relations have similarly employed sit-ins, riots, etc., to keep American attention focused upon the strivings of its Negro and other minorities.

Alternatives

Once the decision maker perceives himself in a situation of choice, he must concern himself with the behavior alternatives available to him. The set of alternatives that he perceives or considers may be the same or different from the total set available. For example, a staunch partisan, whether Democratic or Republican, would ordinarily decide to vote his party's ticket, that is, consider only one response as possible in the election situation. In some instances, however, he may consider another alternative: withholding his vote from his party. The set of behavior alternatives "considered" therefore is: to vote the party ticket or to withhold the vote. Such a partisan would hardly consider voting for the opposition party or a minority party, although, realistically, these are among his total set of objectively available alternatives. For a less partisan decision maker the latter alternatives would be within the perceived set under consideration.

One of the principal motivations for consulting specialists and experts is to aid one's perception of the *total* set of available alternatives in a situation of choice. A physician is likely to see a wider range of treatments for an ailment than a layman. We go to lawyers with legal problems so that they may help us perceive alternative strategies that we might otherwise miss. A President, confronted by the military maneuver of a foreign power, will turn to his Secretary of State, Defense Secretary, Ambassador to the United Nations, and other official advisors for analyses of and suggested responses to the problem; each may suggest a different subset of alternatives, which, even when put together, may fall short of the total available set.

The distinction between the *total set* and the *perceived subset of behavior alternatives* serves as an analytical aid to keep alive the possibility that all objectively available alternatives *may not* necessarily be under consideration by a particular decision maker in a particular situation of choice. For example, a poor person who needs to borrow money rarely believes it is within his prerogative to shop around for favorable interest rates. Truth-in-lending legislation is designed to make such a loan seeker aware that he does have such alternatives, and thereby broadens his "considered" subset by adding alternatives from the total available set.

Outcomes and Payoff Functions

The possible outcomes of a choice have been called by many other names: goals, purposes, ends, objectives, future states of affairs, etc. We have already noted in our discussion of future-descriptive statements that goals are future events that are only mental images in the present. Every choice requires thought *in the present* about possible future states of affairs that *could* be outcomes of the various alternatives available.

A *payoff function* refers to the *value* or *utility* placed by the decision maker upon each of the perceived or anticipated outcomes of choice. These are the evaluational judgments in which the decision maker ranks or rates the possible goals relative to each other. Should an available ten dollar bill be expended on clothing, books, medical care, or dining out? Different individuals would assign different utilities or values to each of these possible outcomes; that is, they would rank them differently.

Since each person's precise evaluational yardstick is different from every other's, the concept *subjective utility* has been useful in describing this aspect of the decision process. Society and its groups may indeed make patterns of utility among individuals somewhat similar, but rarely if ever precisely the same. The payoffs that different outcomes represent for different individuals must be dealt with not only as a highly subjective phenomenon, pertinent to each and only each decision maker alone, but, as Homans points out, each individual's payoff function may vary with time and situation.

A gourmet diner may ordinarily spend his ten dollars on food, except immediately after having completed a gourmet meal. The opportunity for another meal at this moment promises a very low payoff for him. In the mathematical sense, a payoff function refers to the variations in degree of value placed upon the alternative outcomes by the particular decision maker under varying conditions and at varying times.

Instrumental Information

Two types of information are needed by the decision maker in order to help reduce his uncertainty about the behavior alternative he should select. The first type could be called *means-ends information,* or that information which identifies which particular outcome will actually occur if a particular alternative is chosen. To illustrate, let us say that a decision maker in a particular situation of choice perceives three possible outcomes: *A, B,* or *C.* Among the behavior alternatives immediately available to him are: *w, x, y,* and *z.* Which of these four alternatives is related to which of the outcomes?

Assume that *A* will ensue from alternative *w, B* from either *x* or *y,* and *C* from *z,* as follows:

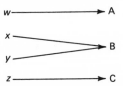

If the decision maker anticipates his highest payoff from the achievement of *C,* he will choose *z* as the most appropriate alternative. He could not do this without information regarding the relationship between the particular alternatives and the particular outcomes. Were he to choose alternative *w* instead of *z,* he would be producing outcome *A* instead of his preferred *C.*

If our hypothetical decision maker prefers *B* as his "best" outcome, his uncertainty about which alternatives to choose would be reduced from four (*w, x, y,* and *z,*) to two (*x* and *y*). He would now find it important to have a second type of instrumental information, namely *probability information.* What is the probability that a particular outcome will ensue if a particular behavior alternative is chosen? If our decisionmaker has evidence that x is likely to produce B three out of ten times whereas y is likely to produce B seven out of ten times, his rational choice would be alternative y.

In such a situation, it is easy to see how well-confirmed empirical information can be most important in the making of a decision. For example, if carefully controlled laboratory experiments demonstrate that a particular antipolio vaccine will immunize human beings in 99.7 cases out of every 100, public health officials can very confidently recommend that all citizens present themselves for vaccination. If the experimental results indicated a probability of only 70 in 100, the public health officials would feel far less confident about carrying on a mass immunization program. Similarly, if a politician running for office knows that he has the regular support of 8 out of 10 members of a particular social group, he is likely to expend more effort trying to raise the relative support in some other, less certain group, thereby, presumably, improving the probability of his election. He would, in other words, choose the behavior alternative most likely to reduce his risk of losing the election.

Often decision makers will base their probability estimates upon fairly objective and validated evidence drawn from experience or experimentation. More often, this probability estimate is a purely subjective one. *Subjective probability* refers to personal estimates about a particular action producing a particular outcome.

Subjective probability estimates may or may not conform with objective mathematical probability in a decision situation. In one experiment, for example, beginning bus drivers were matched against trained drivers in steering a bus between two posts. The two groups were compared on the basis of the risks each took and the success achieved. Some of the beginners attempted to drive the bus through an impossibly narrow gap between the posts, whereas the experienced drivers almost never did. It was found that the experienced not only performed far more successfully than the inexperienced but also took less risk. Since each attempt to drive between two posts involved a judgment regarding the probability of success, the experiment indicated the extent to which subjective probability assessments could vary with experience and training.[14]

---

[14] John Cohen, "Subjective Probability," *Scientific American*, November, 1957, pp. 128 ff. Cohen suggests that, on the basis of studies of subjective probability, certain classes of criminals may differ from their law-abiding fellow citizen only in being more sure that they will escape detection, that is, they may have a level of maximum risk taking quite different from that of others. The relevance of this for the study

Subjective probability has a particular relevance for the structure of personal belief systems generally, hence for styles of decision making. Following World War II, a number of studies of ideological dogmatism revealed a great deal about the psychological characteristics of the dogmatic individual and the consequences of these characteristics for his behavior.[15]

One of these studies assumed that objective reality is represented within a person by certain beliefs or expectations which, to one degree or another, are accepted as true, and other beliefs or expectations that are perceived as false. In this way, all cognitive systems may be viewed as organized into two interdependent parts: a belief system and a disbelief system.

The extent to which a person is able to receive, evaluate, and act upon relevant information from outside his current belief-disbelief system, unencumbered by irrelevant factors in the situation which may arise from either within himself or from the outside, determines the degree to which he is dogmatic. An open-minded person evaluates and acts upon information in terms of its own merits; in this sense, he endeavors to have subjective probability estimates coincide as closely as possible to objective, mathematical probabilities. The *closed mind* has difficulty in separating information from its source, particularly if it is an authoritarian or charismatic source to which this particular person is attracted.

The closed mind tends to accentuate the difference between its own belief content and that of others, exhibiting severe intolerance toward those with differing beliefs. The greater the degree of dogmatism, the more will contradictory empirical events be denied. The greater the dogmatism, the more likely that new experiences will be forced into rather than modify existing belief-disbelief systems. Dogmatism was also found to have an important influence on time perception; the greater the dogmatism, the more will the present time be perceived as relatively unimportant in its own right. Further,

---

of risk taking in politics is impressive. How many wars and revolutions have been initiated in the certainty of success? How many minority party nominees in one-party districts have campaigned with a personal sense of assurance that this time the majority party would be beaten? See also, N. T. Feather, "Subjective Probability and Decision Under Uncertainty, *Psychological Review*, (1959): 150–164.

15 Eric Hoffer, *The True Believer* (New York: Harper, 1951); T. W. Adorno, et al., *The Authoritarian Personality* (New York, Harper, 1950); George Orwell, *1984* (New York: New American Library, 1951); and Milton Rokeach, "The Nature and Meaning of Dogmatism," *Psychological Review*, 61 (May 1954): 194–204. Rokeach's investigations later resulted in *The Open and Closed Mind* (New York: Basic Books, 1960). The observations here are drawn from Rokeach.

the greater the dogmatism, the greater the willingness to condone and risk the use of force. If each human generation produces dogmatic personalities and dictators, whose wishful thinking and subjective probability assessments lead them into violent political adventures, the political costs of coping with such decision makers may obviously be high for a society; witness the wars and riots that have filled the history of the twentieth century.

The act of deciding therefore consists of a number of analytically distinguishable components, according to contemporary decision theories: the decision maker; the perceived situation of choice; the set of all behavior alternatives, and the subset of those that are perceived; the possible outcomes; the value placed by the decision maker on each possible outcome; and the instrumental information that relates alternative with outcome and estimates the probability that the former will produce the latter.

Rationality

The Renaissance produced the hope that man could decide his future by the exercise of his reason. Seventeenth-century rationalism argued that the capacity for reason was deductive in character, that is, an a priori procedure by which knowledge could be produced by the logical derivation of propositions from basic premises. By the nineteenth century, an empirical dimension had been added to discussions of the reasoning processes of men. From these were derived various nineteenth- and twentieth-century conceptions of rational choice.

The *rational person* is one who has a stable and well-organized system of preferences, as well as a skill in computation that permits him to calculate which of the alternative courses of action available to him, will permit him to reach the highest attainable point on his preference scale. Theoretically, he need only have plenty of information and sound computational capacities in order to arrive at an optimal rational choice, the behavior alternative calculated to produce his most preferred goal. If he were *knowingly* to select any other alternative less likely to produce his most preferred outcome or some outcome lower down on his scale of preferences, his decision behavior would be considered, by definition, as *irrational*.

However, most human decision making proceeds from extremely inadeqate information, limited perception of available alternatives, much ambiguity about future states of affairs, shifting rankings among preferred outcomes, and, as we learn from studies of subjective probability, immensely poor computational skills. Under these circumstances it is a rarity to find the decision maker who is rational or the decision that has been rationally made. The notion of rational choice is further undermined by various psychic mechanisms that have been found operative in postdecision *dissonance reduction.*

The term *rationalization* was employed by Ernest Jones in 1908 to describe Freud's hypothesis that apparently irrational acts are often justified by distorting the mental processes involved and by providing a verbal explanation that sounds plausible. Thereafter, rationalization acquired the connotation of falsification and deception in order to cloak a motive, defend a value system, and otherwise protect the self or one's group. A somewhat less disparaging approach to this type of rationalizing behavior as an aspect of decision making is the theory of *cognitive dissonance* developed by Festinger.[16]

In general, a relation between two things that occur together may be called dissonant if, in some way, they appear not to belong together or fit together. Cognitive dissonance refers to this kind of relation between cognitions which exist simultaneously for a person. If that person knows two things, for example, one about himself and the other about the world in which he lives, which somehow do not fit together, that person may be said to experience cognitive dissonance.

As in the case of other human motivational or need states, cognitive dissonance gives rise to activity aimed at reducing or eliminating the dissonance. "Successful reduction of dissonance is rewarding in the same sense that eating when one is hungry is rewarding." Dissonance reduction is, in effect, a process of modifying a belief, reconciling two or more beliefs or cognitions, or, as in the case of the dogmatic personality, somehow incorporating a new cognition into the existing belief system through some process of distortion, self-deception, or falsification. Since belief systems are so often linguistic, dissonance reduction frequently takes the form of purely verbal rationalization.

In one study, for example, a sect of people predicted that, on a given data, a catastrophic flood would overwhelm most of the world,

16 Leon Festinger, *A Theory of Cognitive Dissonance* (Evanston, Ill.: Row-Peterson, 1957).

but that those in the sect were among the chosen who, according to messages from the gods, were to be picked up by flying saucers before the cataclysm occurred. Four days before the predicted event was to take place, most members of the sect gathered in the home of the member who received the messages from the gods to wait together for the arrival of the flying saucer. When it failed to arrive at the indicated time, the group went their separate ways, interpreting the events of that particular night as a rehearsal for the real pickup. However, on the appointed day of the catastrophe, when the event failed to occur, a further message arrived from God which, in effect, said that He had saved the world and prevented the flood because of the faith of this group. With profound sincerity, the members of the sect went forward to spread the message. A skeptic would probably denounce the entire sequence of events as fakery, but deception was not at all evident in the religiosity emitted by the members themselves.[17]

In a subsequent study, the theory of cognitive dissonance was examined as an aspect of postdecision belief behavior. The theory suggests that when a person chooses one of two alternatives, all the items of information which favor the unchosen alternative will be perceived by the decision maker as dissonant. In such a state, psychic pressure to reduce the cognitive dissonance will be created. Some 225 female subjects were asked to rate each of eight items, such as an automatic coffeemaker, on desirability, choose between two of them, and then rate each of the articles again. In addition, some of the subjects were exposed to a mixture of good and bad information about the alternatives after their choice was made. The findings supported the prediction that choosing a "bad" alternative would create dissonance and that attempts to reduce the dissonance would ensue by making the chosen alternative seem more desirable and the rejected alternative less desirable.[18]

Thus, decison making does not end with the selection of an alternative. Conceptions of rationality, dogmatism, rationalization, and cognitive dissonance point to postdecision reactions to later events and new information. The findings further underscore the process aspects of decision. A particular human decision is but one in an

[17] Leon Festinger, H. W. Riecken, and S. Schacter, *When Prophecy Fails* (Minneapolis: University of Minnesota Press, 1956).
[18] Jack W. Brehm, "Postdecision Changes in the Desirability of Alternatives," *Journal of Abnormal and Social Psychology,* 52 (May 1956): 384–89.

endless chain that goes on as long as the decision maker survives as an organism.

ROLE THEORETICAL PERSPECTIVES ON DECISION MAKING

The assumptions of rationalism and hedonism (pleasure-pain responses) in the above models of decision making are sometimes viewed as objectionable or inadequate by many behavioral scientists. The emphasis upon the individual decision maker as the unit of analysis may also be considered incomplete. These models are criticized for drawing attention away from such problems as incomplete information, drift and chance in the decision process, and the group context within which the decision maker behaves. Role theoretical approaches to decision making are among the attempts to locate the decision maker in his social environment and to take that environment into account in his decision process.

Role is an ancient theatrical term referring to the parts for each player that were written on scrolls. The theatrical usage of the term "role" has relatively similar meaning for the usage of social psychology. Biddle and Thomas draw the connection quite clearly.

> When actors portray a character in a play, their performance is determined by the script, the director's instructions, the performances of fellow actors, and reactions of the audience as well as by the acting talents of the players. Apart from differences between actors in the interpretation of their parts, the performance of each actor is programmed by all of these external factors; consequently, there are significant similarities in the performances of actors taking the same part, no matter who the actors are.

> . . . Individuals in society occupy positions, and their role performance in these positions is determined by social norms, demands, and rules; by the role performances of others in their respective positions; by those who observe and react to the performance; and by the individual's particular capabilities and personality. The social "script" may be as constraining as that of a play, but it frequently allows more options; the "director" is often present in real life as a supervisor, parent, teacher, or coach; the "audience" in life consists of all those who observe the position member's behavior. The position member's "performance" in life, as in the play, is attributable to his familiarity with the part, his

personality and personal history in general, and more significantly to the "script" which others define in so many ways.[19]

Ways of Defining Role

The countless approaches to role theory and definitions of the term may be summarized in a number of ways. Biddle and Thomas suggest that *role* has been used as a way of referring to (1) persons, (2) behaviors, and (3) both persons and behaviors at the same time. When referring to persons, *role* usually indicates the whole *behaver* as a person or kind of person. The role name may particularize the person according to his behavior; e.g., "babysitter" is of course a person who is sitting as a baby watcher. The role name may be a reference to a position being filled, as "the teacher," "the chairman," etc. *Role* has also been used in the basic sense of distinguishing one's self from others, in such references as "self" and "ego" and "alter."

The second use of *role* refers to *behavior* as such. The more specific terms employed by this usage are *role enactment, role behavior, behavior pattern,* and *role performance.* All of these refer to the overt behaviors and actions that are characteristically associated together or expected in certain social situations. "His performance as a student was commendable." Such an observation refers to the performance of expected behaviors in a school situation. When applied to behaviors, *role* may also refer to prescriptions or norms of behavior, that is, what it is that is expected rather than what it is that has actually been performed; e.g., "He ought to act more like a teacher than he does."[20] *Role* has also been employed with evaluative and sanctioning connotations.

The third usage described by Biddle and Thomas pertains to *both persons and behaviors.* Usually *role* in this sense refers to the behaviors of particular persons with respect to particular positions, offices, or statuses. To speak of "the teacher role" could, in this

[19] Bruce J. Biddle and Edwin J. Thomas, *Role Theory* (New York: Wiley, 1966), p. 4. Quoted with permission of the publisher. The Biddle-Thomas volume is perhaps the most comprehensive survey of conceptual history, definitions, and research in the field of role theory. Other significant surveys appear in T. R. Sarbin, "Role Theory," in Gardner Lindzey (ed.), *Handbook of Social Psychology* (Cambridge Mass.: Addison-Wesley, 1954), Vol. I, pp. 223–258, and Jack J. Priess and H. J. Ehrlich, *An Examination of Role Theory: the Case of the State Police* (Lincoln: University of Nebraska Press, 1966), and Lionel J. Neiman and J. W. Hughes, "The Problem of the Concept of Role—A Re-survey of the Literature," *Social Forces,* 30 (December 1951): 143–149. See also, Michael Banton, *Roles* (New York: Basic Books, 1965).

[20] Cf. *task expectations,* in Chapter 1.

usage, refer both to the performance of particular persons and the task expectations associated by the group with the position "teacher."

The many definitions of *role* may also be grouped under the following three broad categories: those definitions that relate role to normative culture patterns; those that treat role as a person's orientation to his situation; and those that equate role with what a person actually does as a position incumbent.

NORMATIVE CULTURE PATTERNS   Linton states that a role consists of "attitudes, values, and behavior ascribed by the society to any and all persons occupying [a position]." In this definition, the phrase "ascribed by society" contains a postulate of consensus; i.e., members of society have the same expectations for incumbents of the same position.[21]

Newcomb advances two different definitions in the same place; one is similar to Linton's. In the first instance, Newcomb defines a role as "the ways of behaving which are expected of any individual who occupies a certain position." However, later, he defines a role as "behavior of the occupants of a position—not . . . all their behavior as persons, but . . . what they do as occupants of the position." Newcomb's definitions are an example of the differentiation made between expected behavior and actual behavior of position incumbents.[22] The main point of agreement among the definitions with a normative orientation is that they view *role* as referring to the expectations that others ascribe to an individual as an occupant of a position rather than to what he actually does as a position incumbent.

ORIENTATIONS TO SITUATIONS   This second type of definition embraces among others, the formulations of Stanfeld Sargent and Talcott Parsons. Both treat role as "an individual's definition of his situation with reference to his and other's social position." That a role is situationally determined is one of the points emphasized by Parsons.

> It is a fundamental property of action . . . that it does not consist only of *ad hoc* "responses" to particular situational "stimuli" but

[21] Ralph Linton, *The Cultural Background of Personality* (New York: Appleton-Century, 1945), p. 77.

[22] Theodore M. Newcomb, *Social Psychology* (New York: Dryden Press, 1950), p. 280.

that the actor develops a system of "expectations" relative to the various objects of the situation.

The most elementary components of any action system, then, can be reduced to the actor and his orientation to an object world. As role constitutes a "sector of [this] total orientation system," it is organized "about expectations in relations to a particular interaction context." These expectations "are integrated with a particular set of value-standards which govern interaction with one or more alters in the appropriate complementary roles." There is a reciprocal aspect of these value standards for expectations which govern the inter-action systems of ego and one or more alters. Parsons states that this reciprocal aspect must always be borne in mind, "since the expectations of an ego always imply the expectations of one or more alters." It is in this system of reciprocity that the notion of sanctions enters into role theory. "Sanctions" is used by Parsons to indicate "both positive and negative responses by alter to ego's response."

> What an actor is expected to do in a given situation both by himself and by others constitutes the expectations of that role. What the relevant alters are expected to do, contingent on ego's action, constitute the sanctions. Role expectations and sanctions are, therefore, in terms of the content of action, the reciprocal of each other. What are sanctions to ego are also role expectations to alter, and *vice versa*.

In carrying out his role, an actor (ego) will attempt to elicit the favorable and avoid the unfavorable reactions of significant others (alters). An actor must know the role and expectations of others in order to operate smoothly in his own role. Thus, in Parsons' conceptualization, a position incumbent's role is defined by situational factors.[23]

WHAT THE PERSON ACTUALLY DOES   According to Kingsley Davis, a role "is the manner in which a person actually carried out the requirements of his position." This definition ignores the expectational dimension and removes role from the context of situational factors

---

[23] *Reference group* and *reference persons* may serve as more empirically ascertainable factors in role behavior, as we shall see in the discussion of reference group below. The quotations are from Talcott Parsons, *The Social System* (Glencoe, Ill.: Free Press, 1951), pp. 38–39.

and normative culture patterns. Role here is whatever behavior is elicited by the stimulus of incumbency in a position.[24]

Roles as Building Blocks of Personality

Personality theory as a distinct approach to the study of human behavior has had its fluctuations in popularity. As recently as 1957 two distinguished reviewers in the field, Hall and Lindzey, noted that "in spite of the deepening interest of psychologists in personality theory, there is no single source to which the student can turn for a survey of existing theories of personality." Almost at the same time two other reviewers, Blake and Mouton, concluded that "the hoary tradition that treats personality as a distinct area of theory and research was further destroyed in 1957–8." The latter continued: "Although the idea of an inclusive category of personality will continue to have appeal in parlor and poolroom, the same is not so true in systematic psychology." In 1964, Berelson and Steiner found that "except for the clinical literature, there is (within psychology now) little concern with individual personalities or with personality *per se.*"[25]

In political science, interest in personality theory has been mainly associated with the "Great Man" theories of history (according to which history is "made" by strategic and significant individuals), elite and leadership studies, psychoanalytic studies of political personalities, and the electoral psychology associated with voting behavior. Hall and Lindzey remind us that a number of schools of personality theory have been active in psychology: Freud's psychoanalytic theory, in which the id, the ego, and the superego comprise three major aspects of personality; Jung's analytic theory, which evolves a system of relationships among ego, personal unconscious, collective unconscious, persona, anima, shadow, and self, the latter being the fully developed and fully unified personality; Murray's personology, which views personality as the governing organ of the

---

24 Kingsley Davis, *Human Society* (New York: Macmillan, 1949).
25 C. S. Hall and G. Lindzey, *Theories of Personality* (New York: Wiley, 1957), vii; R. R. Blake and J. S. Mouton, "Personality," *Annual Review of Psychology* (1959), pp. 203–32; B. Berelson and G. A. Steiner, *Human Behavior; An Inventory of Scientific Findings* (New York: Harcourt, Brace and World, 1964), p. 63. See also Alex Inkeles, "Personality and Social Structure," in R. K. Merton, *Sociology Today* (New York: Basic Books, 1959), pp. 249–76, which shows the relationship between role and "modal personality" in a particular culture. For a comprehensive survey of the literature, Edgar F. Borgatta and William W. Lambert (eds.), *Handbook of Personality Theory and Research* (Chicago: Rand McNally, 1968).

body, ceaselessly engaged in transformative functional operations from birth to death; Lewin's field theory, in which the person is a structural concept set apart from everything else in the world and functioning as such within a "life space" that serves as his psychological environment and whose behavior is a consequence of valences and vectors; the reinforcement theories of Dollard and Miller, based upon conditioned reflex, habit, and secondary drives; Rogers' self theory, in which the organism learns a pattern of conscious perceptions in values of the "I" or "me" to which all parts of the phenomenal field or totality of experience are related; Murphy's biosocial theory; and the social psychological theories of Adler, Fromm, and others, to mention only the major formulations.

Gardner Murphy's "biosocial" approach introduces role into personality theory as follows:

> In summary of our thesis regarding roles, we have attempted to show (1) that society, with its system of mores, and with the self-maintenance mores more or less central in the pattern, does not merely "mold" people, but requires from them the enactment of specific roles in accordance with their place in the system; (2) that not all roles are easily accepted, but that many require effort, and indeed frequently put a strain upon the individual; (3) that a given person must enact several different roles (sex, class, etc.) at once, and that their integration is no obvious or mechanical matter; (4) that roles derived not merely from primary obligations, but also in response to the roles of others (there is not only melody but counterpoint); (5) that in consequence of all this the individual develops balancing or complementary roles, so that he is a complement both to others and to himself; and (6) that it is thus a long way from the simplest economic determinism to a realistic role psychology based ultimately upon recognition of self-maintenance factors.[26]

Sherif and Cantril provide an attitudinal emphasis, using the key term "ego" instead of "personality" or "self":

> ["Ego"] has acquired many scientifically objectionable connotations. . . . The "ego" consists, in the last analysis, of a constellation of attitudes which can be designated as ego-attitudes. . . .

> We can perhaps take as a matter of everyday experience the fact that most of the affective fixations (attitudes) which determine, delimit, focus, and shape the selectivity of experience and response

---

[26] Gardner Murphy, *Personality* (New York: Harper, 1947), p. 794.

to various stimulus situations are connected with the individuals, situations, or institutions to which a person is in some way related. Attitudes are toward *my* parents, *my* school, *my* gang, *my* church, *my* nation, *my* boss, *my* friend, toward *my* friend's rival, *my* father's competitor, *my* country's enemy, and so on. Most attitudes have the characteristic of belonging to *me*, as being part of *me*, as psychologically experienced. . . .[27]

Churchman and Ackoff develop a theory of personality derived entirely from the individual's decision process; an individual's personality consists, empirically, of the cumulation of his past chosen alternatives. Every time a decision maker selects one from a set of alternatives, he is adding a brushstroke to the portrait that comprises his personality. Thus, an individual's personality essentially requires an aggregate analysis of the sum of his deeds or action choices.[28]

Self and Ego

The *self* concept emerges for the individual when in his experience he becomes a social object to himself. He becomes such an object only as he learns of himself through the gestures of others toward him. The infant or young child may begin to know about himself as a distinct object because of the activity parents, siblings, and peers may have directed at him. The child, when he is at the center of some social activity (such as feeding or washing) and the gestures (including linguistic gestures) of the others associated with this activity, is learning about himself as an object in the group's environment. He is learning information about the self, the social activity of which he is the center, the gestures and language associated with the activity, and the symbolic pleasantness or unpleasantness of the activity and its outcomes. Such are the behavioral roots of hedonism, Bentham's pleasure-pain theory, and modern behaviorism.

Among primitive peoples, according to George Herbert Mead, the first vague distinctions noticed between the self and the physical organism led to the notion of a "double." Each individual was thought to possess a thing-like self which was distinct from the immediate organism and the object of the activities of other people

[27] M. Sherif and H. Cantril, *The Psychology of Ego-Involvements* (New York: Wiley, 1957), pp. 92–93.
[28] C. W. Churchman and R. L. Ackoff, "An Experimental Definition of Personality," *Philosophy of Science* (1947).

or the individual concerned. Each individual's "double" was both part of the body and separable from it. This became the basis for viewing the soul as a separate entity. All this is comparable to the imaginary companions which young children frequently create as part of their experience.[29]

Primitive society was unspecialized, so that the individual and his double were at the center of group activity only occasionally. The primitive individual, therefore, had a relatively narrow base from which to differentiate the self from other objects, particularly from other persons, in the environment. This was quite different from the broad base for self-differentiation in modern societies. The modern child knows about the self from: sustained attention of family and friends; his personal name, which consists of two or three components; the highly organized educational system, which focuses upon developing *his* particular capacities; and the Western acceptance of the philosophy of individualism. Whereas the primitive child had very little information about himself as a distinct social object, the modern child can hardly escape civilization's ways of gesturing at and to him about his "self." Freud referred to this societal gesturing as "the superego."

Most theorists, then, agree that the concept *personality* and its companion concepts *self* and *ego* touch upon various characteristics that, taken together, help distinguish man from other biological creatures. First, there is the capacity for self-objectification, that is, perceptually discriminating between oneself and other objects in the environment. This may be stated in the first person as: "I" can think of "me." "I" can conceive of "myself" as an object. There is also the evaluative and symbolic aspect, that is, the ability to develop attitudes toward oneself, which, as we have seen, is decidedly a human capacity.

Second, there is much theory among psychologists that suggests a distinctive subsystem of human personality, the *ego*. The distinction between *ego* and *self* in the literature is not too clear, but a useful distinction could perhaps be stated here. The self may be considered the *individual's* perception of his physical and psychological separateness. Regardless what the view of others may be, the individual's views of that separateness and of the collection of learned roles of which he is aware adds up to his self. The ego, on the other hand,

[29] Anselm Strauss, *The Social Psychology of George Herbert Mead* (Chicago: University of Chicago Press, 1956), pp. 226–227.

may be that role or subset of roles whose primacy provides the "direction" or "leadership" components to the individual's behavior. The ego, in this sense, is the leading role or roles.[30]

A third characteristic of personality upon which there is much agreement is the distinctively human capacity for learning *social roles*, that is, general group-prescribed patterns of behavior to be performed in relatively standard situations in order to promote certain personal and group goals.

Socialization and Role Learning

Brim defines *socialization* as a "process of learning through which an individual is prepared, with varying degrees of success, to meet the requirements laid down by other members of society for his behavior in a variety of situations." He equates this process with role learning. Role learning, or socialization, occurs throughout the individual's life as he enters new statuses. Sociologists, according to Brim, have tended to neglect role learning during childhood and have dealt mainly with the individual's entrance into roles during the adult period of life.[31]

Between the time an infant is born and the time it enters an occupation, well over twenty years of living and learning usually transpire. The learning, acquired by direct observation or through some means of communication, usually includes general notions about "types of people" and the "things" each type does. If asked to name "types of people" that he knows about, a typical seven-year-old will probably produce a list along the following lines (from an actual interview):

mother	baseball player	spies
father	football player	T.V. fixers
baby sister	mailman	housebuilders
brother	milkman	churchworkers
teacher	spaceman	policeman
doctor	president	fireman
nurse	governor	furniture makers
pilot	babysitter	

[30] See also Ernest R. Hilgard, "Human Motives and the Concept of the Self," *American Psychologist*, (1949): 374–382.

[31] Orville G. Brim, Jr. "Personality Development as Role-learning," in I. I. Iscoe and H. W. Stevenson (eds.), *Personality Development in the Child* (Austin: University of Texas Press, 1960), pp. 127–159. Chapter 8 below surveys socialization theory as it relates to the acquisition of political roles.

The child is, of course, naming standard positions whose names he has learned, in this case, by the age of seven.

If a child names a position, he will ordinarily also be able to identify at least one thing that "such a person usually does." In other words, he can name a task expectation that he and others ordinarily associate with the position name; e.g., the doctor "makes us well when we are sick." Most individuals may name many positions for each of which he has learned to have certain task expectations. Relatively few, however, will themselves learn and perform the specific activities or tasks.

The child who thinks of a "doctor" as a "type of person" who "makes us well when we are sick" may, after years of medical training himself learn scores of specific "things" that doctors do. His role learning will have included the acquisition of specific role activity information, such as: the recognition of human body parts and their characteristics; handling of diagnostic procedures and equipment; recognition of pathological conditions; prescription of therapy to correct bodily malfunctions; patterns of professional conduct; etc. Once learned, the generalized "doctor" role becomes a significant part of the personality, or ego, of this individual. He will have also, over the years, learned many other roles whose general patterns of activity are prescribed by socializing groups within his society, e.g., student, churchgoer, money earner, consumer, sweetheart, husband, father, businessman, citizen, taxpayer, etc. If the sum of all these learned roles constitutes this physician's objective personality, the self, then, is his own subjective perception and evaluation of his *total* role structure. His "ego," on the other hand, consists of the principal role, that is, physician in this illustration.[32]

Theories about the manner by which roles are learned, especially by children, are numerous. George Herbert Mead identified language development and the activities of play as fundamental mechanisms for role learning. Spoken language is that vocal gesture that tends to arouse in the individual the same attitude that it arouses in others, at the same time mediating the social activities that give rise to the process of taking the role of the other.

This "taking the role of the other" is a significant aspect of play. Kagan calls attention to the mechanism of *identification*, in which

---

[32] In sociology, the field of *individual disorganization* usually deals with deviances and problems of the self, the ego, or the role aspects of personality. Some well-known types of individual disorganization include: juvenile delinquency, alcoholism, sex deviancy, unemployment, suicide, divorce, criminality, corruption, and social mobility.

the child adopts the behaviors of some model whose attractive goals he wishes to command. Identification with various models in varying degrees of intensity adds to the child's repertoire. Piaget emphasizes the imitative aspect. In his view, role learning takes place through various forms of representational thought—by imitation, symbolic play, and cognitive representation. Maccoby posits "that all role-taking is imitation, but not all imitation is role-taking. . . . A child's imitation of someone with whom he interacts may properly be called 'taking the role of another' only if the action imitated is inappropriate for a child and is appropriate instead for the occupant of some other position or status. . . . A child acquires a repertoire of actions by practicing covertly the actions characteristic of the adults with whom he interacts most frequently and who control the resources that he needs." Since the young child is almost completely dependent upon others, learning by covert role playing occurs more frequently in early childhood than at any other time of life. Many adult role behaviors learned in childhood may not be used until the situation arises in which the individual can appropriately play the adult role.[33]

Some theories of personality and decision making have begun to adopt the view that the human actor is essentially an information storage and retrievable system, with program and other capabilities analogous to those of electronic computers. In such models, the person is considered to be an active hypothesis-testing organism capable of receiving, storing, analyzing, and reconstructing information. Such information may be organized and stored into sets called roles, each role set theoretically consisting of several kinds of information.

Role Information

More specifically, roles may be thought of as consisting of *cues* and *information units* communicated to and acquiring meaning for the individual as a consequence of his exposure to numerous socializing groups during his life. We may postulate several types of informational content for *each* learned role: *nominative* information; *instrumental* information and associated *prospective* information; and

---

[33] Mead is quoted from Strauss, *op. cit.*, pp. 227–8; Jerome Kagan "The Concept of Identification," *Psychological Review*, 65 (1958): 296–305; Jean Piaget, "Role-Taking in Childhood and its Consequence for Social Learning," *Child Development*, 30 (1959): 239–252.

punitive information with associated *risk* information. The five types of role information may be briefly defined as follows:

NOMINATIVE   Every group process involves the creation and transmission of cues, including role names, for discriminating among segments of the environment. Some obvious role names are: "father," "mother," "president," "doctor," "astronaut," "teacher," "businessman," "babysitter," etc. The activities normally associated with these role names could be carried on without a role name, but the attachment of a nominative linguistic term to the activities adds significant reenforcement of the role learning and role behaving. For example, a person may engage in the buying and selling of goods without being called by the role name "merchant." However, when these activities are labeled as a "merchant's" they acquire, at least in the American culture, added connotations, including, for example, the expectation that the role is being performed in a marketplace or commercial establishment. In the teaching and learning that make up the socialization process, use of this role name normally could facilitate the acquisition of "merchant-like" behavior.

INSTRUMENTAL   Social groups communicate information about the goals they seek and the conduct they deem instrumental in the achievement of these goals. A labor union may have among its immediate goals a guaranteed annual wage and certain fringe benefits. To achieve these goals, the leaders and members may adopt such presumably instrumental activities as: contract renegotiation; strike action; picketing the White House; support of a particular candidate for mayor; and a letter-writing campaign. Whether or not these activities are *in fact* instrumental is immaterial; what counts is the union's belief that they are instrumental.

This aspect is seen in the definition of roles suggested by Gross, that is, individuals (1) in social locations (2) behave (3) with reference to expectations.[34] In some ways, instrumental information is the same as the child's desire to command the attractive social goals possessed by the model, as theorized in the literature on identification as a mechanism of role learning. The child whose hero is a President of the United States is far more likely to seek and learn information about "what Presidents do" than the child who has no

---

[34] Neal Gross, Ward Mason and Alexander W. McEachran, *Explorations in Role Analysis* (New York: Wiley, 1958).

such model. The youthful hero worshipper may never become President, but he is quite likely to engage in much covert learning and perhaps eventually exercise the learned behaviors in some pertinent adult role such as party leader or public official.

PROSPECTIVE   A person will perform instrumental activities in part because he believes these activities have some prospect or probability of contributing to the achievement of the sought-after goal. Whether the probability estimate is his own or one adopted from another person is immaterial. We saw examples of this in connection with the earlier discussion of subjective probability. A man acting in the role of baseball pitcher may actually improve his pitching (instrumental activity) by rubbing a rabbit's foot that *he believes* will maximize the prospect of winning the game; the connection between the rubbing and the belief system is, of course, more behaviorally important than the connection between the rabbit's foot and the pitching.

PUNITIVE   Groups emit socializing messages containing information about the punitive measures they may use to discourage role behaviors that fail to be instrumental. The bulk of the literature of sanction, punishment, and avoidance behavior deals with the perceived punitive capacities of such groups in the eyes of the actor. Thus the union member who crosses his union's picket line during a strike undoubtedly expects to be ostracized if not ejected from membership. The Congressman who votes against a bill supported by an influential organized group in his district may expect to be "punished," perhaps by that group's withdrawal of support in his next election campaign along with other possible punitive measures. In both examples, however, the actor, while fully aware of a group's punitive resources, may discount such measures as not likely to be administered against him (a probability estimate) or, if administered, not likely to "hurt much" (another probability estimate). In other words, he evaluates not only the punitive measure but also the risks associated with it.

RISK   A group may make known, implicitly or explicitly, how it is organized to deal out its punitive measures. From such implied or declared information, the decision maker gauges the punitive risks he runs as he contemplates performing the instrumental activities related to a particular role. The Congressman from a closely contested district runs greater risk of reelection defeat if he offends some organized group than does the Congressman from a "safe" one-party constituency. All the latter has to do is obtain his party's nomination, while the former must not only be nominated by his party but also attract a winning coalition of interests in a highly competitive campaign situation.

Role Structure

A *role structure* may be conceived as the total and particular set of roles and their information units stored in the decision maker's memory in his lifetime. The role structure (similar to the concept personality in some usages) is, accordingly, the individual's subjective organization of the roles he has become informed about in the course of his learning.

A role, in this sense, is equivalent to a socially learned mental preparation for the performance of prescribed and relatively standardized patterns of response to specific, probably recurrent situations of choice; failure to perform is perceived by the actor as carrying certain risks he may deem punitive to himself.

Each role in the role structure theoretically has some or all of these types of information. The role structure is a relatively organized set of learned roles in relatively stable relationship to each other in the cognitive structure of particular individuals. On the average, it has been estimated, a mature and civilized adult may learn from twenty to forty roles in his lifetime, with sufficient information about each to make these central to his behavioral responses to the environment.

Role and Choice

In a role-informational conception of personality, the individual is influenced in his choices by the relative weights of different roles in his role structure, particularly those among his ego roles. These weights derive from the sum total of information units, probability estimates, and attitudinal dimensions associated with each role. Consider the voting response of a Republican Catholic in the 1960 presidential choice between Republican Protestant Nixon and Democratic Catholic Kennedy. If the weight of his Republican role is greater than that of Catholic, he will predictably cast his ballot for

Republican Nixon. If his Catholic affiliation and role carry more weight in his role structure, he will vote for Catholic Kennedy. If his roles as Republican and Catholic are of equal weight, he will suffer crosspressure and abstain from making a presidential choice.

The accompanying diagram examines a person whose role structure hypothetically consists of only nine roles: father, husband, Caucasian, lawyer, political party official, landowner, Southerner, Democrat and conservative. Each role is designated by R and a subscript: $R_1 \ldots R_9$. Associated with each of these roles is a set of instrumental activity descriptions learned by the individual; these are designated by the letter a plus subscripts. Let us assume that only a total of twenty-one specific instrumental activities have been learned relevant to the nine roles. For example, one of the learned instrumental activities for the role of Democrat might be "vote the party ticket."

The diagram suggests various aspects of the role-structure model.

Role Structure Diagram

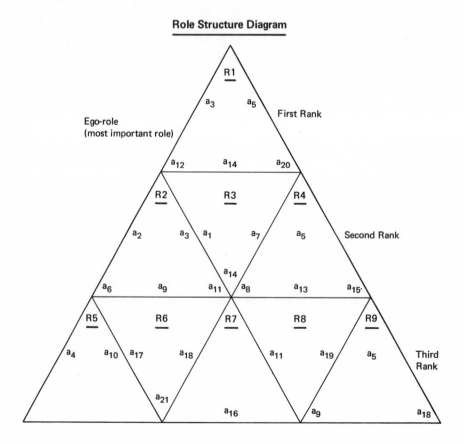

To indicate the relative importance of the particular roles to this hypothetical individual, the diagram indicates that R_1 is of first importance, the next three below are of second rank, and the five roles at the bottom of the triangle are of third rank. Thus, if this decision maker had to choose between an activity associated with R_5 and R_8, he would have great difficulty because both are of equal rank or weight within his role structure. Notice that R_1 is designated as the "ego role" because it is of first importance, in this case, probably the lawyer role.[35]

The twenty-one instrumental activities are distributed among the nine roles, with some appearing in more than one role; e.g., activity a_{11} is, in this example, associated with R_2 and R_8. The activity could be something like "protect the safety and honor of the ladies of the household," a role activity that would be common to both, say, husband and Southerner roles.

From general knowledge of behaviors usually learned in connection with these particular roles, we may hazard many guesses about the personality of this hypothetical nine-role individual. It might even be possible to predict his probable behavior in certain situations; e.g., as a member of the platform committee of a national nominating convention dealing with public policy on racial integration of the public schools. The reader may make his own speculations.

The importance of role structure for decision making, however, has been of little interest in most political research. March, for example, is concerned with the rank ordering of roles and behaviors only as an aspect of a formal theory of influence. Studies of electoral behavior, particularly those at the Survey Research Center at the University of Michigan, touch upon role conflict as a producer of attitudinal cross-pressures, for the more cross-pressured the voter, the later his voting decision and the more likely he will continue to change his mind until later in the election campaign.[36]

The effect of role upon choice may be inferred from a number of studies of role conflict. One study of highly active and progressive union leaders revealed that these individuals perceived their union

---

[35] For a review of gestaltist and other theories of ego as a silent cognitive organizer, Martin Scheerer, "Cognitive Theory," in Gardner Lindzey (ed.), *Handbook of Social Psychology* (Cambridge, Mass: Addison-Wesley, 1954), Vol. I, pp. 111–114.

[36] James G. March, "Measurement Concepts in the Theory of Influence," *Journal of Politics*, 19 (1957); Angus Campbell et al., *The American Voter* (abridged edition; New York: Wiley, 1964), pp. 42 ff.; B. R. Berelson et al., *Voting* (Chicago: University of Chicago Press, 1954), pp. 130 ff.

role as a "calling" in the interest of humanity, requiring a high sense of obligation to fulfill the leadership tasks, a sense of humility about one's own indispensability, and a body of experience that comes with having risen from the rank and file. The job satisfaction of these leaders could not be measured in terms of hours since union officer salaries were not significantly greater than that of the ordinary union member and the hours were certainly much longer in view of the concentration of union activity in the evening. The circumstances thrust upon these progressive union leaders created constant strains with their roles as husbands and fathers. Their own expectations and those of their families included such nonunion role activities as spending greater time with family, dealing with the spouse as wife rather than co-worker, developing a middle-class rather than a proletariat style of life, etc. A discussion of role strains among American elected public officials suggests similar difficulties in the individual's adjustment and decisions.[37]

There is also a situational aspect to the relationship between role and choice. One study examined the racial and action attitudes of the members of two organized groups: one an urban property-owners association, the other a labor union. Among the membership of each group were 151 who had overlapping affiliations. As members of the property-owners association, these 151 individuals acted consistently in an anti-Negro manner, particularly in connection with efforts to resist Negro residential penetration. In the labor union situation, however, in which there was a well-implemented policy of granting Negroes complete job equality, these same persons acted uniformly in a pro-Negro manner.[38]

While students of political behavior have only recently begun to employ role theoretical approaches to investigation of decision making and political socialization, there is some indication that the trend is likely to grow.[39]

[37] Alvin W. Gouldner "Attitudes of 'Progressive' Trade-Union Leaders," *American Journal of Sociology* (1947): 389–92; William E. Mitchell, "Occupational Role Strains: The American Elective Public Official," *Administrative Science Quarterly* (September, 1958): 210–228; and Oscar Grusky, "Role Conflict in Organization: A Study of Prison Camp Officials," *Administrative Science Quarterly*, 3 (March 1959): 452–472. Other studies in role conflict: J. W. Getzels and E. G. Guba, "Role Conflict and Personality," *Journal of Personality*, 24 (1955): 74–85; and John and Jeanne Gullahorn, "Role Conflict and Its Resolution," *Sociological Quarterly*, 4 (1963): 32–48.

[38] Joseph D. Lohman and D. C. Reitzes, "Deliberately Organized Groups and Racial Behavior," *American Sociological Review*, 19 (June 1954): 342–348.

[39] Heinz Eulau, *The Behavioral Persuasion in Politics* (New York: Random House, 1963), and *Political Behavior in America* (New York: Random House, 1966); K. Prewitt et al., "Political Socialization and Political Roles," *Public Opinion Quarterly*, 30 (1966): 569–582.

REFERENCE GROUPS AS THE CONTEXT OF CHOICE

In 1939 Chapman and Volkman hypothesized that the individual's level of aspiration or estimation of his own future performance on a task were anchored in a *frame of reference* consisting of social groups in the individual's psychic environment. College students were asked to predict on a scale their respective performances on a task. The college students were divided into three groups. One of these was told that a group of laborers had performed the task and achieved a specific average score; a second was given an average score presumably produced by other college students; the third was told that college professors had received a given score. The experimental hypothesis: That the college students would predict their own scores as *comparisons* with those of these "anchoring groups," that is, predict their own scores as likely to be lower than the professors', the same as the college students', and higher than the low-status group of laborers. This is exactly what was demonstrated by the results.[40]

The Development of Reference Group Theory

Working from the same theoretical perspective, in 1942 Herbert Hyman employed the term *reference groups* in describing how each individual judges his own status according to values he believes held by groups significant to him. The individual's conception of his own status relative to that of others changed experimentally in the direction of the principal reference group in the individual's mind at different times, according to Hyman's findings.

Newcomb then applied the reference group approach to a study of student values at Bennington College. Newcomb found that some reference groups act as positive and others as negative references. Freshmen at Bennington were usually girls from wealthy and conservative families. However, the faculty, the student leadership, and the majority of the older student body tended to be political liberals. It was found that most freshmen tended to shift from conservative to liberal attitudes on public issues by the time they reached the senior year. Some students, however, retained the conservative atti-

40 D. W. Chapman and J. Volkman, "A Social Determinant of Levels of Aspiration," *Journal of Abnormal and Social Psychology*, 24 (1939).

tudes that they brought from their families. For the latter, Newcomb found that the college was a negative reference group, whereas the family remained a positive reference group. For the students shifting in the liberal direction, it was demonstrated that the college community had become an increasingly positive reference group.[41]

Several years later, in an evaluation of the classic study of the American soldier during World War II, Merton and Kitt employed the reference group concept in explaining certain anomalous findings of the study. The study compared the attitudes of green soldiers (not yet in combat), green replacements (men incorporated into units that had seen combat), and combat veterans with respect to (1) readiness to go into combat, (2) self-confidence in leading men, and (3) physical fitness. It was found that the green soldiers were the most eager to go into combat, followed by the green replacements, with the combat veterans last. Green replacements had the least confidence about leading men but at the same time judged their physical fitness to do so the same as green soldiers and better than the veterans. In explaining the seemingly contradictory results, Merton and Kitt suggested that the green replacements aspired to the more esteemed status of the combat veteran and had adopted in part the latter's attitude toward combat. Among these attitudes were the reluctance to fight and the belief that only combat experience makes one fit to lead.[42]

During the 1950s the reference group approach spread rapidly.[43] Trends in usage were reviewed by Shibutani, who found three general definitions of the concept. The first designates that group which serves as a point of reference in making comparisons or contrasts, especially in forming judgments about one's self. Reference group, in this sense, serves as a standard or checkpoint which an actor uses in forming his estimate of the situation, particularly his own position relevant to it.

A second usage is anticipatory. It refers to that group in which the actor aspires to gain or maintain acceptance, that is, that group

[41] Herbert H. Hyman, "The Psychology of Status," *Archives of Psychology,* 269 (June 1942); Theodore M. Newcomb, *Personality and Social Change* (New York: Dryden Press, 1943).

[42] Robert K. Merton and Alice S. Kitt, "Contributions to the Theory of Reference Group Behavior," in R. K. Merton and P. F. Lazarsfeld, *Continuities in Social Research* (Glencoe, Ill.: Free Press, 1950), pp. 40–105.

[43] The scope and development of the approach is surveyed in Herbert H. Hyman and Eleanor Singer (eds.), *Readings in Reference Group Theory and Research* (New York: The Free Press, 1968).

whose claims are paramount in situations requiring choice by the actor.

A third usage emphasizes the perceptual influence of reference groups. In these definitions, reference group signifies those groups whose norms are used as anchoring points in structuring the actor's perceptual field. Through direct or vicarious participation in a group, one comes to perceive the world from that group's standpoint. Thus, a reference group could be any collectivity, real or imagined, envied or despised, whose perspective is assumed by the actor.

Shibutani's own recommended definition of reference group touches upon many aspects of the approach:

> A reference group, then, is that group whose outlook is used by the actor as the frame of reference in the organization of his perceptual field. All kinds of groupings, with great variations in size, composition, and structure, may become reference groups. Of greatest importance for most people are those groups in which they participate directly—what have been called membership groups—especially those containing a number of persons with whom one stands in a primary relationship. But in some transactions one may assume the perspective attributed to some social category—a social class, an ethnic group, those in a given community, or those concerned with some special interest. On the other hand, reference groups may be imaginary, as in the case of artists who are "born ahead of their times," scientists who work for "humanity," or philanthropists who give for "posterity." Such persons estimate their endeavors from a postulated perspective imputed to people who have not yet been born. There are others who live for a long distant past, idealizing some period in history and longing for "the good ole days," criticizing current events from a standpoint imputed to people long since dead. Reference groups, then, arise through the internalization of norms; they constitute the structure of expectations imputed to some audience for whom one organizes his conduct.[44]

Shibutani further expands the meaning of the notion "perspective" as an activity involving the "definition of the situation." What a man does depends largely upon his "definition of the situation." Further, the manner in which one consistently defines a succession of situations depends upon his organized perspective. A *perspective*, then, is an ordered view of one's world—what is taken for granted

[44] Tamotsu Shibutani, "Reference Groups as Perspectives," *American Journal of Sociology*, 60 (May 1955): 562–569.

about the attributes of various objects, events, and human nature. It is an order of things remembered and expected as well as things actually perceived, an organized conception of what is plausible and what is possible; it constitutes the matrix through which one perceives his environment. The fact that men have such ordered perspectives enables them to conceive of their ever-changing world as relatively stable, orderly, and predictable. One's perspective is an outlined scheme which, running ahead of experience, defines and guides it. Perspectives are continually subjected to the test of reality. All perception is hypothetical. Because of what is taken for granted from each standpoint, each situation is approached with a set of expectations; if transactions actually take place as anticipated, the perspective itself is reinforced. It is thus the confirming responses of other people that provide support for perspectives. Reference groups are the main ingredients and organizing factors in the development and retention of perspectives.[45]

Turner's definition of reference group is essentially the same as Shibutani's, with the additional dimensions of role taking. By imputing roles to others, the actor anticipates responses to his own potential behavior in much the same way that he anticipates the reactions of a reference group.[46]

Reference Groups and Political Choices

In addition to the Bennington study of the effect of reference groups upon the liberal and conservative attitudes of students, numerous other investigations have tended to confirm the usefulness of this approach to decision making. Studies of voting behavior consistently find that an individual's party preference is likely to be the same as that of his closest associates. The child's preference tends to be the same as the father's; husbands and wives tend to vote for the same candidate. To a lesser degree, individuals vote the same way as their friends and co-workers. In the commercial realm, individuals often decide to purchase products or look at television programs

[45] *Ibid.*, pp. 563–569. Also, Alberta E. Siegel and Sidney Siegel, "Reference Groups, Membership Groups, and Attitude Change," *Journal of Abnormal and Social Psychology* (1957): 360–364.

[46] Ralph Turner, "Role-Taking, Role Standpoint, and Reference Group Behavior," *American Journal of Sociology*, 61 (January 1956): 316–28. Also, B. Cohen, "The Process of Choosing a Reference Group," in J. Criswell et al., *Mathematical Models in Small Group Process* (Stanford: Stanford University Press, 1962); J. Sherwood, "Self Identity and Referent Others," *Sociometry*, 28 (March 1965).

suggested by trusted others rather than on any perceived merits. News writing by reporters has been found to be influenced by the reporter's perception of his audience as a reference group.[47]

Perhaps the most dramatic circumstances for observing the effect of reference groups upon decision making is community disaster. In a study of four community disasters involving large-scale explosions and tornadoes, it was found that conflicting reference groups and contradictory roles resulting from multiple-group membership were significant factors affecting individual behavior in critical situations. "What was the first thing you thought of after the disaster struck? What was the first thing you did?" The greatest number of respondents indicated that the choice they faced was one between the family and other groups, principally the employment group or the community. Most persons favored loyalty to the family or to friendship groups, rushing to contact or rejoin their families. Certain roles—policemen, firemen, sometimes refinery workers—that involved substantial learning precisely in anticipation of disaster responded by staying on the job, subordinating all other reference group considerations to those required by their training.[48]

Students of political behavior have yet to make extensive use of reference group theory. A principal hurdle is perhaps the fact that the term lacks adequate operational definition and, like "magnetism," is not likely to be amenable to direct observation except by inference from other events.

An Illustrative Use of the Conceptual Perspective

VOTER AND NONVOTER ROLES IN ELECTION BEHAVIOR

The voter's situation of choice on Election Day has, in the last three decades, been the object of innumerable voting studies provid-

---

[47] Henry W. Riecken, "Primary Groups and Political Party Choice," in Eugene Burdick and A. J. Brodbeck (eds.) *American Voting Behavior* (Glencoe, Ill.: Free Press, 1959); J. W. Riley, Jr., and M. W. Riley, "Reference Groups in the Communication Process," in R. K. Merton et al. (eds.), *Sociology Today* (New York: Basic Books, 1959), pp. 538–561; I. de S. Pool and I. Schulman, "Newsman's Fantasies, Audiences and News Writing," *Public Opinion Quarterly*, 3 (1959): 145–158.

[48] Lewis M. Killian, "The Significance of Multiple-Group Membership in Disaster," *American Journal of Sociology*, 57 (January 1952): 309–314.

ing data about typical responses by individuals with various role characteristics and reference group influences.

Two basic sets of alternatives are available to the eligible voter: (1) to vote or not to vote, and (2) to vote for one party's candidate or another's. Different role and reference group structures respond to these sets of alternatives differently. In connection with the decision to vote or not to vote, the President's Commission on Registration and Voting Participation called attention to two particularly American aspects of the voter's situation of choice:

> It is a tribute to the vitality of our Republic that since the founding of our Nation, we have never canceled or postponed an election scheduled by the Federal or State constitutions or by statute. No civil war, world war, epidemic, or depression has halted our electoral machinery.
>
> It is also significant that throughout our history of unhindered elections, we have maintained a system of voluntary voting. Nothing in this country makes voting mandatory—unless it is the conscience of the voter himself.[49]

In other words, the election as a time of voter decision making has been regularized to an extent unknown in other nations. As a consequence, to a degree not yet measured by research, the American voter approaches the decision of voting or not voting with none of the anxieties experienced by his counterpart in other nations. Elsewhere, in fact, there are circumstances under which the decision to cast a vote may also involve a decision about risking one's life. In the United States, the voter, most of the time and in most places, is free to respond to whatever role, reference group, and other influence may come to mind.

The President's Commission found the political party to be the most influential of the relevant reference groups.

> By far the most important psychological factor affecting an individual's decision to vote is his identification with a political party. A strong Democrat or Republican, as our studies show, is much more likely to cast a ballot than a person who feels little or no allegiance to a party. When an election is expected to be close, the strong partisan is even more inclined to vote.[50]

[49] *Report of the President's Commission on Registration and Voting Participation* (Washington, D.C.: Government Printing Office, 1963), p. 5.
[50] *Ibid.*

Angus Campbell suggests that ego strength may be an important factor in a citizen's decision to go to the polls. A feeling of skill in decision making may be an aspect of ego strength. "People begin at an early age to sense their own capacity to manage the world around them. We think that some people develop a self-confident, positive attitude with which they meet the problems of everday life, while others see themselves as characteristically giving way in the face of environmental pressure, unable to manage the conflicting forces which they encounter."[51] Campbell also reports that political detachment and voting irregularity are found to a disproportionately large degree among persons and groups who are isolated from the larger society. The larger the number of group memberships which a person has, the more likely that he will cast his ballot. In other words, the nonvoter has few social roles in general and probably no political roles in particular that he esteems enough to perform. Put in terms of reference groups, the nonvoting decision maker has in mind few, if any, reference groups whose expectations include the act of exercising his franchise.

Thus, from a variety of conceptual perspectives, the decision *not* to vote becomes a positive, rational act. Low self-esteem, or little ego strength, may place ego satisfaction through voting very low among a citizen's payoffs. From a role perspective, a limited or ambiguous role structure affords few behavioral cues suggesting that voting is a desirable act; this is particularly true if the partisan or citizen roles are lacking. Finally, from the reference group perspective, the fewer groups the decision maker has in mind, the less is the chance that there will be one of them to provide the psychic pull to vote.

Conversely, those who *do* vote are more likely to be men than women. Warren E. Miller, looking at the woman's role in modern society, concludes that "many American women of today still reflect in their own behaviors and attitudes the expectations which society had for women of another generation." In rural areas, "politics is a man's business." Previous generations produced fewer educated women, making irrelevant the fact that formal education facilitates participation in politics. Among parents of young children, wives consistently vote less regularly than do their husbands.[52]

51 "The Passive Citizen," *Acta Sociologica*, 6 (1962): 9 ff.
52 "The Political Behavior of the Electorate," in Earl Latham et al. (eds.), *American Government Annual, 1960–1961* (New York: Holt, Rinehart and Winston, 1960), pp. 40–48.

Very young voters and very old voters tend to get to the polls less regularly, if at all, than voters in the age range between thirty and fifty-five. At the youthful side, the new voter is, of course, unaccustomed and perhaps nervous about his new role as an elector. Young voters are also less settled in their group affiliations through marriage, occupation, residence etc., hence remain less influenced by such reference groups. At the older end of the scale, there are the obvious inhibitions created by physical infirmity. There is also, particularly among those over seventy, a tendency toward withdrawal and isolation associated with retirement.

According to Miller, "the relationship between income and turnout has remained as regular and dependable as death and taxes." Of all the families with income under $2,000 in 1948, 54 in every 100 had eligible voters who failed to go to the polls; in the late 1950s, this level remained approximately the same at 48 percent. On the other hand, persons with family incomes of $5,000 and over failed to go to the polls during this period in only 17 or 18 percent of the cases. However, dollar income is, as every student of electoral behavior appreciates, simply a convenient quantitative way of summarizing a number of group factors that go with income. The poor are likely to be less educated, less occupationally skillful, less affiliated with social and political groups, less complicated in reference group structure, and less ego-involved in political life.

Family income distribution, however, is hardly a static condition of American life. Despite the justifiable complaint that the value of the dollar has declined, proportionately more American families are receiving relatively higher incomes than ever before in American history. In 1935–1936, about 82 percent of the families had annual incomes of $2,000 or less. By 1948 the percentage dropped to 25. In 1965, as few as six percent of American families had annual incomes of less than $2,000. Acknowledging that $2,000 in 1965 was equivalent to about $800 in 1936 purchasing power, and setting aside the moral issue of economic justice for the poor, one inescapable inference is that, in the last thirty years, a significantly larger proportion of American families have a larger number of dollar units with which to make economic decisions.

The spreading practice in decision making about economic matters has had an apparent correlated consequence for the practice of decision making in political matters. Contemporary interest in participatory democracy is possibly a reflection of the rapidly growing numbers of Americans with experience in economic decision making, in contrast to earlier decades when decision opportunities were fewer and decision skills less. Thus, for example, only about 52 percent of the voters eligible to cast their ballots in presidential elections turned out in the early 1930s; participation approached 70 percent during the 1960s. Perhaps the most fundamental relationship between relative increase in income and relative rise in voting turnout is the simple fact that ego involvement and decision experience in the former carried over into the latter.

Collective Decision Making

Decision theorists have speculated about the distinction, if any, between choice as an individual act and choice as the collective act of individuals in a group. One significant distinction is that the group establishes a decision rule, that is, the conditions under which an "ultimate" decision making authority shall prevail. These collective decision rules are usually overt, costly to the group, and endowed with a quality called legitimacy. Decision rules may be classified into three basic types: verbal, violent, and numerical. Each type employs a characteristically different method for signaling that the group has reached a choice. The method of words does something with language, as in the filibusters of the U.S. Senate or the confirmed hypotheses of scientists. The method of violence does something with weapons, from brandishing them to destroying an adversary with them. The method of numbers, usually employing votes, seeks to measure the existing ratio between consent and dissent within the group. In addition to its decision rule, the collective as decision maker is also confronted with the necessity of perceiving and analyzing its situation of choice. Some members may see no predicament demanding a decision, although others do. Situational analysis, for all its importance, is a little-developed aspect of decision theory.

6

Theoretical Aspects of Group Choice

Individuals and groups are distinct types of "decision makers." Although choice is generally considered a personal act, decisions can also be made by individuals acting collectively. A family ordinarily acts as a collective decision maker, with much informality. On the other hand, a nation and its constituent parts—the legislature, the bureaucracy, the courts, the electorate, etc.—arrive at collective decisions with much formality. The family decision is somehow a different kind of event from the decision of any one of its members, just as the decision of a legislature is somehow distinct from that of any one of its legislators.

What marks the difference between individual decision making and collective decision making? Early sociologists, perhaps influenced by the general will conceptions of Rousseau, wrote of *group mind* as a part of a mystical "super-individual" with an existence separate from that of the individuals composing it. Emile Durkheim and Gustave LeBon were considered group mind theorists. These men and their successors tended to focus upon the behavior of crowds and mobs, and on crazes and other types of "abnormal" collective action. Later writers, such as Walter Lippmann and John Dewey, concerned themselves with the study of *publics;* Jose Ortega y Gasset examined *masses,* and Hadley Cantril *social movements.* Today, sociology has a major subfield called *collective behavior,* which usually gives only passing mention to collective *decision* behavior as such.

Upon reviewing the analytical components of the decision process noted in the preceding chapter, a number of differences between individual and collective decision become apparent. As a *type of actor*, the collectivity seems to be more numerous than any one individual; yet, from the decision point of view, what type is the group whose choices are all made for it by a single person? It would also seem that a group, with its many pairs of eyes, could more readily perceive a situation-of-choice; but, what of those failures in collective perception that are so often capitalized on by a skilled dissenter or some charismatic personality? As for the perception of decision alternatives, many eyes are again usually considered better than a single pair; yet, many political arrangements, such as the two-party system, devote enormous energy to reducing the available alternatives to a number small enough to be manageable for collective choice. In short, the components of *individual* decision making seem compounded and complicated in *collective* decision making, but most analytical distinctions between the two soon blur. Yet, there *is* a distinction.

VERBAL, VIOLENT, AND NUMERICAL COLLECTIVE DECISION RULES

The critical question about *collective* decision making is put as follows by Buchanan and Tulloch: "How shall the dividing line between collective action and private action be drawn? What is the realm for social and for private or individual choice?" This is invariably the first important choice that the group must make before it can proceed to anything else.

The Group's Decision Rule

Since decision making is inescapably an individual act, collective action requires some method for summarizing individual decisions on behalf of group objectives. Buchanan and Tulloch elaborate the problem further:

> The selection of a decision-making rule is itself a group choice, and it is not possible to discuss positively the basic choice-making of a

social group except under carefully specified assumptions about [such] rules. We confront a problem of infinite regression here. Individuals cannot competently choose between collective and private action in a particular area until the results of alternative choices are analyzed. Private action, at its simplest, presents little difficulty; the ultimate decision-maker is assumed to be the acting individual. However, collective action is wholly different. Before it can be properly assessed as an alternative to private choice, the ultimate decision-making authority must be specified. Is a simple majority to be controlling? Or must collective decisions be made only upon the attainment of full consensus? Or is there a single-minded ruling class or group? The individual's evaluation of collective choice will be influenced drastically by the decision rule that he assumes to prevail. . . . How is the rule itself chosen?[1]

The "problem of infinite regression" is a fundamental and compelling one when the collectivity initially considers what shall be its first decision rule. Failure to make such a rule reduces the prospect of any collective decision; the collectivity may have a common purpose, but it is not likely to be able to make decisions about implementing it. This condition is frequently observed when factions within new political communities contend with each other, defect, revolt, or initiate "wars of liberation." Their problem is to create the basic design of a national decision rule and to determine who shall follow it. Often civil wars are expressions of major dissatisfaction with the existing decision rule. Prior to the American Civil War, for example, the South had become unhappy over its disappearing access to the Presidency, its deteriorating balance-of-power position in Congress, and its diluted veto power in the Democratic national convention. The Southern states seceded in the expectation of setting up a new collectivity with "better" decision rules. "Infinite regression," therefore, refers to the group's incapacity to remain a group if it fails in that initial decision: the choice of a rule by which decisions shall be made by the collectivity.

As Buchanan and Tulloch correctly point out, "The attainment of consent is a costly process." Not only is there a cost in the decision act itself but also a cost estimation that must be made by the individual member concerning the drawing of a line between his private choice and that of the collectivity. He must find it advantageous or profitable to agree *in advance* to a decision rule which

[1] James M. Buchanan and Gordon Tulloch, *The Calculus of Consent* (Ann Arbor: University of Michigan Press, 1962), pp. 5–6.

he realizes could occasionally work to his disadvantage. He must expect the benefits by and large to exceed the costs. Basically, this cost estimation involves weighing the value of the collective objective against the concessions that may have to be made in giving up personal prerogative. If there is distrust within the group, the odds are against agreement about anything, and particularly about a stable collective decision rule. The "group" is likely to fall apart. On the other hand, mutual trust and intensely shared goals will tend to facilitate the critical initial choice of a decision rule.[2]

The characteristics of collective decision rules are (a) overtness, (b) cost, and (c) legitimacy.

When an individual makes a choice, his procedure for doing so may be covert and private. If he is at all ambivalent or hesitant, this state of mind may be repressed or concealed. Within the individual's mind, there is no need to make ambivalence overt or to measure its degree. In collective decision making, however, the requirement is quite different. Something overt and observable must occur if the group is to recognize that it has arrived at a decision. Further, the decision rule needs to provide members and observers with some measurement of the relative degrees of consent and dissent regarding the alternatives. The sociologist Simmel referred to this as a need for "some quantitative ratio of harmony and disharmony." In short, the collective decision rule, if it is to be practical, must be observable and, in some sense, measurable.

A second characteristic of collective decision rules is their costliness. As each of us has undoubtedly experienced, making personal choices is often a laborious act. Sometimes we conclude that some goals may simply not be worth the decision-making effort; e.g., the decision between two low-quality movies or the decision between two objectionable candidates for public office. Such personal decision costs rarely require public accounting in quite the same way that the costs of a collective decision do. If the collective decision rule calls for a public election, that election must be paid for from the public treasury. Political parties and legislative assemblies expend substantial private and public resources for the implementation

---

[2] *Ibid.*, p. 7. Another approach to the economic theory of constitutions and collective decisions is offered by James S. Coleman, "Collective Decisions," *Sociological Inquiry* (Spring 1964): 166–181. Coleman attempts to show how rational self-interested actors can engage in collective decisions without falling into a Hobbesian war of all against all. See also Julian Feldman and H. E. Kanter, "Organizational Decision Making," in James G. March (ed.) *Handbook of Organizations* (Chicago: Rand McNally, 1965).

of party and public decision rules. If, as in the international community, the decision rule involves the exercise of military force, this too is obviously costly. The yardsticks of cost are of course many, and money is only one of them.

Legitimacy, the third characteristic of a collective decision rule, is perhaps the most elusive. Legitimacy involves attitudes of acceptance and expectations of consistency. Acceptance is sometimes inferred from the absence of challenge and dissent. From this point of view, a legitimate decision rule is one that remains unchallenged or survives challenges, acquiring with use the authority of precedent. For example, the state party-ticket winner-take-all practice in the Electoral College procedure for choosing the President has been challenged from time to time over several generations, yet it remains the legitimate procedure. Similarly, in international politics, war continues to be an accepted mode of decision; the entire body of international law of war is premised upon this legitimacy.

Examination of the human experience in creating and applying collective decision rules suggests that most may be classified according to three basic types: the method of words, the method of violence, and the method of numbers. Definitions and examples of verbal, violent, and numerical collective decision rules follow.[3]

The Method of Words

The method of words employs spoken and written signals, usually in the form of language, as means for consummating a choice. Language, we must remember, is a tool. Language enables one group member to tell another something about the situation of choice as seen by the *first person*. Language also reveals the first person's preference about things. Language is an aid to perception, and perception is a vital aspect of the decision-making process, particularly in situations of choice, perceived behavior alternatives, and instrumental information.

Imagine some cave-dwelling Mr. Flintstone giving his spouse a verbal directive: "Let's get moving!" Imagine the lady-of-the-cave

[3] A somewhat similar typology is offered by Anatol Rapaport, *Fights, Games and Debates* (Ann Arbor: University of Michigan Press, 1961). According to Rapaport, the object of the *fight* is to eliminate the opponent. The *game* is a conflict situation in which decisions are made in order to outwit the opponent. The *debate*, on the other hand, endeavors to convince the opponent, mainly through communicative activity.

dissenting with a simple "No!" The next step in this collective decision process will depend on the family decision rule. If Flintstone is a man of action as well as the principal decision maker, he will probably grip the lady's curls and yank her along. If the family has a more verbal style, Flintstone may inquire: "Why not, dear?" To help the family along its verbal route to decision, Mrs. Flintstone might reply: "The baby is sick" or "My leg is broken." The verbal exchange facilitates the group decision process by providing Mr. Flintstone with new data and new perceptions regarding the difficulties associated with his proposal to "get moving." Knowing more about the capacity of the group to move, he may now reconsider and perhaps withdraw the proposal. A collective decision has thus been reached.

How does the verbal type of collective decision rule meet the test of explicitness in providing a measure of the ratio between consent and dissent? Manifestation and measurement vary for at least three kinds of verbal rule: (1) those verbal rules that manifest variations in amount and intensity of communicative activity, as in the cases of Quaker meetings and Senate filibusters; (2) those verbal rules that involve definition of linguistic terms, as we often find in ideological debates; and (3) those verbal rules which require that linguistic statements be submitted to the tests of observation and measurement, as in the presentation of evidence in courts and the empirical validation of scientific hypotheses.

The collectivity moves itself toward decision with the first type of verbal rule by observing rates and intensities of communicative activity. A Quaker meeting is of this type. Quakers do not decide by voting. Instead, words and gestures flow back and forth until the "sense of the meeting" is reached. The specific, overt event that indicates such a "sense of the meeting" is the significant decline in the amount and intensity of the discussion, leading eventually to a discontinuation of discussion and prolonged silence. When there is nothing further said, all members of the congregation assume that the points of disagreement have been expressed and adjusted.

Another example of this first verbal type of decision rule is the privilege of unlimited debate in the United States Senate, the rule that makes possible the filibuster. This is a talking activity if ever there was one! Whether conducted by Southern senators against a civil rights bill or liberal senators against private control of a satellite telecommunication corporation, the filibuster is a verbal yardstick of the intensity of dissident feeling of a minority in the Senate. A filibuster may decide the fate of a proposed piece of legislation. Aware that today's majority on one issue may contain elements of tomorrow's dissenters on another, the members of the Senate are most reluctant to circumscribe this precious decision rule regarding unlimited debate.

A second verbal type of decision rule invokes the logic of linguistic definition.[4] Verbal communication continues until a particular terminology and definition prevails. A collective decision may be manifest in the agreements reached regarding the use of terms in, for example, the statute writing of legislative assemblies, the platform writing of political parties, the writing and interpreting of constitutions, and the definitional issues in ideological propositions. A substantial part of the civil rights movement has been a struggle over the definition of the term "equal." At one time the Supreme Court interpreted the law of the land to mean that "equal" rights of Negroes were not infringed upon if provision was made for "separate but equal" schools, public accommodations, etc. This conception of equality was unacceptable to many Americans, and the Supreme Court was repeatedly asked to clarify its definition. In the 1954 school integration cases and others, the Court removed the "separate but" phrase, and "equality" took on the connotation of "equal access" and "equal opportunity." The verbal decision rule had, for the time, led to a terminological redefinition by the Federal courts.

There is a third variety of verbal rule, perhaps not ordinarily noticed as a type of decision rule. This third type submits the meaning of language to the tests of observation. A "fact," after all, is only a verbal statement about the *observable* characteristics of a state of affairs in the world. The observations may be made by each of us personally or by others who report to us what they have seen. Lawyers reconstruct the circumstances of an event by calling on witnesses to testify. Newspapermen report events by going out to observe them personally or by interviewing others who have. The biochemist in the laboratory gathers observations about the reaction of Virus A to Chemical X, and then reports the frequency of that particular reaction in some professional journal. Each of these individuals is reporting *his* observations verbally.

The trouble begins when different persons see the same event differently. The Japanese movie *Rashomon* illustrates dramatically

4 See Chapter 3.

how the very same event may be seen and interpreted very differently by different persons. Ordinarily, one man's word may be sufficient to raise an issue, propose a hypothesis, or win acceptance of a piece of evidence; however, according to the scientific rules, that individual's word alone can never be sufficient to establish a "fact." If only one source offers the information, we may—we must—be skeptical, particularly since a biased or erroneous observation may misdirect important decisions, such as a judgment of murder in a court or an act of war between nations.

Scientists, therefore, are people who are in constant, fairly systematic controversy about "facts" that bear upon topics of concern to them. In recent years we have seen how noted physicists argued about the *rate* of fallout resulting from atomic tests. That controversy was more or less decided by developing and applying instruments to measure fallout rate. Then the argument shifted to the amount of fallout that may contaminate food and endanger health and genetic normality.

In this way, scientists in every field of knowledge regularly argue with each other. Their main professional pursuit consists of producing observations about the environment that dependably explain relations in that environment. Fundamentally, their verbal procedures work as follows. A statement is made that "when variables A and B occur together with some observed degree of frequency, then event E tends also to occur." For example, "when humidity (variable A) is high and air pressure (variable B) is low, then rain (event E) tends to occur." That is science. A statement is made in a relatively standard form. Its elements are subjected to observation. The relationships among the elements are measured as to degree and frequency. Confirmatory observations decide the question raised by the hypothesis, a part of a verbal decision rule.

But the evidence is not always well confirmed or politically acceptable. Sometimes a scientist may find himself characterized as "subversive" or "treasonous" for his statements. In earlier ages, men like Galileo found themselves charged with heresy. Such a man makes statements reporting his observations about the environment and invites others to verify his statements by looking at the same phenomenon (thereby following the decision rule of scientists). Others, however, may refuse to look, for fear of being tricked or bewitched into giving up long-held beliefs. Before Galileo, for example, men generally believed the following statement about falling objects: "If one object weighs 100 times as much as another object, the first object will fall to earth 100 times as fast as the second." Philosophers and gentlemen argued the logic of this statement for centuries in universities and in salons. Galileo, however, submitted the statement to an observational test. He actually dropped two objects of unequal weight from an upper gallery of the leaning tower of Pisa, and found that, as an observable matter of fact, the objects fell at relatively equal speeds. That evidence should have decided the matter—and eventually it did. But, first, as we know, Galileo was berated by those committed to earlier beliefs.

The cost of the method of words will be discussed in a later section of this chapter. Notice, however, the ancient saying: "Talk is cheap." Skepticism notwithstanding, if talk prevents serious misperception or error of judgment, talk must be counted as cheap because of the greater costs it may prevent.

On the legitimacy of verbal decision rules, more will be said below. At this point, simply note what proponents of democracy and liberty traditionally say about the legitimate grounds for freedom in discussion in arriving at collective decisions:

> So far as the society exists by dynamic process, it exists for and by the mutual interchange of conceptions and convictions about the good to be obtained in human life and the methods for its attainment. It thus exists for and by a system of social discussion, under which each is free to give and receive, and all can freely join in determining the content or substance of social thought—the good to be sought, and the way of life in which it issues. Now, such discussion is also . . . the essence of democracy.[5]

The Method of Violence

Ordinarily, the method of violence assumes the use of physical means—rocks, bullets, atom bombs—to eliminate those who disagree by placing them in a condition of extreme pain, discomfort, deprivation, or reduced resources.

Most human beings have come to believe that damage to the human body, aggravation of physiological needs such as thirst or hunger, and loss of life are deprivational, and, therefore, *most* human beings submit when confronted with the prospect of such depriva-

---

[5] Ernest Barker, *Reflections on Government* (New York: Oxford University Press, 1942), p. 19. See also, Edith Becker Bennet, "Discussion, Decision, Commitment, and Consensus in 'Group Decision'," *Human Relations* (1955), pp. 251–273.

tion through violence to themselves. However, there is a significant difference between "most" and "all." The difference always comes as a surprise and a shock to tyrants who, despite their extensive use of the method of violence, find that *some* people, such as martyrs and members of an underground, continue to disagree regardless of risks to life and limb. This is the essence of Patrick Henry's call for "liberty or death."

Violent decision rules almost always involve throwing objects at each other—rocks, bullets, bombs—and taking things away from each other, such as life, health, and property. Over the centuries men have excercised great ingenuity in the perfection of instruments of violence. Some of these may be observed in international wars in which the arsenals of great nations are devoted to efforts at mutual destruction of people and property. Domestic violent decision making occurs in revolutions and civil wars. Genocide and purges conducted by those who control a government are aimed at the physical removal of entire minorities. Assassinations, coups d'etat, and other types of political murder are also familiar manifestations of decisive violence. From the medieval rack to modern brainwashing, physical torture has also been a recurrent method of violence.

How do the users of the method violence go about making explicit and measuring the ratio of consent and dissent? There seem to be at least three basic procedures: (1) the weapons-and-willingness procedure; (2) the nonverbal threat; and (3) the actual employment of weapons.

The first procedure tests the availability of weapons and the possessor's willingness to use them in a situation of severe disagreement. Counting other nations' weapons is the major preoccupation of spies and embassies around the world. In making guesses about which nation is capable of disagreeing with which other, information about weapons on hand is essential. Although neither could stand up alone against the United States or the Soviet Union, Israel and Egypt, for example, have sufficient weapons on hand to be able to disagree with each other quite meaningfully. Fidel Castro's past disagreements with and threats against the United States would seem silly if it had not been for the sudden placement of nuclear missiles on that island by the Soviet Union; this converted the Cuban-American dispute into a Soviet-American one. Since the United States and the Soviet Union are the two nations with the largest and most destructive supply of weapons on hand, all nations having disputes with other nations are, of course, eager to draw these two into the argument. With such Goliaths of weaponry involved, every small dispute may thus take on special meaning for the entire world. Often it takes as much, if not more, effort on the part of the United States and Soviet Union to *stay out* of small-nation or local disputes as it does to intervene. Thus, for Castro's Cuba to threaten an attack on the United States is ludicrous—except in the context of supporting assertions from Russia.

To own a rifle or even 33,000 nuclear warheads is one thing. To be willing to fire is quite another. A terror-stricken rifleman incapable of pulling the trigger is worse than no rifleman at all; he is preventing effective use of the weapon and may be distracting his fellow soldiers to the extent that they may need to boost his courage or take the weapon from him. Similarly, the nation with the overwhelming arsenal of 33,000 nuclear warheads that betrays an unwillingness to use them in disagreements with another equally powerful nation might as well have saved the money it spent for these warheads. A nuclear stockpile is meaningless without the willingness to use it "if necessary."

It is probable that the installation of missiles in Cuba in 1962 was in fact a Soviet test of American willingness to use its weaponry decisively in objection to Soviet nuclear warheads in Cuba. Adolph Hitler made such tests of Franco-British willingness to use weapons in the Rhineland in 1936, Austria in 1938, the Sudetenland and Czechoslovakia in 1939, and finally in Poland. Franco-British hesitancy at each probe set the stage for the next test. Hitler's probes were hardly different from the Soviet Union's in Berlin in 1948, in North Korea in 1948 and 1949, in Cuba in 1962, and elsewhere. The consistent and explicit response of the United States at each test was a demonstration of willingness to use its weapons on hand: the airlift in Berlin, the war in North Korea, the quarantine of Cuba, etc. This willingness was decisive.

A second procedure of ratio finding among the violent decision rules is the nonverbal threat. A *verbal* threat is usually a combination of verbal and violent methods, that is, a combination of weapons display and threatening communication. A nonverbal threat is a gesture without words, whose implications are usually ambiguous. The nonverbal threat goes somewhat further than weapons display and indications of willingness to use them; the nonverbal threat may actually set some of the weaponry into place and operation *as though* it were already being expended. There is much bluff as well as ambiguity associated with this technique. The presence of the Seventh Fleet in the Straits of Formosa during the Quemoy-Matsu crisis between Communist China and our ally Nationalist China is an example of nonverbal threat. The ambiguity of this technique, however, may lead to grave misreadings of intentions, as in the case of the withdrawal of American forces from South Korea in 1949–1950, which was interpreted by Communist China as evidence of American disinterest in the future of this area.

A third procedure for ratio measuring is the accounting that takes place with the actual employment of weapons. The aggressive talk of military extremists and advocates of preventive war notwithstanding, the truly skillful party to violent decision rules is always reluctant to fire his weapons. A bullet shot is a bullet expended, forever gone. The strategies of violence are often more conservative than is recognized: "It's cheaper to scare them than to kill them." The employment of weapons is costly and risky. The skillful employer of the method of violence will do so when he estimates a high return at a low cost, which is what happened when Mussolini invaded Ethiopia in 1935 and Nehru took over Goa in 1961.

Whichever the technique of ratio measuring, the method of violence must rest upon the availability of physical means for destroying an adversary or reducing his capacity to disagree during the collective decision making process. The costs of violent methods of decision are relative, ranging from apparently low-cost border harassments to the exorbitant arms races of major nuclear world powers. The legitimacy of the method of violence is usually justified by the absence of any other effective type of decision rule.[6]

The Method of Numbers

The third type of decision rule is the method of numbers. The numerical unit usually used is the vote. The numerical method gives the ratio of consent to dissent its most explicit and precise quantitative expression.

Although voting with wooden pellets or ballots goes as far back as the third century B.C. in India and the first century B.C. in Rome,

---

[6] For a critique of various theories of violence and a view of violence as an aspect of a political bargaining process, see H. L. Nieburg, *Political Violence* (New York: St. Martin's Press, 1969).

voting and numerical procedures for reaching group decisions became a matter of philosophical discussion only as recently as the Middle Ages. At that time, the medieval Roman Catholic Church adopted voting procedures, particularly in papal elections, and embarked upon a theoretical discussion of the reasons for counting votes one way rather than another. The method of numbers, therefore, is a relatively recent invention compared with the antiquity of verbal and violent methods.

The principal element of the numerical decision rule is the vote. In general, this type of decision rule allows the faction with the greatest number of votes at the time of decision to commit the entire collectivity to a course of action. The collective decision process is thus directed toward the mobilization of the greatest number of votes. Since votes are precisely quantifiable, it is possible to reduce to explicit ratios the proportions of agreement and disagreement within the total eligible body of voters. Within this basic quantitative framework, the combinations and permutations of specific voting arrangements seem infinite, varying with collective responses to questions such as the following:

1. Who shall be permitted to participate in the group's elections? This has usually been argued as a question of suffrage. In the last two hundred years, popular sovereignty has been given practical effect in the decision making of nations by successive extensions of the suffrage. One by one, property restrictions, religious restrictions, racial restrictions, restrictions based upon sex, and other impediments have been set aside as more and more of the populations of the world have acquired the vote.

2. How shall the units of influence, that is, the votes in the final decision, be apportioned among the eligible participators? The issue of apportionment of votes is a recurrent one. In the medieval systems, societies were divided into classes, which led to the apportionment of voting strength roughly on the basis of "one class, one vote," as in the early arrangements in Britain's parliament. Apportionments have since been made in a growing variety of ways, and today in the United States we see prevalent the principle "one man, one vote" which is presumably the ultimate measure of equality of persons in a society.

3. When may the method of numbers be employed in the col-

lectivity's decisions? When does voting take place? The arrangements are many: at some time during a crisis; after a given
number of readings of a proposal; at regular intervals of time
(as in most American elections to public office), and so on.
The occasion for a vote may profoundly affect the outcome
of an election, since opinion and participation may vary greatly
with crisis, season, and even day of the week. (Relative turnout is largest on Sundays.)

4. What quantitative performance, or ratio of consent to dissent,
    shall signal a conclusive decision on behalf of the entire group?
    Unanimity? A majority of three-fourths, two-thirds, or one-
    more-than-half? A plurality? Should the computed proportion
    be based upon a denominator of all those eligible to vote or
    only of those actually voting? Shall there be a system of
    weighted voting? Whatever the specific ratio and procedure
    of computation, the numerical method does make quantitative
    clarity feasible. Politicians who understand this precision in a
    world beset by political ambiguities cherish the method of
    numbers.

5. In what manner shall the votes be gathered and counted?
    What counting procedures shall be used? A secret ballot may
    very well produce different results from a *viva voce* system.
    Announcement of the vote in one time zone may influence the
    returns in another; East Coast and Midwestern presidential
    election returns have consequences on the West Coast.

6. What activities for influencing each voter's decision shall be
    permitted prior to the final vote? Voters marched to the polls
    under duress obviously behave differently from those who
    may or *may not* vote if they so wish. One of the permitted
    activities most characteristic of democracies is the campaign-
    ing carried on by political parties. Competitive electioneering
    in the United States is probably the most vigorous in the world
    and has probably been a great stimulus to the growth of this
    nation's free press, the relatively high level of information in
    the electorate, and the general responsiveness of American
    politicians to their constituencies.

Obviously the debate regarding the voting arrangements can be
interminable. Once inaugurated, however, a method of numbers may
have important consequences.

While election administration as such is somewhat costly to the collectivity, it is the competitive electioneering that leads to the greatest expenditures. The merits of such costs may perhaps be measured only in comparison with the costs of the verbal and violent types of decision rule. As for the test of legitimacy, a method of numbers often becomes so legitimate that its modification may require substantial political ingenuity, as any legislator who has ever led a campaign for reapportionment will testify.

The Prevalence of Mixed Methods

Collective decision rules are rarely pure types as just described. More commonly, particularly in well-developed and formalized political system, a mixture of methods exists. For example, the United States Senate employs a combination of numerical and verbal methods, usually arriving at decisions by a vote, but frequently enough allowing a filibuster or a committee discussion to decide an issue. In the international arena, all three methods exist side by side: usually verbal in the ideological contest, numerical in the United Nations and similar international agencies, and violent in the wars among competing political systems.

The history of the three types of decision rule—words, violence, and numbers—has yet to be written. Offhand, however, it seems that the method of violence enjoys the greatest antiquity and continues to be our most primitive procedure. Language developed long after brute force, and with its invention came the method of words. Mankind has done a great deal over the last 5,000 years to improve the use of language as a tool of collective decision making. The development of rules of logic, grammar, and scientific procedure continues, but a glance at our daily press promptly reminds us how much further mankind has yet to go. The numerical type of decision rule is of most recent vintage; it is scarcely five centuries old. There is much to be learned about the numerical method, particularly the consequences of various numerical arrangements for the behavior of politicians and citizens. It is difficult to generalize from the experience of older nations in order to help design decision rules for the emergent nations of the contemporary world. We know even less about the best mixture of methods: To what extent can words be separated from violence? How do we go about displacing bullets with ballots?

Procedural Legitimacy and Decision Costs

Why is it that some political collectivities tend to prefer one decision type over others? A talking community such as the British, where the legislative assembly is called Parliament (from the Old French term meaning "to speak"), engaged in internal violence for nearly a millennium, yet remained predisposed toward the method of words until finally the latter prevailed. On the other hand, nations dominated by military experiences, such as those in Latin America, continue to rely mainly on methods of violence. Some nations, such as the United States with its daily stock market reports and baseball statistics, seem to prefer the method of numbers. What are some of the factors that influence these decision rule preferences?

Probably the most important considerations relate to certain underlying assumptions held by different collectivities, assumptions about the nature of man, the prospects for achieving agreement among men, the conclusiveness and hence legitimacy of collective decisions, and the costs of the different types of decision rule.

What does the nature of man have to do with different decision rules? Those who prefer the method of words usually think of man as a rational animal, capable of using language as an instrument of reason and capable of acquiring thereby new perceptions about old problems. Those who prefer to resort to violence usually think of man as a beast of narrow vision to be whipped along toward agreement or even destroyed if excessively unruly. Those who prefer the method of numbers think of man as a self-oriented and self-interested creature whose preferences are changeable and whose support—in numbers—can be solicited, delivered, and counted up.

Similar differences may be found in the assumptions about the prospects of collective agreement and cooperation among men. The word users tend to think that the prospects for human consensus are excellent; the users of violence incline to believe that the chances are small. Those who prefer numerical methods tend to be probabilistic; the chance of agreement among men is variable, but 50-50 often enough to justify resort to numerical arrangements that may be computed and recomputed.

Regarding the degree of consensus desirable, word users seem to incline toward a preference for *total* agreement. Some of the worst dogmatics are found among ideological totalitarians, for whom anything short of total belief in The Word is heresy. And our worst murderers are found among the military totalitarians, for whom anything less than total acquiescence is grounds for war to the death. On the other hand, the users of numerical decision rules tend to be great respecters of relativism in the belief that *partial* agreement may very well be honorable. Those who prefer the method of numbers also tend to assume that few things are as transitory as today's coalition and that "half a loaf is better than none."[7]

How conclusive are group decisions? If *legitimacy* consists of group acceptance of actions arising out of preestablished procedures, then *conclusiveness* is essentially a matter of the legitimacy of a collectivity's decision rule. There are different group assumptions about the legitimacy of the several types of decision rule. For those who prefer the verbal rule, talk could be endless, and this, in a negative way, may be decisive. Thus, a filibuster may properly go on for a long time, probably leaving the issue at hand decided in favor of the status quo. Similarly, those who incline toward the method of numbers tend to believe that votes can be taken again and again, particularly as new support is located. Both talkers and voters also tend to view collective decisions as cumulative rather than conclusive; each decision is viewed as a step forward from the last decision, but rarely, if ever, as a final step. Only total destruction appears to be—yet never is—final and conclusive, and this, of course, is the preferred procedure of the users of violence.

Because methods of words and numbers tend to deny the finality of group choices, collectivities encounter the problem of "infinite regression" noted by Buchanan and Tulloch. As a group that is organizing itself approaches the establishment of that initial collective decision rule, suspicion or competition for influence may easily lead to acts of impatience and destruction by those seeking a "final decision." To become legitimized, a decision rule has to withstand the test of use under conditions of controversy, which is least possible when establishing the *initial* decision rule. The odds, unfortunately, favor resort to the method of violence, followed by reversion to preorganizational relationships.

Finally, there is the issue of costs and risks. Which of the three methods is cheapest and least risky in money, human effort, or other

---

[7] See William H. Riker, *The Theory of Political Coalitions* (New Haven: Yale University Press, 1963), who takes the position that politics is an allocation process wherein decision making is a process of coalition building.

kinds of cost? Which type of rule allows the highest community decisional benefit at the lowest cost and least risk? The answer depends upon the yardstick used to measure expense. The method of words is usually assumed to be low cost, but think where we all could have been if the men who unleashed the first nuclear chain reaction had used "cheap" (poorly confirmed) hypotheses. Users of violence tend to think this method less costly than others because results seem to be achieved more quickly. The violent, however, almost always fail to take into their accounting the price implied by the stricture, "He who lives by the sword dies by the sword." The method of numbers also seems fairly low cost to many until they count how many hundreds of millions of dollars are expended in the competitive elections of Western countries, particularly in American presidential elections.

To shout diatribe *at* The Establishment is different from pronouncing the law *as* The Establishment. To overthrow a regime by violence is different from managing the instruments of violence to maintain law, order, and justice. To be influential as a voting minority is different from becoming the winning, hence the governing, majority. In every case, if a minority fails to have the skill, knowledge, and direction needed to manage itself and its nation were it to become a majority, it does its own cause and the entire body politic a great disservice. It is important not only for the minority but also for the community as a whole to protect itself, through its institutional arrangements for collective decision making, against incompetent minority leaders who happen to win office.

From this point of view, it is possible to grasp the critical significance of certain institutional arrangements designed to channel the method of words toward maximum benefit for the community as a whole, including the preparation of minorities for the responsibilities of governance. Verbal decision rules are significant in revealing disagreement within the existing consensus. This is perhaps the basic motivation for protecting freedom of speech, freedom of the press, freedom of inquiry, the right of petition, and all of the elaborate assurances of due process before the law which give dissenters time to articulate and an opportunity to alter, if possible, the perceptions of the other members of the collectivity.

The traditional defense of these communication freedoms is based, as we have noted, on the assumption that men are rational and that rational men will respond to logical debate. But, as a matter of fact, we find that men are rarely rational. Perhaps a better motivation for protecting these freedoms may be found in some of the consequences of verbal rules in practical operation. For example, when articulated dissent signals divergent perceptions of a situation, a group may in fact be strengthened by this information. The collectivity may not only begin to see the environment differently, but may also improve its control over it.

Further, when words of dissent provide the group with new evidence about the preferences and beliefs of smaller parts of the group, this may give the entire collectivity a better impression of the differences out of which it must build a consensus. Sociologists who have observed deviant behavior in groups such as the Quakers and the Army found that:

> . . . deviant members are important targets toward which group concerns become focused. Not only do they symbolize the group's activities, but they help give other members a sense of group size, its range and extent by marking where the group begins and ends in space. In general, the deviant seems to help give the group structure, a visible "shape." The deviant is someone about whom something should be done, and the group, in expressing this concern, is able to reaffirm its essential cohesion and indicate what the group is and what it can do.[8]

To put it another way, the dictator, who tolerates no ideology other than his own, who allows no opposition press, who stifles freedom of speech and inquiry, and who warps due process before the law into a tool of oppression, cuts off his nose to spite his face. That dictator puts himself in the unenviable position of sooner or later falling out of touch with the realities of his regime. Indeed, the most difficult lesson for totalitarians to understand is the experience of all their predecessors in history: The greatest evil in governing a people is to deny them the right to see evil, hear evil, and speak evil. This is the fatal flaw in every totalitarian regime.

Since the method of violence continues to be so prevalent, what are some of the institutional arrangements or rules of the game that prevail in order to maximize the collective usefulness of this method? It is an inescapable feature of the human condition that, in the absence of other decision rules, physical might becomes the most

---

[8] Robert A. Dentler and Kai T. Erikson, "The Functions of Deviancy in Groups," *Social Problems* (Fall 1959): 98–107.

significant way of "making right." The nation without weapons capacity, without willingness to use such capacity, and without a record of skill in weapons employment is a nation with little influence in international decision making. In a world in which wars continue to be legitimate, peace *and* safety demand practical adjustment to the method of violence.

As for domestic violence, there is the right to bear arms, as written into the U.S. Constitution, and the right of revolution, as so clearly stated in the Declaration of Independence. It is an irrefutable fact of history that the opportunity and the capacity to disagree by employing violence is as much a part of the struggle for human liberty as is freedom of speech and association. Only when opportunities for disagreement are improved or nonviolent methods of decision making are assured, do the violent methods atrophy.

In numerical decision rules, we find the most practical demonstrations of theories of dispersed power. The principle of majority rule is revealed in all its simplicity and strength when analyzed as a type of collective decision rule. In this light, freedom of assembly and association may be seen as valuable aids in the practice of the method of numbers. Of the three types of decision rule, the method of numbers is perhaps the only one with the potentiality for infinite improvement and constant reduction of decision costs.

SITUATIONAL ANALYSIS BY THE GROUP

One of the major components of decision making is the *situation of choice*. Situations consist of "selectively perceived patterns of relationships among events, objects, conditions, and other actors that are organized around a focus which is the center of interest for the decision maker." The individual decision maker may perceive his situation of choice accidentally, by deliberate analysis, through advice by others, or in some other way. Institutionalized groups—sometimes accidentally, more often deliberately—endeavor to regularize various aspects of their situations of choice. The purpose of such regularization is, for the most part, simply to avoid the traumas of surprise situations as well as to give all members a fair opportunity to pull themselves together for the decision act. Thus, legislatures such as Congress have standard occasions for collective decision. This is also true in bureaucracies and courts. Political parties and organized interest groups are particularly resistant to surprise situations of choice and sometimes go to great lengths to avoid them.

What, then, constitutes *situational analysis?* In its broadest sense, the decision maker's *situation* refers to the conditions of his environment that impinge upon his behavior. To understand the manner in which an individual responds to his environment, it is necessary to know what *he sees* of that environment and what it *means to him*. In their pioneering study of acculturation, Thomas and Znaniecki described this with the term "definition of the situation." In his experimental field theory, Lewin argued that the individual's "life-space" or psychological environment was functionally an integral part of his behavior.[9]

One attempt to summarize theoretical features of the "dimensions of situations" was made by Shartle, who identified the following as empirically observable situational variables: distance, structure, stability, threat, newness, status, leadership climate, value climate, supply-demand ratio, and duration. Shartle does not understate the difficulties of situational analysis.

> A situation may be defined as a complex of events occurring at any given time. The events are thus components of the situation. No two situations are exactly alike. Two persons placed in the same physical environment, say, an office, may agree on certain events that form the situation, and disagree on others. An observer may present a third picture, describing the situation that both persons are in. . . . The development of dimensions of situations is a difficult task, but there have been sufficient studies of organizations so that a large number of events can be listed and classified.[10]

Three of Shartle's situational dimensions are *temporal* in character.

(a) How new is the situation to the decision maker? The newness of a situation may introduce elements of caution and restraint that may make behavior difficult to predict. This is why institutionalized collectivities are so reluctant to deal with spontaneous, ad hoc, or spurious situations. Familiar situations that may be handled by fa-

---

[9] W. I. Thomas and F. Znaniecki, *The Polish Peasant in Europe and America* (Boston: Badger, 1918); Kurt Lewin, "Group Decision and Social Change" in E. E. Maccoby et al. (eds.), *Readings in Social Psychology* (New York: Henry Holt, 1958), pp. 197–211.

[10] Carroll L. Shartle, "Value Dimensions and Situational Dimensions in Organizational Behavior," in *Proceedings of the Tenth Annual Meeting, Industrial Relations Research Association* (1958), pp. 303–313.

miliar patterns of response are preferred as grist for the institutional decision mill.

(b) How long has the situation existed? If it is of long duration, it may be guessed that the collectivity has "adjusted" to the situation, hence reducing the prospect of decisions leading to change. For example, if the deprivations of a political minority have long endured, it becomes difficult for the rest of the collectivity to see such conditions as a situation requiring group action. Whether it is the social plight of a racial minority or the inequities that malapportionment brings to an urban community, the older the situation, the more difficult it is to get the community to perceive it as "due for a change."

(c) How stable is the situation in which choice is to be made? Are the elements in the situation likely to remain in relatively consistent relation to each other? Stability refers to the "steady states" or "equilibrium" aspects of a situation. The less stability, the greater the uncertainty and, presumably, the more intense the search for information to reduce that uncertainty. Conversely, the more stable the situation, the more readily can the group "program" responses to it. Control over the agenda of its decision time is perhaps one of the most valued resources of an institutionalized group.

A second type of situational variable in Shartle's list is *spatial*. What is the physical distance of the decision maker from the problem or situation that will be acted upon? Behavioral scientists have recently become interested in the behavioral consequences of "territoriality," that sense of possession or involvement with geographical environment that apparently motivates persons as well as animals. From this point of view, the closer the physical proximity of the situation to the decision maker, the greater its salience for him and the more likely will it provoke a response. A taxpayer is usually more willing to pay the price of a police force if there have been recent robberies in his own neighborhood or a fire department if he has seen a neighbor's house burn down. The family with an elderly retiree to support is more likely to applaud a social security retirement system. The closer an international aggressor comes to one's own borders, the greater is one's devotion to international arrangements for collective security.

Several situational variables relate to the *social structure* within which the situation occurs.

(a) Where in the status structure is the decision maker? A high-status individual or group is likely to be better informed, perceive a wider range of available alternatives, and be more willing to act with independence. Members of low-status groups are likely to be more dependent upon their leaders for decision cues.

(b) How structured is the group environment within which choice is to take place? Are the goals relatively well defined and explicit? Is the position structure readily identified? Is it relatively clear which persons are responsible for the tasks of particular positions? Has the socializing of position incumbents been sufficiently regularized to make the behavior of incumbents predictable? Are relations among groups fairly well defined? The less structured the group environment, both internal and external, the less predictable the interaction among situational elements.

(c) What is the "leadership climate" within which collective action takes place? Because leaders are specialized individual decision makers within the group, their characteristics—perception, initiative, information, value preferences, and so on—are particularly strategic in defining situations of choice for the collectivity. If the "climate" provides leaders' actions with legitimacy and support as well as opportunities for personal as well as collective satisfactions, leadership impact upon the situation of choice is likely to be substantial. On the other hand, a decision-making climate that is constrictive and punitive to leaders is likely to produce in them attitudes of caution, inflexibility, and even withdrawal.

(d) A situation's "supply-demand ratio" refers to the available resources perceived by the decision maker as relevant to the situation of choice. If the problem is hunger, how does the size of the available food supply relate to the estimated need? If the problem is employment, what is the ratio between the number of unemployed and the number of available jobs. As often happens, a group that sees itself without necessary resources for meeting a large need may be unwilling to acknowledge that a situation of choice confronts it. This ostrich attitude is a particularly familiar one in poverty-stricken communities.

Finally, a fourth set of situational variables appears to be *psychological*. The psychological aspects of a situation of choice can of course become as numerous as the analyst's conceptual categories. For example, what is the typical cognitive structure of the members of the collectivity? What are the perceptual tendencies of the group? What is the general distribution of attitudes and expectations regarding the many elements in the situation of choice? Two psychological variables given particular attention by Shartle:

(a) How threatening is the situation to the decision maker? The greater the apparent threat, the more likely will the group react to the situation in a manner intended to reduce or eliminate the threat.

(b) What is the prevailing "value climate" in the situation? Will the outcomes preferred by individual members and leaders fall into rankings similar to those of the group as a whole? Or are the payoff priorities within the group poorly correlated? The less correlated the value structure, the more reluctantly will the collectivity perceive the situation as one requiring action.

These four general types of variables are, then, theoretical aspects of any collective decision situation. Situational analysis is obviously a complex process. First, the situational variables must be perceived. Then they must be analyzed. This is accompanied by all the other psychological and collective actions associated with collective decision making.

The consequences of perception and analysis of the situation of choice vary. If situational analysis leads to the collective conclusion that a situation of choice does exist, the group may (a) choose one among its perceived alternatives, (b) postpone or decline to choose among the perceived alternatives, or (c) remain indecisive or inert, suspended in the decision-making process, as it were. Each of these outcomes is a "decision," although sometimes terms such as "indecision" or "non-decision" are applied. On the other hand, if situational analysis leads to the collective conclusion that a situation of choice does *not* exist, the group will not proceed further into the decision process.

In politics, particularly competitive politics, it is common for leaders or bureaucratic organizations to be charged with "inaction" in the face of "crisis situations." The charge, of course, usually comes from some subgroup or faction of the community, and the charge is based upon this subgroup's perception of a situation as "critical," requiring choices to be made. (Much of the recent violence in the black ghettos, for example, has purportedly been aimed at making the American people and its leaders aware of the desperate economic and social condition of most black Americans.) Leaders in public office or in political bureaucracies, given the demands for other kinds of action from other subgroups, may not share such a perception or evaluation. "Inaction" or "non-decision" may therefore be a deliberate act of choice, of "wait and see."

To cope with complex situational analysis, groups and organizations tend to pay substantial attention to the problem of regularizing and institutionalizing their situations of choice. It will be recalled that behavior becomes institutionalized when, to a relatively high degree, its patterns become stable, uniform, formal, and general. In this sense, bureaucracies, legislative assemblies, judiciaries, political parties, and similar political institutions attempt to set forth fairly explicitly their decision rules and their institutional situations of choice.

An Illustrative Use of the Conceptual Perspective

PRESIDENTIAL VETO AS A LEGISLATIVE DECISION RULE

On the Federal level collective decision makers would seem to be the Chief Executive in the executive branch, the two houses of Congress on the legislative side, and the nine-member Supreme Court at the pinnacle of the court system. However, these simple appearances are deceiving; a great variety of collective decision makers and decision rules may be found in each branch.

The President's veto stands as one of the most influential individual decision events in the national government. However, the veto is only one aspect of the President's constitutional participation in the collective decisions of statute making. Section 7 of Article I of the Constitution describes the statute-making decision rule in detail:

> Every bill which shall have passed the House of Representatives and the Senate, shall, before it becomes a law, be presented to the President of the United States; if he approves he shall sign it, but if not he shall return it, with his objections, to that House in which it shall have originated, who shall enter the objections at large on their journal, and proceed to reconsider it. If after such reconsideration, two-thirds of that House shall agree to pass the bill, it shall be

sent, together with the objections, to the other House, by which it shall likewise be reconsidered, and if approved by two-thirds of that House, it shall become a law. But in all such cases, the votes of both Houses shall be determined by yeas and nays, and names of the persons voting for and against the bill shall be entered on the journal of each House respectively. If any bill shall not be returned by the President within ten days (Sundays excepted) after it shall have been presented to him, the same shall be a law, in like manner as if he had signed it, unless the Congress by their adjournment prevent its return, in which case it shall not be a law. [Another paragraph of Section 7 includes under this procedure "every order, resolution, or vote to which the concurrence of the Senate and the House of Representatives may be necessary."]

Thus, the Founding Fathers made the President an integral part of the law-making process whether he exercises a veto or not. The reasons are fully discussed by Hamilton in *Federalist Paper* No. 73. In defense of the separation of powers among the various branches of government, Hamilton noted the "propensity of the legislative department to intrude upon the rights, and to absorb the powers of the other departments." If he had no capacity to exercise a veto over legislative acts, the President would be "absolutely unable to defend himself against the depredations" of the Congress. In fact, "he might be gradually stripped of his authorities by successive resolutions, or annihilated by a single vote." The veto power also "establishes a salutary check upon the legislative body, calculated to guard the community against the effects of faction, precipitancy, or any impulse unfriendly to the public good, which may happen to influence a majority of that body."

Of course, the Founding Fathers were responding to the governmental system of eighteenth-century Britain. There, an angry Parliament had stripped the king of his major executive powers, but had left open the possibility that an angry king might forcibly attempt to end all such arrangements. The Founding Fathers preferred to guarantee both political branches a proper and lasting respect for each other's resources and, to this end, devised the veto of the President on the one hand and the congressional capacity to override a veto on the other.

According to Hamilton, a qualified, or partial, veto could be more readily exercised than a total veto. If as much as one-third of each House concurs in the President's objections to the bill, this, the Founding Fathers believed, would be a sufficient minority to command the respect of the majority. The President would not stand alone but would in effect be responding to a minority large enough to make executive branch execution of the law difficult. "When men, engaged in unjustifiable pursuits, are aware, that obstructions may come from a quarter which they cannot control, they will often be restrained by the bare apprehension of opposition, from doing what they would with eagerness rush into, if no such external impediments were to be feared."

Presidential participation in statute making is an excellent example of the skill with which the Founding Fathers applied the method of numbers in designing collective decision rules for the new national government. Much of their discussion had to do with their anticipation of behavioral responses that politicians might make to various legislative voting arrangements. What they could have only intuitively surmised is the mathematics of the distribution of power they arranged. In fact, one such mathematical analysis has been developed only very recently. Shapley and Shubik devised a "power index" for making an a priori mathematical evaluation of the division of power among members of a numerous body such as Congress. The "power" of an individual member depends on the chance he has of being critical to the success of the winning coalition. Thus, if fifty-one votes are necessary to win a division in the Senate, the pivotal fifty-first vote would be the most powerful; without it, the majority could not be accomplished. That fifty-first vote would therefore bring the highest price if it were for sale, while a fifty-second vote would bring nothing since it would not be necessary. Assuming that each member of the body had an equal chance of becoming "pivotal," he could be credited with having $1/n$th of the power, there being n members in the winning set of votes.

Shapley and Shubik computed the power indices for the three statute-making bodies—House of Representatives, Senate, and President—and found them to be in the proportion 5:5:2. Relative to the two other bodies as a whole, the President has a power index of 1:6. On the other hand, the indices for the President (as a *single* person), a *single* congressman, and a *single* senator (computations were made when the Senate had 96 members) resulted in the proportion 350:2:9, respectively. Thus, the President *as the particular person* capable of making or breaking a piece of legislation is 175 times more powerful than any one congressman and about 39 times more powerful than any single senator. Shapley and Shubik observe:

In a multi-cameral system such as we have just investigated [that is, Congress and the President], it is obviously easier to defeat a measure than to pass it. A coalition of Senators, sufficiently numerous, can block the passage of any bill. But they cannot push through a bill of their own without help from the other chamber.[11]

Such behavioral consequences of the mathematics of the statute-making decision rule are as the Founding Fathers intended. Congressmen, senators, and president would, because of their respective numerical strength within the decision rule, soon realize that they would "need each other" to pass even the most self-interested legislation, but that no legislation was likely to pass if a numerous minority coalition intensely opposed it. The majority could get what it needed if it did not strike at the interests of a substantial minority. What assured this was not any mystical rendering of "majority will" or "minority right," but a specific decision rule whose numerical requirements left no other alternative.

[11] L. S. Shapley and Martin Shubik, "A Method for Evaluating the Distribution of Power in a Committee System," *American Political Science Review*, 48 (September 1954): 787–792. For comment on the power index, William H. Riker, "A Test of the Adequacy of the Power Index," *Behavioral Science* (1959), pp. 120–131.

Leadership and Participation

Some individuals more than others are involved in and skilled at making decisions, and these seem to be among the principal attributes of leaders. Such persons are the subject of that literature referred to as elite and leadership theory. Leadership also appears to be contingent upon acceptance as such by followers. The emergence or selection of a leader is also related to the tensions and values operative in a particular situation. Theorists in this field have taken innumerable other perspectives upon leaders: as exercisers of authority; as controllers of others; as autonomous persons; their significance for statecraft as policy-makers; as distinctive personality types; and as products of a recruitment process. The particular skills of leaders and their numerous roles have also been studied. However, leaders seem most distinct from nonleaders in their behavior in decision situations and in the intensity of their participation in the affairs of political and other groups. As a consequence of the leader's high ego-involvement and the group's need for executives, the investing and divesting of persons with incumbency in offices and other positions, usually under conditions of conflict or competition, is also a process of substantial theoretical and practical interest.

Leaders as Specialized Decision Makers

7

Whenever two or more persons engage in collective activity, at least one of them seems to dominate some or all of the others, for some or all of the activities. Many social scientists enjoy referring to this dominant-submissive pattern as "the pecking order."

More seriously, Plato considered the recruitment and training of leaders as the principal concern of the state. The job of a ruler, he said, is not only to maintain the organization of the society but also to perfect the moral character of its citizens. The two tasks are inseparable; ruling is primarily an educational enterprise, and education has as its primary goal the perfection of the virtues of the citizen. The most virtuous of these, according to Plato, would of course become the community's philosopher king. This view of politics and political leaders may seem somewhat quaint until one notices the size of the educational budgets of the major powers in the world today, particularly the United States, and counts the amount of time that major leaders around the world spend on the propaganda-educational aspects of their work.

According to Seligman, "Politics by leadership is one of the distinguishing features of the twentieth century."[1] In the United States

[1] Lester G. Seligman, "The Study of Political Leadership," *American Political Science Review*, 44 (December 1950): 905–915.

particularly, the communications revolution wrought by television, radio, and the mass distribution of newspapers has given most citizens a sense of personal connection with the nation's best-known political leaders. By contrast, most principal leaders in other countries and in previous centuries have been "known" only from their portrait hanging in some prominent corner of the citizen's home.

A second twentieth-century development has been the transformation of a concept, *popular sovereignty*, into a vital group phenomenon called the *mass electorate*, enormous numbers of voters mobilized by large-scale political parties whose leaders are the acknowledged dominant power holders in the community. With certain significant differences in practical operation, leadership of mass parties and mass electorates has been a feature of both totalitarian and democratic regimes, and greater popular participation seems to be the promise of the centuries ahead.

As one approaches the study of leadership, two factors seem indisputable. First, leadership is an essential component of group life. No one can be a leader in isolation; a leader, by definition, needs other people to lead. A second factor is the general quality of specialness ordinarily attributed to leaders. For that matter, the isolation of attributes that seem most special—skill, position, articulateness, motivation, special traits, and so forth—has been one of the major pursuits of students of political leadership.

ELITE AND LEADERSHIP THEORIES

Few aspects of political life have had such a profusion of theoretical and conceptual writings as the subject of leadership. Perhaps the simplest explanation for this outpouring is the view that, for most of us, the leader appears to be the human individual writ large. If we can understand how leaders behave and why, we may perhaps better grasp the behavioral dynamics that pertain to all individuals. Another explanation may relate to the availability of data about leaders; the persons most observed and best described in any civilization are its heroes and great men. An ancient tradition in historical writing, in fact, is that history is "made" by the personalities and deeds of great man. Historians and biographers continue to search assiduously for those *crucial decisions* by *crucial persons* that have presumably altered the entire course of human affairs.

From Plato to Durkheim

Plato and Aristotle, however, inaugurated another great tradition in leadership theory that gained renewed attention during the nineteenth century in the writings of Gaetano Mosca and Vilfredo Pareto. In describing the philosopher king who would rule the ideal state, Plato was referring to an individual selected from a special class of individuals, the guardians. The guardians were a specially endowed and trained "higher" class who were responsible for protecting the community against foreign enemies and maintaining peace among citizens at home. To the kingship form, Aristotle added rule by aristocracies and polities (or democracy). Throughout the Middle Ages and most of the Renaissance, however, the main attention of political theorists remained focused upon the single leader or "Great Man" conception of leadership, largely a response to the prevalence of popes and kings as the major types of political chiefs of these periods.

Mosca and Pareto, on the other hand, noted the multiplicity of leaders in nineteenth-century political communities and introduced the concepts of *ruling class* and *circulation of elites*. Pareto concerned himself with the nonlogical or irrational behavior of human beings, which he believed was based upon sentiments—"residues," in his obtuse terminology. Pareto argued that different social classes possess residues in varying proportions.

The governing elite is always strongly motivated by the residues he called "combination" and "persistence of aggregates." A governing elite remains in power only so long as it remains willing to use physical force and to manipulate the masses by appeals to their sentiments. If one elite loses its ability or willingness to use force, it is overthrown by new leaders; that is, there is a "circulation of the elite." For Pareto, "history is a graveyard of aristocracies."

Mosca, on the other hand, started with the premise that, despite theories of kingship and majority rule, most societies have always been ruled by minorities or oligarchies. He argued, therefore, for a classification of oligarchies rather than of governments, himself noting a number of oligarchic types: military and priestly aristocracies, hereditary aristocracies, aristocracies of landowners, aristocracies of liquid wealth (money), and aristocracies of merit. From these arises the "ruling class" in every society.[2]

The French sociologist Emile Durkheim, in his famous study of suicide published in 1897, shifted theoretical attention from elites and leaders per se to the *relationship* between leaders and followers. The society with clear-cut, stable values which precisely define the status of each member produces high morale or perfect integration; Durkheim calls this *solidarité*. In contrast, where values and beliefs are uncertain or changing rapidly, the society suffers a disorientation which he calls *anomie*.

In his analysis of suicide rates, Durkheim expected to find a rising suicide rate during periods of economic depression. This tendency could easily be associated with disrupted life patterns and the sudden necessity to restrain individual wants. Durkheim was astonished, however, to observe that suicide rates increase during periods of rising prosperity. He theorized that sudden affluence, like sudden poverty, produces feelings of disorientation in the populace. "People no longer feel sure about what is possible and what is not, what is just and what is unjust, which claims or aspirations are legitimate and which go beyond measure . . . thus, the appetites of men, being no longer restrained by a public opinion, now bewildered and disoriented, do not know any more where the bounds are before which they ought to come to a halt." In short, the society suffers from *anomie*.[3]

The society also suffers from a failure of leadership. If the sheep are scattered, the shepherd must lie smitten. In a nation where an essential part of the ruler's obligation is military victory, the defeat of his armies frequently leads to his overthrow at home. In a country where the maintenance of prosperity is a primary obligation of business leaders, periods of large-scale unemployment and economic depression are likely to lead to a radical rejection of businessmen and their economic ideology. Passage through a state of anomie is often traumatic and revolutionary in consequence.

[2] Gaetano Mosca, *The Ruling Class*, trans. by Hannah D. Kahn (New York: McGraw-Hill, 1939); Vilfredo Pareto, *The Mind and Society*, ed. and trans. by Arthur Livingston et al., 4 vols. (New York: Harcourt, Brace, 1935). See also, Robert A. Dahl, "A Critique of the Ruling Elite Model," *American Political Science Review*, 52 (1958): 463–9.

[3] Quoted by Sebastian de Grazia, *The Political Community* (Chicago: University of Chicago Press, 1948), p. 3.

A strong impetus to the study of *personal traits* of particular leaders was generated by a concern for the charisma associated with some of them. The sociologist Max Weber gave the term special meaning. He used charisma to refer to that capacity for leadership that rested upon something "extraordinary" and innovative in the personality or personal style of the particular leader. Whereas most leaders claim political legitimacy on traditional or legal-organizational grounds, the charismatic leader, whether he is seeking legitimization or not, has his unusual personality upon which to rest his status. In earlier theories of charisma, this extraordinary personal attractiveness was thought to be a matter of divine grace, as in the case of religious prophets. Later charisma came to be associated with persons who were expansive, forceful, and breakers of established routines. The charismatic leader also receives some intense loyalty from his followers. Mahatma Gandhi, Adolph Hitler, Franklin D. Roosevelt, Winston Churchill, Dwight D. Eisenhower and Fidel Castro have been referred to as charismatic leaders. From the point of view of systematic research, however, the concept has been of relatively little utility, although it has acquired much usage in popular conversation.[4]

Recent Theory

During the 1940s, the studies of social and political leadership were particularly prolific. Seligman, in surveying that literature, found several conceptions of leadership. From the work of Elton Mayo and others at the Harvard Business School, it became evident, according to Seligman, that problems of morale, coordination, and efficiency in large-scale organizations were essentially problems of leadership, particularly in the informal relationships within the organization. Chester I. Barnard considered leadership the "strategic factor" in systems of cooperation. A similar concern for the implications of leadership for the management of organizations pervades the work of others investigating industrial and public administration. Within this framework, leadership was considered an organizational function or position.

[4] H. Gerth and C. W. Mills (eds.), *From Max Weber* (New York: Harper, 1953); James Davies, "Charisma in the 1952 Campaign," *American Political Science Review,* 48 (December 1954): 1083–1102; W. Friedland, "For a Sociological Concept of Charisma," *Social Forces,* 48 (October 1964): 18–26; K. J. Ratnam, "Charisma and Political Leadership," *Political Studies,* 12 (October 1964): 341–355.

Still another approach viewed leaders as a distinctive type of personality. Harold D. Lasswell, introducing psychoanalytic theory to the study of political persons, made the earliest, most seminal contributions regarding political personality. On the one hand, Lasswell viewed the political personality as one in which private motives are displaced onto public objects and rationalized in terms of the "public good."[5] In another formulation, he classified distinctive leadership "character structures," namely, agitator, theorist, and bureaucrat. In general, he viewed leaders as "power seekers" who devote themselves to the capture and use of government.[6]

Other investigators and theorists, somewhat fruitlessly, sought personal traits as the key variable in identifying leaders. Thus, it was hypothesized that leaders are taller, stronger, heavier, more energetic, better looking, more intelligent, more ambitious, more persistent, great initiators, and even more "surgent," a term that includes talkativeness, cheerfulness, geniality, enthusiasm, expressiveness, alertness, and originality. The traits, however, were difficult to define operationally; the research found few correlations.[7]

Seligman found the most universal attribute of leadership to be relational, that is, dependent upon some people's acceptance of others. This relation could be seen from two perspectives. First, leadership is a function of acceptance by followers. Without such acceptance, there is no leader. Secondly, the selection of a leader is related to the tensions and values of a particular situation. As for any other collective decision, members initiate the decision process about leadership as a consequence of a perceived situation of choice. The tensions and values that become salient in such situations are, according to the theoretical literature, significantly related to who is chosen leader.[8]

What concepts and perspectives on leadership are more currently employed? A recent survey provides a convenient inventory that highlights nine major conceptual approaches to leadership theory.[9]

---

[5] Harold D. Lasswell, *Psychopathology and Politics* (Chicago: University of Chicago Press, 1930).

[6] Harold D. Lasswell, *Power and Personality* (New York: Viking Press, 1962).

[7] Ralph M. Stogdill, "Personal Factors Associated with Leadership: A Survey of the Literature," *Journal of Psychology*, 25 (January 1948): 35–71. Another comprehensive survey of the leadership literature is Cecil A. Gibb, "Leadership," in Gardner Lindzey (ed.), *Handbook of Social Psychology* (Cambridge: Addison-Wesley, 1954), Vol. II, Chap. 24.

[8] Seligman, *op. cit.*

[9] Lewis J. Edinger (ed.) *Political Leadership in Industrialized Societies* (New York: Wiley, 1967). Chapter 12 of this volume provides a thorough and authoritative in-

1. *Leadership authority.* Studies of this type focus upon the relational inequality endorsed by the group and providing the legitimacy with which leaders make and enforce policy. This approach underscores the fact that decision prerogatives are not equal throughout a collectivity. In fact, the collectivity approves more or less specific inequalities which become the authority or power of its leaders.

2. *Leadership control.* This perspective tries to measure the extent of the leader's ability to elicit conforming behavior within the group through some actual or perceived capacity to provide or withhold benefits and apply sanctions. Presumably, according to these studies, the degree of control is a direct function of the size of the leader's stick or carrot. Another way of examining control is to consider it as the consequence of an exchange or transaction between leader and led in which something is given and something received by both.[10]

3. *Leadership Autonomy.* How capable is the individual of "rising above his environment" and employing his own behavioral yardsticks to his views and actions? The more the person is independent of environmental factors, the greater is his autonomy as a leader.

4. *Leadership skills.* This conceptual concern follows the tradition that leadership capabilities may be acquired through training. Such training requires that the prospective leader acquire knowledge about the nature and application of managerial methods to gain compliance by group members with behaviors instrumental to achieving group goals.

5. *Statecraft.* When the leader is part of some sovereign entity, such as a nation, or a subcomponent, such as a legislative assembly, it is possible to judge his success or failure in the exercise of authority by his achievements with respect to the stipulated goals of the sovereign entity. Thus, the political leader who neglects the defense of his nation, which is usually the most carefully stipulated of collective goals, may be accused of failure in statecraft.

6. *Policy making.* This is the perspective that emphasizes the

---

terdisciplinary bibliography of the leadership field. See also, Carl Beck and J. Thomas McKechnie, *Political Elites* (Cambridge, Mass.: M.I.T. Press, 1967); Harold D. Lasswell and Daniel Lerner, *World Revolutionary Elites* (Cambridge, Mass.: M.I.T. Press, 1966).

[10] Cf. Chapter 4 on transaction theory.

decision-making aspect of leadership. Such studies examine the process by which leaders choose among alternative goals, courses of action, and even among subordinate decision makers, as in the case of appointing the proponent of one public policy rather than another to take charge of some governmental bureau.

7. *Leadership roles*. Burgeoning interest in role theory has led to a number of role conceptions of leadership. One conception examines the office occupied or sought, also concerning itself with the rights and duties associated with the position. A second role conception gives special attention to the group's expectations about the behavior of incumbents of leadership positions. A third role approach focuses upon the behavioral style of leaders, particularly as style relates to their use of coercive, manipulative, persuasive, and other modes of interaction with other actors.

8. *Leadership personality*. How do the attitudinal and behavioral patterns of individual leaders differ from the general characteristics of other members of the group? The earlier interest in personality traits has in recent years been broadened to include studies of attitudes and observable patterns of behavior such as expressiveness.

9. *Leadership recruitment*. How do the processes of selecting leaders influence the acquisition of leadership status on the one hand and the advancement of particular types of persons to positions of leadership on the other? This perspective is particularly relevant to the discussion below regarding investiture process.[11]

LEADERS AND DECISION SITUATIONS

The conception of political leaders as specialized decision makers in special group decision situations is well expressed by Froman.[12] People differ in their predispositions to act, according to Froman. These predispositions differ in content, in the ordering of preferences, and in the intensity with which preferences are held. As a consequence, one of the most important ways in which leaders and

[11] For a particularly thorough evaluation of research in the field of leadership theory, Edwin P. Hollander and James W. Julian, "Contemporary Trends in the Analysis of Leadership Processes," *Psychological Bulletin*, 71 (1969), 387–397.

[12] Lewis A. Froman, Jr., *People and Politics* (Englewood Cliffs, N.J.: Prentice-Hall, 1962), esp. pp. 38–48, also Chap. 4.

followers differ is in the nature of their values, attitudes, and beliefs. Froman then enumerates several propositions about the differentiating characteristics of leaders, many of which are supported by the findings of empirical investigators.

1. "Leaders have more values relating to why they are in the group." Often their private goals are very closely tied to the achievement of group goals, and they are very much aware of the overlap as well as the distinctions.

2. "Leaders are more intense about their values." They are far more reluctant to give up valued objectives and actions than nonleaders and are often confronted with the necessity of revitalizing follower loyalty to group values.

3. "Leaders have more beliefs concerning the group and the group's relations with other groups, the government, issues affecting the group, etc." This is another way of saying that leaders are more knowledgeable and better able to assimilate new information regarding group-revelant beliefs.

4. "Leaders are more intense than nonleaders in their attitudes." Whether favorable or unfavorable to particular values, beliefs, events, and objects, the leader's attitude structure is more responsive to stimulation and more likely to trigger intensely held attitudes. Thus, leaders are more likely to give attitudinal guidance to nonleaders as the group confronts new factors in the world around it.

5. "Leader's attitudes are more resistant to change." As a consequence, for example, leaders are more likely than nonleaders to be hard bargainers and to resist being "pushed around."

6. "Leaders are more likely to act on the basis of their attitudes." Compared to most members of the group, leaders are much busier making decisions, a characteristic emphasized in the general approach of this chapter. The intensity and stability of leader attitudes make it more economical and, in many ways, easier for the group to let them lead the way to collective decisions.

7. "Leaders are more issue-oriented, that is, much more sensitive to events and problems that create a 'situation of choice' for the group."

8. "Leaders are more concerned with 'position issues,' those problems and alternative courses of action that tend to be concrete, related to reality, and measurable by some precise

unit of analysis." Leaders, for example, concern themselves with the issue of war and peace not only by reiterating their devotion to peace, but also by asking questions about defense budgets and specific international negotiations.

9. "Correlatively, therefore, leaders are more interested in material satisfactions than are nonleaders." Leaders are, for example, more impressed by defense budgets being raised or lowered than by symbolic reaffirmations of devotion to peace.

10. "Leaders tend to differentiate themselves from nonleaders and leaders of other groups more than do nonleaders." This self-conscious differentiation takes place in a number of ways. Use of a title such as "president" or "director" may be all that is necessary to differentiate the leader. During discussions or negotiations with other groups, a leader may distinguish his own position from that of others within his group. If there is a degree of professionalism associated with a leadership role, the leaders of these groups often acquire a sense of fraternity and mutual regard for each other that they cannot and do not share with their respective members.

Froman next describes how the distribution of acquired resources among any group of people is determined by (a) the kind of people involved in the decision-making process and the resources they have to bring to bear on others and (b) the type of decision-making process in which advantages are being distributed. Following a theoretical formulation developed by Robert A. Dahl, he describes four situations of decision-making interaction: (1) leaders interacting with leaders, (2) nonleaders interacting with nonleaders, (3) leaders interacting with nonleaders in a situation in which nonleaders elect leaders, and (4) leaders interacting with nonleaders in a situation in which the nonleaders do *not* elect leaders. These four systems, respectively, are called: bargaining, discussion, democracy, and hierarchy.[13]

	LEADERS	FOLLOWERS
LEADERS	*Bargaining*—The resources of these actors are large.	*Hierarchy*—Leaders are *not* elected by nonleaders.
FOLLOWERS	*Democracy* — Leaders are elected by nonleaders.	*Discussion*—The resources of these actors are small.

[13] *Ibid.*, Chap. 4. The table is adapted from Froman's at p. 52.

Decision making under conitions of *bargaining* involves people who are well-informed about the issue at hand, who have strong attitudes about it, who control a substantial amount of resources, and who are interested in the prospective material benefits. The bargaining process, as we have seen in a previous chapter, involves offering others something in return for something else. The outcome is literally a "deal" or, in more political terms, a "compromise." Bargaining requires skills, decision opportunities, and resources greater than are likely to be available to nonleaders.

In decision making by *discussion* nonleaders interact with nonleaders. A number of the actors' resources, such as information, skill, interest, and material resources, are likely to be modest. Decision making under such circumstances tends to be inconclusive, usually with each participant "saying his piece" and withdrawing to his original position without changing any other minds.

Democracy is the type of decision-making situation in which leaders interact with followers under conditions in which the followers elect the leaders. Leaders must talk the language of the followers, deal in evaluative judgments, work within the context of a followers' relatively small amount of information, seek to reinforce their committed followers, activate latent followers, and hope favorably to change the minds of a number of those who are nonfollowers or opponents.

Hierarchy is a decision situation characterized by interaction between leaders and nonleaders in which the leaders are not elected by nonleaders. In bureaucratic organizations, leaders in situations of hierarchy are recruited by appointment, promotion, tenure, etc., and not by election. Under such conditions leaders tend to be task-oriented, that is, particularly concerned with the relationship between current activities and the achievement of certain stated goals. In hierarchy, too, people tend to be sensitive to superordinate-subordinate relationships, often attempting either to circumvent, modify, or preserve these relationships. In other words, in hierarchy, leaders and followers tend to focus their activities upon modification of the hierarchy relationship itself as well as upon the performance of group tasks.

Nonleaders, it should be emphasized, are not simply people who are in some way *less than* leaders, say, in information, intensity of attitude, or motivation. Lane's studies show that many nonleaders are positively affirmative about wishing to remain followers. Lane conducted extended interviews with fifteen American urban male voters drawn as a sample from a list of 220 in a housing development where income ranged from $4,000 to $6,500 (as of 1957). Most were white, married, fathers, blue-collar workers, in their thirties, Catholic, native-born but with a variety of nationality backgrounds, and a wide spread of formal education. In general, most of these men denied that social class is important in America, asserted that the working class gets its share (and they along with it), were willing to match their moral virtues against any man's (although unwilling to do the same for their economic status), felt that the upper classes undoubtedly deserved to be "upper," and, in various ways, expressed an unwillingness to face the prospect or requirements of greater equality of opportunity and income. Among the other generalizations that Lane believed could be derived from his data were these:

The greater the emphasis in a society upon the availability of "equal opportunity for all," the greater the need for members of that society to develop an acceptable rationalization for their own social status.

The greater the strain on a person's self-esteem implied by a relatively low status in an open society, the greater the necessity to explain the status as "natural" and "proper" in the social order.

People tend to care less about *equality* of opportunity than about the availability of *some* opportunity.[14]

PARTICIPATION AS A LEADERSHIP ATTRIBUTE

If nothing else, leaders are psychologically the most involved members of the group. From the point of view of sheer activity, they are also probably the busiest participators in its affairs. Ego-involvement and intense participation are clearly identifiable special characteristics of leaders.

Involvement for leaders is a special amalgam of personal and group motives in relation to which participative activity becomes a deliberate allocation of personal resources. Thus, it is not outlandish for a President who refers to *"my* country" to be thinking of the entire United States in the same highly personal way that most home-owning Americans might think of *"my* house." And if a President works an eighteen-hour day, seven days a week, as most contemporary presidents do, it is precisely because he is the most intensively participating member of the nation.

[14] Robert E. Lane, "The Fear of Equality," *American Political Science Review,* 53 (March 1959): 35–51.

Following the tradition of Lord Bryce, Mosca, Michels, and others, Truman calls attention to the existence of an "active minority" in almost all groups.[15] What do we know about these "actives" or, as some theorists prefer to call them, "influentials"?

Participation in politics takes a variety of forms, depending upon the structure and complexity of a political system. In the United States, among many types of political activity, voting is perhaps the most widely experienced form of participation. To this we may add such forms of participation as holding public office, rendering military service, membership in and financial contributions to political parties and associations that take stands on public issues, activity in political campaigns, active discussion of political affairs, and communication with legislators and other officials. This list includes many of the activities that students of political participation use as yardsticks in their researches. If we note that over 99 percent of the eligible voters in the Soviet Union usually participate in the elections of that country while only between 60 and 70 percent of the eligible American electorate participates in presidential elections, the difficulty in defining "participation" meaningfully becomes quite apparent.

Expert testimony about the extent of political activity in the United States offers varied estimates. Tocqueville in the 1840s and Bryce in the early 1890s both found the number of politically active citizens in the United States "astonishing." Bryce expressed the belief that it was fifty times as great as in England. Woodward and Roper have concluded that "the few act politically for the many"; they estimate that three-fourths of the citizens are inactive politically, only one-tenth are "very active," and probably one in fifty, that is, two percent, have "political influence." De Grazia estimated that there are only a few hundred persons in each state of the Union and a few thousand in Washington, D.C., who can be included in the top rank of "active politists." Referring to politically active and influential persons, Agger and Ostrum found, by their criteria, that only 1 percent could be called "active advisors," while as many as 51 percent of the American population consists of political nonparticipants.[16]

15 David B. Truman, *The Governmental Process* (New York: Knopf, 1955), pp. 139–140.
16 Julian Woodward and Elmo Roper, "Political Activity of American Citizens," *American Political Science Review*, 44 (December 1950): 872–85; Alfred de Grazia, *The Elements of Political Science* (New York: Knopf, 1952), pp. 87, 92; Robert Agger and Vincent Ostrum, "Political Participation in a Small Community," in Heinz Eulau, S. J. Eldersveld, and M. Janowitz (eds.), *Political Behavior* (Glencoe: The Free Press, 1956), pp. 138–48.

One comprehensive study of participation in voluntary groups suggests that the number of persons participating in *any* kind of voluntary association is highly exaggerated by scholars. Nearly 36 percent of the sample investigated had no associational affiliation whatsoever (church affiliation being excluded from the study). Such membership as did exist was highly concentrated; 15 percent of the sample held 51 percent of the total membership and 16 percent of the sample held all associational officerships. More than a third of those with associational affiliation belonged to only two types of group: religious-sponsored or fraternal. Only five percent of the affiliated belonged to organizations that could be classified as "military, patriotic, or political," and among these were many veterans' organizations. Thus, the percentage in purely "political" associations was exceedingly small. Even though American society is reportedly made up of "joiners," there are fewer joiners than commonly supposed, with control of voluntary associations concentrated in the hands of relatively few highly active leaders.[17]

Other research indicates that not only are the same people *generally* active as well as *politically* active, but also that activity in voluntary associations serves as a stimulus to greater political involvement. Maccoby studied one voluntary association organized to foster a community recreation program. He examined evidence of participation before and after the formation of the association. It was found that 68 percent of the associated members voted in 1949, but only 49 percent of the nonmembers had voted. In 1951, the voting rate of the association members rose to 74 percent, with only 43 percent of the nonmembers voting. Out of every three association members who had been nonvoters in a 1949 primary election, two became voters in 1951. On the other hand, of every three nonvoters in 1949 among nonmembers, only one became a voter in 1951. Thus, the association members were more likely to *be* voters, *remain* voters, or *become* voters if they had not previously voted. This tendency was greater among the "high actives" in the association. Two ordinarily nonparticipative types of persons—females and Negroes—showed the same effects of associational membership; both tended to go to the polls in greater numbers in 1951.[18]

[17] John C. Scott, Jr., "Membership and Participation in Voluntary Associations," *American Sociological Review*, 22 (June 1957): 315–26. Scott reports that similar conclusions may be drawn from a dozen or more other studies reviewed by him.
[18] Herbert Maccoby, "The Differential Political Activity of Participants in a Voluntary Association," *American Sociological Review*, 23 (October 1958): 524–532.

Ego-involvement of the "Actives"

What are some of the characteristics of the "actives"—those who participate at least by voting and, in some cases, by participating in political campaigns, making financial contributions, and activity as regular workers in party organizations? Numerous studies of voting behavior indicate that the most significant attributes of the activist in American politics are higher education, higher income, higher occupational status. The active voters are also more likely to be male, older, Republican, urban dwellers, home-owners, Protestants, Caucasians. These latter characteristics vary in degree and significance in different localities and under different political conditions.[19]

Berelson ascribes the greater political interest of upper class groups to the fact that the "wealthy are alert to political effects upon their interests." They have, he suggests, a feeling of potency plus partisanship which stimulates their interest. According to Eulau and Schneider, civic responsibility is heightened when one feels one's actions have an impact on the political process; it is worthwhile to participate because one's own political role is significant and effective. Perhaps the most direct evidence, particularly as it relates to decisional activity of leaders, is found in Dahl's study of the power structure of New Haven. Participation in local political decisions he found is: greater among citizens with high incomes than among citizens with low incomes; greater among citizens with high social standing than among citizens with low social standing; greater among citizens with considerable formal education than among citizens with little; greater among citizens with professional, business, and white-collar occupations than among citizens with working-class occupations; and greater among citizens from better residential areas than among citizens from poor areas. Dahl calls such participators in local political decisions the "Better-Off."[20]

Dahl observes that few decisions by government affect citizens generally and uniformly. Most governmental decisions have mean-

[19] Perhaps the best survey of voter and other forms of political participation is Robert E. Lane, *Political Life* (Glencoe, Ill.: The Free Press, 1959).

[20] Bernard Berelson et al., *Voting* (Chicago: University of Chicago Press, 1954); Heinz Eulau and Peter Schneider, "Dimensions of Political Involvement," *Public Opinion Quarterly* (Spring 1956): 128–42; Robert A. Dahl, *Who Governs?* (New Haven: Yale University Press, 1961), Chap. 26.

ingful and immediate consequences only for a relatively small part of the population at any one time. Only those citizens who expect the decisions to have important and immediate consequences for themselves try to influence the outcome. As the character and consequences of decisions change, some of the actors change; there is "an ebb and flow in the numbers who participate." There is much looseness in the relationship between leaders and followers. Only a small proportion of the citizens will have much *direct* influence on decisions in the sense of directly initiating proposals for policies subsequently adopted or successfully vetoing the proposals of others. Such influence as there is is usually related to decisions that determine the kinds of policies to be emphasized, the amount of resources to be put into them, the development of specific proposals, and the implementation of policies when sufficient consensus has been successfully negotiated. In New Haven there were only a *very few* leaders with *generalized influence* of some degree in most areas of policy; leaders and subleaders tended to be influential only in relatively few, specialized areas of policy, for example, urban redevelopment and public education.[21]

Leadership is related to political pluralism by Presthus. Acknowledging that occupation is typically the primary *personal* factor in leadership status, Presthus emphasizes the *social* or *institutional* relations that are also significant. For example, a local political leader's command of resources often rests upon his access to and alliances with state and national centers of political and economic resources. His personal leadership resources thus depend a great deal upon the commitments he can make of the resources—economic, organization, symbolic, etc.—of one or another of these other centers. Presthus identified several types of community leadership: *political* leaders (holders of public office and long-term participants in political party affairs), *economic* leaders (with positions in business, commerce, industry, or finance), and *specialist* leaders (often in education or welfare).[22]

Role theory and the psychology of the ego afford more theoretical insights into the special types and degrees of participation of group leaders. In Chapter 5, social roles were viewed as the building blocks

---

[21] *Ibid.,* passim. Issue specialization was early identified by Ralph H. Smuckler and George M. Belknap, *Leadership and Participation in Urban Political Affairs* (East Lansing: Michigan State University Press, 1956).

[22] Robert Presthus, *Men at the Top* (New York: Oxford University Press, 1964), pp. 7–8, 50.

of personality. One diagram viewed the individual's role structure as a system of role ranks or priorities. The hypothetical person represented in that diagram, it will be recalled, possessed nine roles— five of third rank, three of second rank, and one, the ego role, of first rank. The ego role was presumably the most directive and influential in the role structure.

As Sherif and Cantril found in their survey of the experimental literature relating to ego-involvement, "All attitudes that define a person's status or that give him some relative role with respect to other individuals, groups, or institutions are ego-involved."

> Whether these attitudes stem from some biological drive or whether they are derived from some non-instinctual source (from some social value or norm), any attitude is ego linked which functions to shape, delimit, or point to our relative position. In the United States, for example, the individual derives and experiences a general status from such reference groups as white or Negro; native or foreign-born; upper, middle, or working class; worker, employer, or independent; Catholic or Protestant. And one derives and experiences more specific status from his relative position in membership groups, that is, as the father of a family, a newcomer in a gang, an active member of his union, a key skilled worker in a factory. Directories such as *Who's Who*, compiled for the purpose of making it possible "to place" a person, describe individuals entirely in terms of their reference and membership characters.[23]

It follows, then, that a person who is more ego-involved in a group is more likely to be a leader of the group. Even the most gregarious and motivated person is rarely likely to be *the* leader in more than one or two groups although he may well be *a* leader in a larger number. The number of ego roles any individual, even the most active, is likely to have is necessarily limited. The personality with too complex a role structure would have trouble juggling the many cross-pressures impinging upon him from his group statuses. The skillful leader may perhaps do this with finesse, carefully weighing one group's expectations against another's, noting the relevance of each particular decision situation to his various roles, and deliberately estimating the degree of his ego-involvement in the group concerned with each situation.

Evidence of ego-involvement may, according to Sherif and Cantril,

---

23 M. Sherif and H. Cantril, *The Psychology of Ego-Involvement* (New York: Wiley, 1947), pp. 96–97.

be readily inferred from numerous factors. One of the most obvious kinds of evidence is clothes, especially clothing worn by persons whose ego roles are significantly related to various customary forms of dress, as in military or religious groups. Contemporary advertising of commercial products as well as image making in entertainment and political life are deliberately designed to "hook in" audience ego or "self-identification."

Ego-involvements are by no means unchangeable. Attitudes and information that comprise a person's role structure may change and develop in a variety of ways. This is usually best observed in the development of occupational roles and in the acquisition of a leadership status. Studies of children, in fact, indicate that before a child can participate in a group, a certain degree of ego development must take place so that the child can see himself in some definite relationship to the other children as required by group situations. In play and other types of group activity, children find their "places" and acquire experience regarding appropriate role performances; they also assume positions associated with leadership or followership.[24] Entrance into and elevation to a leadership status within a group is a process of personal role adjustment and ego-involvement as much as one of position definition by the group.

Perhaps one of the best examples of the convergence of occupational career and political leadership role is the lawyer in American politics. "No occupational group stands in more regular and intimate relation to American politics than the legal profession. Lawyers make up a large proportion of American politicians at all levels and in all branches of government, in the political parties, and in other political organizations."[25] The activities, status, training, role expectations, and values associated with the profession of lawyer in the United States have been uniquely appropriate to the extra-professional role of politician. Ego-involvement in the one is readily transferred to ego-involvement in the other. The route, in terms of group positions, is fairly direct: from law school to practice in a public court system; next, to party affiliation and involvement in public affairs; and then to election as a legislator or other public

24 *Ibid.*, p. 182.
25 Heinz Eulau and J. D. Sprague, *Lawyers in Politics* (Indianapolis: Bobbs-Merrill, 1964), p. 11. Also, Joseph A. Schlesinger, "Lawyers and American Politics: A Clarified View," *Midwest Journal of Political Science*, 1 (May 1957): 28; Donald R. Matthews, *The Social Background of Political Decision-Makers* (Garden City, N.Y.: Doubleday and Co., 1954).

officer. The ego role can readily be professional, partisan, or public, all at the same time or in sequence.

The converse of such high ego-involvement is found among the "followers" in American politics. The Survey Research Center at the University of Michigan devised an index of political involvement that consisted of scale responses to two questions concerning how much the respondent "cared" and how much he "paid attention" to politics. As might be expected, citizen participation in the voter role varied directly with a sense of involvement; 58 percent of the least involved and 88 percent of the most involved actually voted. Similar results were found with respect to "sense of political efficacy," an index based upon scale responses to five questions. Based on this survey, more than one-third of the eligible American electorate failed to experience either a sense of political involvement or political efficacy, according to the findings employing this measure. The egos of these many millions of Americans are obviously involved elsewhere than in politics.[26]

INCUMBENCY AND THE INVESTITURE PROCESS

Positions, we have seen, may be conceived as standardized sets of task expectations; personalities may be viewed as role structures. Yet, the individual who knows how to perform the tasks of a carpenter need not necessarily be employed in the position of carpenter. Or, conversely, a carpenter position may exist in an organization and no one be available to fill it. Groups have positions and offices; persons have personalities and roles. When person and position are brought together in a relatively stable relation, a *state of incumbency* may be said to exist. The process—a decisional one—by which incumbency is affirmed may be called the *investiture process*.[27]

In the incumbency relationship, the members of the group expect a particular person to fulfill by appropriate role behavior the task expectations that constitute a particular position. More precisely, incumbency reflects a consensus among the members of a group

26 Survey Research Center data cited in V. O. Key, Jr., *Public Opinion and American Democracy* (New York: Knopf, 1961), Chap. 8.

27 The empirical literature on succession, incumbency relationships, or investiture is almost nonexistent. Two excellent studies dealing with succession in educational and business organizations are Richard O. Carlson, "Succession and Performance among School Superintendents," *Administrative Science Quarterly*, 6 (September 1961): 210–227, and Donald B. Trow, "Executive Succession in Small Companies," *ibid.*, pp. 228–239.

concerning which particular person is to be held accountable for the performance of task expectations included in a particular position set.

Incumbency exists only so long as the members of a group agree that it should exist. Usually the consensus is made known by some observable event, which may be called a *legitimizing event*. Legitimacy, an ancient and politically significant concept, has usually been defined, as it is here, as referring to those procedures and events that assert the group's willingness to assign power and authority to particular individuals incumbent in particular offices. The legitimate leader is one who has arrived in his position by some preestablished and accepted procedure.[28]

In the course of history, men have employed a variety of legitimizing events for the political investiture process. Birth and the rule of primogeniture have provided one such procedure, particularly for royal succession in monarchies. In warrior societies, a kind of trial-by-combat, in the sense that winning military leaders also become major political leaders, has been employed. Appointment by the principal officer of the governmental organization is still another way of legitimizing incumbency, particularly in communities where governmental and political bureaucracies have become well established. In recent centuries, mass participation communities have made election by eligible voters one of the most prevalent procedures of investiture.

An investiture process, therefore, particularly for leadership positions, has several aspects. First, the group must reach a collective decision about the particular legitimizing event that will normally confirm the state of incumbency of a particular person in a particular position. If the legitimizing event is ambiguous or unacceptable to a substantial minority in the group, the duties and powers associated with the office may be challenged, or two or more persons may claim the office. This is seen in rival claims to thrones or in contested elections.

---

[28] The importance of legitimizing mechanisms in shaping group members' reactions to its leader-spokesman is explored in James W. Julian, Edwin P. Hollander, and C. Robert Regula, "Endorsement of the Group Spokesman as a Function of His Source of Authority, Competence, and Success," *Journal of Personality and Social Psychology*, 11 (1969), pp. 42–49. Conversely, leader's risk deviating from their followers' preferences in proportion to their sense of the legitimacy of their means of selection. Edwin P. Hollander, James W. Julian, and Richard M. Sorrentino, "The Leader's Sense of Legitimacy as a Source of His Constructive Deviation" (Office of Naval Research Technical Report 12, Project Number 177-269, July, 1969).

A second aspect of the investiture process is the examination and evaluation of candidates' role backgrounds to determine the appropriateness of that background for the fulfillment of the position task expectations. Even under procedures of royal succession by birth, the issue of competency may occur in connection with establishment of regencies. In electoral systems, of course, examination of candidate qualifications is familiar in nominating and election campaigns. The candidate's training, attitudes, policy preferences, and even appearance become grist for the investiture mill.

Once an individual's incumbency is determined, a third aspect appears in connection with his accountability for fulfilling the task expectations of the group. In modern democracies, for example, accountability is encouraged by such practices as frequent elections, limited terms of office, arrangements for recall, and procedures of impeachment. More extreme approaches to accountability include assassination, revolution, and sometimes international war.

The investiture process has its installation or investing rituals, such as the coronation of kings or the swearing in of presidents. The termination of an incumbency has also acquired numerous types of *divesting rituals*, such as the transfer of a gavel or mace from the old to the new leader, or a farewell address. Divestiture processes are numerous and familiar: resignation, termination of a term, retirement, death, and, sometimes, discontinuation of the office itself.

In selecting persons for incumbency in positions of leadership, organized groups, particularly political ones, tend to make their investiture procedures increasingly regular, overt, and representative of significant subgroups within the organization. This tendency often contributes substantially to the viability of the organization.

Harold Lasswell makes an important distinction between "mystical democracy" and "instrumental democracy," applying considerations relevant to the investiture process:

> The slogans of the former justify the exercise of authority without emphasizing the procedure by which official personnel is recruited. Instrumental democracy not only justifies the exercise of authority in the name of common ends; it is careful to demand that the personnel of authoritative agencies be chosen by a procedure which involves the participation of most if not all the community.[29]

[29] Harold D. Lasswell, *The Analysis of Political Behavior* (New York: Oxford University Press, 1958), p. 138.

In this sense, modern totalitarian regimes identify themselves with mystical democracy, whereas most of the older democracies are clearly instrumental in their concern for widely participative legitimizing procedures for public leadership selection.

The investiture and divestiture of rank-and-file members of a group are usually less explicit than the leaders'. One of the great anomalies of organizational and group theory is the difficulty in drawing a precise line between membership and nonmembership. Membership may be entirely voluntaristic, that is, contingent upon the predisposition and effort of the prospective member. In a street-corner gang or a friendship group, membership may involve little more than attendance, that is, physical presence. The concept of "the open society" assumes easy investiture procedures for all wishing to become members. Membership in an American political party may simply require enrollment on the public register of voters. On the other hand, such colloquial phrases as "the cold shoulder" or "the freeze" refer to the ability of group members to reject informally prospective members or to ostracize incumbent members.[30] The individual who includes himself voluntarily as a member may just as readily divest himself of membership by resigning, absenting himself, or otherwise allowing interactions with the group to discontinue.

Divestiture procedures take a variety of forms, from divorce in the marital group to excommunication in the church. Withdrawal of citizenship and suffrage rights are among the most significant membership divestiture acts of political communities.[31]

In summary, the theoretical literature generally considers the leader's status as necessarily a concomitant of group membership in which other members accept him in that status. Those who become leaders tend to have the same attributes as other group members, only in greater degree and intensity. This is particularly the case

[30] In experiments with college students, it was found that individuals who go through a severe initiation to gain admission to a club or organization tend to think more highly of that organization than those who do not go through severe initiation. Elliot Aronson and Judson Mills, "The Effect of Severity of Initiation on Liking for a Group," *Journal of Abnormal and Social Psychology*, 59 (September 1959): 177–181.

[31] Several types of selection mechanisms employed in recruiting individuals for political roles and public office are enumerated by Lester G. Seligman, "Political Parties and the Recruitment of Political Leadership," in Edinger, *op. cit.*, Chap. 10: (1) Self-recruitment, wherein the individual is the initial and primary instigator of his candidacy; (2) sponsorship, in which the candidacy is advanced by an interested group; (3) conscription, which involves drafting the candidate to run for office; and (4) co-optation, whereby the candidate is invited and enlisted on a relatively informal basis to join those already in positions of leadership.

with respect to ego-involvement and decisional effort. Finally, most groups, as an aid to their stability, devise fairly explicit processes for investing particular positions of leadership on particular persons.

An Illustrative Use of the Conceptual Perspective

COLLECTIVE PORTRAITS OF PRESIDENTIAL PARTY LEADERS

The principal titular and formal leaders of the Democratic and Republican national parties have included the presidential and vice-presidential nominees and the national party chairmen. What attributes have these individuals tended to possess? Numerous studies have undertaken to provide collective portraits.

The Presidents

One way of characterizing the presidents of the United States is to describe what they are *not*. In the view of Sidney Hyman, a "natural aristocracy" of presidential leadership is the "residue" of such a process of exclusion and subtraction.

From the total U.S. population, Hyman subtracted (1) all females and all males who (2) were not within the age group from thirty-five to sixty-seven years, (3) had not been born as American citizens, and (4) had ethnic lineage incompatible with that of "the English alliance"; all men who were (5) currently ill or (6) who had experienced spectacular marital difficulties; or who were (7) non-white, (8) non-Protestant (written before the election of a Catholic in 1960), (9) Southerners (written before the election of Lyndon B. Johnson —who referred to himself as a Southwesterner); as well as all men (10) who come from small states, (11) who have been conspicuously identified with big city life, (12) whose family origins cause "unease" to our middle and upper classes; and finally all (13) lawyers publicly identified with a specialized clientele, (14) all individuals identified with a special segment of the economic community (Big Business, Big Labor, etc.) and (15) all without some experience in major offices of government, whether at the international, national, or local level. Each of these criteria of exclusion obviously removes millions of individuals at a time, leaving a tiny group "in the neighborhood of one hundred men."[32]

Hyman might have added one other rule of exclusion: self-exclusion. Stating one's unavailability or voluntarily retiring from politics—common in American experience—is relatively unusual behavior among leaders in other nations of the world. Among American presidents, Washington's retirement at the end of his second term, despite popular enthusiasm for his continuation in office, was voluntary and in the public interest; Washington wished to set a precedent not prescribed in the Constitution regarding limited tenure in the Presidency. Others retire as a result of sheer physical exhaustion, as did President Polk. Some do so because they are confounded by rapid shifts in public events and opinion. After President Hoover's resounding defeat in his 1932 race for reelection, many Republicans began to talk of drafting ex-President Calvin Coolidge for the nomination in 1936. Coolidge's response to this was:

> I have been out of touch so long with political activities that I feel I no longer fit in these times. Great changes can come in four years. These socialistic notions of government are not of my day [referring to the anticipated policies of the New Deal]. When I was in office, tax reduction, debt reduction, tariff stability and economy were the things to which I gave attention. We succeeded on those lines. It has always seemed to me that common sense is the real solvent for the nation's problems at all times—common sense and hard work. When I read of the new-fangled things that are now so popular, I realize that my time in public affairs is past. I wouldn't know how to handle them if I were called upon to do so. That is why I am through with public life forever.[33]

Presidents are chosen from nominees offered by the two major parties. However, prior to the first national nominating conventions in 1832, there were ten major candidates for the Presidency, nominated by a variety of informal means. Six of these became President: Washington, Adams, Jefferson, Madison, Monroe, and John Quincy Adams. Four others may be called "opposition titular leaders": C.C. Pinkney, DeWitt Clinton, Rufus King, and Henry Clay. A social

[32] Sidney Hyman, *The American President* (New York: Harper and Brothers, 1954), pp. 231–232.
[33] Henry L. Stoddard, *It Costs To Be President* (New York: Harper and Brothers, 1938), p. 145.

composite of these ten men would be: a Virginian, a lawyer, a member of the Episcopal Church, about fifty-five years old when first a candidate for President, a Harvard graduate, the son of a father in a professional occupation. Typically, these men had substantial experience in government positions: as members of the Constitutional Convention in Philadelphia, as elected state officials, as members of the United States Senate, as officials in the foreign service, and as members of the Cabinet.

From the founding of the convention system in 1832 through 1956, according to the studies of the Brookings Institution, some 306 different individual candidates for major-party presidential and vice-presidential nominations polled over three percent in convention votes, that is, enough to count them, even loosely, as serious candidates. About 177 of these were presidential candidates in at least one convention, and 63 received nominations during the 1832–1956 period under study.[34]

What kinds of personal and social characteristics did these presidential and vice-presidential nominees have? From what states did the nominees come, particularly in view of the importance of large states in the Electoral College and the regional-balance principal in most ticket making? For this period, twelve first-time presidential nominees came from New York, seven from Ohio, and four from Illinois, these being among the largest and most politically competitive states in the Union between 1832 and 1956. California, New Jersey, Pennsylvania, and Virginia each had two presidential nominees, and nine other states had one each. The pattern of regional balance on the national tickets was as follows. The Democrats composed each of the eight successive tickets from 1864 to 1892 with a Northeastern leader and a Midwestern teammate. In six of the same eight election years, the Republicans composed party tickets that were the exact opposite: a Midwesterner together with a Northeastern leader. Between 1896 and 1924, the Northeast and Midwest were the regions with the greatest representation in both parties. Since 1928, the South received renewed attention from the Democrats, and the West from the Republicans.

The average age of presidential nominees was between fifty-one and fifty-four, whereas, curiously enough, vice-presidential nominees ranged, on the average, from 53 to 57. (Presumably, a Vice President

---

[34] Paul T. David, Ralph M. Goldman, and Richard C. Bain, *The Politics of National Party Conventions* (Washington, D.C.: Brookings Institution, 1960), Chap. 7.

should have prospects of living longer than the Presidents he may have to succeed!) With respect to formal education, 15 presidential nominees went to law school, 14 had other college or university training, 6 had secondary school only, and 5 had only elementary school training. Among the vice-presidential nominees, 18 went to law school, 26 had other college or university education, 6 had secondary school only, and 6 others elementary school only. The nation's major political leaders hardly appear to be members of an exclusive educational elite.

Most presidential and vice-presidential nominees began their careers in some specific private occupation, often one to which they could retreat when not holding public office. The practice of law is clearly the principal occupation of most nominees: 24 lawyers among the presidential nominees and 45 among the vice-presidential. Ranking far behind the lawyers are publishers, editors, business executives, and farmers.

The government experience of these leaders is directly relevant to their availability for nominations at particular times, as it offers both learning opportunities and occasions for demonstrating political skill. Nearly half of the first-time presidential nominees, notably during the nineteenth century, have had state legislative experience. About three-eighths have served in the House of Representatives and another three-eighths in the Senate, again mainly during the nineteenth century. The next largest proportion have been governors, for the most part during the present century. Another important source of government experience has been Federal appointive office. A similar pattern was found for first-time vice-presidential nominees, with somewhat less experience in governorships but substantially more experience in local government.

Is there an ideal type of presidential nominee? The Brookings Institution study drew the following conclusion about presidential nominees during the period 1896–1956.

> Able political leaders who are still in the prime of life and who have come up through elective executive office in states where politics is vigorous and competitive, without necessarily having as yet taken on the characteristics of a "father-image." This appears to be the type that has been preferred by the Democratic party in its first-time presidential nominations of recent decades when the type was available. . . .

The Republican party, on the other hand, seems to have had a fondness for "untypical" nominees. Wendell Willkie was probably the most outstanding example of untypicality, with his total lack of previous governmental experience. Dwight D. Eisenhower, with all his eminence as a five-star general and in other respects, was a reversion to an earlier pattern of American politics and was one of the most untypical of the possible choices when first nominated. Charles Evans Hughes . . . was untypical as the only Supreme Court Justice in history who has been nominated for President. . . .

The other five first-time Republican nominees . . . were able executives whose affiliations with the business community were close and well known. . . . Their careers have included various elements of distinguished public service and evidences of capacity for the cultivation of the electorate. . . . Their origins lay in the populous two-party states where presidential elections have generally been won or lost.[35]

Party Leaders

At the pinnacle of the formal structure of the national parties is the national party chairman. On the Democratic side, some 28 different persons occupied the national chairmanship between 1848, when that position was created, and 1959; on the Republican side, there were 41 national chairmen, commencing with the founding of this party in 1856.[36] These national chairmen, as a group, may be described as follows:

Most have been in the forty-five to forty-nine-year-old age category when first elected to the chairmanship, with Democrats on the younger side and Republicans on the older. The father of the "typical" chairman was employed in the middle range of occupational skills usually as a farmer or proprietor-manager-official. Most chairmen were Presbyterians (particularly Republicans) and Catholics (particularly Democrats). Episcopalians were in third rank among religious affiliations represented.

Chairmen usually had been born in New York, Pennsylvania, or Indiana, and, at the time of election to the chairmanship, most tended to be natives of the state in which they were born rather

[35] *Ibid.*, pp. 160–161. Quoted with permission of the Brookings Institution.

[36] Findings regarding characteristics of national party chairmen are based upon unpublished research by this author in connection with a Brookings Institution study of trends in national party leadership. See also Ralph M. Goldman, *The Democratic Party in American Politics* (New York: Macmillan, 1966), p. 130.

than transients from other states. Most held either the LL.B. or a
high school diploma, with Democrats tending to have slightly less
formal schooling. Most had extensive experience as party officers,
that is, as state party executives, as national party staff, as national
party executive officers, and on the national committees. In brief,
they were usually persons with long-standing attachment to party
organizational activity in states with highly competitive party politics who worked their way up through the local and state party
hierarchy as "organization men." Chairmen generally had private
occupations as professional persons or public officials, the latter in
state legislatures or appointive Federal posts.

National chairmen, although formally elected by the national committee, are so often close associates of the party's presidential nominees that a comparison of attributes with those of the nominees is
of particular interest. For example, we find confirmation of prior
research regarding age relations between heads of state and their
propaganda ministers. Smith found that propaganda ministers tend
to be half a generation or more younger than the heads of state they
serve.[37] In general, presidential nominees have tended to be in the
age range of fifty to fifty-four compared with forty-five to forty-nine
for national chairmen. More specifically, when a particular presidential nominee is matched for age against his national chairman,
43 nominees were older than their chairmen, 9 fell into the same
age group, and 26 presidential nominees were younger than their
national chairmen. The latter figure may in part be attributed to the
factional character of American national parties. If, as is frequently
the case, "Young Turks" capture the major prize—the presidential
nomination—from the "Old Guard," some consolation prize is almost
invariably offered the older generation of leaders, and this is often
the national chairmanship.

While presidential nominees and national chairmen have tended
to come out of higher occupation homes, the national chairmen have
come from the less advantaged of the two. Similarly, presidential
nominees have belonged to "high status" churches, whereas national
chairmen, particularly on the Republican side, have come from
"lower status" churches. Catholics in America have found political
parties an important channel of social advancement and achievement

---

[37] Bruce L. Smith, "The Political Communications Specialists of Our Times," B. L.
Smith, H. D. Lasswell and R. D. Casey (eds.), *Propaganda, Communication and
Public Opinion* (Princeton: Princeton University Press, 1946), p. 67.

particularly in the Democratic party. In recent years, the Democrats have recognized this by frequently reserving the national party chairmanship for a Catholic. Presidential nominees have had substantial higher education, particularly in the field of law; on the other hand, a substantial proportion of national chairmen have completed only elementary or secondary school.

Of particular political relevancy is the state of residence of presidential nominees and national chairmen at the time of first nomination or election. For the presidential nominees, the most frequent place of residence has been New York or Ohio. Among national chairmen, New York and Ohio have been similarly predominant, this ascendancy shared by Pennsylvania and Massachusetts. These states have been the homes of, at one time or another, powerful political machines and, almost invariably, vigorously competitive party politics. It should be no surprise that they are also major training grounds for party leadership of a highly competitive national party politics.

Politicization

The human individual is born into a world made up of groups, and many of these groups are actively interested in *socializing* him to their particular interests, preferences, and modes of behavior. Of the many types of groups—kinship, locality, age, faith, sex, educational, ethnic, occupational, friendship, political, and perhaps others—the political are concerned most with the civic education of the individual. Yet, all groups with which he comes in contact may influence the political behavior of the individual in one way or another; all these groups endeavor to communicate socializing messages, many with political implications, to the individual. Perception and cognition theories help us to understand how socializing groups may influence what we see and know of our political environment. Learning theories suggest how such information may be incorporated into our behavioral responses, particularly as attitudes and expectations. A fruitful concept in political research has been *attitude,* as indicated by the importance of Gallup Polls and the findings of the many major studies of American voting behavior. Another significant aspect of the socialization process is the situation in which it occurs, which may affect the manner and degree in which socializing messages may be accepted. Of growing interest in recent years is the process and consequences of the political socialization of the young. Adult socialization has received somewhat less attention, except to the extent that political propaganda may be considered an instrument of adult political socialization.

8

Elements of the Socialization Process

Almost before he can utter his first cry, the newborn child is a candidate for membership in many, many groups. He is an object of great interest to significant persons in different groups, and soon he is an audience for many messages from them. Mother and father often have a conception of the "kind of child" they would like to see develop. The family minister sees him as a prospective communicant. The local school board starts planning for his arrival as another pupil. The local party leader looks ahead to a new voter. Thus, groups and group leaders begin making claims on an individual's social and psychic life very early in his career. Each endeavors to socialize him in a particular group-oriented way.

The *socialization* of the individual is a process of social development resulting from the cognitive and attitudinal "inputs" of the many groups in the individual's environment. These inputs do not produce a "mechanical man" for they are infinite in variety, combinations, and relative influence upon the individual. The resulting personality, while it may have much stability and regularity of structure and content, is nonetheless continually changing, the rate of change undoubtedly varying at different periods of a normal lifetime; adolescence, for example, is generally believed to be a period of rapid change among Americans.[1]

[1] The research findings substantially confirm the proposition that the behavior of group members is significantly influenced by the composition of and stimuli from

Political socialization may be considered simply that type which affects the political roles, political responses, and the political culture of a community generally. Also distinguishing political socialization are its most active socializing agencies, that is, political groups such as government, secular schools, political parties, organized interests, and mass media.

GROUPS AS SOCIALIZERS

The scientific literature on socialization and the related field of child development is large. However, it is a field with "a large number of ill-assorted concepts and very tentative hypotheses." The literature about particular theoretical aspects of socialization, such as the agencies of socialization, the perceptual, cognitive, and attitudinal consequences of socialization, and the stimulus situations that evoke responses to which the individual has been socialized, is perhaps somewhat better developed.[2]

Definitions of the concept socialization are numerous. Child uses the term to describe "the whole process by which an individual, born with behavioral potentialities of enormously wide range, is led to develop actual behavior which is confined within a much narrower range—the range of what is customary and acceptable for him according to the standards of his group." Berelson and Steiner refer to socialization as "the training or molding by which an individual is made a member of a particular society, i.e., how the infant becomes a child, the child an adult." They add: "Since the socializing is necessarily done by people who are already members of a society, the process provides continuity for the society's intangibles by passing on its traditions, customs, skills, mores, morals, etc—that is, its culture—from one generation to another."[3]

---

the group to which they belong. Multiple group membership simply adds complexity to the basic hypothesis. W. W. Haythorn, "The Composition of Groups: A Review of the Literature," *Acta Psychologica*, 28 (1968): 97–128. It should also be noted that the field of social psychology is premised upon the above proposition.

[2] A comprehensive survey is found in David A. Goslin (ed.), *Handbook of Socialization Theory and Research* (Chicago: Rand McNally, 1969). See also, John A. Clausen (ed.), *Socialization and Society* (Boston: Little, Brown, 1968), and Irvin L. Child, "Socialization," in Gardner Lindzey (ed.), *Handbook of Social Psychology* (Cambridge: Addison-Wesley, 1954), Vol. II, p. 687. See also Bernard Berelson and Gary A. Steiner, *Human Behavior* (New York: Harcourt, Brace and World, 1964); John E. Anderson, "Child Development: An Historical Prespective," *Child Development*, 27 (June 1956): 181–196.

[3] Child, *op. cit.*, p. 655; Berelson and Steiner, *op. cit.*, p. 38.

Socialization Groups as Communicators

In the simplest sense, socialization is the process by which a group tells an individual what to do when. (Like any audience, the individual may hear only a portion of the message and behave only in part as directed.) If this is the essence of the process, it is, to some theorists, appropriate to analyze it according to the model of communication described in an earlier chapter; the communicator communicates a content through channels to an audience with some effect.[4]

As noted in Chapter 1, society contains many types of groups and organizations in which individuals find themselves, through birth or other chance circumstance, or with which they may affiliate as a matter of their own choice. The general types of groups noted earlier, with parenthetical illustrations of possible subtypes, included:

kinship (the family)
locality (neighborhood, nation)
age (children, adults)
faith (Protestant churches, Catholic church)
sex (women, men, transvestites)
educational (nursery school, college, alumni association)
ethnic (Caucasian, Negro, Oriental)
occupational (carpenter, machine operator, physician)
friendship (cronies, social clubs, sororities)
political (political parties, organized interests, governing organizations)

This is hardly an exhaustive list of group types or subtypes. The range would become very large if we were to attempt to list all *specific* groups. For example, anthropologists have produced enough knowledge about kinship groups in nearly all cultures to enable us to make generalizations about *the family* as a type of kinship group in any culture. We also know about *American families* and distinguish them from families in other societies. However, when we

---

[4] This statement of the socialization process is adopted by Fred I. Greenstein, *Children and Politics* (New Haven: Yale University Press, 1965), pp. 12–15. Greenstein's formulation: (1) who (2) learns what (3) from whom (4) under what circumstances (5) with what effects?

speak of *the John Doe family in Tennessee,* as distinct from all other American families, we are inevitably going to find additional distinctive characteristics. The same problems of classification occur in every other category; e.g., all educational groups, of which universities are a subtype, of which Yale is one specific and distinctive case. Each *specific* socializing group (Yale) usually has its own unique formulation of the socialization messages of a more comprehensive *subtype* (universities) and the even more comprehensive *general* group type (educational groups). Thus, in American society alone, there are many, many millions of general and specific socializing groups—many communicating similar socialization messages and others with relatively unique messages.

The particular socializing communicator is rarely an entire group. The individual usually hears from some specific group member what he is expected to do and what attitudes are commendable. The source may be a leader or some other authority figure: a parent in the kinship group, a teacher in his educational group, the president of his fraternity, his job supervisor, a crony, a peer member of the group, or an "opinion leader."[5] The group as a whole, on the other hand, may become a socializing source when it produces, for example, a collective statement of "instructions" for new or prospective members, such as may be found in textbooks, programs of training, job descriptions, statutes, and constitutions.

Socializing messages need not always be linquistic. Often important socializing information or attitudes are conveyed by models that may be imitated. Copying qualities and behaviors is perhaps the oldest manner for socialization. Whether in the form of hero worship or apprentice training, whether the fine quality of honesty displayed by a young George Washington in his report about cutting down the cherry tree or the cheerful endorsement of aggressive-but-fair play by a Willie Mays, imitation of models continues to be a pervasive approach to socializing-message formulation in every society.

[5] The concept *opinion leader* has attracted much interest in political sociology, particularly in connection with studies of mass communications and voting behavior. Elihu Katz concluded, in a survey of relevant studies, that "opinion leaders and the people whom they influence are very much alike and typically belong to the same primary groups of family, friends, and co-workers." Further, "despite their greater exposure to the media, most opinion leaders are primarily affected not by the communication media but by still other people." For example, the electorate consists of networks of interconnected individuals through which mass communications are channeled. "The Two-Step Flow of Communication: An Up-to-Date Report on an Hypothesis," *Public Opinion Quarterly,* 21 (Spring 1957), 61–78.

On the other hand, as societies become more verbal and more specialized, language tends to grow in importance as an instrument for carrying socialization messages. These messages may touch on a great variety of topics of interest to groups:

1. The group's conception of and general attitudes toward the environment, often stated as an ideology or a philosophy
2. The group's description of its general goals and its justification of their significance
3. The group's view of its own structure and boundaries
4. Identification of those events or situations to be of particular importance to its members
5. Information about the task behavior expected of members, along with information about possible punitive consequences that the individual may risk if he fails in his performance

In short, the messages advise the individual what to look for, what to like, what to do, and what to know in order to do it.

Over long periods of time, the individual is bombarded with these messages in differing intensities on particular occasions. For example, faith groups often carry on their most intensive socializing work during the individual's early childhood. There are the great socializing ritual occasions over a lifetime: confirmation into a church; graduation from a school; enrollment in a political party; weddings; christenings; burials. Occupational socialization goes on most intensively during late youth and early adulthood. With the prolongation of the individual life-span and creation of elaborate provisions for retirement, gerontologists and educators are becoming increasingly concerned with the continued socialization of older citizens.

The group, then, when viewed as a socializing agency, is essentially an educational—some would say propaganda—organization, providing its target individuals and audiences with goal and behavioral information, reinforcement of attitudes and expectations, and perceptual guidance.

A review of man's history suggests that, at different epochs, different types of socializing groups became predominant. In the Greek city-state, the family was apparently the major center of socialization. During the Middle Ages, the Church became the major socializer in the Western world. As kingdoms and nation-states emerged from the feudal order, the monarchy and the town became the principal socializing sources, later aided by the Protestant churches, particularly in America, secular schools and political parties assumed major responsibilities as socializing agencies. In the twentieth century these several types of socializers were joined by still another, the military services, which with the prevalence of universal military training often become a specifically political agency. The processes of contemporary socialization are complicated, however, by the pervasive and subtle influence of television. Significant amounts and types of behavioral cues are learned by the young as they watch TV, a process that is often put forward as an explanation of the predisposition toward violence found among young people in America.

It may be useful to survey briefly the generalized goals about which the various types of socializing groups usually communicate. The multiplicity of socializing agencies will again become evident as will the great overlapping among them.

A *kinship group* starts with a biological circumstance, namely, mating that produces offspring. Whether by biogenetic relationship, common ancestry, or legal procedures such as marriage certification or adoption, families and other kinship relations are established and may be terminated. The large body of family and household law produced by most developed societies and political communities is testimony of an overriding human interest in this type of group. In many societies, social and religious, as well as political, groups are very interested in protecting and maintaining families, expecting to work through them to achieve their own socializing objectives.

But family *as* family carries on its own elaborate goal and role instruction, for there are husband and wife roles, mother and father roles, son and daughter roles, sister and brother roles, not to mention the elaborate permutations and combinations that include uncles, aunts, grandparents, and cousins.

These represent almost as large a variety of behavioral expectations as there are individual personalities to perform them. The behaviors that represent "fine son" or "good aunt" or "loving wife" are numerous indeed.

A *locality group* arises out of the circumstance of spatial proximity. Physical proximity becomes a matter of significance in an age in which men can circle the earth in a matter of hours. Thus, in addition to neighborhoods, communities, and regions, there is increasingly the entire world as a locality grouping. When combined with political factors, these locality groups acquire other designations: precinct, township, city, county, state, and nation. The political importance of locality roles is readily illustrated by such designations as European, African, Southerner (vs. Northerner), Westerner (vs. Easterner), etc.

A *faith group* arises, historically speaking, from speculation about the relationship between human beings and the rest of the cosmos. Religions, churches, denominations, sects, congregations, and religious orders are the kinds of groups that offer sets of beliefs regarding the universal social order. Such groups usually consist of clerical leaders and rank-and-file communicants, with behavioral guidelines for both these roles. Faith groups often provide the most basic and generalized information and attitudes about human conduct, usually in the form of creeds and moral systems. The tone, style, and basic ethical concepts of political communities are often set by the socializing content of their faith groups.

Several types of groups are premised upon *sex differences.* Although originally an observable distinction based upon anatomy, the old male-female dichotomy has become complicated by social and psychological factors associated with the biological attributes. The roles of man and woman have come to have many gradations of behavior pattern. As for the political relevance of sex difference, we need only recall the history of the suffragettes and other women's rights movements. In recent years, homosexuals have begun to organize politically in order to protect certain rights to equal treatment as citizens.

With more than twenty million Americans over sixty-five and nearly half the population under twenty-five, the nation has become keenly aware of its *age groups.* The distinction between old and young is an ancient one; often it has been the principal ground for political controversy. It was not long ago, however, that men were old if they reached the age of forty. The remarkable prolongation of human life in most Western countries in the last century, with all of the concomitant social and economic legislation resulting from that longevity, has tended to divide the population into relatively self-conscious and often well-organized age groups. The consuming interest in juvenile delinquency is, after all, a concern for the socialization pathologies of adolescents. Consumer products for teenagers constitutes one of the richest manufacturing sectors of the American economy today. Since the Townsend Movement of the 1930s, senior citizens have mobilized some of the strongest lobbies in the nation.

Ethnic groups arise from certain anatomical and cultural distinctions, usually referred to as *race*. The specific attributes making for racial variation are widely studied and controverted. Like any other criterion of group distinction, race is as much a consequence of attribution by others as it is a deliberate self-recognition by ethnic group members. In fact, there is hardly a racial type—Caucasian, Negro, Oriental, or other—that does not become divided into many subtypes. Further, as individuals, many may have a sense of ethnic identity that others do not. In contemporary America, for example, much can be inferred about a particular person's socialization and his political orientation if he refers to himself as "Colored," "Negro," "Black," or "African."

People in *occupational groups* interact on the basis of productive skills and activities which result in the exchange of goods and services usually for monetary remuneration. The Department of Labor publishes a *Dictionary of Occupational Titles* which contains literally tens of thousands of job positions. These have been summarized by the Census Bureau into broad occupational categories that include: professionals, farmers and agricultural workers, executives, skilled workers, semiskilled workers, unskilled workers, and other types. Individuals performing occupational roles may group together in a variety of ways. A number of different types may be brought together according to manufacturing or production establishment; individuals with the same occupation may unite into guilds or unions to protect and promote the particular occupation.

In past generations, a man's occupation consumed the bulk of his time and attention during his lifetime; once socialized to his job, little further occupational socialization would be necessary. In contemporary America, however, a revolution in occupational socialization seems to be imminent as a consequence of rapid technological change (8,000 new occupations have been created in the last generation and 6,000 others have become obsolete), automation, and increased leisure. There is the real prospect that the same individual may pass through two or three careers—and attendant socializations—in a single lifetime.

A friendship or *sociability group* is one whose members interact primarily as a consequence of mutual affect, probably during recreational or leisure-time circumstances. A great variety of gangs and clubs could fall into this category. These groups often have no apparent or articulated goal other than the experience of pleasant companionship while "passing the time." The friendship component in political relationships, however, is a fundamental one and often reinforced by friendship groups.

Political groups, which most concern us here, are those related to the self-governance of men. They have specialized into a variety of types already noted: political parties, organized private interest associations, governments, bureaucracies, publics, electorates, etc. Socialization to these groups involves communication about, for example, what it takes to be a "good" citizen, Democrat, Republican, civil servant, voter, etc.

Inevitably the definitions and goals for each of the above group types are difficult to defend. A fraternity is, after all, *both* an educational and a sex-type group; but who is to say it is not also a friendship group? Today's politician cannot escape making his own definitions and working with the consequences of yesterday's socialization processes. With luck, however, he may have an opportunity to affect the direction of the next generation's socialization experiences.

GUIDES TO PERCEPTION AND KNOWLEDGE

The socializing group seeks nothing less than to mold its audience's perceptions, structure its knowledge, direct its attitudes, and influence the pattern of its responses. Relevant to these objectives are innumerable theories of perception, cognition, attitude, and learning, although it is difficult to draw points at which one of these aspects of behavior ends and another begins. At what point does perception become cognition? How, if at all, may we distinguish between learning and cognition? How do attitudes differ from opinions and expectations?

Perception

No person can experience or know his environment without his senses becoming involved. *Perception* has been called the "first event in the chain that leads from the stimulus to action."[6] Perception has

---

[6] E. G. Boring et al., *Foundations of Psychology* (New York: Wiley, 1948). For a succinct and thorough review of the perception theory literature, S. S. Zalkind and T. W. Costello, "Perception: Some Recent Research and Implications for Administration," *Administrative Science Quarterly,* 7 (September 1962): 217–235.

also been described as that "set of variables that intervene between sensory stimulation and awareness."[7] The object or segment of the environment that is perceived is variously referred to as "stimulus," "phenomenon," or "percept." Whatever it is "out there," it must alter light, sound, odor or otherwise affect sensory stimulators in order to create sensations in the sense organs. Perception, then, is a complex process by which "people select, organize, and interpret sensory stimulation into a meaningful and coherent picture of the world."[8]

Early psychological behaviorists reduced behavior to simple stimulus-response relations: any stimulus to which an organism has been conditioned will recurrently produce the same response from that organism. Perception theorists, however, subsequently called attention to the active part that the organism—the person—plays in how he receives the stimulus, organizes it, and interprets its meaning. Since the individual is unable to experience everything around him all at once, the perceiving process becomes one of narrowing the total field to those parts selected for attention or those parts that have some *apparent* experience content. Perception, in this usage, deals with our awareness of the objects and conditions around us and depends very much upon the impressions these objects make upon our senses. Although perception is the way things look to us, or the way they sound, feel, taste, or smell, it also involves, to some degree, an understanding, awareness, recognition or "meaning" for the perceiver.[9]

When is this recognition or meaning acquired? Despite extensive experiments with various forms of sensory perception, the answer is hardly conclusive. For example, in one experiment more than 1,000 chicks were tested on some 100 objects. Through a clear plastic container the chicks were presented with eight objects of graded angularity—from a sphere to a pyramid—during the first forty minutes of their visual experience after birth. The chicks were hatched in darkness to exclude any opportunity for postnatal learning. They pecked ten times oftener at the sphere than they did at the pyramid. The experiment clearly demonstrated that newborn chicks have a distinct preference for rounded shapes.[10] What was *not* clear was

[7] Charles E. Osgood, *Method and Theory in Experimental Psychology* (New York: Oxford University Press, 1953).
[8] Berelson and Steiner, *op. cit.*, p. 88.
[9] Floyd H. Allport, *Theories of Perception and Concept of Structure* (New York: Wiley, 1957), p. 14.
[10] Robert L. Fantz, "Form Preferences in Newly Hatched Chicks," *Journal of Comparative and Physiological Psychology*, 50 (October 1957): 422–430.

whether this perference had been acquired without learning or whether the prenatal experience of the chicks hatching in a sphere (the egg) may have had something to do with the predisposition.

A similar experiment was performed with human infants. Does the human infant have an innate or rapidly learned skill in form perception which introduces a measure of order and meaning into what would otherwise be a chaotic jungle of sensations? Facial patterns are among the first environmental stimuli for the infant. Therefore, infants were presented with three flat objects the size and shape of a human head. On one was painted a stylized face in black on a pink background. A second had the features rearranged in a scrambled pattern. The third was a solid patch of black at one end with an area equal to that covered by all the features. The forty-nine infants tested were from four days to six months old; the focus and duration of their visual attention was measured. As predicted, the infants looked most at the "real" face, somewhat less often at the scrambled face, and largely ignored the control pattern. Perceptual development undoubtedly proceeds rapidly from the infant's first recognition of the facial configuration. "Social perception follows with the child's recognition of precise detail in the facial pattern, with subsequent perception of subtle details of expression that may reveal the other person's attitude or thoughts."[11]

Substantial evidence indicates that the things we perceive are very much influenced by our cognitive and attitudinal relationship with them. Wittreich calls attention to our normal reaction to a person walking away from us. We see his image shrink in size but we know that, in fact, he is not shrinking. Therefore, we make an unconscious correction and "see" him as retaining his full stature. Past experience suggests to us what his true stature is with respect to our own. Any dependable expectation about the future requires that he have the same true stature when we next encounter him. Our perception is thus a prediction; it embraces the past and the future as well as the present.

Perception is not only closely related to the learning process, but also involves a conception of one's own self-image, needs, values, and purposes as much if not more than it involves the image of the object perceived. The emotional relationship between people, for example, also conditions how they see each other. In one experiment, married couples were asked to view their partner walking and peer-

[11] Robert L. Fantz, "Pattern Vision in Young Infants," *Psychological Record*, 8 (1958): 43–47.

ing through windows of rooms with distorted shapes. They were asked to make the same observation of a stranger. The more newly wed the couple, the more promptly they recognized the distortion of the room as his or her spouse entered it. The recognition of distortion was significantly less prompt when the stranger entered. Faced with the perceptual choice of seeing their partner or the room distorted, the newlyweds—presumably still in the glow of courtship —chose the latter.[12]

Perception in politics follows the same pattern, according to the Stanford Studies in International Conflict and Integration. Events during the summer of 1914 are a vivid illustration of how an international crisis may spiral as a consequence of leader perceptions. The Austro-Hungarian leaders had long been suspicious of the Serbians as agents of Tsarist Russian expansionism. Thus, with the assassination of the Archduke Francis Ferdinand in late June, 1914, the Austro-Hungarians perceived the act as an injury to themselves and as dangerously threatening. Serbia, they believed, must be punished and the Austro-Hungarian Empire "preserved at all costs." In moving to preserve itself, the Empire started a chain of events that led from one distorted perception to another. Germany's Kaiser Wilhelm was in an ambiguous position, on the one hand, seeking to preserve the status quo and, on the other, feeling as threatened as the Austro-Hungarians. The Kaiser agreed to let the Austro-Hungarians take care of Serbia, expecting nothing more than a local war.

England, France, and Russia failed to make unmistakably clear their determination to defend Serbia. In Vienna, the Austro-Hungarians saw only the prospect that the Russians would object but not intervene and that England would remain noncommital. The Russian response, however, was an attempt to "deter" Austria-Hungary by a "partial" mobilization. The Russian troop movements were perceived by the Kaiser, however, as intolerable and threatening, whereupon he invoked the Schleiffen Plan, a course of military action designed to protect Germany from a two-front war. The Plan called for an attack on France. This brought Great Britain into the war and started an irreversible chain.

A similar ambiguity in American intentions when it withdrew from Korea in 1948 is generally credited with leading to the Communist attack upon South Korea in 1950. The experience is said to

---

[12] Warren J. Wittreich, "The Honi Phenomenon: A Case of Selective Perceptual Distortion," *Journal of Abnormal and Social Psychology*, 47 (July 1952): 705–712.

have left a great impression upon President Kennedy, who recalled it as he faced the Cuban missile crisis in October, 1962. He promptly acted to make crystal clear American intentions by establishing a strict naval quarantine around that island to halt the missile build-up.

"Perception is always part of a larger *adaptive* act which brings some but not all qualities of objects into our experience. We are not randomly and helplessly responsive to stimuli; drive structures (i.e., goals and purposes) are fundamenal guarantors of this selectivity." In other words, "perception is directed and organized in terms of goal sets." What we see is what we hope will help us achieve an objective; the wish is father to the percept.[13]

Perception of objects, then, is to a large extent determined by culture and the group life of the individual. An average person's perception of the world is affected by his party, his club, his church, his place of work, the newspaper he reads, and by his group membership in general. And from these groups, in their socializing efforts, he receives values and knowledge which, in the special combination they make as part of his personality, affect his perceptions.[14] Perception is, therefore, also a personal and goal-directed reaction subject to needs and attitudes of the individual.[15]

In an experiment conducted during the last few weeks of the 1960 presidential election campaign, eighty members of the Young Democratic Club and thirty-nine members of the Young Republican Club of the University of Illinois were given a fifty-item interpersonal perception questionnaire. Each item consisted of a six-point scale whose polar points were a pair of logically opposite adjectives or nouns (cooperative-independent, indecisive-cocky, etc.) Each respondent scored himself, Kennedy, and Nixon on the questionnaire.

13 George S. Klein, "Cognitive Control and Motivation," in Gardner Lindzey (ed.), *Assessment of Human Motives* (New York: Grove Press, 1960), Ch. 4.

14 J. S. Bruner and C. C. Goodman, "Value and Need as Organizing Factors in Perception," *Journal of Abnormal Psychology* (1947): 33–44.

15 An excellent review of this affective aspect of perception may be found in Noel Jenkins, "Affective Processes in Perception," *Psychological Bulletin*, 54 (March 1957): 100–127. See also, Berelson-Steiner, *op. cit.*, Ch. 4. Neurophysiologists, however, continue to complain that our knowledge of sensory perception is grossly inadequate. The chairman of one medical symposium summed up the reported research as follows: There are factors controlling sensory data as it goes up the nerve pathways to the brain. Perhaps there is already modulation and distortion before reaching the perceptual centers in the head. In other words, by the time any sight, sound, smell, taste, or tactile sensation gets to the brain, it may already be far removed from reality. The new research suggests that experience not only modifies the higher centers, but also all the traffic carried by the sensory pathways as well. Reported in *Newsweek*, May 11, 1964, p. 89.

It was found that, despite the fact that members of the two parties did not differ in their self concepts, they did differ significantly in their perceptions of the two presidential candidates. However, the tendency to differentiate between self and the opponent was *not* significantly stronger than the tendency to differentiate between self and the preferred candidate for either party group. In other words, the adversary partisan designations of the candidates led to a *perceived difference between Kennedy and Nixon* which proved inconsistent with the *lack of difference between the candidates and the respondents* themselves.[16] What we see, therefore, depends a good deal on what we already know. Perception and cognition are apparently inextricably related.

Cognition

Although the problem of knowing is an ancient one, cognitive theory in behavioral science is a recent and relatively controversial area of investigation. The main thrust of theoretical work in this field places its referents somewhere between the source of a stimulus and the organism's adaptive behavior or response. *Cognition* is generally concerned with the *organization* of representational structures of perception of both internal and external phenomena.

The main elements of cognition are "bits" of knowledge about one's self, other people, and the world. These "bits" presumably are made up of language, pictures, and other phenomenal representations for which cognition serves as an integrating process. E. C. Tolman argues that cognition deals with holistic or "molar" behavior or total acts, involving the full participation of the individual as an organism with a capacity for psychic organization. This psychic organism interacts as an entity with his environment, or with what Lewin calls his "life-space." In cognitive theory, this environment is actually an internal representation or *perceptual map* of that outside world and the organism's place in it. The self or ego construct is the crucial element in this point of view. It is the ego that cognitively structures and integrates the perceptions mediated within the regions of the organism and registered on its neural centers. The central organizing influence of the ego or the self involves the person's "awareness of being, of functioning" and results from a

16 J. E. McGrath and M. F. McGrath, "Effects of Partisanships on Perceptions of Political Figures," *Public Opinion Quarterly*, 26 (Summer 1962): 236–248.

process of continuous evaluative interaction with the environment. In short, the capacity for purposiveness in individual development is as essential to the organization of a person's ego as it is for organizing his social groups. Valued purposes are associated with the emergence of the ego, and the ego is the center of the cognitive process of the individual.[17]

Cognitive theory (and learning theory as well) have received a substantial and unexpected spur from the technological development of electronic computers.[18] Alterations in the molecular structure of neurons as a result of chemical changes in the synapse are thought to be theoretically analogous to the magnetizing of cathode ray tubes in computers. Information storage is accomplished by the same binary coding system. The human brain is composed of more than ten billion nerve cells available to serve as storage units for binary data, whereas computers can store only several million "bits." Behavioral researchers continue to work on this analogy in a field known as "computer simulation of cognitive processes."

Each human organism lives through a unique environmental experience and acquires a unique cognitive collection of information bits. To the extent that there exist similarities in experience and information, there also exist similarities in attitude and behavior pattern among persons. However, in view of the infinite number of combinations of experience and information, individuals are *invariably* unique. Similarly, each person's self or ego, role structure, goal orientations, and value priorities constitute a unique combination. Thus, of necessity, each individual becomes the sole judge of the worth he attaches to each of his life experiences and to the information he holds in mental storage.

Out of these factors there comes a circularity in the relationship between goals and information. Goals are suggested to an individual

[17] Martin Scheerer, "Cognitive Theory," in Gardner Lindzey (ed.), *Handbook of Social Psychology* (Cambridge, Mass.: Addison-Wesley, 1954), Vol. I, Ch. 3. Significant related works include: Leon Festinger, *A Theory of Cognitive Dissonance* (New York: Row, Peterson, 1957); Fritz Heider, "Attitudes and Cognitive Organization," *Journal of Psychology*, 21 (1946): 107–112. Also, Jack Brehm and Arthur Cohen, *Explorations in Cognitive Dissonance* (New York: Wiley, 1962); Douglas Lawrence and Leon Festinger, *Deterrents and Reinforcement* (Stanford: Stanford University Press, 1962); Leon Festinger, *Conflict, Decision and Dissonance* (Stanford: Stanford University Press, 1964).

[18] For example, W. Ross Ashby, "Simulations of a Brain," in Harold Borko (ed.), *Computer Applications in the Behavioral Sciences* (Englewood Cliffs, N.J.: Prentice-Hall, 1962), Chap. 19; Edward A. Feigenbaum and Julian Feldman, *Computers and Thought* (New York: McGraw-Hill, 1963). A popular review of this area may be found in Marvin L. Minsky, "Artificial Intelligence," in *Scientific American* Editors, *Information* (San Francisco: W. H. Freeman and Co., 1966).

by socializing groups, then modified by his experience and other acquired information. The more favored goals will activate the individual to expend substantial information cost in the acquisition and organization of information if the new information appears to facilitate achievement of the goals. As the individual's cognitive structure grows, so do his ego and goal images as well as the values, attitudes, and expectations associated with each of them. So it goes through a lifetime, hastened along and sometimes substantially influenced by the individual's socializing groups.[19]

Learning Theory

After the organism perceives an environmental stimulus and incorporates that experience in some way into his cognitive structure, it remains stored there until a subsequent event excites it as part of a response pattern. The response pattern that takes into account the newly stored information is presumably different from previous response patterns of a similar type; that is, the newly stored information presumably has a modifying consequence for behavior. This is also called *learning*.

Like other behavioral concepts, learning is a theoretical construct which must be inferred from observed behaviors. According to Kuhn, learning takes place when, as a result of experience, a given stimulus (input) elicits a different response (output) than it did before. A critical aspect of learning is the adaptation process, that is, the process of discovering what is possible and then selecting a preferred behavior from among the possible alternatives. According to Estes, "learning" is "almost universally defined and measured in terms of a change in the probability, or frequency, with which a given stimulating situation evokes a response (or instances of a response class) that has been designated as 'correct' by the experimenter."[20]

[19] The relevance of learned goals and "rational" decisions relating to them is worth recalling at this point. Herbert Simon's discussion in *Models of Man, Social and Rational* (New York: Wiley, 1957), at pp. 198–199, regarding "bounded rationality" is particularly appropriate. If information is the reduction of uncertainty, rationality in this context is the reduction of uncertainty about choices likely to bring into reality currently envisaged goals. The discussion of cognitive dissonance below is closely related to such phenomena as psychic anxiety resulting from informational uncertainty and disorientation.

[20] Alfred Kuhn, *The Study of Society* (Homewood, Ill.: Dorsey Press, 1963), p. 57; W. K. Estes, "Learning Theory and the New 'Mental Chemistry'," *Psychological Review*, 67 (July 1960): 207–223. Surveys of the development of learning theory may be found in Louis P. Thorne and A. M. Schmuller, *Contemporary Theories of Learning* (New York: Ronald Press, 1954) and E. R. Hilgard, *Theories of Learning* (Revised ed.; New York: Appleton-Century-Crofts, 1956).

Learning is the gerund form of the verb "to learn," indicating that most theorists are concerned with a dynamic process. Their big question is: By what discernible psychic steps does acquired information become incorporated into the cognitive structure so as to have consequences for subsequent behavior? Thus far, psychologists have identified several factors that seem to occur in many learning situations, namely, (a) association of stimuli or stimulus response events, (b) reinforcement, and (c) motivation. *Association* usually refers to some connection in time between two events, e.g., lightning and thunder, which usually occur in close temporal sequence. Contiguity, or association in space, may be a significant aspect of this connection. Such connections, usually in the physical world, provide occasions for the individual to form associations. S-R, or stimulus-response association, suggests that the learner *directly* associates a stimulus event with a *particular* response, e.g., the red traffic light that the driver immediately associates with the learned response of engaging the brakes of his car. Some psychologists try to explain *all* association as S-R association.

Reinforcement is another significant aspect of learning. An act or event that has a satisfying effect—escape from punishment, achievement of a goal, relief from fear—will be learned, according to reinforcement theory. Reinforcement requires that stimuli be presented in pairs: the first to become associated with a response pattern, and the second to reward an appropriate response. Some theories of reinforcement call for a third factor involving need-reduction or drive-reduction. An organism that is attempting to reduce a need or to satisfy a drive is said to be *motivated*. Motivation presumably leads the organism to expand substantial energy and run through an extensive number of trials in order to find the response that leads to the reinforcer.

In classical conditioning experiments, such as Pavlov's at the turn of the century, a neutral conditioned stimulus, e.g., a bell, is paired with an unconditioned stimulus, e.g., food, the latter evoking an unconditioned response, salivation. After repeated pairings of the two stimuli, the conditioned stimulus (bell) will elicit a response similar to the unconditioned response (salivation). This acquired response is called the *conditioned response* (CR).

Conditioning experiments also consider a converse process called *extinction*, that is, the weakening of conditioned response. Extinction is obtained usually by presenting the conditioned stimulus (e.g., a bell), but withdrawing its paired relationships with the unconditioned stimulus (food). A process called *spontaneous recovery* occurs when a conditioned response that has been extinguished recovers (spontaneously) some of the strength lost in extinction after an interval of rest.

Instrumental learning differs from classical conditioning in that the learner takes an active part and *emits* responses instead of having the responses elicited from him. In this type of learning, also called "operant conditioning," a response by the learner is itself instrumental in producing a reinforcing stimulus. The response which produced the reinforcement becomes stronger, that is, more likely or probable to occur, whereas that which is not reinforced becomes weaker. B. F. Skinner has emphasized the importance of instrumental learning in the socialization process by pointing out how socializing agencies, such as schools and government, often use reinforcements to shape behavior. For example, as we have previously noticed, charitable giving is encouraged by the Christian ethic that prevails in the United States. Congress has reinforced this behavior by allowing tax deductions for it. In time, taxpayers in many instances began to give in order to obtain the deduction rather than the ethical satisfaction. Beliefs, customs, and group goals may be learned through the operation of instrumental learning, particularly during such periods as crises when there may be heightened disposition to perceive connections and retain associations.[21]

Avoidance learning is an important type of instrumental learning and is based upon *negative* reinforcements, stimuli that are painful, uncomfortable, or fearsome, and hence to be avoided. Avoidance learning relates to avoiding or preventing the unpleasant situation *before* it occurs. *Escape learning* is the process of learning how to get away from or eliminate an unpleasant situation after the individual is already in it. In general, avoidance learning is motivated by anticipated punishment, that is, the application of a noxious or unpleasant stimulus. Yet, despite the fact that punitive measures are widely employed by society, many questions have arisen regarding the effectiveness of such procedures in controlling behavior. The following conclusion about punishment is by Morgan and King:

> Punishment . . . does not permanently weaken a habit that has been learned under strong motivation. If the punishment is strong enough, it may completely suppress the habit, but this leaves the

21 B. F. Skinner, *Science and Human Behavior* (New York: Macmillan, 1953).

individual in a conflict between fear and other motives. If the punishment is mild, it temporarily suppresses the habit and gives an opportunity for other responses to be learned. Without such alternative responses, mild punishment does little good. When an individual has already learned many alternative responses, mild punishment may serve as a cue for what is "wrong" and thus indirectly encourage him to do what is "right."[22]

Comprehensive general theories of learning are numerous. They are only briefly reviewed here. Connectionist theory, for example, assumes that learning takes place through the "connections" which are "stamped in" the synapse through constant reaction to given stimuli. From this point of view, learning is defined as a link between two or more neurons.

Conditioning theories emphasize the adaptive feature of the learning process, in which all reactions are seen as physiologically motivated and leading to the elimination of tension-producing stimuli. According to one conditional theorist, learning is a reinforcement of habit; according to another, learning is a process by which reflexes are modified.

Gestalt theory views learning as primarily a matter of insight, in which the learner grasps some "essential unity" in the stimulus or in nature. Gestaltists believe that the learning process is an attempt on the part of the organism to achieve a balance or state of equilibrium when confronted with a disequilibrium. The similarities between gestalt theory and the psychic organization element of cognitive theory are appreciable.

The functionalist school considers learning as a social process in which practical results are essential. The basic rationale of man's responses may be found in the need for survival. One of the most influential functionalists was John Dewey, for whom learning was a process by which men adjust to their environment, which in turn is hostile, problematical, a source of uncertainty. Festinger's theory of cognitive dissonance may be considered a product of the functionalist position.

Cognitive Dissonance

The relationship between an individual's cognitive structure and personality structure as these interact with the social structure con-

[22] C. T. Morgan and R. A. King, *Introduction to Psychology* (Third ed.; New York: McGraw-Hill 1966).

stitute the main elements of the theory of cognitive dissonance. *Cognitive structure* refers to the individual's phenomenological representation of himself and the world, that is, the set of ideas maintained by him and relatively available to his conscious awareness. Cognitive structure is an important aspect of the person's total *personality structure*, the latter being a more inclusive phenomenon encompassing all psychological aspects of the person whether or not he is aware of them. *Social structure* refers to the patterns of interactions among people as they engage in behaviors appropriate to their social positions. Positions involve patterned behaviors, repetitive acts that are linked with the behaviors of others; the focus of positions is not on the activities of particular individuals, but on activities which are shared by the incumbents of any given position type and observed within the context of the role performances of these incumbents. In the course of such patterned interactions, the incumbents develop shared definitions of themselves and of their environment, and these definitions come to be known as *culture.*

The notion of *structure* should be regarded here as a set of elements and the relations among them. Cognitive structure, personality structure, and social structure, therefore, consist of sets of elements and relations among them. For this reason, cognitive as well as the other structures are often theoretically analyzed as though they had organization properties, such as association, hierarchy, and integration, or could be in states of disorganization, such as inconsistency, imbalance, or dissonance. Out of the latter condition of imbalance or dissonance, Festinger argues, arises significant individual activity aimed at dissonance reduction.[23]

Cognitive dissonance, according to Festinger, refers to a relation among cognitions (knowledge, opinions, or beliefs about the environment) which exist simultaneously for a person. In general, two cognitions are dissonant with each other if, considering these two cognitions alone, the obverse of one follows from the other. For example, a person may "know" that "capitalism will destroy itself." He (obviously an orthodox Marxist) also "knows" that the United States and other capitalist nations are maintaining remarkable economic development. These obverse cognitions have produced

---

[23] William A. Scott, "Cognitive Structure and Social Structure: Some Concepts and Relationships," in N. F. Washburne (ed.), *Decisions, Values and Groups* (New York: Pergamon Press, 1962), Vol. 2, pp. 87 ff.; Festinger, *Theory of Cognitive Dissonance, op. cit.* Festinger's theory and supporting research are discussed above in Chapter 5.

much Marxist cognitive dissonance and for some have led to modification of cognitions, that is, Communist revisionism.

In Festinger's view, "the existence of cognitive dissonance is comparable to any other need state. Just as hunger is motivating, cognitive dissonance is motivating." Cognitive dissonance, therefore, gives rise to activity oriented toward reducing or eliminating the dissonance. Successful reduction of dissonance is rewarding in the same sense that eating when one is hungry is rewarding. Thus, the existence of dissonant or "nonfitting" relations among cognitive elements gives rise to psychic pressures to reduce dissonance or avoid its aggravation. These pressures may result in manifest behavioral changes, cognitive restructuring of perceptions, avoidance of commitments, or cautious exposure to new information or opinion.

Dissonance may also be a major motivating factor in the "strain toward symmetry" noted in Chapter 2 on communication. This suggests another explanation for the importance attached to communicative activity in a democratic system, namely, the reduction of cognitive dissonance. In fact, a politician's principal skill may well be the management of language and symbols so as to create or reduce cognitive dissonance for the constituencies with which he deals.

ATTITUDES AND EXPECTATIONS AS SOCIALIZING COGNITIONS

Among the most important types of cognitions acquired by the individual from socializing groups are attitudes and expectations. Opinions are usually considered overt behavioral manifestations of these two.

Attitude

The concept *attitude* is one of the great "discoveries" of modern behavioral science. It is a theoretical construct, like magnetism, electricity, or gravity, in that an attitude cannot be seen or otherwise directly observed; it must be inferred from observable events. For example, the presence of magnetism must be inferred from the observable behavior of two metals as they are attracted toward each other. Similarly, an attitude must be inferred from the response of a person to objects and situations in his environment; the response may be verbal or some other behavioral manifestation.

The concept attitude was well accepted by 1935 in sociopsychological studies. In that year, Gordon W. Allport synthesized the definitions of the concept in the statement below. A year later, a significant new device was added to the analysis of American politics when the Gallup Poll offered its first presidential election forecast. Gallup predicted a Roosevelt landslide, whereas the authoritative *Literary Digest* Poll forecast a Landon victory. The latter proved so wrong that the *Literary Digest* ceased publication shortly thereafter. Today, scientific sampling of public attitudes is a big business, serving the advertising, communications, and political "industries" of the nation.

An attitude, according to Allport, is:

> . . . a mental and neural state of readiness, organized through experience, exerting a directive or dynamic influence upon the individual's response to all objects and situations with which it is related.[24]

Examination of the components of this early definition suggests that, even in the light of more recent knowledge, the components continue to serve as relevant intentions. "Mental and neural," for example, would probably be lumped together today by contemporary physiological psychologists as "neural" factors. The functional analogy between nervous system and electronic computer, each as an integrated information transmitting and storing system, recommends the discard of the old distinction between mental and neural.

Similarly, "state of readiness" may now be viewed as that awareness or sensitivity that results from the presence or imprimiture of information on some part of the molecular structure of a neuron. Thus, a person who has never seen or touched a hot stove will have no information in his neural system regarding the hotness of stoves and the risks of being burned. By actually touching a hot stove or accepting a verbal warning against doing so, he may of course become "sensitized," that is, arrive at a state of readiness for avoiding direct contact with hot stoves.

[24] "Attitudes," in C. M. Murchison (ed.), *Handbook of Social Psychology* (Worcester, Mass.: Clark University Press, 1935), pp. 798–844.

Cognitions, we have seen, are acquired through experience.[25] That experience may be of various types: direct, vicarious, linguistic (hence representational), or symbolic. In his lifetime the human individual experiences many millions of objects and situations, toward all of which he develops attitudes or constellations of attitudes. Out of this accumulation of experience comes the "organization" described in the earlier discussion of cognitive structure and personality structure. Information and attitudes associated with a first encounter with an object or situation will affect subsequent responses to the same or similar objects and situations. Attitudes then become organized when one attitude is associated regularly and consistently with other attitudes. Love of one's own family domicile, for example, has much to do with love of homes generally, love of community, and love of country in which the home is located.

To the extent that a previous attitude predisposes the individual to certain objects and situations, that attitude exerts a dynamic influence upon the individual's responses. Learning theorists are concerned with investigating how such attitudinal dynamisms work.

Attitudes have been more or less successfully "measured" by behavioral scientists. More specifically, several attributes of attitudes have been defined in a measurable manner, that is, operationalized. Thus, every attitude has a *target*, that is, an object, situation, event, relationship, or symbolic representation—sometimes real and sometimes not—toward which it is directed. An attitude may then have these measurable attributes with respect to the target:

1. Direction
2. Degree
3. Intensity
4. Saliency

[25] We need not digress very long into the old nature-nurture argument whether genetic or environmental influences are more significant in the development of the individual. However, some fascinating discoveries are being made about genetic influences on neural structures. The lowly freshwater planarian is a type of flatworm with a rudimentary central nervous system, a blind-ended gut, no circulatory system, and a distinct head end that exerts control over the rest of its body. Experiments reveal that the planarian can grow a new "brain" if the original is removed. It will also accept transplants from other planarians. It is possible to grind up and feed a dead planarian to living ones, producing behavioral responses uniquely in the experience of the deceased planarian among those still living. Hugh McCann, *Science Digest*, October, 1960, p. 3; Jay Boyd Best, "Proto-psychology," *Scientific American*, February, 1963, pp. 55 ff. It has already been suggested that the same principle be applied in higher education, that is, that professors be ground up and fed to students in lieu of textbooks.

DIMENSIONS OF AN ATTITUDE

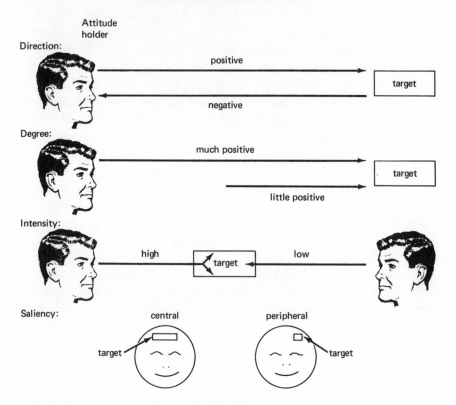

Probably the basic dimension of an attitude is its *direction* toward or away from, for or against its target. The object, situation, event, or relationship is "liked" or "disliked." If the individual is favorable to or attracted by the target, he is said to have a *positive affect* toward it. If he is unfavorable or repelled by the target, he has a *negative affect*. Thus, a favorable attitude is one in which we are predisposed toward the target, in a state of readiness to lend it our support or evaluate it among "good things." If the attitude is unfavorable, its target is in the class of "bad things." "Good" and "bad" are, of course, ancient evaluative categories.

Measuring the direction of an attitude is often simply a matter of inquiring if the person favors or opposes some target. "Are you for or against Eisenhower?" If this question were asked some time near the end of World War II, nearly all Americans who knew of the General's leadership of the European crusade against the Axis would, in admiration and gratitude, respond, "Yes." However, if the question were: "Are you for or against Eisenhower *for Presi-dent?*" a different distribution of responses would result, perhaps 55 percent favorable and 45 percent unfavorable. The first question had a single target, "Eisenhower"; the second had two, "Eisenhower" and "President." In the second question, while the broad positive affect for Eisenhower in the mid-1950s might influence many responses in a favorable direction, other famous names—Taft, Stevenson, etc.—were also favorably associated with "President." In other words, the targets in the second question were numerous and in complicated relationship to each other; therefore, a simple unidirectional response was no longer to be expected.

Attitudes vary in *degree*. For example, two individuals may hold generally positive attitudes toward some target. One, however, may be mildly favorable and the other strongly favorable. Degree may sometimes be measured by words: "very much" is more than "a little"; "love" is stronger than "like," and so on. In attitudinal research, the respondent is often asked to rate on some scale presented him the degree to which he holds a particular attitude. Special scales, such as Guttman scales, are designed so that cumulative responses to several questions may provide a more accurate measure of degree.

Intensity of attitude refers to the tenacity with which it is held. On the above chart, this is suggested by the extent to which the arrows representing attitudes are "hooked in" to the target. Ordinarily, degree and intensity correlate positively; a high degree of affect is likely to be held with some tenacity. Nevertheless, the two attributes are different. It is quite possible to hold a mild attitude with great tenacity. For example, consider the individual who, asked if he likes drinking alcoholic beverages, responds: "Oh, I can take it or leave it." He is neither strongly for nor strongly against alcoholic beverages, and he may hold this moderate attitude with substantial intensity.

Saliency is a fourth measurable attribute of attitudes. Open-ended interviews and projective tests are often used by investigators to discover the saliency of a particular target in the attitudinal structure of an individual, that is, whether the target is "on the top of the individual's mind." This dimension relates to the central or peripheral location of the target in the individual's perceptual and cognitive systems. Here again, there is often a dimensional correlation with other attributes; a central or salient target is often the object of a high degree of affect intensely held. The things we do not have "at the top of our minds" are likely to be peripheral matters of mild or low-intensity affect.

Opinion

Unlike attitudes, *opinions* are usually considered overt responses to actual situations. Opinions rest upon one attitude or a constellation of attitudes. Most targets in the environment are made up of a complex of objects, situations, and events. A person may have an attitude toward each element in the complex, particularly if he has had earlier experience with each of them. However, there may also be unfamiliar elements in the complex which, under the circumstances, he will associate with the elements that are already known. The overt response which results from the individual's network of attitudes toward particular elements in the complex target is his opinion.

Put another way, opinions are situational, that is, overt and tentative responses which serve as guides to action in dealing with the problematical situations confronting the individual. In responding to a situation, particularly an unfamiliar one, the individual assesses the relevant targets in the environment, recalls his past experience, and recapitulates attitudes that seem relevant. More or less self-consciously, then, the individual works out a definition of the situation and a conception of appropriate action (based upon his attitudinal complex) in dealing with it. He *may* or *may not* act in accordance with his opinion, depending upon such other factors as resistance from the environment and confidence in his opinion. Thus, a diner in a restaurant may express the opinion that "the best thing to do with this meal is to toss it out." Whether or not he actually does so will depend upon his attitude toward restaurants, those dining with him, and the propriety of such a dramatic reaction to poor food. His expressed opinion will be the vector resulting from a complex of relevant attitudes, but his actual behavioral response will be the vector of evaluations more comprehensive than his attitudes, including an estimate of the risks involved.[26]

[26] The above survey is based upon E. L. Hartley, R. E. Hartley, and Clyde Hart, "Attitudes and Opinions," in Wilbur Schramm (ed.), *The Process and Effects of Mass Communication* (Urbana, Ill.: University of Illinois Press, 1954), pp. 216–250.

Expectation

An *expectation* is an attitude combined with other elements. These additional elements seem to be temporal, predictive, and instrumental. From the *temporal* point of view, an expectation is always a present mental conception of some prospective future event or behavior. An expectation is akin to a goal or purpose, the latter being a presently envisaged future state of affairs desired by the individual. An expectation, on the other hand, need not be desired, that is, its attitudinal direction may be either favorable or unfavorable.

The *predictive* aspect of an expectation not only anticipates the future event or behavior but also views its probability. Whether the grounds for such anticipation is a scientific analysis or a strong wish, this probabilistic element makes the expectation predictive, such as the expectation that Jones will win the election or the expectation that Smith will successfully fulfill the task expectations associated with the position he holds.

The *instrumental* aspect of an expectation is closely related to the attitudinal in that the anticipated event or behavior may be contributory to some goal or purpose of the holder. Brown's "high expectations" of Jones' performance in a particular public office may be an anticipation that Jones' actions will be instrumental in the advancement of Brown's goals.

In brief, expectations are a future-oriented, goal-related, probability-estimating type of attitude or opinion.[27]

SOCIALIZING SITUATIONS

An important factor in the socialization process is the situation or setting in which the socialization occurs. In Chapter 5, we noted how the individual decision maker faces his situation of choice. In Chapter 6, we examined the group analyzing its situation of choice. In the socialization process, the situation or setting is relevant to another aspect of behavior, that is, to the reception of cognitive and affective information. The socializing situation, in other words, may influence the recipient's perception and learning.

[27] Expectation is related to the phenomenon of subjective probability discussed in Chapter 5. The predictive element of an expectation may be based upon either a personal or subjective probability estimate or an objective mathematical probability judgment derived from systematically observed and quantified evidence.

The expressed opinions of other members of a group may create a "situation" that changes the views of an individual. This has been demonstrated in a number of perception experiments. In one of these, a group of eight individuals was instructed to match the length of a given line with one of three unequal lines. Each member of the group announced his judgment publicly. However, in the midst of this procedure, one individual found himself suddenly contradicted by the entire group. This contradiction was repeated again and again in the course of the experiment. With the exception of the one minority individual, the others were accomplices of the experimenter who signaled when they were to render wrong but unanimous judgments. The person in a minority of one, faced perhaps for the first time in his life with a unanimous majority, was then permitted to modify his response. In one-third of all the estimates made by these minority individuals, judgments were modified in the direction of the majority's. On the other hand, the rest stood firm despite the pressure of the majority. Differences between subjects who yielded and those who remained independent were examined. The importance of several situational elements was demonstrated. Independent judgments were maintained (a) if the majority was slightly less than unanimous, (b) if the majority consisted of fewer than three persons, and (c) as the objective size of the error of the majority in matching the lines grew. There were, of course, obvious (but uncontrolled in this experiment) variations in the personality attributes of the yielders and the independents.[28]

The socializing group is a kind of propaganda organization. If we accept the communication model of socialization, such a view is not farfetched. After all, socializing groups are engaged in instructional attempts, not all of which are successful. The "disobedient" child is "unsocialized" according to the yardstick of some unsuccessful socializing agent—say, parent or teacher. The very same disobedient behavior may be perfectly in accord with the recommended behavior of a competing socializing group, say, his playmates or a street gang. In the manner of other propaganda organizations, therefore, the socializing group may, as one tactic, endeavor to shape the socializing situation in order to reinforce a learning association in some desired manner. Thus, socializing instruction is usually more

[28] S. E. Asch, *Social Psychology* (New York: Prentice-Hall, 1952), Chap. 16; and also "Effects of Group Pressure Upon the Modification and Distortion of Judgments," in Harold Guetzkow (ed.), *Groups, Leadership, and Men* (Pittsburgh: Carnegie Press, 1951).

acceptable, hence more successful, in a family or a school situation in which there is an atmosphere of group affection and trust.

The discussion in Chapter 2 of Newcomb's model of communicative act noted how "strain toward symmetry" is facilitated by favorable attitudes ("attraction") of communicator and audience toward each other as persons. This, too, has been confirmed experimentally. Two groups of subjects were presented with identical communications, one rendered by a "trustworthy" communicator and the other by an "untrustworthy" one. The topics had to do with antihistamine drugs, atomic submarines, steel production shortages, and the future of movie theaters. A typical trustworthy source was a medical journal and a typical untrustworthy one was *Pravda*. The content of each communication was intended to change the opinion held by each subject on a topic. When before-and-after opinions in the two experimental groups were compared, it was clear that opinion change was influenced by the credibility of the source. Untrustworthiness decreased audience acceptance of the content material.[29]

Standard, recurring situations may serve as the conditioned stimuli for evoking socialized behaviors. For example, driving on a highway safely is possible only because the automobile industry and most state governments have carefully standardized the driving situation. A person in the role of "driver" must be certified as having learned standard responses to standardized features of vehicle operation and traffic movement: slowing the vehicle at intersections, driving to the right of the road, and responding to road sign instructions.

Socializing situations may be perceived and understood differently by those who are socializers and those who are targets of their socializing efforts. This is nowhere better illustrated than in the administration of penalties for crimes. Society identifies certain activities as "criminal," or antisocial, in its laws. Crimes are subdivided into many types, presumably according to seriousness (degree to which society perceives each type as antisocial) which facilitates the assignment of penalties. The more serious the crime (e.g., murder), the more serious the penalty (e.g., death sentence). The classification of crimes and associated penalties has become quite refined. For example, a "robbery" is the taking of another's property from his person or in his immediate presence by the use of violence or intimidation, whereas "burglary" is the breaking into a house with

29 Carl I. Hovland and Walter Weiss, "The Influence of Source Credibility on Communication Effectiveness," *Public Opinion Quarterly*, 15 (1952): 635–650.

the intent to commit theft or other felony. Robbery and burglary draw different legal penalties.

In all of this matching of punishment to crime, society's legislative *assumption*—largely untested in any scientific way—is that known punishments will become part of the socialization of all its members and will deter them from committing such crimes. A subsidiary assumption, also untested, is that an applied punishment will deter actual criminals from doing the evil deed again.

The criminal may, and often does, see the socializing situation quite differently. He may be a member of a subculture—ghetto, drug, or other—that views most prevailing social norms as hostile or warranting exploitation. From the point of view of *his* subculture socialization, the *successful* criminal may be something of a subculture hero—skillfull, well-to-do, and unapprehended by the "enemy," the law enforcement agencies of the community. For such a person the system of legal penalties becomes a choice among risks; should he risk two years of prison for robbery or five years for burglary, for example? The decision will rest on the confidence he has in his skills and the size of the "take" he expects from the "job." The deterrent force of the legal penalties is likely to be a minor influence, if any at all, in the prospective criminal's mind. He has been listening to his subculture's, and not society's, socializing messages. His socializing situation is hardly what the lawmakers have assumed.

Let us assume that this criminal is caught, tried, and imprisoned for the period specified by law. Will the punitive experience deter him from ever performing a crime again? The evidence on recidivism, or repetition of punishable acts upon release from internment, hardly supports such an expectation. "Repeaters" are a disproportionately large part of the prisoner population of the United States. The legislative *assumption* is that the prison experience will teach the criminal a "lesson," that is, socialize him to more law-abiding ways. This assumption fails to take into account the demonstrable fact that prisons and rehabilitation centers are populated by a very large proportion of criminals, addicts, and other types of social delinquents who find the primary-group life of prison more secure and structured than any other they have known. For these "repeaters," getting "back in" is more like "coming home" than punishment for wrong-doing. The prison community itself socializes them to its norms through a reward-and-punishment system perhaps much more meaningful to the imprisoned criminal than any devised by society at large.

Thus, socializers and their targets may be operating from highly different socializing situations. Socializers may *assume* a role and reference group structure in their targets that has no reality in fact. A potential social delinquent may be more concerned about the disapproval of his subculture peers than about the penalties of a hostile legislature or law enforcement system. If the criminal code were constructed around the psychodynamics of the typical criminal himself, it would have to be largely rewritten.

POLITICAL SOCIALIZATION

Recorded human history is, by and large, a tale of public attempts to socialize the human animal. Medicine men and tribal chieftains prescribed rules of conduct on a relatively ad hoc basis much like the circuit judges of medieval England. With the development of written language came an interest in setting down in writing some of the principal prescriptions of acceptable social conduct. One of the most venerable and influential of these is the Decalogue, or Ten Commandments, that governed the ancient Israelites, presumably written by "the finger of God" on two tablets of stone for Moses.

The Commandments, mainly constraints stated in the negative ("thou shalt not"), were and continue to be fundamental guides to civic socialization. Safety of person underlies the commandments not to kill or bear false witness. The integrity of the family as the basic social unit is supported by the commandments to honor father and mother and not to commit adultery. Property is presumably protected by the stricture against stealing or coveting what is thy neighbor's. The other commandments establish the monotheistic Judeo-Christian religious systems of the Western world. The Ten Commandments are, in short, one of man's oldest efforts in civic education.

The political community is the most comprehensive secular group in which most individuals hold membership. Only in recent centuries have political communities, that is, city-states and nation-states, taken on the task of doing their own socializing. In former times, religious and military leaders did most of the politicizing work of the community, although this practice is hardly extinct. This meant communicating cognitive and affective information regarding such questions as: Wherein lies the ultimate sovereignty (most authoritative source of decisions) of the community? Is the voice of God speaking through a pope or a king? Or is the voice of the people speaking through elected leaders? What persons and activities would ensure order and justice without denying the community the benefits of dissent and change?

In his concern for citizenship training, Plato developed an entire analysis of politics that viewed the state primarily as an educational organization whose effectiveness and health was directly contingent upon the quality of political education. In his *Politics* Aristotle stated the problem in part as follows:

> All would agree that the legislator should make the education of the young his chief and foremost concern. [There are two reasons for taking this view.] In the first place, the regime will suffer if education is neglected. The citizens . . . should always be educated to suit the regime. . . . The type of character appropriate to a regime is the power which continues to sustain it, as it is also the force which originally creates it. The democratic type of character sustains and creates democracy; the oligarchal type creates and sustains oligarchy. . . . In the second place every capacity . . . requires as a condition of its exercise some measure of previous training and some amount of preliminary habituation. . . .

Thus, the political community that fails to transmit its dominant political beliefs and attitudes or its preferred types of civic personality to its young soon finds itself going through unwanted transformations of government. Democracies have become dictatorships, and dictatorships have become democracies, usually because inadequate attention has been given to the great array of problems associated with the transmission of civic values to the young.

In the twentieth century, certain totalitarian nations have given formidable attention and resources to the training of their youth. In the Soviet Union the child in nursery school is a "Little Octobrist." At the age of nine he becomes a "Young Pioneer." At about fourteen "chosen" children enter the Komsomol, the Young Communist League. Only between 30 and 40 percent of the children at this age are admitted into what amounts to a ten-year program of politicization. Only the best of the Komsomols become adult members of the Communist Party. Even outside the Komsomol in the ordinary Soviet schooling process, the political aspects of education are explicitly matters of instruction concerning the dialectic-materialistic outlook, including science from a Marxist-Leninist point of view. Antipathy for the non-Soviet world and devotion to the development of the "Soviet Man" are central aspects of this political education.[30]

In Nazi Germany, the Hitler Jugend (Hitler Youth) were similarly organized and indoctrinated. The *Nazi Primer* emphasized the inequality among men, the biological superiority of the German race, the evil role of the Jews, the ethics of Hitler-worship, and the joy of life in the soldier-state. Like the Komsomols, the Jugend was not only a socializing agency but also a recruiting mechanism for leaders in the adult Nazi Party.[31]

Not that political education went unnoticed among the Founding Fathers! Jefferson was most concerned with this topic. He was particularly pained by the evil effect of slavery on masters and their children:

> The whole commerce between master and slave is a perpetual exercise of the most boisterous passions, and most unremitting despotism on the one part, and degrading submissions on the other. Our children see this, and learn to imitate it; for man is an imitative animal. This quality is the germ of all education in him. From his cradle to his grave he is learning to do what he sees others do. If a parent could find no motive either in his philanthropy or his self-love, for restraining the intemperance of passion towards his slave, it would always be a sufficient one that his child is present. But generally it is not sufficient.

Elsewhere, Jefferson comments on the problem of planning for elementary schools:

> Is it a right or a duty in society to take care of their infant members in opposition to the will of a parent? How far does this right and duty extend?—To guard the life of the infant, his property, his instructions, his morals? The Roman father was supreme in all these: we draw a line, but where?—Public sentiment does not seem to have traced it precisely.[32]

---

[30] Merle Fainsod, "The Komsomols: A Study of Youth Under Dictatorship," *American Political Science Review*, 45 (March 1951): 18–40; G. K. Hulicka, "Political Education in Soviet Schools," *Soviet Studies*, 5 (October 1953): 138–150; Zev Katz, "Party-Political Education in Soviet Russia, 1918–1935," *Soviet Studies*, (January 1956): 237–247.

[31] Herbert Lewin, "Hitler Youth and the Boy Scouts of America," *Human Relations*, 1 (1947–1948): 206–227; Julius Gould "The Komsomol and the Hitler Jugend," *British Journal of Sociology*, 2 (December 1951): 305–314.

[32] Saul K. Padover (ed.), *Thomas Jefferson: On Democracy* (New York: Pelican Books, 1939), pp. 98, 90.

Thus, nearly every major political philosopher since Plato has focused in part upon the problems of citizen training. However, political socialization, as a distinctive area of behavioral investigation, with the exception of the American Historical Association studies of the late 1920s and the Charles E. Merriam studies of the early 1930s, is a product of the 1950s. Merriam's work was a cross-cultural study of the institutions most directly concerned with the political instruction of children and youth: the school system, youth groups, political parties, private associations, and governmental bureaucracies. The studies were mainly impressionistic and, in fact, failed to refer to the family as an agency of political socialization. Merriam's summation volume in the nine-volume series is a classic for its success in orienting the reader to the multicultural aspects of this subject and for the inspiration it provided later investigators.[33]

Political Socialization of the Young

In 1959, a social psychologist, Herbert H. Hyman, gave further impetus to this field with publication of an inventory of recent empirical psychological studies. These studies revealed that tendencies toward political participation, political orientation, and authoritarian or democratic attitudes among adults usually have origins in earlier stages of development. At a very early age, for example, a significant sex differentiation in political participation was observed. Hyman also found a progressive development of positive political orientation as children grew older and advanced in their schooling. However, at different stages of development, youth of different economic classes tended to differ appreciably in party preference, self-identification with such groups as the "working class," and similar affiliative attitudes.

With respect to agencies for politicizing children, Hyman found much agreement that the total family structure—both parents and the relationships among all family members—is clearly the most influential agency. However, parental influence does become somewhat systematically attenuated by the changing social and political en-

[33] Charies E. Merriam, *The Making of Citizens* (Chicago: University of Chicago Press, 1931). This early literature is surveyed in Fred I. Greenstein, *Children and Politics* (New Haven: Yale University Press, 1965), Chap. 1. Harold D. Lasswell, one of Merriam's most eminent students, dealt with political socialization in an essay urging further study. His "Democratic Character" is perhaps one of the most stimulating statements about the distinctive characteristics of leadership personality in democratic societies. *Political Writings* (Glencoe, Ill.: The Free Press, 1951).

vironment encountered by each succeeding generation. To a significant degree, this generational factor seems to promote youthful departures from parental positions on party affiliation, ideological orientation, and such matters as tolerance for nonconformity.

In the 1960s several politicization studies appeared which reported substantial new collections of data. Easton and Hess investigated childrens' attitudes in Grades 2 through 7 as well as in high school, later extending their original study to include some 17,000 children in eight major and medium-sized American cities. In another project, Greenstein studied 659 children in Grades 4 through 8 in New Haven, Connecticut. Following the Merriam tradition of cross-national studies of political culture and civic education, Almond and Verba examined samples of 1,000 in each of five nations: the United States, Great Britain, Germany, Italy and Mexico. Some of the major findings of these investigations are reported below.[34]

The Easton-Hess studies were concerned with the target content of particular attitudes developed by children during elementary school years, e.g., their perceptions of political figures and organizations and their conceptions of the role of citizens in the political system; the institutional and personal agencies from which these political attitudes and behavior are acquired; and the pattern of attitudinal change and growth as the child matures. They found that children are aware of and involved with political objects, at least in an attitudinal way, as early as ages seven, eight, and nine. Among the principal Easton-Hess findings were the following.

The young child's relation with the political system begins with a strong positive attachment to this country; the United States is seen as ideal and superior to other countries. The young child perceives figures and institutions of government as powerful, competent, benign, and infallible, and trusts them to offer him protection and help. The child's initial relationship with governmental authority

[34] Robert Hess and David Easton, "The Child's Changing Image of the President," *Public Opinion Quarterly*, 24 (1960): 632–644; David Easton and Robert Hess, "The Child's Political World," *Midwest Journal of Political Science*, 6 (1962): 229–246; Fred I. Greenstein, *op. cit.*; David Easton and Jack Dennis, "The Child's Acquisition of Regime Norms: Political Efficacy," *American Political Science Review*, 60 (March 1967): 25–38. The full Easton-Dennis report is in *Children in the Political System* (New York: McGraw Hill, 1969). Also, Roberta Sigel, "Political Socialization," *Annals of the American Academy of Political and Social Science*, 351 (September 1965). The closely related perspective of "national character" is reviewed in Bernard C. Hennessy, "Psycho-Cultural Studies of National Character," *Background* (Fall 1962): 27–49. Other significant research is reported in Kenneth P. Langton, *Political Socialization* (New York: Oxford University Press, 1969) and "Special Issue on Political Socialization," *Harvard Educational Review*, 38 (Summer 1968).

is with the President, whom the child sees in highly positive terms indicating his basic trust in the benevolence of government. The young child's trust in the political system is expressed not only by a view of figures and institutions as benign, but also through a view of the citizen's obligation to be a good person. The child's image of political parties develops somewhat later, and the nature of the difference between the two major parties is not clearly defined in his mind.

Greenstein examined similar aspects of political socialization, particularly the acquisition of political information and motivations for political actions. Greenstein's general findings may be summarized as follows:

The child's first conception of political authority seems to have more affective than cognitive content. The child, like the adult, has a quite firm impression that figures such as the President of the United States are important, but he has no clear understanding of what these individuals do. Contrary to the often expressed skepticism and disfavor that adults manifest about political leaders, the affective response to political leaders among children is strikingly positive—a finding that confirms the Easton-Hess data. Children acquire party attachments before they can make more than the most fragmentary distinctions about the nature of political parties, about what parties stand for, even about who the parties' public representatives are. Among the levels of government, the Federal is the first about which there is awareness of both an executive and a legislative component; the state level is the last about which learning takes place.

While the political socialization studies have tended to focus on the content of the political information of children and their attitudes toward that content, another significant feature of these studies has been the attention given to the sources of this information. In the United States at least, the most influential socializing agency is clearly the family with respect to the more salient objects of information and attitude: political parties, major political figures such as the President, and the various levels of government. However, other agencies make themselves felt fairly early in the child's development: teachers, neighbors, relatives, peers, media of communication, and those personages whose views and behavior are reported through the media. As the youth becomes an adult, he is more frequently aware of organized group socializing messages, in business, on the job, and in social relations. These now become significant sources of political information and points of view.

In dealing with the importance of such agencies of politicization, we must remember that each *general* type of agency (family, school, peers, media, party, etc.) includes innumerable *particular* agencies, each of which transmits a somewhat different informational and attitudinal content. Although Democrats and Republicans are both political parties, hence the same general type of group, as particular groups they certainly transmit significantly different information. Out of the heterogeneity of *particular* socializing agencies comes great variety of political information and attitude.

The five-nation study of Almond and Verba produced 5,000 interviews revealing some significant variations in political cultures and processes of politicization. Some of the findings of the Almond-Verba study are particularly relevant here.

Of the five nations studied, large majorities of the respondents in the United States, Great Britain, and Germany felt that their national governments had some important impact on their personal lives, placed a favorable evaluation upon the general governmental output, and, not surprisingly, tended to have a substantial amount of basic information about the politics of their countries. The Mexicans, on the other hand, tended to see little effect on their own lives from the activities of their national government, tended to be somewhat parochial and alienated from their government's output, and, by the simplest measures, appeared poorly informed about politics. The Italians fell between the two extremes in their views about the personal consequences of governmental activity and its general value. The saliency of the citizen role in the United States, Great Britain, and Germany was thus confirmed.

The citizen role also has its participative aspect. About three-fourths of the Americans and Britons claimed that they take part in the discussion of politics and other types of political communication without, for the most part, any sense of restriction. Although political communicative activity was also substantial in Germany, a far greater proportion of Germans felt seriously restricted. In Italy and Mexico, the proportion communicating about politics dropped markedly, accompanied by a rise in feelings of substantial restriction.

Should the individual be an active participant in the affairs of his community? A large number of Americans and Britons believed so, while few Italians felt such an obligation to participate. Germans and Mexicans were somewhat more ambivalent. Associated with actual participation and sense of obligation was the individual's subjective sense of political competency. Asked what the individual citizen could do about an unjust local or national governmental regulation, three-fourths of the Americans felt subjectively competent about getting something done. The British and the Germans felt competent in lesser numbers.

The Almond-Verba study provides much information about the agencies of political socialization and their relative success in the five nations. The authors begin with the assumption that *nonpolitical* patterns of relationship and attitudes toward authority may, analogously, have important consequences for a citizen's relationships and attitudes toward political authority.

> The patterns of interpersonal relations within the family, the school, and, to a lesser extent, the job, are likely to take forms different from those within the political system. They are likely to be less formal. Decision-making in such situations does not involve membership in formal parties or participation in a formal election system; it is more likely to consist of an expectation that one will be consulted, if only tacitly, before decisions are made; or that one is free to express one's point of view when decisions are being considered. Democracy in the more intimate primary groups is expressed in the tone of relations and in implicit norms.[35]

Asked to recall how much influence they had in *family* decisions during their adolescence, respondents in the United States and Britain led the others in perceived influence over family decisions. The lead of the British and Americans is even greater in connection with perceived opportunities to complain about family decisions.

Remembered participation in decision making at *schools* appears as another relevant nonpolitical source of politicizing experiences. Respondents were asked to report on the recalled opportunity to discuss and debate political and social issues at school. American respondents showed a sharp and significant contrast with those of the other four countries. About 40 percent of the Americans indicated that there were such discussions and that they took part. The next closest were the British, 16 percent with such recollections.

The study also found that, over all, an individual's current sense

[35] Almond-Verba, *op. cit.*, p. 274.

of political competence (that is, perceived capacity to change unjust regulations, etc.) was demonstrably connected with remembered participation in family and school decisions. Individuals with no more than elementary or secondary educations derived a more intense sense of political competency from remembered participation in school discussions, debates, and decision making than (a) those who, with the same education, lacked such opportunities or (b) those with higher education regardless whether they did or did not have such opportunities. In short, the less-education citizens with a sense of political competency derived this mainly and most recently from their school experiences. On the other hand, high-education types, at least during their adult years, acquired less from home and school than from direct personal participation in political organizations of one kind or another.

> If an individual has had the opportunity to participate in the family, in school, or at work, he is more likely than someone who did not have the same opportunities to consider himself competent to influence the government. . . . Our data suggest that education on the secondary level or above can replace family participation, and to some extent school participation, as a factor leading toward political competence. . . . Those with higher education, this suggests, do not need the push toward a sense of political competence that participatory family and school experiences might provide, for there are so many other factors that operate to make them politically competent. . . . Work-place participation does not have as broad an effect upon one's sense of political competence as educational attainment does; it is a much narrower factor, which does not produce as basic a set of changes in one's intellectual capabilities, values, or social situation.[36]

The Almond-Verba study, therefore, clearly sets forth the general schema of socializing agencies in the countries investigated. The family and the school are most likely to be basic for the creation of any sense of political obligation and competency. Among those individuals who proceed beyond the secondary school, membership in political organizations becomes the principal politicizer. Those respondents who were members of voluntary associations and other types of political organizations, when compared with those who were nonmembers, perceived themselves as more competent citizens, tended to be more active as participants in politics, and were able

---

[36] *Ibid.*, pp. 299 ff.

to know and care more about politics. Even passive membership, when compared with nonmembership, produced significant differences in the sense of political compentence. It should be added that political organizations yield a larger sense of political competence and involvement than do nonpolitical organizations.

Adult Politicization

Until recently most studies of the socialization process have been limited to the periods of childhood and adolescence. Socialization theorists, however, have come to recognize that the individual continues to be "modified" throughout his life as a consequence of socializing influences.[37] The phenomenon of adult socialization, therefore, has begun to claim much attention in studies of occupations and professions. Another important body of relevant adult socialization literature may be found in studies of immigrants and college students.

The classic study of immigrant socialization is W. I. Thomas and Florian Znaniecki's *Polish Peasant in Europe and America.*[38] Five volumes of case materials about the life of Polish immigrants before and after they came to America led the authors to postulate two basic personality types, each with a different socialization pattern. The "Bohemian" was that type whose desire for new experience so far outweighed his desire for security that he was completely adaptable to the ways of his social environment. The "Philistine," on the other hand, was so completely rooted in an established way of life that any change was unacceptable, even if that change appeared to be objectively beneficial to him.

Because of the prevalence of Philistines among Polish immigrants, socialization into the American system was difficult for most of them. This difficulty was aggravated by the great heterogeneity of American groups to which the immigrant found it necessary to adapt himself. While the Philistine immigrants managed to resist adaptation, the pressures nonetheless produced a substantial measure of

---

[37] For example, Howard S. Becker and Anselm Strauss, "Careers, Personality and Adult Socialization," *American Journal of Sociology*, 62 (1956): 253–263; Robert K. Merton et al. (eds.), *The Student Physician—Introductory Studies in the Sociology of Medical Education* (Cambridge Mass.: Harvard University Press, 1957); Orville G. Brim, Jr. and Stanton Wheeler, *Socialization After Childhood* (New York: Wiley, 1966).

[38] W. I. Thomas and Florian Znaniecki, *Polish Peasant in Europe and America* (New York: Knopf, 1927).

personal disorganization among them. This personal disorganization was magnified among their children, whose interest in becoming Americanized led to substantial parent-child conflict and alienation.

The pattern identified by Thomas and Znaniecki was, of course, apparent in other immigrant groups and may today have its counterpart in the black nationalism found among certain segments of the Negro population. In the case of the immigrants, it was not until the third generation that descendants of immigrants were sufficiently educated and Americanized to "spin off" from the ghettoes into other neighborhoods of the city and suburb.

College students, including foreign students, have also been a source of data about young adult socialization.[39] A study of 600 undergraduate girls at Bennington College in Vermont revealed that students experienced a change in their political and economic attitudes during college attendance. The shift involved a movement from a more conservative to a less conservative general viewpoint. The principal socializing agencies appear to have been the faculty and the upper-division student body.

The "liberalizing" effect of the college socializing experience is challenged by the findings of Jacob. Much of the difficulty lies in the definition of liberalism. Jacob finds little evidence to support any significant shift toward *political* liberalism in terms of ideological and policy positions. On the other hand, there was much evidence to support a shift toward psychological liberalism: open-mindedness, flexibility, tolerance, and adaptiveness.

Study of the political socialization of foreign students in the United States continues to be conducted, with varying results. These studies are likely to be of growing significance as the United States becomes more and more committed to international educational activities. In general, foreign students at American colleges and universities tend to suffer substantial disorientation—sometimes *anomie*—as they try to learn and evaluate American educational and social customs. For most, the competitive education milieu and the

[39] A pioneer study is Theodore M. Newcomb, "Attitude Development as a Function of Reference Groups: The Bennington Study." in *Readings in Social Psychology*, ed. by E. E. Maccoby, T. M. Newcomb, and E. L. Hartley (3d ed., New York: Holt, Rinehart and Winston, 1958); Philip E. Jacob, *Changing Values in College* (New York: Harper, 1957); F. D. Scott, *The American Experience of Swedish Students; Retrospect and Aftermath* (Minneapolis: University of Minnesota Press, 1956); Richard D. Lambert and Marvin Bressler, *Indian Students on an American Campus* (Minneapolis: University of Minnesota Press, 1956); Herbert Passin and John Bennett, "The American-Educated Japanese," *Annals of the American Academy of Political and Social Science*, 95 (1954): 83–107.

substantial range of student social freedom calls for unfamiliar behavioral norms whose acquisition depends a great deal upon the availability of guidance from older foreign students from the same country. At the end of the educational stay in America, a substantial number of foreign students once again suffer "culture shock" upon return to the home country, whose political and social life they now find constrictive. It is not unusual for such students returning from America also to find themselves with a political stigma placed upon them by anti-American elements at home. In such cases, the difficult alternatives are either to remain "deviant" or to remove the stigma by becoming actively anti-American.

Propaganda

In some respects every socializing group, including government, is a propaganda organization endeavoring to modify the conduct of its members, or audience. World Wars I and II produced a substantial interest in the concept and activities associated with propaganda.[40] Much of what happened in the name of propaganda could be reduced to Pavlovian conceptions of conditioned reflex and learned behavior; a cartoon caricature of the hated enemy would presumably suffice to activate patriotism and heighten contribution to the war effort. Pavlov's experiments had, in fact, become sufficiently influential at the time to lend an overriding conditioned-reflex orientation to the study and practice of propaganda. Wartime propaganda was soon followed by peacetime commercial advertising, particularly in the United States. As a consequence, the study of propaganda received exceptional impetus and support from government and industry.[41]

Propaganda has been described as language aimed at large masses; that is, words and other symbols such as pictures, transmitted through press, film, radio, and television, so as to reach huge audiences. "The intention of the propagandist is to influence mass attitudes on controversial issues."[42] In another place, propaganda is

[40] For example, see Alexander L. George, "Prediction of Political Action by Means of Propaganda Analysis," *Public Opinion Quarterly* (1956): 334–345.

[41] A basic reference guide is Bruce Lannes Smith, Harold D. Lasswell, and Ralph D. Casey, *Propaganda, Communication, and Public Opinion* (Princeton: Princeton University Press, 1946). A classic text is Leonard W. Doob, *Public Opinion and Propaganda* (New York: Holt, 1948). An excellent contemporary survey may be found in Clarence Schettler, *Public Opinion in American Society* (New York: Harper, 1960).

[42] Smith, *op. cit.*, p. 1.

defined as "the use of covert actions by a person to influence the response of other persons in situations that usually involve conflict or competition so that the welfare of the propagandist will be benefited."[43]

The student of propaganda is usually confronted with the problem of differentiating it from education or socialization. Ordinarily, propaganda is differentiated from education on the basis of self-awareness on the part of the audience. In propaganda, opinion and conduct are presumably influenced in such a manner that the audience adopts the opinions and conduct without itself making any search for rationalization or logic. Education, however, while also attempting to influence opinion and conduct, calls upon the audience to seek understanding for itself regarding the bases for accepting the suggested opinion or conduct. Socialization differs from propaganda in that its objectives are long run, pervasive, and, as far as the socializing agency is concerned, noncontroversial.

Obviously the definitions of education, socialization, propaganda, and advertising are more a matter of taste than of logic. All involve a communication process in which the source is attempting to affect the attitudes, opinions, and behaviors of some target audience: to purchase a product; to contribute more to the war effort; to render service and loyalty to the goals of the socializing group; or to learn effectively the information and values presented in the educational program. If anything distinguishes propaganda from the others, it is perhaps the claim that government propagandizes but business advertises. Further, if the influence attempt relates to some short-run or imminent political or policy event, it is usually called propaganda.

An Illustrative Use of the Conceptual Perspective

THE SOCIALIZATION OF MEMBERS OF CONGRESS

Most members of Congress are not novices to legislative politics. Many have had experience as state legislators, and among those in the Senate there is often a background of experience in the House of

---

[43] Schettler, *op. cit.*, p. 380.

Representatives. Each congressman has therefore learned much from his prior campaigns and officeholding. Yet, most congressmen are likely to say that such service "prepared me somewhat" or "provided a partial understanding of the legislative process and some idea of what to expect." They will suggest that national and state legislative bodies "differ markedly." In support of congressional reform, Woodrow Wilson wrote in 1885:

> The newly-elected member always experiences great difficulty in adjusting his preconceived ideas of Congressional life to the strange and unlooked for condition by which he finds himself surrounded. No man, when chosen to the membership of a body possessing great powers and exalted prerogatives, likes to find his activity repressed and himself suppressed, by imperative rules and precedents which seem to him to have been framed for the deliberate purpose of making usefulness unobtainable by individual members. Yet such the new member finds the rules and precedents of the House to be.[44]

IN THE HOUSE

While still in his home constituency, the new member receives from the Clerk of the House a copy of the pamphlet *Information for Representatives-Elect,* which contains basic information about his salary, allowances, office facilities, and similar matters. The rest of his socialization to membership in the House comes to him, however, from many other sources: established members of his state's congressional delegation, often regardless of party affiliation; newly recruited staff assistants with extensive experience on Capitol Hill; an established leader of his party in Congress with whom he may strike up a friendship; colleagues on committees to which he may be assigned; friendly Washington lobbyists and newspapermen with whom he may have ties through constituents back home; and occasionally, study of the published professional literature on Congress and its operations. One of the main activities of the Democratic Study Group, an informal caucus of Democratic liberals in the House, has been to provide a continuing seminar through which to

---

[44] From Woodrow Wilson, *Congressional Government* (New York: Houghton Mifflin, 1885), p. 61, quoted by Charles L. Clapp, *The Congressman* (Washington, D.C.: Brookings Institution, 1963), pp. 9–10. Many of the present observations and quotations are drawn from Clapp. See also, A. Kornberg and N. Thomas, "The Political Socialization of National Legislative Elites in the United States and Canada," *Journal of Politics,* 27 (1965): 761–775.

help orient freshmen Democratic representatives, most of whom tend to come from highly contested, high-turnover urban districts.

Perhaps the most critical "recommended behaviors" communicated to freshmen representatives are the following:

> The main rule of the game is "thou shalt not demagogue thy colleagues." We acknowledge that a person does a little bit of demagoguery with his people, but snow is for the folks. . . .

> There is another rule that you shouldn't do harm to a colleague if you can avoid it. You have to live with these people. You need their votes just as they need yours. . . .

> Another rule is the rule of convenience. Whatever is most convenient for the majority of the members will be respected. Along the same line is the idea that agreements made between leaders on both sides will be respected and followed.[45]

Clapp devotes two chapters to a "Lecture for Freshmen" derived from discussions at a round-table conference of nearly two score Democratic and Republican members of Congress. In brief, the behavioral advice for freshmen who wish to succeed includes the following:

Participate wholeheartedly in your committee work; if possible, develop a specialty but stay away from substantive interests that happen to fall within the jurisdiction of another committee. Spend time on the House floor and in the cloakrooms learning parliamentary procedure, engaging in informal negotiations, but, above all, making friends with colleagues and House staff. Hire Capitol Hill professional staffers; they are a shortcut to self-socialization. Defer to the House leadership, even at the expense of the Senate or the President. Respond to mail from home promptly and engage in activities that will give you a "district image." Be sure to be thoroughly informed upon any subjects to which you may address yourself in your initial floor speeches.

Some of the behavioral roles associated by the round-table members with "typical" House members were: infighter, operator, worker, specialist, craftsman. Other, somewhat unconventional role types, included: needler, comedian, summarizer, protector of the public purse, objector, conscience of the Congress, technician, dean of a state delegation, demagogue.[46]

---

45 *Ibid.*, pp. 13–14.
46 *Ibid.*, Chap. 1, passim.

IN THE SENATE

The efforts of Senate socializing agencies have been somewhat more closely studied and reported.[47] Although most men who run for the Senate are experienced politicians, their politicization as senators begins, as for others, in the campaign. "Political campaigning forces a man out of a comfortable cocoon of self-imposed uniformity within which most of us live. It results in an acute awareness of the vast differences in the conditions, interests, opinions, and styles of life of the American people and a detached tolerance toward this diversity."[48]

The prospective senator, during his campaign, becomes aware of the organized and not-so-organized interests in his state to which he will have to respond while in office. He learns of the pattern of denunciation and diatribe employed by the party opposition in his state, which may reinforce his own partisanship as no other experience can. Given the half million dollar cost of the average Senate campaign, he becomes expert in the formal and informal aspects of public accounting for funds received and disbursed, learning as well the countless forms of nonpecuniary income and expenditure. What better preparation for making judgments about the economics of national government in one of the most expensive political systems in the world?

> They are not the same men that they were before the campaign began. A Senate campaign is a unique educational experience for the candidate, if for no one else. Those who have gone through the experience learn much about their future constituents, their conflicting interests, opinions, and biases, in the process. A candidate learns, too, that most of his constituents expect contradictory behavior from him: he should be above petty politics but he should bring home the bacon; he should run a clean and dignified campaign but he should be a fighter; he should bring his campaign to the voters but he should not spend money doing so; he should frankly state and act on his convictions but represent his constituents. The candidate has become accustomed to the evasiveness, minor deception, and hypocrisy required to satisfy these conflicting expectations. Candidates learn, too, about themselves and the insidious appeal,

[47] Notably in William S. White, *Citadel, The Story of the United States Senate* (New York: Harper, 1956), and Donald R. Matthews, *U.S. Senators and Their World* (Chapel Hill: University of North Carolina Press, 1960).
[48] *Ibid.*, Chap. 4.

when the chips are down, of the doctrine that the end justifies the means.[49]

In Washington, the agencies of senatorial socialization are not unlike those in the House of Representatives. The new senator is expected to serve a proper apprenticeship; "proper" includes acceptance of unpleasant or politically useless committee assignments, keeping his mouth shut, respecting his senatorial elders, and generally accepting a subordinate role in all that goes on. As Matthews observes, however, "Veterans in the Senate remark, rather wistfully, that the practice of serving an apprenticeship is on the way out." A freshman senator, particularly from a heavily contested larger state, is likely to represent many more millions of people than an old-timer and is likely to have to take his constituency more seriously and sooner into account as a reference group than he does his senatorial elders.

Other socializing folkways of the Senate add up to the following behavioral prescription: Be a work horse rather than a show horse; spend most of your time on your legislative homework. Specialize in some subject-matter area early. Never let political disagreements influence personal feelings or destroy senatorial courtesy. Help thy colleague whenever possible and ye shall receive in kind. Act as though you belong to the greatest deliberative body in the world, because you do.

But socialization to the ways of the Senate does not come easy to all freshmen. A former governor who becomes a Senator finds the apprenticeship role something of a demotion. This is also true of some men who enter the Senate after distinguished service in the House of Representatives. Any senator with presidential or vice-presidential ambitions is likely to champ at the apprenticeship bit. Senators from highly competitive constituencies are likely to want to move faster than "normal," as are senators with a liberal ideological orientation. Such departures from traditional senatorial socialization are likely to produce nonconforming behavior, with important consequences for a senator's legislative effectiveness. Matthews, in fact, constructed a "legislative effectiveness" index by calculating what proportion of all public bills and resolutions introduced by each senator were passed by the Senate. This admittedly crude index revealed that the more conforming a senator, the greater is his effectiveness.[50]

[49] Matthews, *op. cit.* (Vintage Books ed.), pp. 73–74.
[50] *Ibid.*, p. 115.

Conflict and Games of Strategy

Theoretically, organized groups, including governments, are systems of cooperation. Some writers contend that politics is primarily more-or-less cooperative efforts to manage the processes of conflict. The theory of games of strategy has recently come into prominence as an approach to the analysis of economic competition and political conflict. Game theory refers to decision makers as "players" interested in employing their resources ("rules") so as to maximize the chances of winning their most favored outcome ("payoff") under conditions of incomplete information. A player's plan for accomplishing this is a "strategy." Series of conflicts may constitute a conflict process, and conflict processes may have residual consequences for political organization. Three such processes may be identified: formalization, socialization, and investiture processes. Formalization conflicts tend to modify task expectations and positions. Socialization conflicts tend to influence role learning and role performance. Investiture conflicts tend to determine which particular person will be incumbent in and responsible for which particular position.

9

Conflict Theories and Processes

As president of the American Political Science Association, E. E. Schattschneider told his colleagues that "the concept of political strategy is . . . a point of view loaded with implications for the study of politics." "Strategy," he continued, "is the heart of politics, as it is of war." In fact, he pointed out, the term "strategy" is borrowed from the language of war and obviously has a great deal to do with human conflict.

> If politics is the management of conflict, it is necessary first to get rid of some simplistic concepts of conflict. Political conflict is not primarily or usually a matter of head-on collisions or tests of strength, for a good reason: intelligent people prefer to avoid tests of strength, about matters more serious than sports, unless they are sure to win.

> Nor is political conflict like an inter-collegiate debate in which the opponents agree in advance on the definition of the issues. The definition of alternatives is the supreme instrument of power; the antagonists can rarely agree on what the issues are because power is involved in the definition. He who determines what politics is about runs the country because the definition of the alternatives is the choice of conflicts, and the choice of conflicts allocates power.

Returning to his comment on political strategy, Schattschneider further observed:

Political strategy deals therefore with the exploitation, use, and suppression of conflict. Conflict is so powerful an instrument of government that all regimes are of necessity concerned with its management. . . . The grand strategy of politics deals with public policy concerning conflict. This is the policy of policies, the sovereign policy—what to do about conflict.[1]

This view places political conflict within the framework of government, itself a distinctive form of *cooperation*. In behavioral theory, on the other hand, the relationship between conflict and cooperation is often poorly delineated. What does seem settled is that the two concepts are intimately connected in social and political behavior and that each is of equal importance.[2]

HUMAN STRUGGLES AND CONFLICT THEORIES

Human struggle and social conflict have held the intellectual interest of men of thought and science for 2500 years that we know of. The Iranian philosopher-poet Zarathustra (660–583 B.C.) gave dramatic expression to the grand conflict between the "powers of Light" and the "powers of Darkness" struggling around and within each human individual. Violence in the relations of men, and the forerunners of men, is apparent in prehistoric evidence. Skills evidently shattered by special artifacts have been found on Chinese soil and provide evidence that even among the first known hominids extreme conflict was practiced. The Bible records an act of fratricide as the most significant fact about the sons of Adam.[3]

[1] "Intensity, Visibility, Direction and Scope," *American Political Science Review*, 51 (December 1957): 933–942 passim.

[2] The conflict theory literature has proliferated remarkably since Jessie Bernard asked "Where is the Modern Sociology of Conflict?" *American Journal of Sociology*, 56 (1950): 11–16. Two recent surveys are: Lewis A. Coser, *Continuities in the Study of Social Conflict* (New York: Free Press, 1967) and N. J. Demergh III and R. A. Peterson (eds.), *System, Change, and Conflict* (New York: Free Press, 1967). Other major bibliographic surveys include: special issue of *Journal of Conflict Resolution*, 12 (December 1968); and International Sociological Association, *The Nature of Conflict* (Paris: UNESCO, 1957). *The Journal of Conflict Resolution* is primarily devoted to empirical studies in this field. Game Theory has, in recent years, added an entirely new theoretical dimension to the literature of conflict theory; Jessie Bernard, "Theory of Games of Strategy as a Modern Sociology of Conflict," *American Journal of Sociology*, 59 (March 1954): 411–424. On the relationship between conflict and cooperation: W. S. Landecker, "Types of Integration and Their Measurement," *American Journal of Sociology*, 56 (1951): 332–340; Robert C. North et al., "The Integrative Functions of Conflict," *Journal of Conflict Resolution*, 4 (September 1960): 355–374; Ralph M. Goldman, "A Theory of Conflict Processes and Organizational Offices," *ibid.*, 10 (September 1966): 328–343; James D. Thompson, "Organizational Management of Conflict," *Administrative Science Quarterly* (1960): 389–409.

[3] Kurt Singer, *The Idea of Conflict* (Melbourne: Melbourne University Press, 1949) is an excellent "genealogy" of conflict theory throughout human history.

According to Greek poetry and thought, the way to solve conflict was to know fearlessly and to sing beautifully of the "true" things. The first Greek to distinguish among forms of conflict seems to have been the poet Hesiod (775 B.C.) who taught that there were two kinds of *eris* (strife): a bad one which incites men to "evil war and battle, being cruel," and a good one which stirs up even the shiftless to toil, making them eager to work in order to overtake their neighbor. Twenty-one centuries later, essentially the same distinction is found in Havelock Ellis's notion that conflict is a universal and beneficial force without which there would have been no world, but that violence is a rare and destructive form of conflict which should be eradicated.

Somewhat fatalistically, Plato viewed war as an inevitable expression of politics and human nature. Aristotle, however, condoned war as a *means* to the end of imposing government upon men. Christianity established the concept of "just war," that is, the relentless struggle against the devil and his works, and Islam had its own holy war against the infidel, who, during the Crusades, was the Christian. Machiavelli, writing in an age of distintegrating empires, emergent nations, and seasonal warfare, reasserted the Aristotelian view that war was one of the Prince's means for preserving his sovereignty. Hobbes believed that struggle was universal and evil, and that it drove men, out of necessity, into compacts with monarchs as a means for maintaining peace and order among themselves; these compacts remained valid only so long as the monarchs more or less effectively kept the peace.

The French Revolution and Napoleon broke apart the uneasy harmonies of the late Renaissance by spreading a strong sense of struggle across nations and continents. A later "era of conflict" was dominated by Bismarck, whose contemporaries Darwin and Marx inaugurated profoundly influential new theories of conflict in the fields of natural history and social science. Darwin's "struggle for existence" hypothesized the "survival of the fittest." Marx, adapting Hegel's dialectical system, interpreted human history as a "class struggle" whose "final" outcome would be communism. Less comprehensive, but no less intellectually influential, were Gumplowicz's theory of racial struggle and Ratzenhofer's theory of conflicting group "interests" within the state.

By the nineteenth century, liberal laissez-faire economists held economic competition, a constrained kind of conflict, to be the most desirable method for achieving the greatest prosperity for the greatest number. Few nations have given more ideological support to this theory than the United States.

But conflict is not always social or political; it is also psychological. For Nietzsche, morality rested upon strength, and strength is the possession of "masters," that is, superior individuals for whom society is but an instrument for enhancing power and personality. More contemporary are the contributions of Freud, for whom nature was a battlefield on which irrational forces strive with one another, equally strong and equally indispensable, at once stimulating and limiting each other.

Simmel felt that conflict is best studied as a form of socialization and civilization. Social conflict, he declared, is a process in which accumulated social tensions are liquidated and through which, in consequence, new and more complex forms of social organization are established.

The study of conflict has been carried on under numerous rubrics: tension, hostility, disjunctive social process, social dynamics, social change, social Darwinism, evolution, sociology of war, group dissociation, competition, cultural disintegration, rivalry, dissent, and mostly recently, theory of games of strategy.

There has been a general tendency for theorists to evaluate social cooperation as "good" and social conflict as "bad." While the human struggle against the hostile forces of nature has always been considered legitimate, greater approval has been given the search for immutable truths through which the environment may be controlled and social organization may exercise such control. At the same time, the conflicts of man against man have never seemed right or good. In this context, the state, or government, has long been viewed as the principal organizer of human society, with force and warfare condoned only as necessary evils in the slow progress toward greater human cooperation.

Contemporary conceptions of conflict are summarized in a thorough survey by Mack and Snyder.[4] Some fifty propositions were drawn as a sample from a much larger inventory. "The distinctions between conflict and non-conflict are fuzzy at best and at worst not

---

[4] Raymond W. Mack and Richard C. Snyder, "The Analysis of Social Conflict—Toward an Overview and Synthesis," *Journal of Conflict Resolution*, 1 (June 1957): 212–48.

made at all," they concluded. Without attempting a formal definition of "conflict," these authors do derive from the literature a set of properties and empirical conditions for identifying and characterizing conflict phenomena and situations.

First, social conflict requires at least two analytically distinct entities or units, such as persons, groups, or organizations.

As in cooperation, conflict implies a minimum of visibility, contact, and interaction (not necessarily face to face) between the two or more parties. Interestingly, at least two persons are also needed to enter a *cooperative* relationship.[5] In fact, it may sometimes be difficult to discern whether the individuals or entities are engaged in a conflict or a cooperative relationship. Consider the case of two individuals working in close cooperation as one of them secretly plots the destruction of the other. Where does the cooperative relationship end and the conflictual one begin? Or, consider the case of the aggressive and possessive lover who would destroy rather than lose the loved one; where does love end and hostility begin?

Second, according to Mack and Snyder, social conflict arises from at least two kinds of scarcity: position scarcity and resources scarcity. *Position scarcity* is a condition in which an object cannot occupy two places at the same time, serve two different functions simultaneously, or perform two or more roles simultaneously. Thus, for example, a Congressman cannot be in his constituency and in his Capitol Hill office at the same time, which may lead to conflicting claims for his presence; nor can a tax dollar go toward military supplies and public housing at the same time; nor can a president be a husband at exactly the same time. There is not enough of the Congressman, the tax dollar, or the president to meet all these requirements *at the same moment*, and this scarcity gives rise to conflicts. *Resources scarcity* is a condition in which the supply of desired objects or "future states of affairs" is limited so that parties cannot have all they want of anything.[6]

A third feature of conflictful behaviors is their intent to destroy, injure, thwart, or otherwise control another party or parties. Generally, a conflict relationship is conceived as one in which the parties

---

[5] See Chapter 1 above.

[6] We shall shortly refer to these scarcities as *conflict topics* involving disagreements over (a) task expectations associated with an organizational or group position, (b) role performances by position incumbents, and (c) conditions of incumbency that place particular persons in particular positions. See Goldman, *op. cit.*

can gain (relatively) only at each other's expense. Thus, the evidential bases for placing behaviors and relationships into a conflict rather than a cooperative classification lie in the intent or object of action.

Fourth, social conflict requires interaction among parties, during which actions and counteractions are mutually opposed. Conflict cannot exist without action, and such action must presumably embody the pursuit of mutually exclusive or incompatible goals or values. However, as indicated above, it is sometimes difficult to identify when some actions are "opposed."

Fifth, conflict relations seem always to involve attempts to gain *control* of scarce resources and positions or to *influence* behavior in certain directions; that is, a conflict relationship involves either attempts to acquire or exercise power or actual acquisition or exercise of power. In this context, *power* is defined as control over decisions regarding disposition of scarce resources and positions. Power is also the basis of reciprocal influence upon the behaviors between or among parties. Conflict thus reflects power strain, in which opposed actions are directed to changing or preserving existing power relations.

Sixth, conflict relations are seen as constituting a fundamental social-action process going on through time and having important consequences. Such conflict processes or relations are said to represent temporary tendencies toward disjunction in the interaction flow between parties. Conflict relations do not necessarily represent a breakdown in the regulated conduct of the parties, but rather a shift in their governing norms and expectations.

Building upon the Mack and Snyder survey, it is possible also to define conflict from a situational point of view. A *conflict situation* may be viewed as a social relationship between two or more parties (persons, groups, or empirically distinguishable entities) in which at least one of the parties perceives the other as an adversary engaging in behaviors designed to destroy, injure, thwart, or gain scarce resources at the expense of the perceiver. As noted earlier, there are many situations in which it is difficult for an observer to tell whether a fight or a love affair is going on. In fact, conflictive behaviors may be so subtle or indirect that even the target party may not know he has a fight on his hands. Thus, it may not be valid to assume that it takes two to start a fight; but it invariably takes two to sustain it. The one who starts may derive motivation from some perceived injury, classification of another party as "an adversary," or sheer attitudes of distrust toward another party.[7]

A party's perceptions and attitudes of distrust may be inferred from his language and behavior toward some aspect of the relationship with the other party. The first party may declare the second an "adversary" or some equivalent. He will declare the other party's intentions and behaviors as costly (in the transactional sense) to himself. He will classify his own intentions and behaviors as defensive and good, in contrast to the adversary's. Of course, if the second party responds in like manner toward the first, a conflict spiral or cycle comes into full swing.[8]

GAME THEORY: A SPECIAL THEORY OF CONFLICT

Chess, checkers, poker, bridge, and similar games of chance and strategy have obvious elements of conflict, decision making, and cooperation. These are, after all, conflicts in which the decisions of each player are contingent upon the decisions of the others. A decision involves the allocation of resources so as to "win," that is, gain *the* (or *part of the*) prize outcome. The fact that all players value the same prize draws them together; the prize is a shared goal in the sense used in theories of cooperation. It is not difficult, therefore, to see how theorists have recently drawn analogies between such games and the "games" of profit making in competitive business enterprise, office holding in a competitive political system, and winning of wars in a world of contentious nation-states.

Although game theory was first propounded in 1928, the 1944 publication of *The Theory of Games and Economic Behavior* by John von Neumann and Oskar Morgenstern of Princeton marked the beginning of contemporary interest in this "special theory" of conflict. As an economic theory, the object was to provide a mathematical approach to business decision making under conditions of competition. Within a decade, however, behavioral scientists in other fields were attracted by the highly suggestive concepts of the theory despite its somewhat limited empirical applications. In an age of large-scale international conflict, military strategists have also been

---

[7] We have in Chapter 4 touched upon the conflict-cooperation consequences of distrust, namely, a decline or discontinuation of transactions associated with a breakdown in communication.
[8] Goldman, *op. cit.*, pp. 335–336.

attracted by the usefulness of game theory concepts for the analysis of their strategic problems.

In both economic and military conflict, the problem for the typical participant is that, while he logically strives to win all that there is to win, he usually controls only part of the resources available to all the participants involved. His gains are very much contingent upon how he and the other participants use their resources. As in transactional behavior, each of a set of decision makers must arrive at some valuation regarding the expenditure of his resources. In a transaction, the valuation was based upon a comparison of what one must give up in order to receive something he wants from the other transactor. In a gamelike conflict, however, the decision maker must determine how much closer his expenditure of resources will take him toward capture of the big prize: maximum sales, profit, victory in war, etc. The theory of games of strategy undertakes, through the use of logic and mathematics, to help each decision maker determine precisely how he can make maximum gains at minimum costs.

Game theory, it must be emphasized, is a formal theory. Like any other formal theory, it deals with an arbitrarily abstracted segment of reality and requires that others accept the author's assumptions about reality. A theory holds constant specified elements in reality in order to facilitate the logical aspects of communication. In presenting the terminology of the theory of games of strategy, we shall attempt to capture, in somewhat simplified form, the definitions of its concepts. However, it will be evident that the application of game theory to the analysis of real situations must necessarily be cautious; the "fit" may be intellectually helpful, but it may provide the decision maker with little predictive knowledge.

Players

Decision makers are often referred to in the theory of games of strategy as *players*. The primary purpose in using the term is to call attention to the fact that the decision maker is involved in a situation of contest or conflict. Some game theorists, however, refer to games-against-nature in which the human player is pitted against the "laws" or "rules" (resources, as we shall see below) of nature. In order to fly his plane successfully to some destination, the airline pilot must know something about the weather conditions (nature) with which he must cope. If weather bureaus give him sound empirical knowledge from which to forecast weather conditions, the pilot can "outwit" nature by circumventing troublesome weather zones or postponing his flight entirely. In this sense, nature may be viewed as a player.

Outcomes and Prospects

As do all decision makers, players in a game are engaged in choosing alternatives *now* that they believe relate to some conceived *future* state of affairs. These future states of affairs may be called *outcomes*. In a game, an outcome is usually the relationships between the players and the reward or goal they seek. Thus, in chess there are only three different possible outcomes for each player: win (by checkmating the opponent's king), lose (by being checkmated), or draw.

The full range of possible outcomes in any game is called its *prospects*. In chess, checkers, poker, and other man-made games, the inventor of the game usually designs a very small range of prospects, limited in number and possible combinations. In real life, however, this is much more difficult to do. In working out a procedure for contesting the Presidency, for example, the Founding Fathers agreed that the man with a majority vote among the presidential electors in the Electoral College would be the winner. How could they anticipate that political parties would years later come on the scene as "players" who, instead of capturing individual electors, would play for entire electoral slates in each state? Nor could they anticipate that the prospects would include not only winning the Presidency but also the Vice Presidency, policy commitments made in party platforms, Cabinet offices, etc. In other words, the political parties came along and expanded the range of prospects and the combinations of outcomes.

Payoff

The prospect of each game has a specific outcome or reward for each player. This reward is called the *payoff*. In chess, the big payoff is *winning*, although this may perhaps also lead to prize money, a championship status, or some other reward. Something less than total victory is the game that ends in a draw, a payoff that is usually "second best" among the preferences of a player. Losing would of course be "third best." What the game theorist tries to analyze are those strategies by which players may maximize their payoffs, that is, get as close as possible to their first preference outcome.

The general structures of available payoffs in any game have been described as (a) zero-sum two-person, (b) non-zero-sum two-person, (c) zero-sum N-person, and (d) non-zero-sum N-person. In the *zero-sum two-person game*, there are, strictly speaking, only two players. The gain of one player is always equal to the loss of the other; the sum of the outcomes for the two players is zero. If John and Jim match pennies, at each turn, the gain of a penny for one is the loss of a penny for the other: that is, 1 minus 1 equal zero. Similarly, if the Democrats and the Republicans "play" for the Presidency, victory for one side is loss for the other, for only one party's nominee can occupy the office.

A *non-zero-sum game*, whether it is a two-person or an N-person (N representing any number higher than two) contest, is one in which the players may share in some division of the rewards; that is, the gain of one is *not* equal to the loss of the other. This requires that the payoff be divisible and that some principle of distribution be applied. For example, only one baseball team can win the championship in the World Series, but both teams share substantially, although unequally, in such payoffs as the box office proceeds.

When a non-zero-sum game has three or more players, several new features of the game situation appear. It becomes possible for two or more of the players to cooperate against the others by pooling resources and making collective decisions during the play. In the course of play, coalitioning may reduce the number of adversaries from several to two. For example, on the race track and in campaigns for a party's nomination, there is a tendency for players to "gang up" on the front-runner in order to reduce his chances of winning without an assist from one or more of them. If the front-runner beats the adversary coalition, he walks off with the whole prize. If the front-runner needs help, e.g., a pivotal number of votes at a party convention, he is likely to "do business" with one or more of the other players. He may pay a high price, say, the vice-presidential nomination, to the player whose support gives him the major portion of the available payoffs, or he may work out a deal with all the other players, giving each something relative to his measure of support, e.g., promise Cabinet positions and other appointments, promise programs of public policy or recognition in the party organization.[9]

Rules

Because of its ordinary usage in daily life, the concept rule is one of the more difficult to grasp in game theory. In ordinary usage, a rule is some established understanding or verbal statement that prescribes what shall be acceptable conduct on the part of an individual, a group, a player, etc. People "break" rules by not conducting themselves in the prescribed way. This leads to the inference that rules are merely words that may be ignored if one is *powerful enough*. In game theory, not the words but the being "powerful enough" is what makes a rule; attention is paid to the resource implications of rules rather than to the prescriptive requirements.

In game theory a *rule of the game* consists of the distribution of resources and the strategic possibilities open to each player in the employment of these resources. In chess, the rules state the power or capacity of each piece, the moves allowable for each piece, the structure of the board on which the game is to be played, and the constraints in the exercise of their resources that each player must follow. Rules may be specified by mutual agreements into which players enter, as in the case of the rules to which major league baseball clubs subscribe or the constitutional rules to which major American political interests subscribed during the ratification of the Constitution. Rules may also be specified by an umpire or third party whose judgment both or all players agree to follow, as in the case of circuit court justices who traveled their circuits in medieval England or of arbitrators who are called in to adjudicate contemporary labor-management disputes.

---

[9] Notice how helpful this aspect of game theory is for explaining why well-organized opponents may be willing to pay a very high price for the support of some uncommitted and less powerful player. In a voting contest, for example, in which there are 101 votes to be cast and 51 are needed to win, a 50-50-1 split would give the single vote a "power index" of 100 percent; it would be up to him to decide which of the major players will win. If the payoff is a zero-sum one, as in the Electoral College choice of President, a powerful player should be willing to pay a very high price to a minority for its critical support, without which the powerful player would have *no payoff at all* to share. The *power index* and its significant implications are developed in L. S. Shapley and Martin Shubik, "A Method for Evaluating the Distribution of Power in a Committee System," *American Political Science Review*, 43 (September 1954): 787–792.

Rules may be specified in terms of the resources that players are willing to use; possession of nuclear weapons is a "rule" of the "international game" only if the possessors have demonstrated a willingness to use them. In Vietnam, for example, American possession of nuclear bombs has *not* been a rule because the United States has tacitly proscribed their use in that conflict. Conversely, by delivering nuclear-tipped intercontinental ballistic missiles to Cuba in 1962, Premier Khrushchev sought surreptitiously to alter the worldwide distribution and placement of nuclear weapons. This attempted rule change was challenged by President Kennedy, who ordered the United States Navy to "quarantine" that island. The Navy proved to be a sufficient "rule" (resource) to prevent further shipment of missiles from the Soviet Union.

As we have seen above, in N-person games it is possible that no one player will have sufficient resources unto himself to win the payoff alone. Such a player may seek out other players with whom to combine resources and coordinate decisions. These collaborations are called *coalitions* and remain in effect only as long as their members anticipate a higher payoff as a consequence of belonging. The division of the reward or proceeds among the members of the coalition in the event of victory is called an *imputation*.

Often enough, a coalition becomes a game-within-a-game in which players exercise rules (apply resources) in order to enforce agreements and keep less advantaged members from breaking away in response to higher bids from adversary players. In real life, the astute politician is a player who sees the advantage in giving all members of his coalition a substantial stake in victory. His political ingenuity is tested when he designs a novel imputation, or division of the proceeds, to take into account the special demands or needs of his coalition members.[10]

---

[10] Shapley and Shubik, *op. cit.*, describe the consequence of coalitioning in a five-member committee in which a majority carries. Arithmetically, each member holds 20 percent of the voting strength of the committee, that is, one vote in five. The "power index" of each member, however, is 33.3 per cent because each member has an equal chance of becoming the pivotal vote in the three-vote majority required to carry a decision. Now, if two of the members form a tight coalition, this, in effect, reduces the five-member committee to a four-member one, for the two-man coalition will always act as a unit. Thus, instead of having what is ostensibly 40 percent of the committee's voting strength, the coalition has a power index of 66.6 percent, requiring only the support of any one of the three other committee members in order to carry its preference. A coalition reduces the relative power of other players; on the other hand, coalitioning by one set of players tends to stimulate coalitioning by another set.

Strategy

The core concept of the theory of games of strategy is the concept *strategy*. Strategy assumes *rationality* in the behavior of the players. In both decision theory and game theory, rationality is a more demanding quality than "sweet reasonableness." A "rational" decision maker or player is strictly a theoretical construct, an artificial being, similar to "economic man" or "political man." It is assumed that the rational player is *completely self-aware* about the priorities among his preferences and has *complete knowledge* about the strategies available to him in pursuit of the payoff. By using logic and all available information, the rational player will *invariably* attempt to maximize his payoff in a manner consistent with his own *payoff function* or ranking of preferences. In game theory, such a rational player is assumed to be incapable of performing any illogical act, although he may commit errors as a consequence of inadequate information.

Given rational behavior (a rarity in the real world), a *strategy*, then, is an overall program of actions which a player adopts in order to achieve a desired outcome or series of outcomes under adverse or conflict conditions. The strategy consists of all the different contingent plans that the player has for deciding along the way how to act next. In game theory it is assumed that the player, because he is rational, can design a strategy that covers *all* possible contingencies. Thus, a strategy might be viewed as a book of instructions which a player could give to a representative to tell him exactly what to do under all circumstances. Needless to say, strategy is very difficult to set out in real life; there are simply too many contingencies to take into account. Even in chess, with its three outcomes—win, lose, or draw—there are many millions of different ways of proceeding through the game.

> The matrix of possible strategies for poker is so large that it has not even been calculated, much less drawn. Consider a radically simplified version of the game which assumes a deck of only three cards, a one-card, no-draw hand, only two players, three bids between them, (the first player gets two, the second, one) and no overbetting. Even this watered-down version of poker involves a matrix of 1,728 boxes, and computing a single best possible strategy for

each player to an accuracy of about 10 percent might require almost two billion multiplications and additions.[11]

Associated with the concept of strategy are several other notions. One is *minimax strategy*. This strategy is adopted by the player who wishes to gain the largest possible payoff when confronted with his opponent's best playing; while taking *minimum* risk, the player aims to achieve *maximum payoff*. This of course assumes a finite number of possible strategies available to each player. To illustrate, assume a zero-sum two-person game between A and B. Assume that A has three possible strategies open to him and B has four possible strategies. The table below shows the scores that A might hypothetically receive as a result of any possible choice of strategies by A and B.

OUTCOME OF GAME BETWEEN A AND B

Strategies available to A	Strategies available to B				Row Minima
	B1	B2	B3	B4	
A1	2	1	4	5	1
A2	2	3	2	4	2
A3	2	—1	1	3	—1
Column Maxima	2	3	4	5	

In the course of this game A will wish to maximize his score and B will wish to minimize his payment to A. If A chooses strategy A1, he is sure to receive an amount, according to this table, not less than the minimum value 1 in the first row, even if B should be able to find out A's strategy. Note that this minimum is indicated in the last column entitled "Row Minima." Similarly, if A chooses A2, he can assure himself a score at least equal to the minimum value 2 in the second row. For strategy A3 his score will certainly not fall

[11] Oskar Morgenstern, "The Theory of Games," *Scientific American*, 180 (May 1949): 22ff. Game theory literature has grown rapidly in the last decade. Some major works, in addition to the original von Neumann and Morgenstern book, include: Kenneth J. Arrow (ed.), "A Symposium on Game Theory," *Behavioral Science*, 7 (January 1962); R. Duncan Luce and Howard Raiffa, *Games and Decisions* (New York: Wiley, 1957); Anatol Rapoport, "Critiques of Game Theory," *Behavioral Science*, 4 (January 1959): 49–66; Martin Shubik (ed.), *Readings in Game Theory and Political Behavior* (Garden City, New York: Doubleday, 1954); Richard C. Snyder, "Game Theory and the Analysis of Political Behavior," in Stephen K. Bailey et al., *Research Frontiers in Politics and Government* (Washington, D.C.: Brookings, 1955), pp. 70–103; J. D. Williams, *The Compleat Strategyst* (New York: McGraw-Hill, 1954). Regular sections on game theory are published in the journals *Behavioral Science* and *Conflict Resolution*.

below −1 in the third row. Strategy A2 will therefore be the most attractive to A since it assures him the largest among the minimum scores listed under "Row Minima." A2 is a minimax strategy for A.

From B's point of view, his strategies B1, B2, B3, and B4 would, in this table, produce payments to A in the amounts of 2, 3, 4 and 5, respectively. Strategy B1 will be most attractive to B and, therefore, his minimax strategy. (It is coincidental that here both the largest row-minimum and the smallest column-maximum equal 2. This outcome, in which the two parties happen to have exactly the same payoffs, is called *saddlepoint*.) In general, then, for strictly determined games, the minimax strategies may be regarded as optimal strategies, and the choice of these strategies will provide a satisfactory solution of the players' problem. In essence, the minimax strategy is the one that is likely to produce the largest payoff with the least risk.[12]

Information State

Game theory is linked to information theory because the rational player, in order to design his best strategy, must carefully analyze all of the relevant factors at any moment. To avoid the risks of error, the rational player must, in the information theory sense, reduce his uncertainty about the state of affairs, both present and future, as much as possible. As a consequence, game theory has focused much attention upon the relevance of information analysis in the conduct of games and conflicts.

At the outset, the player must be thoroughly familiar with the rules, or distribution of resources. He has *perfect information* when he knows everything about the original distribution and subsequent distributions. In chess and checkers each player's original and subsequent resources are completely visible, constituting a situation of perfect information. On the other hand, in poker or bridge, since players are not permitted to see opponents' hands, information is "imperfect." Imperfect information produces an unequal distribution of data among the players. This, in turn, leads to various efforts to rectify the inequality by acquiring information that will reduce uncertainty. Spying is the attempt to learn more about the opponent's resources without his becoming aware how much the spy

---

[12] Adapted from Abraham Wald, "The Theory of Games," in Shubik, *op. cit.*, Chap. 4.

learns. "Signaling" is the term that describes giving information surreptitiously to allies in a coalition. Bluffing consists of attempts to misinform the opponent by "leaks" of information or other misleading data about one's resources or intentions. A double cross refers to the unexpected exploitation of information by one's allies, usually at some critical moment of play. As a consequence of these practices, information analysis runs many risks of misinformation and error.[13]

Such is the extensive and rich terminology of the theory of games of strategy. Because so many people are familiar with the social parlor games to which the theory sometimes refers, the language of game theory has been readily learned and, for many students, captivating in its relevance to conflict situations. Unlike games of chance such as dice, in which impersonal probabilities prevail, the theory of games of strategy has made much of the informational and analytical capabilities of the hypothetical rational player. This assumption relates game theory to other behavioral theories—decision theory, conflict theory, theories of cooperation, and information theory—in a number of significant ways. To some extent, game theory is the theory that links the others together.

The very rigor of the formal theory of games has rendered another kind of scientific service: exposure of (a) the severe limitations of numerous persistent assumptions about human behavior, e.g., human rationality, and (b) the substantial difficulty of testing and applying behavioral theories. Nonetheless, in the last two decades, many attempts have been made to describe political behavior within the conceptual framework of game theory. War-time strategies, international and labor-management bargaining negotiations, national nominating convention developments, political campaign, competitive relations between the President and Congress, and decisions of the Supreme Court: all have been subject to sometimes formal, sometimes informal game theoretical analysis.

The Prisoners' Dilemma

Of particular interest has been a special type of non-zero-sum game called "the Prisoners' Dilemma." This game is thought by many to

---

[13] The earlier discussion of subjective and objective probability is relevant here. See Chapter 5 above. Data that is intersubjectively tested by empirical observation may lead the player to conclusions quite different from those he arrives at through subjective probability estimates in which he is susceptible to misperception due to inexperience, wishing, etc.

be analogous to many everyday life experiences, particularly those of a transactional character in which two parties, such as a buyer and a seller, stand to gain by their interaction despite the fact that they have, in many respects, opposing interests. The Prisoners' Dilemma situation may also be found in an arms race. Experiments with the Prisoners' Dilemma have disclosed the significance of attitudes of trust or suspicion in situations which potentially could lead to either cooperative or conflictual relationships.

The payoff matrices of the Prisoners' Dilemma have the following characteristic: if each person acts only in his own interest, then the result for each will be "bad," for there is an alternative outcome that each would have preferred to the result achieved.[14] The original Prisoners' Dilemma predicament involves a district attorney who holds two prisoners against whom he has a weak case. He presents them with the following alternatives. "The evidence against you is not complete, so each of you has a choice of confessing or not confessing to the crime. If you both confess, your sentence will be five years. If neither of you confesses, your sentence will be one year. If one of you confesses and the other does not, the one who confesses will get a light sentence of only a half year for helping us clear up this case, and the other will be dealt with harshly receiving a sentence of ten years." The prisoners are then separated so that each must make his own decision without information about what the other prisoner has decided. The possible payoffs are summarized in the following matrix:

PRISONER II

		Not Confess	Confess
PRISONER I	Not confess	(1, 1)	(10, ½)
	Confess	(½, 10)	(5, 5)

The first digit in each double entry is the payoff (penalty) of the first prisoner and the second digit is the payoff of the second prisoner. Presumably, a reasonable prisoner would think as follows: "I have two choices, to confess or not confess. If the other prisoner does not confess, I am better off confessing because ½ year is better than 1 year. If the other prisoner does confess, I am stil better off confessing because 5 years is better than 10 years." If the other

[14] Philburn Ratoosh, *Experiments in Non-constant Sum Games* (Berkeley: Management Service Research Center, University of California, 1961).

prisoner follows the same line of reasoning, then they both will receive five years. But it is obvious that both could have received the better payoff of 1 year each if each had not acted solely in his own self-interest.

Thus, in the Prisoners' Dilemma, a "rational player" who, by definition, must strive exclusively for a payoff that maximizes his self-interest, without regard for the other player, finds himself moving necessarily toward something less than his optimum outcome. Other realistic examples of the same kind of situation may be observed in the behavior of persons in a crowded auditorium if someone shouts "Fire!" Wheat farmers who have a choice between restricted or full-production quotas are in a similar situation. So are the parties to an arms race, whether it involves nuclear weapons or rifles. The rational nation or rifleman thinks: "I have two choices, arm or disarm. If the other player disarms, I am better off armed. If the other player arms, I am even more obviously better off armed." If both or all players follow the same line of reasoning, they will not only remain armed, but probably will become involved in an arms race. Yet, if each armed "player" did *not* act solely in his own interest, the consequences could include vastly reduced military budgets, perfection of other conflict techniques (perhaps of the verbal or numerical types), and the probable development of less costly arrangements for mutual physical safety. What, then, are the conditions under which a nation need no longer be its own fortress or a citizen no longer his own policeman? The question carries us back to trust-suspicion attitudes.[15]

Deutsch and Ratoosh have used the Prisoners' Dilemma under experimental conditions to test various hypotheses regarding conditions for trust and suspicion. The Prisoners' Dilemma lends itself particularly well to this type of experiment because the game's essential psychological feature is that there is no possibility in it for "rational" individual behavior unless the condition of mutual trust exists. The investigators define trust as follows: "An individual may be said to have trust in the occurrence of an event, if he expects its occurrence, and his expectation leads to behavior which he perceives to have greater negative motivational consequence if the expectation

[15] For an overview, Anatol Rapoport and Albert Shammah, *Prisoners' Dilemma—A Study in Conflict and Cooperation* (Ann Arbor: University of Michigan Press, 1965); Anatol Rapoport, *Two-person Game Theory: The Essential Ideas* (Ann Arbor: University of Michigan Press, 1966). The study cited below, Morton Deutsch and Philburn Ratoosh, "Trust and Suspicion," *Journal of Conflict Resolution*, 2 (1958): 265–279.

is not confirmed than positive motivational consequence if it is confirmed." A "motivational consequence," according to Deutsch and Ratoosh, is *negative* when it decreases or prevents an increase in the welfare of the individual and *positive* when it increases or prevents a decrease in the welfare of the individual. A person may be said to be "suspicious" of the occurrence of an event if *dis*confirmation of the expectation of the event's occurrence is preferred to its confirmation and if the expectation of its occurrence leads to behavior which is intended to reduce negative motivational consequences. Notice that important features of trust in the Deutsch-Ratoosh study were *predictability* and *expectation*. Furthermore, trust or suspicion are directed at the anticipation of an event rather than at the adversary player.

The investigation found that cooperatively oriented players were more likely to produce trusting behavior even when situational factors did not encourage it. On the other hand, even when situations encouraged trust, those who were competitively oriented were more likely to produce behaviors eliciting suspicion. Only those players who were individualistic seemed influenced by the character of the situation. Such persons decided to expect cooperative behavior from another person by examining the situational aspects of his behavior.

The experiment also found that one individual is more likely to trust another (a) if he believes that the other has nothing to gain from untrustworthy behavior and (b) if he believes he is capable of exerting some influence over the other person's outcome. For instance, congressmen engaged in "logrolling" transactions are doing as much to promote attitudes of trust in each other as they are to acquire desired resources for their constituents.

Trust and suspicion have been subject to scientific investigation only in recent years. The fundamental significance of these behavioral phenomena, often noted in such phrases as "A politician's word is his bond" or "Trust is a necessary antecedent of disarmament," is becoming increasingly apparent to students of politics.

CONFLICT PROCESSES AND CONSEQUENCES

The conceptions *process* and *change* are often stated with some reference to *conflict*. In economics, for example, competition among conflicting interests has been associated in numerous theories with the dynamic progress of economic institutions. In American life this view has prevailed as a kind of ideological necessity; antitrust legislation, for example, presumes that monopolies are resistant to change and that vigorous business competition is as fundamentally good as the family farm and apple pie. Social psychologists have begun to view the "mature personality" as an individual who exposes himself to and deliberately reconciles his role conflicts; in psychological terms, the inner conflicts of certain types of neurotics seem to be a precondition of personal change and growth.

The relationship between conflict and change has held the attention of significant thinkers for centuries. Heraclitus, around 500 B.C., drew a striking analogy between unity and diversity in the universe and the archer's bow. "The universe," he said, "appears to be a taut structure, like the archer's bow, with opposites producing stability in equilibrium and change as the consequence of struggle. . . . All things come into being and pass away through strife."[16]

In the classic Greek view, the state is really a group of persons cooperating for some common purpose. The souls of men achieve their *telos* or most fundamental purpose only through sharing in the life of the group. Therefore, the more rationally organized the society, the greater is man's fulfillment of his unique individual potentialities. The purpose of the state is nothing less than the production of the "best possible" human beings. If a state fails in this respect, the citizens should "allow it to be revolutionized . . . rather than to change to a polity which naturally makes men worse."[17]

Plato identified three factors influencing the behavior of organized societies; reason, spirit, and appetite. Reason impels organizational behavior as a means to understand group purposes and devise ways to implement those purposes. Spirit is the driving element which enables men to resist aggression, to voice indignity at injustice, and to be ambitious and compete. Appetite is the organization response to its material needs. Given these three factors, the ideal organization is one in which rationality is in control and is sustained by spirit and supplied by appetite. Modern versions of the platonic categories may be found in theories of rational collective decision making (reason), conflict as a producer of group integration (spirit),

---

[16] Fragment from Heraclitus, in John Burnet, *Early Greek Philosophy* (London: A. Black, 1930), pp. 136–137.

[17] Quotation from *Plato's Laws*, in Mulford Q. Sibley, "The Place of Classical Political Theory in the Study of Politics," in Roland Young (ed.), *Approaches to the Study of Politics* (Evanston: Northwestern University Press, 1958).

and economic affluence as a lubricant of organizational growth (appetite).

Plato also examined the problem of social disorganization. Such tendencies appear when the predominance of the rational element is destroyed or discounted. As opportunities for disorganization increase, oligarchic elements emerge from divisions in the ruling class. The appetitive element in the organization then begins to usurp the functions of reason, and the appetites become competitive. Under such circumstances, conflict becomes perennial, and agreement is the exception. Such a state is ripe for a tyrant.

Aristotle approached the phenomena of conflict and change somewhat more systematically and empirically; some political scientists believe that the Aristotelian theory of revolution has been little improved upon to this day.[18] According to Aristotle, a *constitution* may be defined as the organization of the entire political community (*polis*) with respect to its offices generally but particularly to that office which is sovereign to all issues. Under the constitutions of democracies (Aristotle called them *polities*), the people are sovereign; in aristocracies, the few; in kingships, full sovereignty rests with a single man.

Whether written or customary, the constitution sets forth the "job descriptions" of the various public offices and regulates participation, or eligibility for and selection to these offices. For Aristotle, participation in office is equivalent to citizenship. Thus, the constitution is the organization of all citizens into positions with duties and prerogatives bearing upon the political community as a whole. Each citizen is a public officer in the broadest sense; each public officer has task expectations set forth for him in the constitution. The constitution also prescribes what kinds of persons (in the sense of personal background and attributes) may become incumbents and according to what selection or investing procedures.

Revolution, Aristotle believed, produces changes in constitutions. Changes may involve shifts from normal to perverted constitutional forms: kingships may become tyrannies, aristocracies become oli-

18 Some noteworthy attempts to develop a theory of revolution include: F. A. de Chateaubriand, *An Historical, Political, and Moral Essay on Revolutions* (1815); Crane Brinton, *The Anatomy of Revolution* (New York: Harper, 1951); Feliks Gross, *The Seizure of Political Power* (New York: Philosophical Library, 1958); Peter Amann, "Revolution, A Redefinition," *Political Science Quarterly*, 78 (March, 1962); D. J. Goodspeed, *The Conspirators; A Study of the Coup d'Etat* (New York: Viking Press, 1961); Chalmers Johnson, *Revolutionary Change* (Boston: Little, Brown, 1966).

garchies, and polities become "democracies," as Aristotle used the latter term. Another kind of change described by him involved shifts in sovereignty from kingship to aristocracy, aristocracy to polity, polity to kingship, etc. Oppression, fear, and contempt cause kingships to become tyrannies; limitations of offices and honors to a narrow circle tend to convert aristocracies into oligarchies; and the wanton license of demagogues leads polities into their less desirable "democratic" form.[19]

The classical approach to analysis of complex phenomena into *structural* and *process* elements continues to be found in every field of knowledge. A familiar example from medical science is the distinction between anatomy and physiology. Anatomy provides a *structural* perspective on the human body by analyzing that body into distinguishable parts or components and establishing, where possible, subsidiary organized relationships among these parts. Thus, the heart is a component of a body subsystem called the circulatory system, in which other familiar components are the veins, arteries, capillaries, etc. Similarly, the structure of the national government of the United States consists of an identifiable number of parts called the executive branch, the legislative branch, and the judiciary, each with its own subsystem of components.

Physiology provides a *process* perspective by examining the interaction through time of the various identified parts of the structure. What the various components of the circulatory system do, for example, from moment to moment, is transfer blood and its contents to various parts of the body. The interaction consists of a heart pumping, a set of lungs aerating, nutrients collected by the arteries, waste collected by the veins, etc. Familiar political interactions in the American national government occur when, for example, the President recommends legislation suggested to him by his party or some organized interest, Congress considers his proposal in the form of a bill, modifies it, and enacts it for his approval or veto; in essence, this is the legislative *process*.

Process frequently refers to a patterned series of changes in a structure. Observers of processes sometimes consider structure as a temporally delimited instance of process; in effect, process called to a halt long enough to examine the general organization of the interacting parts. Observers of structure and process invent modes of

[19] Book V is devoted mainly to this subject. See Ernest Barker, *The Politics of Aristotle* (Oxford: Oxford University Press, 1956), pp. 203–254.

description and analysis that help determine whether changes in a structure over time are random or regular. Terms such as "disequilibrium," "tension," and "conflict" are frequently employed in referring to the conditions under which processes evolve and by which alterations in structure are produced.

Aristotle suggested three characteristic processes by which modifications in constitutional structure occur. One process involved conflicts over the "job descriptions" for the offices comprising the constitution. This is similar to the conflicts over task expectations described in Chapter 1 above. Such conflicts affect the distribution of tasks within the position structure of the organization. Their outcomes have consequences for a *formalization process*.

A second process referred to by Aristotle involves changes in the attitudes, capacities, and moral qualities of those individuals—king, aristocracy, or citizenry—exercising sovereignty in the community. Conflicts directed toward changing such attitudes, capacities, and moral qualities, would, in modern behavioral science terms, produce outcomes that relate to the *socialization process*, as in Chapter 8 above. In essence, if the position incumbents "behave poorly," in the Aristotelian scheme they need to be taught (socialized) to perform better.

A third kind of conflict and change is related to the holding of offices. Presumably, after fighting about the tasks to be performed in a particular office and about the competency of particular kinds of persons to perform them, another evenue of change is to separate individuals from the offices. This is a conflict over incumbency status in which one person may be divested of the office and another invested with it; the result has been referred to in Chapter 7 above as an *investiture process*.

Formalization, socialization, and investiture processes may be viewed as three types of conflict process that have consequences for the structure of organized groups.[20] Each conflict process is a sequence of *conflict cycles* in which initiating events and concluding events of a decisional character set boundaries for the cycle. Thus, a conflict may be initiated by one party's decision to declare another to be an "enemy" whose intentions and behaviors seem hostile. The cycle may conclude with a decision by one or an agreement by both parties. The concluding decision or agreement may have important

---

[20] Goldman, "Theory of Conflict Processes and Organizational Offices," *op. cit.*

consequences for both. For example, in labor-management contro-
versies, a union may win organizational recognition from management, while management may retain the prerogative of hiring and
firing employees. These outcomes also carry with them structural
and organizational consequences, such as the formalization change
that recognizes management's hiring prerogative.[21]

Formalization

As a conflict process, formalization relates to disagreements over
task expectations. We have seen earlier how the goals of an organization may be analyzed into tasks whose performance is assigned to
particular members.[22] Task expectations are designed and grouped
into sets called positions, and group and organization members may,
at different times and under changing conditions, come to hold different task expectations about particular positions. This is especially
true as new organizational goals arise, as new techniques for implementing these goals are discovered, and as new environmental
conditions are encountered by the group.

To reiterate what has been said in an earlier chapter, conflicts
about task expectations among members of an organization are
usually started with questions such as "What is the relationship between the duties of a position and the goals of the organization?"
"Are the particular actions [A_{g1}, A_{g2}, etc., in the chart] specified in
task expectations sufficiently clear, or is more detailed prescription
necessary?" "What is the distribution of duties [task expectations]
among the organization's various positions?" "What resources and
prerogatives are associated with the task expectations of a particular
position?"

Conflicts over task expectations are usually resolved in one or
more of several ways. One resolution occurs when there is a change
of consensus within the group concerning the content of the expectations held by most members. A second mode of resolution occurs
when the task expectations associated with a particular position are

[21] An adversary's *declared goals* may be observed by examining his communications about the demands and outcomes he seeks. *Behavioral consequences*, on the
other hand, depend upon the theoretical interest of the observer. Such an observer
may be interested in measuring the reallocation of resources resulting from the
conflict. Or, as we prefer here, he may be interested in the consequences for organizational development, theoretically stipulated here as outcomes that produce formalization, socialization, or investiture changes.

[22] See Chapter 1.

FORMALIZATION OF A GROUP POSITION*

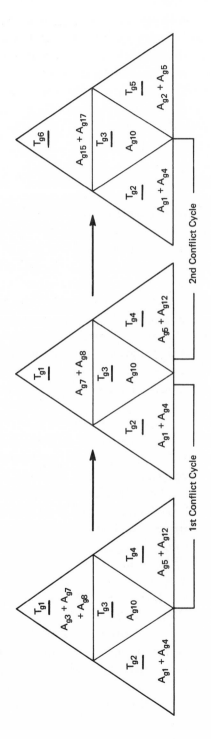

1st Conflict Cycle

2nd Conflict Cycle

* KEY: T_{g1}, T_{g2}, T_{gn} = specific task expectation of group; A_{g1}, A_{g2}, A_{gn} = specific behavioral act associated with a task-expectation by group.

This chart of the formalization process illustrates how two conflict cycles might change the set of task expectations associated with group position. At the end of Cycle 1, Task Expectation 1 has had Activity 3 dropped from its set. At the end of Cycle 2, Task Expectation 1 has been replaced entirely by Task Expectation 6, with its set of Activities 15 and 17. Also, Task Expectation 4 has been replaced by Task Expectation 5, which retains Activity 5 which had been part of Task Expectation 4.

explicitly and formally modified by statute, policy declaration, or constitution. Such modifications may specify new task activities, reassign task expectations to other positions, or discontinue tasks. A third possible outcome of conflict over task expectations involves bringing together into a single position set for the first time task expectations that had previously been unrelated. These various outcomes or resolutions, because they affect task expectations, may be subsumed under the formalization process.

Socialization

Socialization is a process to which we have already given much attention. In essence, this conflict process relates to individual role information and role performances during the conduct of organizational activities. The football player who throws the ball poorly may be instructed by the coach how to throw better. If the instruction is welcomed and the behavior modified, socialization has been a cooperative process. On the other hand, if the player disagrees with the coach about the quality of his performance or the content of the instructions, a disagreement is in progress. In other words, a socialization conflict may occur over the appropriateness of actual performance, in which group members or leaders make reference to an actor's particular behaviors.

As we saw earlier, groups are constantly communicating generalized role information to members. From such information (usually in some linguistic form), a role becomes a mental or neural preparation for the performance of prescribed and standardized patterns of individual activity in certain relatively standardized situations in which the group is interested. Ordinarily when a person's role performance approximates the group's task expectations, that person is said to "have done a good job."

The individual, however, may be unfavorably disposed toward the group, unskilled, a poor learner, or some combination of these. If the particular role performance falls short of the group's task expectations, the resulting conflict usually involves charges of "incompetency," "lax performance," and other negative evaluations of the role performance. If, as a consequence of the socialization conflict, the performance of the individual is modified, he may be said to have "learned a lesson." This lesson may refer to the fact that he became more informed about the appropriate pattern of role

SOCIALIZATION OF AN INDIVIDUAL PERSONALITY *

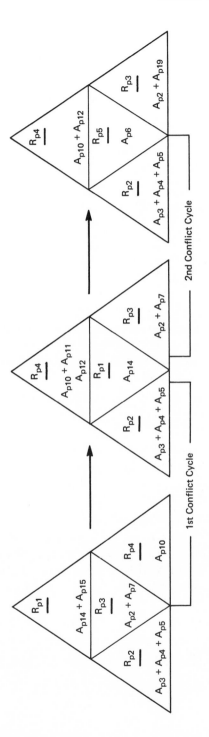

1st Conflict Cycle

2nd Conflict Cycle

* KEY: R_{p1}, R_{p2}, R_{pn} = specific role information of person;

A_{p1}, A_{p2}, A_{pn} = specific behavioral act associated with a person's learned role.

This chart illustrates the socialization process in which the personality (role structure) of the individual, and associated behaviors, are modified from conflict to conflict. At the end of Cycle 1, Role 1 has been reduced to second rank and Activity 15 eliminated from its set, Role 4 and its Activities 10, 11, and 12 have displaced Role 1 at the top of the hierarchy (with Role 4 having had Activities 11 and 12 added to its first-stage set), and Roles 2 and 3 remaining the same. At the end of Cycle 2, Role 4 has lost Activity 11, Role 5 has displaced Role 1, and Role 3 has had its Activity 7 displaced by Activity 19.

activity, acquired greater skill, or lent greater importance to this over other roles.

Socialization conflicts may also arise over the appropriateness of the individual's prior socialization. This usually takes the form of a debate over personal qualifications, or already learned roles. This is the essence of the well-known "a man who . . ." speeches that place candidates for public office into nomination or urge their election by the voters. To ask if a man is qualified for an office is to raise a socialization issue over which there may be disagreement. Such personality issues are familiar features of American politics, and it is sometimes argued that they may be its main issues.

Investiture

Ordinarily, the term "investiture" is used to describe the procedure or ceremony with which kings and other high officials are formally endowed with the duties and prerogatives of an office. In Chapter 7 we first used this term to describe those conflicts that relate to incumbency situations. An *incumbency* was defined as that state of affairs in which a person and a position, that is, a role structure and a set of task expectations, are brought together into sustained relationship with each other and the group. In ordinary language, investiture refers to the process of locating "the man for the job" and putting him in it.

An incumbency exists if there is a consensus among the members of a group concerning which *particular person* is to be held accountable for the performance of the task expectations associated with which *particular position*. Usually the group develops some overt demonstration of this consensus, referred to as a legitimizing situation. A *legitimizing situation* is a procedure or an event or some group act that serves as explicit notice that a group consensus has been reached or terminated regarding a particular incumbency. Familiar legitimizing situations in the American political system are: election by members of the group or constituency; appointment by some authorized public officer; employment from civil service rolls; dismissal for cause; popular recall; and impeachment. Some of these terms refer to divesting acts which indicate a termination of the group consensus about incumbency.

The most obvious occasions for conflict over incumbents are: (1) those in which there are two or more candidates for a position; (2)

INVESTITURE OF AN INCUMBENCY

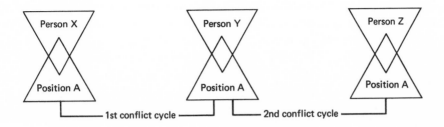

This chart illustrates the investiture process by simply showing how Position A may be filled by different persons - X, Y, and Z - as a consequence of conflict cycles.

those in which a change is sought in the group's definition of the legitimizing situation; and (3) those in which the composition of the electing or appointing authority is challenged. In the American system, for example, the presence of two major political parties tends to assure a choice between at least two candidates for most public offices. Attempts to change legitimizing situations are also common and often subject to much controversy; viz., the continuing attempts to modify the Electoral College procedure for choosing the President. American experience has also seen a great deal of conflict regarding the composition of the investing authority, or who shall have the right to vote.

Historically, a variety of legitimizing situations have been employed by groups and governments to resolve investiture conflicts. An ancient procedure of choice is selection by lot, which is designed to depersonalize and defactionalize controversy by leaving the issue to chance. The accident of birth is another traditional method of placing individuals upon the ruling throne—a procedure, as noted earlier, which combines the laws of genetic chance with the laws of primogeniture. Co-optation is usually a more subtle and selective process, in which "insiders" add to or replace themselves in office by informally recruiting "new blood." Election and appointment, as indicated above, are the most common investiture practices in the American system.

Divestiture, or separation from office, can also be carried out by a variety of techniques. The more peaceful of these include formal procedures for terminating incumbency. In the United States these are most frequently limitations upon length of tenure in office or upon the number of terms permitted, as in the case of the two-term limit for the Presidency prescribed in the Twenty-second Amendment. Regularized procedures for dismissal, recall, or impeachment are also common. More violent practices of divestiture abound in human history and are only relatively less frequent in the American experience. These include: assassination of incumbents; coups d'etat, armed revolutions, purges (particularly in modern totalitarian regimes), and even international wars such as those required to remove from office leaders such as Hitler and Mussolini.[23]

In general, therefore, man's age-old concern with conflict phenomena has led him to theorize extensively about this aspect of human interaction. There have been philosophical justifications and denunciations of conflict. Conflict has been considered both essential to and anathema to self-government. A major stride in conflict analysis has been made possible by the development of the theory of games of strategy. The conflict processes of formalization, socialization, and investiture have been viewed as essential elements in the evolution of all organizational life.

An Illustrative Use of the Conceptual Perspective

THE LEGISLATIVE "GAME" IN CONGRESS

Most of the analytical elements noted in conflict theory and game theory may be identified in the normal activities of Congress. These elements include: regularly participating players, or parties; scarcities that may be converted to payoffs at the conclusion of a contest; resources ("rules") and alliance systems; fairly standardized patterns of conflict interaction; terminal decisional events that somehow re-

---

[23] Useful sources on the more violent techniques: Joseph Bornstein, *The Politics of Murder* (New York: Sloane, 1950); Feliks Gross, *The Seizure of Political Power* (New York: Philosophical Library, 1958); John H. Herz, "The Problems of Successorship in Dictatorial Regimes," *Journal of Politics* (February 1952): pp. 19–40; C. Wright Mills, *The Power Elite* (New York: Oxford University Press, 1956), pp. 139 ff.

solve or conclude the "temporary disjunction" created by a conflict cycle; various types of information states that may critically influence players' strategies; and conflict outcomes that may affect the attitudes of trust among both allies and adversaries. These elements are touched upon in the illustrations that follow.

Choosing Enemies

The "players" in the legislative "game" are able to identify the "enemy" rather precisely. An obvious adversary for every senator and representative is the membership of the opposition party. The convenience of party labels for identifying "friends" and "enemies" is not available within the executive branch or the judiciary. In Congress it has, at least since the Reconstruction Era, become the starting point for choosing sides. The first and foremost of legislative fights is the one at the opening session which determines which party shall organize a particular house, select its senior leaders, and win its committee chairmanships. On organization of their house, most members of Congress vote their party's line. But, while the two-party structure is known to be quite stable, it is equally clear that some, if not most, bills are passed by coalitions different from the party coalitions.[24]

Often providing the basis for factional alignments within and between the two major congressional parties is the presence of *liberals* and *conservatives;* on particular issues these legislators view each other as adversaries. Numerous studies that apply scales of liberalism and conservatism in legislative voting confirm that the adversaries divide on these lines with significant frequency.[25] An alliance between a liberal or conservative minority in one party and its counterpart majority in the other party may make all the difference for the passage of legislation in some sessions. In recent years, the best known of such alliances has been the one between Republican conservatives and Southern Democratic conservatives in the Senate.

A third familiar choice of adversaries in Congress is the one that

[24] See the *Congressional Quarterly Weekly Report,* published in Washington, D.C., for analyses of voting patterns in both houses. The general proposition that legislators tend to vote with their party is examined for its conflict implications by R. Duncan Luce and A. A. Rogow, "A Game Theoretic Analysis of Congressional Power Distributions for a Stable Two-Party System," *Behavioral Science,* 1 (1956): 83–95.

[25] For example, Dean R. Brimhall and A. S. Otis, "A Study of Consistency in Congressional Voting," in John C. Wahlke and Heinz Eulau, *Legislative Behavior* (Glencoe, Ill.: The Free Press, 1959), pp. 384–387.

a legislator makes when he decides to be anti-President or pro-President, regardless of his and the incumbent President's party. This choice is perhaps most often made by members from marginal states or marginal congressional districts in which the presidential coattail may make a substantial difference with respect to reelection. A similar type of choice is made by legislators who acquire reputations as "mavericks," as noted in an earlier chapter. To strike a stand independent of the leadership of Congress can, under certain circumstances, be as impressive as taking a stand against the President of the United States.

Prospects and Payoffs

The payoffs in the congressional game are also fairly explicit. In general terms, passing a law should be considered the maximum payoff in a legislative contest. However, the astute observer of congressional behavior knows that some victories include the *failure* to pass a bill, as well as other nonlegislative accomplishments such as personal publicity, initiation of a public issue, acquisition of political credit, and concessions from the President or other distributors of political currencies. Then, of course, there are many payoffs that come with the substance of legislation itself: to mention the more obvious, the declaration of a national public policy, the allocation of funds in an appropriation, the distribution of prerogatives in a particular area of decision making, the election or confirmation of persons for high office, and the resolution expressing a significant congressional attitude on some topic.

Resources and Rules

The rules of the legislative process in Congress are numerous, and those that are written are voluminous, as we have seen elsewhere. Perhaps the basis of most congressional resources is the fact that, according to the intent of the Constitution, this body is the principal repository of the Nation's sovereignty. This sovereignty is essentially a decisional capacity out of which other allocations of prerogative derive.

Under the Articles of Confederation, the American system started with a parliamentary or deliberative conception of national government's role. The Founding Fathers in the Constitution converted this to a system of powers divided among the several branches, leaving the bulk of the more explicit prerogatives with Congress. In time the claims of the Supreme Court, the growth of the Presidency, and the process of specialization within Congress itself restricted somewhat the gross decision-making capacity of Congress. Yet, Congress remains the primary deliberating and decision-making organ of the national government.

The principal resources of each of its members is his one vote. If he invests that resource wisely through alliances both inside and outside Congress, he may be able to amplify it into a powerful resource in legislative contests. In many respects, the rules and customs of each house have evolved precisely in ways which amplify the prerogatives associated with the votes of certain members, e.g., those with seniority, those who are committee chairmen, and those holding particular offices of a house.

Finally, there are the substantive aspects of choices made by Congress. How much to tax whom is simultaneously a matter of how much Congress will make available to itself for expenditure. A powerful national government is, after all, a government whose power Congress shares.

Conflict Interaction

The mode of conflict interaction in Congress stands at a point midway between the relative informality of the executive branch and the great formality of the judiciary. Conflict situations may develop at any one of several points in the process of legislating. Competing bills may be introduced dealing with the same problem or subject, and each side may find itself at this time making important tactical decisions, such as whether its bills should be introduced collectively or by various legislators individually.

Next, a battle may develop over referral of the bill to one or another committee. Since referrals are rarely formally challenged, this issue may require much behind-the-scenes activity. Patterns of conflict activity within a congressional committee are fairly standard since members' votes on most legislation are usually predictable. The strenuous fight comes when committee members wish to challenge a chairman's attempt to delay or to bury a particular bill. At committee hearings, a conflict may become public if adversaries deside to interrogate witnesses and present competing testimony.

By the time the bill reaches the floor of one of the houses, sides have generally been chosen and votes settled. It is rare that a floor battle will change many votes, but it may accomplish other things; it makes a public record, demonstrates the tenacity of a minority (as in filibusters), or gives the leadership of one or both sides time in which to work out a compromise or face-saving formula.

Similar patterns of conflict then occur when the bill passes through the other house, survives the rigors of a conference committee, and surmounts the hurdle of a possible presidential veto.

While the formal aspect of the legislative process imposes regularities upon conflict patterns related to bills and resolutions, Congress, it must be remembered, is also an informal meeting place for some of the nation's best politicians. Opportunities for nonlegislative contests exist and are frequently exploited. Contests over positions of party leadership, for example, may become the occasion for the demonstration of a particular faction's strength within the party. Such was the case when Representative Gerald Ford of Michigan challenged Charles A. Halleck of Indiana for the Republican leadership of the House; this was widely reported as a contest between the "Young Turks" and the "Old Guard." In 1969, Senator Edward M. Kennedy defeated Senator Russell B. Long for the position of Democratic Majority Whip, which was generally interpreted as a Kennedy bid for national as well as senatorial party leadership. Such contests are normal occasions for intracongressional engagement.

Terminal Decision Events

Conflicts come to a head at numerous junctures in the legislative process. The most overt and dramatic decision event at the end of a controversy is the floor vote. The tally of "ayes" and "nays," even when the outcome is a foregone conclusion, invariably carries an air of suspense. Yet, the truly conclusive floor vote may have been taken much earlier on some procedural or technical motion to change a phrase, to table, or to override the chair's interpretation of a parliamentary question.

Congress also affords many opportunities for its members to conclude their contests out of public view. The best known of these is the prerogative of congressional committee chairmen to "bury" bills. While the charge is often heard that such burials are autocratic, they are more often quite representative of the view of the majority within the committee. Perhaps the least visible of the decision centers is the conference committee for reconciling differences in similar bills passed by each house. Decisions taken "in conference," as we have already seen, may be even more binding than those taken on the floor of either house.

Information-States

In the legislative process, "the record" is one of the most significant means of communicating information about a political conflict. The record is much more than a formal *Congressional Record*, as important as this is. A record may be made during committee hearings, and, in recent years, such hearings have been published with greater regularity. A record may be made in the press, especially when public knowledge is a significant factor in a struggle. In 1955, for example, four unions—the International Ladies' Garment Workers Union, the Amalgamated Clothing Workers of America, the Textile Workers of America, and the United Hatters, Cap and Millinery Workers—organized a Joint Minimum Wage Committee to campaign for an increase in the Federal minimum wage, then 75 cents an hour. This committee sought a climate of information and opinion in Congress that would help advance the legislation through the House Committee on Education and Labor, under the hostile chairmanship of Representative Graham A. Barden. In order to inform and arouse nonlabor, nongovernmental organizations in support of the bill, the Joint Committee asked union locals throughout the country to inform their local political leaders about the proposed legislation and its implications for their community. Community information was then transmitted by local leaders to their representatives in Congress, who very often thereby learned about the bill *for the first time.* This information campaign changed enough votes to put the bill through the House by a narrow margin of five votes.[26]

As parliamentarians, legislators are familiar with the use of the agenda and motions of cloture as devices for bringing conflict cycles to a conclusion. An *agenda* is an order of business which arranges the sequence of issues to be dealt with by a deliberative body. Any particular issue under deliberation must eventually make way for the next item of business or for the termination of a session of busi-

[26] Gus Tyler, *A Legislative Campaign for a Federal Minimum Wage, 1955,* Eagleton Case Study (New York: Henry Holt, 1959).

ness. A major intention of parliamentary procedure is to "push along" with the business at hand, although those who wish to delay and divert usually need to exercise no great ingenuity to devise techniques of obstructionism.

Trust

Few groups of people in the world pay more attention than Congress to ritual and other requirements for maintaining the bond of trust among themselves. The gentlemanly style and language, the club atmosphere, the many opportunities for generating long-standing political friendships even among partisan opponents, and the stern treatment given men who break the atmosphere of trust are evidence of the concern for trustworthiness among the members.

Systems and System Building

Systems theory, popular in mechanics and communication engineering, has captured the interest of political scientists as a possible tool for large-scale or macrocosmic analysis of political phenomena. Some view the political system as a kind of guided missile whose targets are its purposes and whose components operate to adjust the system's course toward its targets. Others consider the political system as a converter that transforms inputs (such as political demands) into outputs (such as public policies). Still another group of theorists use the system concept as a way of dealing with structural analysis and functional analysis of politics at the same time. Whichever the approach used, a basic motivation for systems theories is comprehensiveness. The focus of attention is usually the totality, the overview. This has been reinforced by recent concern for the emergence of new political systems throughout the world, in the new nations and in the international system. The object is to discover what makes some of these systems more effective and more viable than others.

10

Political Systems

Another "first" for Aristotle was his reference to the Egyptian "political system" as one of the oldest on earth. As long ago as 1651, Thomas Hobbes wrote of political systems in *Leviathan.*[1] However, not until recently did the concepts *state* and *system* achieve major status as empirically significant perspectives in political science. In 1953, David Easton wrote a notable critique of the concepts state and power, declaring them useless to the empirical political scientist and recommending *systems analysis,* particularly its notion of *equilibrium.* Within a few years the systems approach, or aspects of it, found its way into a wide range of significant political writing. By the mid-1960s, however, the systems model, although influential, had become the target of criticism and skepticism.[2]

The popularity of the systems concept seems to have been generated from two sources. The first was a general dissatisfaction with political analysis as such. Many behavioral approaches seemed to analyze political phenomena into tiny, often insignificant, fragments with little attention to resynthesizing these analyzed phenomena into

[1] Noticed in Herbert J. Spiro's excellent "Evaluation of Systems Theory," in James C. Charlesworth (ed.), *Contemporary Political Analysis* (New York: Free Press, 1967), Chap. 9.

[2] David Easton, *The Political System* (2nd ed., New York: Knopf, 1971). Easton's most recent formulation may be found in *A Systems Analysis of Political Life* (New York: Wiley, 1965).

theoretical wholes. Just as gestalt learning theory was in part a reaction to behaviorism in psychology, systems theory in political science apparently represents something of a revolt against microcosmic analyses of political phenomena. The concern with systems reflects a revived interest in the relationship of parts to wholes and the integration of parts into wholes. Entire political structures, the dynamic interaction of their parts, and their contributions to the functioning of the system as a whole have therefore come under new examination.

A second source of behavioral interest in systems theory came from the new science of cybernetics and its emphases upon homeostatic systems and the analysis of informational feedback. Cybernetics, in turn, reflects a growing body of systems theory in communications engineering and mechanics.[3]

SYSTEMS THEORY IN THE STUDY OF POLITICS

The effort to design theories of political systems may be summarized under three general headings: political systems viewed as "guided missiles" seeking out political goals; political systems viewed as convertors of inputs into political outputs; and political systems as kinds of structures performing particular kinds of functions.

Systems as Guided Missiles

In 1948 Norbert Wiener coined the term *cybernetics*, which he derived from the Greek word *kubernetes*, or "steerman." This is the same Greek word from which the term "governor" is derived. What interested Wiener was the relationship between input of message signals and outputs of such automatic machinery as the automatic door opener, the proximity fuse, thermostats, and controlled missiles. Cybernetics deals with the systems characteristics that produce the "steering" or control of such mechanisms for the purpose assigned to them. By 1950, viewing people and society as systems amenable to cybernetic study, Wiener wrote *The Human Use of Human Beings*.[4]

---

[3] Walter Buckley (ed.), *Modern Systems Research for the Behavioral Scientist* (Chicago: Aldine, 1968); Oran R. Young, *Systems of Political Science* (Englewood Cliffs, N.J.: Prentice-Hall, 1968).

[4] Norbert Wiener, *Cybernetics* (2d ed.; New York: Wiley, 1961) and *The Human Use of Human Beings* (Boston: Houghton Mifflin, 1950).

An analogy between person and machine may begin with the fact that every instrument created by scientific instrument makers is in some respect a sense organ constructed to record readings remotely through the intervention of some appropriate electrical apparatus. Such instruments, and other machines, may be produced not only to sense information, but also to act on the external world as a consequence of receiving and sending messages. The automatic photoelectric door-opener is a familiar example. When a message consisting of the interception of a beam of light is sent to the apparatus, the message triggers the door, which opens so that the person may go through.

On the basis of such simple message-receiving, machine-actuating procedures, modern engineering has built large and complex automatic mechanisms. These mechanisms receive an *input*, that is, message data, to which they respond with an *output*, or action upon the outer world. If past data is stored in the machine, at some time to be combined with new incoming data, as in the case of the electronic computer or the controlled missile, the mechanism is said to have a *memory*. As the machine performs in response to messages from the environment, the effects of that performance produce further information from the environment, called *feedback*. Thus, just as a thermostat switches on a furnace when its thermometer "reads" that the surrounding temperature is falling lower than some preset level, the same thermostat also "reads" the consequent rise in temperature as feedback, enabling it to switch off the furnace at some desired maximum temperature level.

Thermostats and other cybernetic mechanisms are designed to control mechanical tendencies toward disorganization or disequilibrium. If the designer is able to "fix" his desired state (goal) in some kind of mechanical and informationally "readable" way, just as the thermostat may be set at some desired temperature level, he may guide the action responses of the mechanism so as to counter or reverse the disequilibrium, disorganization, or disorientation. In other words, he may control the tendencies toward entropy. In Wiener's opinion:

> The physical functioning of the living individual and the operation of some of the newer communication machines are precisely parallel in their analogous attempts to control entropy through feedback. Both of them have sensory receptors as one state of their cycle of operation: that is, in both of them there exists a special apparatus

for collecting information from the outer world at low energy levels, and for making it available in the operation of the individual or of the machine. In both cases these external messages are not taken *neat*, but through the internal transforming powers of the apparatus, whether it be alive or dead. The information is then turned into a new form available for the further states of performance.[5]

Three basic questions come into view as soon as we establish a distinction between a *system* and its *environment*.[6] First, what are the operating parts or *components* of the system? How are they coordinated? What activities do they perform? How do they fluctuate, change, grow, disappear, or become replaced? As we shall see below, some theorists feel that this structural-functional concern should be paramount in systems theory, whereas others insist that system components ought to be viewed as a closed *black box* whose inputs and outputs are the significant phenomena to watch.

A second question has to do with the *boundaries* between the system and the environment. What are the boundaries? How are they structured, maintained, and changed? What functions do the boundaries themselves serve? In biological osmosis, for example, the permeability of a membrane is usually its most important characteristic in transactions between one system and another. Similarly, the human being is usually considered an organic system separated from its environment by its skin. Political scientists have tended to view the external geographical boundaries of a nation as the limits of its political system.

Boundary designation, however, has raised more problems for systems theory than it has solved, particularly when the attempt is made to distinguish between a closed and an open system. A *closed system* is presumably one which carries on no exchanges with its environment. It is static, a fixed structure. On the other hand, an *open system* is dynamic in its reception of inputs from the environment, its conversion of them into consumable components *within* the system, and its return of outputs to the environment. In order to continue their existence open systems characteristically seek equilibrium, balancing inputs and outputs in order to maintain the equilibrium state. Distinctions between open and closed systems are made according to the purpose or preference of the theorist; often the same system can be conceived of as either open or closed.

---

[5] *Ibid.* (Doubleday Anchor Edition, 1954), pp. 26–27.
[6] The following is based upon Charles A. McClelland, "The Function of Theory in International Relations," *Journal of Conflict Resolution*, 4 (September 1960): 328 ff.

The third question raised by any distinction between system and environment is the nature of the *interaction* between the two. What is the influence of the environment on the system and of the system on the environment? This question focuses attention upon the interactions or transactions between system and environment. Thus, for example, a guided missile may change the environment by exploding its target as it hits. Conversely, a strike will also result in the destruction of the missile system itself.

These questions have, unfortunately, been of relatively little empirical use in the study of political phenomena. Different authors freely call different political entities "systems." Usually these systems are coterminous with some geographical boundary; a city will constitute an urban political system, a national political system will extend to the nation's official boundaries, and regional or international systems will be similarly designated. The "openness" of a political system will often be correlated with democratic attributes; totalitarian systems tend to be called "closed."

Another concern of the cybernetic school of systems theory is the condition of equilibrium or stability. Easton identified two types of equilibrium associated with open systems. *Stationary equilibrium* exists if the components of the system are held constant over a given period of time, whereas under conditions of *dynamic equilibrium* there is constant activity and change. As components of a system undergo change, the position of equilibrium may always be shifting. "However, if the rate of change has a pattern that consistently repeats or maintains itself, then the process of change is said to have achieved a state of equilibrium."[7]

Another distinction among types of equilibrium are mechanical and homeostatic equilibrium. When a physicist says that two weights are equal, his statement can be confirmed by an independent method such as the spring scale; this scale reflects a *mechanical equilibrium.* The temperature of the human blood, on the other hand, is a *homeostatic equilibrium* system, that is, blood temperature is maintained by processes (such as constriction of the blood vessels) that compensate for environmental disturbances. Homeostatic systems are self-regulatory; they have the capacity to reestablish a predetermined balance among system components. Political systems are frequently referred to as either "dynamic" or "homeostatic."[8]

[7] David Easton, "Limits of the Equilibrium Model in Social Research," in Heinz Eulau, Samuel J. Eldersveld, and Morris Janowitz (eds.), *Political Behavior* (Glencoe, Ill.: The Free Press, 1956), p. 399.

[8] Morton A. Kaplan, "Systems Theory," in James C. Charlesworth, *op. cit.*, Chap. 8.

Feedback becomes significant in the maintenance of system equilibrium. Feedback consists of those input messages from the environment which affect components and component relationships within the system in a way that modifies succeeding outputs. In making public policy, for example, government economists watch such feedback indicators as Cost-of-Living Index, Gross National Product, rate of unemployment in the labor force, and similar economic information usually summarized in the Economic Report of the President to aid the President and Federal agencies in spending, interest-rate, and related economic decisions. The economic data feedback is thus used in modifying certain relationships among components of the American economic system so as to maintain a general state of economic equilibrium.

However, without an explicit "desired state" or goal to serve as its target, no political or other system can remain on course in the same sense that a guided missile does. Specificity of goal or target is a critical element in any dynamic or homeostatic system, including a political one. Some political goals may be quite specific; e.g., the maintenance of a three per cent rate of growth in Gross National Product or the maintenance of full employment to within three or four percentage points of the total labor force. Most political goals, however, are hardly that well qualified. "Equal opportunity" or "free speech" are not amenable to easy calibration.

Some political systems do nonetheless give the *impression* of being guided missiles locked in on vast political targets. Nazi Germany, in its declared thousand-year goal of world domination and its step-by-step progress in that direction, certainly had the appearance of a goal-oriented system that was very much "on target." On the other hand, less millenial political systems such as the United States seem at times to be without goals, literally unguided and constantly out of equilibrium.

Systems as Convertors

Another approach denies the importance of boundaries, equilibrium, etc. The conversion of inputs into outputs by the system is what merits attention, according to this school.

Usually an analogy is drawn to the black-box notion borrowed from the field of electrical engineering:

We imagine that the investigator has before him a black box that, for any reason, cannot be opened. It has various inputs-switches that he may move up or down, terminals to which he may apply potentials, photoelectric cells onto which he may shine lights, and so on. Also available are various outputs-terminals on which a potential may be measured, lights that may flash, pointers that may move over a graduated scale, and so on.[9]

The investigator is supposed to estimate what the outputs of the black box will be from his knowledge of how to manipulate the switches and levers controlling the inputs or the manner in which the black box will respond on the input side to various feedback information it receives. The process is illustrated in the following diagram:

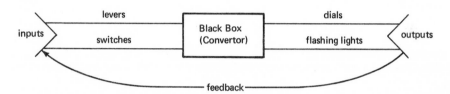

Input-output analysis, therefore, is an essential feature of this approach. A good example is the type of input-output analysis economists have applied to the exchange of goods and services in the American economic system. Because all transactions may be reduced conveniently to dollar units in economic analysis, the results are relatively clear. Below is an illustrative chart showing how a small part of such an input-output analysis of the American economic system might look, in billions of dollars.

On the basis of this input-output analysis, it can be seen, for example, that the agricultural and fisheries industry purchases over $25 billion of its own products, $360 million in rubber products, $180 million in machinery other than electrical machinery, $180 million in coal, gas, and electric power, and $990 million in railroad transportation services. Similar observations may be made about the relative inputs and outputs of all other sectors of the economy.

The full 500-item input-output table from which this illustration is drawn adds up to the total gross purchases and production of the

ILLUSTRATIVE (AND PARTIAL) INPUT-OUTPUT ANALYSIS
OF GOODS AND SERVICES EXCHANGED IN U.S. ECONOMIC SYSTEM
(IN BILLIONS OF DOLLARS)*

		Industry Purchases (Inputs)				
		Agriculture and Fisheries	Rubber Products	Machinery (exc. Electric)	Coal, Gas, Electric Power	Railroad Transportation
Industry Production (Outputs)	Agriculture and Fisheries	25.86	0.01	0.01	0.01	0.03
	Rubber Products	0.36	0.12	0.39	0.01	0.01
	Machinery (exc. Electric)	0.18	0.01	2.69	0.09	0.18
	Coal, Gas, Electric Power	0.18	0.12	0.30	3.71	0.99
	Railroad Transportation	0.99	0.12	0.48	0.43	1.02

* Table is based upon illustrative materials used by Wassily W. Leontief of Harvard, who is perhaps the principal contributor to the development of this analytical technique. The five-item table is only part of a matrix that had 50 or more items in horizontal rows and vertical columns. The 50-item matrix, in turn, was a summary of one that had over 500 sectors. See also, William H. Miernyk, *The Elements of Input-Output Analysis* (New York: Random House, 1965).

entire economic system. Each component of the system—consumer and producer—is seen in relation to all the others, and every number on the chart is dependent upon every other. When this type of input-output analysis is programmed to take into account changes over time, say, each month, quarter, or year, it is possible to see the impact of an input of a million dollars in one part of the economic system upon outputs in other parts. Thus, both governmental and private spending may, if decision makers so wish, be modified to reduce exaggerated consequences for some part of the economic system or to encourage development in others. As indicated earlier, the possibility of reducing all input and output values to dollar units makes it relatively easy to design such an analysis. The same ease, unless it be the input and output of voting behavior, has yet to be achieved in the study of political systems.

Nevertheless, Easton has defended the black box, input-output analytic approach as appropriate to the study of political systems. Easton's argument is as follows:

> The study of politics is concerned with understanding how author-
> itative decisions are made and executed for a society. We can try to
> understand political life by viewing each of its aspects piecemeal.

We can examine the operation of such institutions as political parties, interest groups, government, and voting; we can study the nature and consequences of such political practices as manipulation, propaganda, and violence; we can seek to reveal the structure within which these practices occur. By combining the results we can obtain a rough picture of what happens in any self-contained political unit.

In combining these results, however, there is already implicit the notion that each part of the larger political canvas does not stand alone but is related to each other part; or, to put it positively, that the operation of no one part can be fully understood without reference to the way in which the whole itself operates. I have suggested in my book, *The Political System*, that it is valuable to adopt this implicit assumption as an articulate premise for research and to view political life as a system of interrelated activities. These activities derive their relatedness or systemic ties from the fact that they all more or less influence the way in which authoritative decisions are formulated and executed for a society.[10]

A diagram representing Easton's model, admittedly a primitive one, would appear as follows:

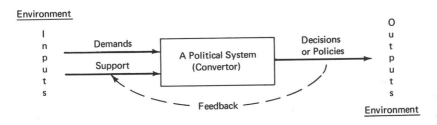

According to Easton, the units of the political system to be observed are *political actions*. The boundary of the political system is to be determined by all those actions more or less directly related to the making of binding decisions for a society. The inputs into the system, which may be conceived as a black box model, are of two kinds: *demands* and *support*. These inputs constitute the raw material or information that the system must process as well as the energy to keep it going. Thus, for example, a particular group in society articulates a demand, say, for a decrease in taxes, which provides the political system with input information. That group also

10 "An Approach to the Analysis of Political Systems," *World Politics*, 9 (1956–57): 383–400. Copyright © 1957 by Princeton University Press. Diagram used by permission of the publisher.

generates support for its demand from within itself and from among its allies in order to energize the system's conversion processes. From this, the system produces its outputs, that is, authoritative decisions or public policies which are binding upon society. These outputs of course have consequences both for the political system itself and for the environment in which the system exists; the Sixteenth Amendment giving Congress the power to lay and collect income taxes certainly produced permanent changes in both the political system's manner of providing fiscal support for itself as well as the American economic system's mode of earning and spending. A political system presumably reaches a state of equilibrium when all demands are satisfactorily met by the public policy outputs.

Another view is of the political system as a "decision machine." Spiro argues that "a political system can exist wherever people are concerned about common problems and are engaged in cooperation *and* conflict in their solution."[11] Spiro would establish the boundary of such a system by defining the extent of the population so engaged.

Once the common problems are recognized, the political conversion process begins. *An issue is formulated* on the basis of the problems perceived, and these problems usually relate to the alternative paths toward shared goals. There then is a *deliberation* of the issue, during which alternatives are contested and evaluated. The deliberative part of the process may lead to a *resolution* of the issue, that is, a choice of one or a combination of the alternatives available. The actions following the resolution may produce a *solution* to the problems originally perceived. If this solution occurs, presumably feedback through the system would indicate that an equilibrium state had been achieved. More usually, only partial solutions occur and feedback information suggests to the system population that new problems or modified old problems require reformulation of the issue.

> Human beings are aware of discrepancies between their present and some wished-for future condition. They try to work toward the future goals which they invent and set for themselves. On the road toward these goals, they encounter obstacles. In order to overcome these obstacles, to solve these problems, they engage themselves in politics, and they form and dismantle political systems. Sometimes they approach closer toward their goals, sometimes they move or

---

[11] Herbert Spiro, "An Evaluation of Systems Theory," *op. cit.*, p. 172. See also his excellent *Government by Constitution* (New York: Random House, 1959), pp. 17–42.

are moved farther away from them, sometimes they forget about them as a result of changes in the perspective of their consciousness, and sometimes they substitute new goals for old ones. Usually all of this is going on simultaneously, all over the earth. And as men are engaged in the political process—actually, in many simultaneous political processes—they change their consciousness of the possible. Often they expand their awareness of that which they recognize as possible. In recent centuries, since the time of Hobbes, they have increasingly recognized the converse, namely, that whatever may be possible can be achieved ultimately only through politics. I am tempted to paraphrase the motto of a large chemical corporation: "Better things for better living through politics!"[12]

Bertram M. Gross proposes that a social system should more deliberately identify the system-states it wishes to achieve in order that its political components may have explicit guidance in the processing and converting of issues into policies. Gross points to the great success of national economic accounting, particularly in the United States (e.g., the Economic Report of the President) and England.

National economic accounting uses models for structuring the complex information which summarizes states of the system, both past and present as well as desired and undesirable. Bertram Gross illustrates with three economic concepts: per capita Gross National Product, net investment in relation to GNP, and the balance of international payments on current (or commercial) account. Each concept has been carefully defined and well operationalized quantitatively. As a consequence, the economic system of a nation may be summarized and interrelated as shown in the following chart.

MULTIPLE USE OF SYSTEM STATE CONCEPTS*

System-State Concept	National Performance	National Goal	Criteria Critic A	Critic B
Annual increase in *per capita* GNP	2%	4%	5%	4%
Net investment in relation to GNP	12%	12%	10%	15%
Balance of payments, current account (Millions of $)	200	—250	0	—300

* Bertram M. Gross, *The State of the Nation: Social Systems Accounting* (London: Tavistock Publications, 1966), p. 11.

12 Spiro, "An Evaluation of Systems Theory," *op. cit.*, p. 174.

The "criteria" part of this chart makes explicit that different decision makers may wish to apply different achievement yardsticks to planning judgments. Critic A obviously wants a higher per capita *GNP* than Critic B does. On the other hand, Critic B would like to see a higher net investment performance. With these kinds of system data, it becomes feasible for them to argue their differences about goals and values.

A similar systems approach to the components and goals of American society, argues Gross, would require the development of well-defined and well-operationalized social indicators that could be incorporated annually into a "Social Report of the President." For example, the grand national goal of "abundance" would need to be translated into "intermediate abstractions" of relatively observable and quantifiable components such as: growth in national output, price stability, and output of specific services on goods.

It has already been established that such intermediate abstractions can be kept track of on a quantitative basis. On the other hand, many of the other "grand abstractions" with which we describe the goals of American society need substantial specification and refinement, not to mention better quantitative performance measures. For example, how shall the great goal of "equality" be translated into intermediate abstractions such as fair employment and equitable income distribution so as to be measurable from year to year? How can the grand goal of "order" be specified in terms of law enforcement, due process, and fair procedures? How can the goal of "a well-informed and rational people" be converted into operationally measurable units of formal education, scientific and technological productivity, or similar measures?[13]

The usefulness of transactional concepts in understanding political systems as convertors becomes apparent at this point.[14] If, for example, the inputs and outputs of the political system were classified as *political currencies*, it could be possible to observe and count system conversions in units such as *incumbencies, shares* and *commodities*. An input, for example, might be a demand for more shares in the prerogatives of the system, leading, perhaps, to new policies regarding shares allocations; extensions of the suffrage are of this type. Or the political system may decline to meet the demand for new shares and instead convert the demand into a commodities out-

13 *Ibid.*
14 See Chapter 4.

put; legislation providing for increases in welfare benefits or for a guaranteed annual income might be the "price" paid for denying some sought-after rearrangement of the suffrage laws. Transaction theory affords additional conceptual range for formulating units of interaction among the components within the political system as well as between the political system and its environment.[15]

Structures with Functions

Earlier we examined briefly the perspective of structure and process. We cited the distinct orientations of anatomy (structure) and physiology (process) in medicine. A structural analysis is an examination of the elements or components of some phenomenon at one point in time. A process analysis, on the other hand, examines the interaction of these components with the passage of time. If the purpose of studying a process is to discover consequences that follow from the interactions among the components of the structure or to specify functions served by the dynamics of the system, a systems analysis may become a *structural-functional analysis.* Functions are performed by structural components insofar as their interactions and activities satisfy demands upon the system under observation. An automobile, for example, is a *functional* transportation system only insofar as its fuel, motor, and wheel components interact in such a way as to satisfy the demands of a driver for transportation from one place to another.[16]

The structural-functional theoretical framework has been extensively developed by Talcott Parsons and Marion Levy. It has been most directly applied to American phenomena by William C. Mitchell. Gabriel A. Almond and James S. Coleman have attempted a comparative examination of state systems from the same perspective.[17]

15 For a statement of this perspective, Ralph M. Goldman, "The Political Context of Arms Control: A Systems Approach," *Journal of Conflict Resolution,* 7 (September 1963): 618–646; also, same author's "A Transactional Theory of Political Integration and Arms Control," *American Political Science Review,* 63 (September, 1969): 719–733.

16 A succinct survey of functional and structural-functional approaches may be found in William Flanigan and Edwin Fogelman, "Functional Analysis," in Charlesworth, *op. cit.,* Chap. 4. The logic and theoretical utility of functionalism have come under severe criticism in recent years; e.g., I. Horwitz, "Sociology and Politics: The Myth of Functionalism Revisited," *Journal of Politics,* 25 (May 1963), and Donald Martindale (ed.), "Functionalism in the Social Sciences," *The Annals* (February 1965).

17 Talcott Parsons, *The Social System* (New York: Free Press, 1951); Talcott Parsons and Edward Shils (eds.), *Toward a General Theory of Action* (Cambridge: Harvard University Press, 1951); Talcott Parsons, with Robert F. Bales and Edward

Some of the general features of structural-functional analysis which establish its connection to systems theory include the following. (1) The unit of analysis is the whole system. (2) Particular functions are postulated as necessary for the maintenance of the system, much the same as homeostatic equilibrium in systems theory. (3) Structural-functionalists are interested in the functional interdependence of the structural components within the whole system, which often leads them to study the relationships between subsystems and the whole system.

For Parsons, a *function* is whatever action contributes to the maintenance or development of a system. All action systems, he writes, have certain "functional imperatives" which he calls "pattern maintenance," "goal attainment," "adaptation," and "integration." If the structure of values endorsed by the actors of the system are maintained by its patterns of interaction, this meets a functional requirement of the system. The system should also make it possible for valued outcomes and rewards to be achieved by actors either as individuals or collectivities. The adaptation function refers to the system's capacity to adjust to the environment in which it operates, whereas the integrative function refers to the solidarity in relations among system components.

Since all human action is goal-oriented, according to Parsons, the question still unresolved is how to define a well-functioning system or a satisfactory system-state. Are all the actions presumed to be contributory to the *declared goals* of the actors "functional"? In order to be able to purchase food, housing, and other consumer goods in the modern economy, individual members or units of the economic system need to earn income. Farmers earn income by engaging in one set of system-supporting activities and thieves another; both share in the consumption goals of the system. Are the activities both "functional"? Are there *empirical behavioral consequences* apart from the *declared* goals of the actors that are relevant to system maintenance and development? Parsons does not resolve this analytical difficulty.

Levy, on the other hand, takes a less goal-oriented view of functions within a structure. In his approach, a *function* is a state of

Shils, *Working Papers in the Theory of Action* (New York: Free Press, 1953); Marion Levy, *The Structure of Society* (Princeton: Princeton University Press, 1951); William C. Mitchell, *The American Polity* (New York: Free Press, 1962); Gabriel A. Almond and James S. Coleman (eds.), *The Politics of the Developing Areas* (Princeton: Princeton University Press, 1960). The following discussion is based upon the Flanigan-Fogelman evaluation.

affairs or a condition which results from the operation of a structure through time. A *structure* is a pattern of action through which functions operate. This is an attempt to be empirical rather than teleological, emphasizing that functions are those activities that may be *observed* rather than those that are *evaluated* according to some yardstick of system outcomes.

The differences between Parsons and Levy once again underscore the analytical difficulties that confront a rational actor in a system on the one hand and a scientific observer of a system on the other. A declaration of goals for the system may be quite different from an anticipation or prediction of outcomes of system activity. If a Democratic poll-taker predicts a Republican victory on the basis of his survey data, he is no less a loyal Democrat; as a scientific observer of public opinion, he has no alternative but to predict the behavioral consequences of whatever relationships may be revealed in his investigation.[18]

Following Parsons, Mitchell suggests four essential functions performed by the political system, which in Aristotelian fashion he calls "the polity." These functions are: (1) the authoritative specification of system goals; (2) the authoritative mobilization of resources to implement these goals; (3) the integration of the political system as a whole; and (4) the allocation among components of the system of values and costs of system operations.

The comparative study of political systems is the object of theoretical work by Almond and Coleman, who view a political system as "that system of interactions to be found in all independent societies which performs the functions of integration and adaptation . . . by means of the employment, or the threat of employment, of more or less legitimate physical compulsion." In other words, "the

---

[18] *Declared goals*, as noted in Chapter 9, are relatively explicit and overt. They may be found by a straightforward content analysis of the linguistic statements of the actors. Systems analysis begins to run into difficulty when it looks for *undeclared goals* of the actors, that is, those objectives that are either secretly held by the actors or not even at a conscious level, as in the case of the Freudian "death wish" and similar wishes.

Analysis becomes even more difficult when an observer of the system (who may or may not be one of its actors) looks for the *empirical behavioral consequences* of system activity. Such an observer must necessarily have a theoretical perspective from which he examines system activity and evaluates the consequent events and behaviors as "functional" or not. Declaredly, for example, the automobile was invented to provide another form of human transportation. However, from a behavioral consequence point of view, an anthropologist might examine the functional relationship of the automobile to, say, courtship patterns in America, an economist might see it as a generator of widespread distribution of individual income, and a military analyst could be interested in the armament function that is always potential in the automotive industry. Each behavioral-consequence analyst would of course have his own aspect of the system in mind and his own criteria of functionality.

political system is the legitimate, order maintaining or transforming system in the society." The special properties of a political system include these: (1) enough comprehensiveness to include all the interactions which affect the use of or the threat of use of physical coercion; (2) interdependence of components, as revealed when a change occurs in one of the subtypes of interaction which is followed by changes in all the other sub-types; and (3) boundaries, so that it is evident where the political system begins and other systems end.[19]

When Almond and Coleman refer to political structure, they have in mind the patterns of human interaction by means of which order is maintained. These structures, when examined for their inputs and outputs, perform certain political functions. The functional inputs include political socialization, political recruitment, interest articulation, interest aggregation, and political communication. The functional outputs are the activities of rule making, rule application, and rule adjudication, which are akin to the legislative, executive, and judicial processes.

Systems theory generally and structural-functional approaches to systems particularly compel the student of politics to attend to some of the most comprehensive aspects of political life. If the collective goals of a society are "to form a more perfect union, establish justice, insure domestic tranquility, provide for the common defense, promote the general welfare, and secure the blessings of liberty to ourselves and our posterity," how indeed does the political system of that society operate over time to implement, modify, or change those goals? How are the many component parts of the political system to be structured so as to interact effectively to achieve these goals? How are the interactional processes to be labeled, observed, measured, and modified in order to be "functional"? Systems concepts bring into focus macrocosmic considerations. Such considerations may be matters of historical interest in older political systems; they tend to be of vital significance for newly emergent nations whose leaders and citizens aspire to master their own collective destinies.

DEVELOPMENT OF DYNAMIC POLITICAL SYSTEMS

In the generation following World War II, the number of sovereign nations in the world has almost trebled. The membership of the

[19] Almond and Coleman, *The Politics of the Developing Areas*, pp. 7, 11.

United Nations rose from the 46 signatories in 1945 to more than 120 today. Although new nation-states have been emerging ever since the Renaissance, the most recent developing nations have been a subject of consuming interest for political scientists during this post-World War II era. What experience of democratic or American systems can be useful for the management of these new systems? What do we know of these new systems that would better permit the older American system to accommodate to the changing world political environment? How can inputs from the American system, perhaps in the form of foreign aid of one sort or another, be directed to produce outputs amenable to preferred goal-states? How can the old and the new national systems, seen as subsystems, be managed to produce a well-integrated and peaceful world political system? These kinds of questions are perhaps akin to studying how an airplane flies at the same time one is piloting it; it is likely to produce an anxious pilot.

These questions, of interest to the field of comparative politics, are currently considered under the specialized rubric *political development*. However, according to Riggs,

> The established modes of analysis in comparative government tend to break down when confronted with the realities of non-Western politics. One apparent solution was simply to add a new noninstitutional category of "non-Western" system to the prevalent typologies. This could be done, however, only by admitting that formal structures were not definitive, and that governments were essentially reflections of an underlying dynamism or "political culture." An early protagonist of this view was Gabriel Almond, who suggested that all political systems might be classified under such sociological headings as Anglo-American, Continental European, totalitarian, and "pre-industrial."
>
> Almond himself soon moved beyond this position as the many variations among non-Western politics became evident. A broad spectrum was soon drawn between "traditional," "transitional," and "modern."[20]

In general, the students of political development have made brave attempts to tackle, both theoretically and empirically, the characteristics of political systems across the board—their common attributes,

[20] Fred W. Riggs, "The Theory of Political Development," in Charlesworth, *op cit.*, Chap. 16.

where they came from, how they came into being, what sustains them, and where they are going. Among the attempts were those of Deutsch and Cutright. Deutsch embarked upon a program of cross-national comparative studies for which he identified numerous quantitative indicators of "social mobilization." A similar quantitative approach is represented by Cutright's statistical index of levels of political development, measured in terms of parliamentary and elections records, degrees of political stability, and other quantitative criteria. Still another quantitative approach to the comparison of political systems is made by Banks and Textor.[21]

Broad theorization about "stages" and "types" of political development has been prolific; the following is a sampling of the analytical categories offered thus far. Organski suggests four stages of political development: political unification, involving effective political and administrative control over the system's population; industrialization, in which the accumulation of capital is made possible; national welfare, during which problems of distribution of power, goods, and services are paramount; and abundance, during which technological automation creates problems arising out of affluence. In his examination of transitional political systems, Shils suggests five categories: political democracy, tutelary democracy, modernizing oligarchy, totalitarian oligarchy, and traditional oligarchy. Kautsky also has five categories: traditional aristocratic authoritarianism, domination by nationalist intellectuals, totalitarianism of the aristocracy, totalitarianism of the intellectuals, and democracy. Apter employs a two-way classification in which there are three authority types (hierarchical, pyramidal, and segmental) and two value types (instrumental and consummatory). Huntington prefers to study political development as a matter of institutionalization, in which the attributes of adaptability, complexity, autonomy, and coherence serve as yardsticks of change. Pennock suggests that the study of political development include such phenomena as political culture, informal political institutions, governmental and constitutional arrangements, as well as "the operation of the whole." Riggs prefers to build upon the developmental tests formulated by the Committee on Comparative Poli-

---

[21] Bruce M. Russett, H. R. Alker, Jr., Karl W. Deutsch, and Harold D. Lasswell, *World Handbook of Political and Social Indicators* (New Haven, Yale University Press, 1964); Philips Cutright, "National Political Development; Measurement and Analysis," *American Sociological Review*, Vol. 28 (April 1963): 253–264; Arthur S. Banks and Robert D. Textor, *A Cross-Polity Survey* (Cambridge, Mass.: M.I.T. Press, 1963).

tics of the Social Science Research Council, namely, equality, capacity, and differentiation.[22]

Systems theorists and students of political development also give much attention to the matter of political subsystems. These, too, are variously identified. One approach, for example, starts from the premise that political systems continue to be the major organizing factor in modern civilization. As new collective purposes are discovered, defined, and commonly accepted, it is the political system and its various specialized subsystems that ultimately play the major role in the preservation of these collective purposes and their implementation. In the case of democratic societies, the personnel of the constitutional system have become sufficiently restrained, the centers of decision making in the community sufficiently dispersed, and the procedures for channeling social conflict so adequate for their containment that individuals and groups are assured a maximum measure of safe play in the conflict cycles occurring among themselves. As more and more aspects of relationships within the political system become matters of organized cooperation, the areas of political conflict become increasingly specialized and the avenues for their expression and resolution increasingly refined. In this developing way subconstitutional systems of cooperation and conflict emerge. In short, subsystems within the political system are, by and large, a consequence of series of transactions in political currencies leading to political specialization.[23]

Over all, the attempts to produce theories of political systems have been less than fruitful. What systems theorists have best accomplished is the directing of attention to the macrocosmic aspects of politics. The "big picture," whether national or international, is the focus of analytical attention for the systems theorists. A second contribution has been the revival of interest in the relationships between structure and function, between the static and the dynamic. The system must be examined as a living, moving, changing, growing entity. In an age whose political communities are clearly living,

[22] Based upon Riggs' survey, *op. cit.* The theoretical works cited by Riggs include: Kenneth Organski, *The Stages of Political Devolopment* (New York: Knopf, 1965); Edward Shils, *Political Development in the New States* (The Hague: Mouton, 1962); John H. Kautsky, *Political Change in Underdeveloped Countries: Nationalism and Communism* (New York: Wiley, 1962); David E. Apter, *The Politics of Modernization* (Chicago: University of Chicago Press, 1965); Samuel P. Huntington, "Political Development and Political Decay," *World Politics*, 17 (April 1965): 386–430; J. Roland Pennock, "Political Development, Political Systems, and Political Goods," *World Politics*, 18 (April 1966): 413–434.

[23] Goldman, "The Political Context of Arms Control," *op. cit.*

moving, changing and growing, the systems approach may yet demonstrate its utility for the architects of developing and future political systems.

SYSTEMS ARCHITECTURE IN AMERICA

Americans are among the world's most inveterate builders and rebuilders. This interest in the architectural problems of design and construction is relatively pervasive, ranging from the styling of automobile models to the reformation of political systems. By those who object, Americans are characterized as "tinkerers." By others who view this as a manifestation of adaptiveness, Americans are seen as "social engineers" whose inventiveness and pragmatism are vital resources for national survival and development.

Types of Architects

In the political field, these architectural concerns and efforts seem to be characteristic of several types of people working within the constitutional arrangements. Chief among these types: reformers, planners, policy scientists, futurists, and practical politicians. These individuals, in the language of systems theory, are most deliberately attentive to the specification of political and social goals for the system, system adaptiveness and maintenance, realignments, among system components, and similar system aspects of American politics.

Reformers

Few nations have been as accepting of reformism as the United States. Reformers generally support the goals of a society and the present overall political system. What distinguishes reformers is dissatisfaction with particular features of the structure or process within the system. Often the reformer is more interested than the ordinary citizen in achievement of the system's goals, and his dissatisfaction reflects his impatience or frustration with inept or inefficient machinery for accomplishing results. If political pathology seems to be the consequence of some existing arrangement, get a new arrangement! For example, when legislators seemed chronically corrupt in the late nineteenth and early twentieth century, reformers proposed removing the legislative function or critical aspects of it to the people-at-large through the initiative and referendum.

Reformism has been thoroughly reflected upon and reported in textbooks by political scientists. Hardly a textbook fails to include, at the end of each chapter or section, some review of current proposals for reforming the feature of the political system just described. For example, one famous text in American government includes the following suggestions for improving features of government:

State governments should strengthen themselves by "regenerating" their legislatures, toning up their civil services, improving their administrative methods, modernizing their county and other rural local governments, and utilizing the newer techniques of long-term planning.

To improve voter turnout at the polls, simplification of registration procedures, simpler ballots, less frequent elections, and clearer statements of the issues are needed.

The shortcomings of party organization and financing could be met by supporting these out of the public treasury, together with extention of the provision of the Corrupt Practices Act to cover primaries.

For improving relations between Congress and the President, a standard array of reformist proposals is offered, including adoption of a cabinet system of government, providing Congressional floor privileges for Cabinet members, and creation of a legislative-executive council.

This sampler of reform proposals is drawn from the chapters in a single text; the practice is typical. Rarely does a reformer offer the empirical grounds upon which others might base confidence that his proposals would work as desired or even that some of them have already worked elsewhere. Reformers often seem drawn to panaceas or to the appearances of "greener grass" in someone else's backyard.[24]

Charles Hyneman, in several pages, enumerates examples of the reformist inclinations of political scientists. These are, he notes, but

---

[24] From Frederic A. Ogg and P. Orman Ray, *Introduction to American Government* (10th ed.; New York: Appleton-Century-Crofts, 1951), passim.

a "few items selected either because of the high prestige they have enjoyed" or because of the "boldness with which social action of highest significance is urged." Such preoccupation with social engineering, he says, "pervades our literature."

The entire system of American government, for example, is appraised, with proposals for reform, in such books as: William Y. Elliot, *The Need for Constitutional Reform* (1935), Arthur C. Millspaugh, *Democracy, Efficiency, Stability* (1942), and Arthur N. Holcombe, *Our More Perfect Union* (1950). The American Political Science Association has sponsored several special committees to review and evaluate proposals for change: Committee on Congress, *The Reorganization of Congress* (1945); Committee on Political Parties, *Toward a More Responsible Two-Party System* (1950); and Committee on American Legislatures, *American State Legislatures* (1954). Other reform oriented works include: Leonard D. White, *The City Manager* (1927), Pendleton Herring, *Presidential Leadership* (1940), James M. Burns, *Congress on Trial* (1949), and Paul T. David, Malcolm Moos, and Ralph M. Goldman, *Presidential Nominating Politics in 1952* (1954).

Reviewing the consequences of this political science interest in social engineering, Leonard D. White has observed:

> Political scientists took a major responsibility for the reconstruction of municipal government, the hottest of our governmental problems in the first decade of the century. They led the way in the reorganization of state governments in the second and third decades. They were influential in the drive for a short ballot and better election procedures. They were chiefly responsible for educating the American public to the necessity of a budget system. They began the long process of discussion that finally, with the powerful help of circumstances, reversed the historical direction of American foreign policy.[25]

Planners

The *scientific management* movement began early in this century with the writings of Frederick W. Taylor on the application of the methods and spirit of science to the deliberate control of man's economic and organizational life, particularly its production as-

---

[25] Quoted by Charles S. Hyneman, *The Study of Politics* (Urbana: University of Illinois Press, 1959), p. 121.

pects.[26] Between World Wars, "Taylorism" developed into a world-wide movement devoted to the efficient and effective implementation of man's goals by highly trained managers following scientific principles of analysis and organization. This meant seeking "facts" through "research" and "measurement." Corporate and governmental managers were presumed to be amenable to the approaches of scientific management.

The organizational and managerial emphasis of scientific management gave a special direction to the planning movement that arose from the tribulations of the Great Depression of the 1930s. While the characteristic activities of planning are undoubtedly as old as government itself, the post-Depression planning movement, particularly in the United States, had an explicit public administrative mold to it. *Planning* came to mean the pursuit of *publicly articulated objectives* through *public agencies*, both presumably created and supported by legislatures and other representative institutions. The spirit of the administrative planner is succinctly summarized by Dwight Waldo:

> Planning is the means by which the discipline of Science applied to human affairs will enable man to incarnate his purposes. It is the inevitable link between means and ends. Moreover, it is in itself an inspiring ideal. For once it is realized that there is no natural harmony of nature, no Divine or other purpose hidden beneath the flux and chaos of present planlessness, it becomes immoral to let poverty, ignorance, pestilence, and war continue if they can be obliterated by a plan. Although there is some disagreement as to the nature and desirable limits of planning, students of administration are all "planners."[27]

The dramatic growth of governmental organization under the New Deal, with its accompanying mobilization of economic and political resources to overcome the disruption of the Depression, gave proponents of planning a new status in public affairs. Thus, the periodical *Plan Age* began publication in 1934. In the December, 1936, issue of this journal, George B. Galloway reviewed "American Proposals for Central Planning" that had been publicly offered or implemented during the preceding four or five years. These coincidentally included proposals by such ideological opposites as Senator LaFollette and the

---

[26] For historical background, Leland H. Jenks, "Early Phases of the Management Movement," *Administrative Science Quarterly*, 5 (December 1960): 421–447.

[27] Dwight Waldo, *The Administrative State* (New York: Ronald Press, 1948), p. 67.

United States Chamber of Commerce, each favoring creation of a national economic council. Galloway noted the New Deal's unprecedented array of planning agencies, including the National Emergency Council, the National Planning Board, the Science Advisory Board, and the Central Statistical Board.

The professional literature on planning was particularly prolific in the decade between 1935 and 1945, and included such volumes as: George Soule, *A Planned Society* (1932); Arthur N. Holcombe, *Government in a Planned Democracy* (1935); Barbara Wooton, *Plan or No Plan* (1935); Lewis L. Lorwin, *Time for Planning* (1935); Findlay MacKenzie (ed.), *Planned Society; Yesterday, Today, and Tomorrow* (1937); Leonard Doob, *The Plans of Men* (1940); George B. Galloway, *Planning for America* (1941); Sir William H. Beveridge, *Full Employment in a Free Society* (1945); Barbara Wooton, *Freedom Under Planning* (1945); Friederich A. von Hayek, *The Road to Serfdom* (1944); and Herman Finer, *The Road to Reaction* (1945).

The Hayek and Finer books climaxed the decade's writing with a "great debate." Hayek condemned the contemporary trends toward planning as a socialist threat to individual liberty, very much on the order of Nazi Germany. He vigorously opposed the centralism of the collectivists; he argued, however, that a system of social service could be compatible with free enterprise. Because public planning raises the question "planning by whom for whom?" the consequence, he declared, means enforced inequalities by some groups over others. Hayek called scholars and intellectuals who support the scientific attitude "totalitarians in our midst." In a final global warning, Hayek stated that national planning cannot be accomplished without international repercussions, while planning on an international scale requires naked force.

Finer's response is equally vigorous. Finer denied that the alternatives are as extreme as either total freedom of competition or total collectivist regimentation as Hayek anticipated. Rather, economic planning and responsible government, Finer claimed, are perfectly compatible. Finer described a plan as "a series of well-concerted laws, separate as to substance but integrated and then carried into further detail by a series of rules and orders, made by officials deputed thereto, and controlled by the standards enacted in the statutes and subject to parliamentary or judicial revision or both." In this way, "the legislature is the heart of the planning process for it is here that the less authoritative and less definite programs of the parties enter for definition and authorization."[28] For Finer the big issues of planning are the provision of an economic service which hitherto thas been subject to the rule of prices and the market and creation of a nonarbitrary way of balancing services and liberty.

Through the 1940s and 1950s, the planning function was increasingly accepted as a differentiated component of governmental organization at all levels. Professional planners found themselves on the staff rather than the line side of such organizations. Private citizens also participated in public planning as members of advisory groups and planning councils. Planning commissions were a popular committee-type arrangement for cutting across established governmental departments in order to obtain a comprehensive planning viewpoint. City and regional—usually multicity—planning agencies were also growing in number and professional quality. By the 1960s planning had become a special field of public administration concerned with projecting ongoing trends into the future, establishing priorities among parts of that future, and then building economic, social, and physical environmental factors into the blueprint. Around the world, national economic planning agencies became impressively popular.

The planning movement is more a profession than a movement today. The planning approach is a well-established responsibility of major public agencies. For example, Federal departments concerned with the domestic economy, such as Labor, Commerce, Agriculture, and interior, are constantly peering into the future by extrapolating current trends of all types, planning that future accordingly. Department of Defense planners ponder such matters as the future economic consequences of peace and disarmament. Other agency planners respond to problems of the physical environment, that is, air and water pollution, destruction of recreational and natural resources, and health risks in food, drug, and other consumer products.

What frustrates planners most, of course, is their inescapable inability to keep up with the geometric growth of technological change.

Policy Scientists

In an attempt to establish an intellectual relationship between empirical scientists and public policy-makers, Harold D. Lasswell and

[28] Finer *Road to Reaction*, pp. 26, 213.

others have promoted the notion of a *policy science*. In his presidential address to the American Political Science Association, Lasswell argued that "within a rich intellectual tradition [such as that of political science] the most significant task is to construct a continuing institutional activity by which central political [theory] is related continuously to [contemporary] events as they unfold."

> It is abundantly clear that the impact of science and technology does not occur in a social vacuum, but in a context of human identifications, demands and expectations. I make the modest proposal that it is appropriate for political scientists, in company with other scientists and scholars dealing with human affairs, to improve our procedures of continuous deliberation upon the potential impacts of science and technology upon human affairs.[29]

In earlier statements Lasswell made a number of suggestions regarding useful conceptual tools that might help in developing what he came to call "a policy science." An observer, no matter how scientific in the procedures and empirical tests of his investigations, is nonetheless a citizen of his political community and a creature of his society. He usually shares its values and remains committed to many if not all of its goals. Lasswell tried to make clear that the two interests are *not* incompatible. Hyneman, for example, pointed out how much admiration was expressed for Harold Gosnell's *Getting Out the Vote*, a volume which produced significant new scientific knowledge about the correlates and conditions of nonvoting, but which also contained Gosnell's personal judgments and advice about ways in which a society as devoted to participation as the American can go about promoting greater turnout at the polls. In Lasswell's view an observer such as Gosnell should indeed produce scientific generalizations about the state of affairs in the past, then add his own guesses, based upon the data, regarding the alternate possible courses these trends are likely to take into the future. The observer should then evaluate these expectations according to existing social and political preferences.[30]

More specifically, Lasswell suggested that leaders and citizens of

[29] Harold D. Lasswell, "The Political Science of Science," *American Political Science Review*, 50 (December 1956): 961–979. The following quoted paragraph is from the same source.

[30] The concept of policy sciences was introduced in the volume by Daniel Lerner and Harold D. Lasswell, *The Policy Sciences* (Stanford: Stanford University Press, 1951). The reference to Gosnell's work (Chicago: University of Chicago Press, 1927) is in Hyneman, *op. cit.*, p. 108. Lasswell's early statements about the observational model indicated may be found in his *World Politics and Personal Insecurity* (New York: Free Press, 1965) and *The World Revolution of our Time* (Stanford: Stanford University Press, 1951).

a democratic society need to be skilled in three different types of intellectual activity if they are to make rational public policy decisions. He labeled these types "goal-thinking," "scientific-thinking," and "trend-thinking."

Goal-thinking is the process of analyzing and selecting the ends toward which decisions are presumably directed. *Scientific-thinking* requires the formulation of generalizations that are confirmable by observation and which identify the determinative relationships among variables involved in behavior and situations. *Trend-thinking* is a way of "sketching the plains, plateaus, and mountain chains of the continent of events comprising past, present, and future." Heinz Eulau refers to these types of thinking as a methodological problem involving nothing less than finding ways "to connect statements of value or preferences, statements of fact and statements of expectation." From this point of view, three kinds of data are needed for policy decisions. Goal-thinking is essentially the analysis and selection of those objectives or future states of affairs toward which the decisions are to be directed; scientific-thinking is the analysis of the limiting empirical conditions within which decisions and actions must be taken; and trend-thinking is the analysis of past tendencies as they provide a basis for estimating future probabilities.[31]

One specific analytical device suggested by Lasswell for helping relate the three types of thinking is the *developmental construct*. Briefly, this is a statement of expectations concerning the future, usually expressed in certain core concepts. An example is Lasswell's own notion of "garrison state," a phrase which summarizes his own expectation, based upon trend analyses, that modern nation-states are likely to become increasingly committed to military activity and the production of military goods. In his discussion of the garrison state, Lasswell proceeds to identify the "good" and "bad" of such prospects, offering advice about what might be done to avoid the "bad." A developmental construct, then, is supposed to be descriptive of the emerging future; it "throws the time axis—the 'from what toward what'—into relief." In other words, "a developmental construct characterizes a possible sequence of events running from a select cross-section of the past to a cross-section of the future."[32]

31 Lasswell, *World Revolution of Our Time*, p. 5. Heinz Eulau, "H. D. Lasswell's Developmental Analysis," *Western Political Quarterly*, 11 (June 1950): 229–242. Eulau provides a thorough critique of Lasswell's "developmental construct" concept.

32 Lasswell, *World Revolution of Our Time*, pp. 4–5. See also, "The Garrison State and Specialists in Violence," *The Analysis of Political Behavior* (New York: Oxford University Press, 1948), Part II.

Eulau criticizes the developmental construct notion as "an ideal-type exaggeration of the relationships between empirical and hypo-thetical (or past and future) situations." Rather than serving as a prediction, a developmental construct is more of a speculative model which, of course, may be useful in suggesting significant hypotheses to be tested. If trends are themselves the finding of tested hypo-theses, they may presumably acquire additional significance for policy purposes if embedded in developmental constructions.

Since it is the special function of policy to achieve valued goals, a first step in the creation of relevant developmental constructs is the clarification of the political goals to be realized by decision making. A trend may be explainable by a general law or hypothesis, and it may predict a future event to the extent that the general law is valid. A developmental construct is, on the other hand, an interpretation of trend data by the policy maker concerned with a goal. The be-havioral scientist can serve the policy maker by conceptualizing and producing knowledge about the empirical environment of the latter's decisions. When he himself produces developmental constructs or converts scientific terms into such constructs, the behavioral scien-tist himself takes on the role of policy maker. This is a shift in roles that is perfectly legitimate, according to Lasswell. However, it must be done explicitly, with its intellectual implications clearly recog-nized.

The policy science approach has not developed into an intellectual movement. However, it has been accompanied by a significant shift in relationships between academic scientists and public policy makers that has been going on over the past generation. This shift was succinctly described by Donald Hornig, Special Assistant to the President of the United States for Science and Technology, in an address to The Academy of Political Science in 1966.

> At a much earlier time Jefferson and Franklin, both of whom were scientists, did consider science important in the affairs of the fledging republic, but not through public involvement. As you know, Franklin founded the American Philosophical Society, and he and Jefferson alternately were presidents of the Philosophical Society. But neither of them saw a place for science in government or gov-ernment in science. And for more than a century therefore, science was remote from the thoughts of the nation. The nineteenth century was the century of the practical man, of Yankee ingenuity, of the inventors like Thomas Edison. . . . The theoretical man was gen-erally held in low repute, at least outside the universities.

The situation is entirely different now. Not only does the President have a science advisor, but so do the Secretaries of State, Agriculture, and Interior. . . . And all three military services have Assistant Secretaries for Research and Development. . . . Forty percent of the top four grades of the civil service are occupied by scientists and engineers, and fifteen percent of the federal budget, fifteen billion dollars, is spent on research and development.

Substantially all this evolutionary change has occurred in the last twenty-five years, and most of it in the last ten years. Scientists entered the high councils of the military service during the last war. They joined the political fray afterward, in the debates over the international control of atomic weapons and the question of whether atomic energy should be under civilian or military control domestically. They have never left the arena since.[33]

According to a recent report of the National Science Foundation, scientists and engineers, broadly defined, account for well over 125,-000 of the Federal government's white-collar workers. A very small number of these, however, can be considered consistently influential in Washington decisions on scientific matters—only about 900 in one estimate, 400 in another, and 200 in still another. Government science advising during the mid-1960s has been characterized as "a sort of Harvard-MIT-Bell Telephone-Cal Tech situation, with lines out to a few Eastern universities and to Palo Alto, Berkeley, and the RAND Corporation." One reporter notes that "far more troublesome to those who receive advice from Washington's new class of scientific watch-dogs, consultants, and policy makers has been the seemingly simple matter of figuring out what is a scientific question in the first place, and what is a scientific answer." For example:

The following statement was made [in 1962] before the Joint Committee on Atomic Energy by Air Force seismologist Carl F. Romney: "Based on all the information now available, we can conclude that it is feasible to design a detection system, based entirely outside the Soviet Union, which is capable of detecting explosions of about 1 kiloton in granite, 2–6 kilotons in tuff, and 10–20 kilotons in alluvium." As a statement of fact, it was agreed to by government scientists. Yet the old quarrel over our detection capabilities immediately broke out anew among them. Why? They were arguing about many things—whether the Soviet Union would go to the expense of developing weapons below that threshold of detection, whether such

[33] "Science and Government," in Sigmund Diamond (ed.), *Proceedings of the Academy of Political Science,* 28 (April 1966).

weapons would be worth not only the cost of them but the oppro-
brium of getting caught—whether, in fact, such weapons would have
any decisive military value at all. In other words, they were arguing
about Soviet intentions and Soviet strategy, not about science. Failing to appreciate the distinction, many people continue to invoke
the scientist of their choice in support of their own test-ban and
disarmament positions in the happy belief that they are citing un-
challengeable scientific authority.[34]

The distinction between scientists-in-policy-making and policy
scientists is likely to be a difficult one to draw for some time to
come. Inescapably the relationship between science and policy making is likely to have substantial consequence for the future architecture of the American political system.

Futurists

The forecasting of possible future states of civilization and the assessment of their respective relative probabilities has not only been
of interest to reformers, planners, and policy scientists, but also to
a new "breed" known as *futurists*.[35] This approach is new in at least
two respects. First, futurists have given a primary role to technology
and technological innovation as the headwaters from which flow
future developments in all fields of human affairs. Secondly, this
approach accepts forecasting as an essential element in human survival, taking the view that forecasting the future can become a rigorous intellectual discipline in its own right.

In 1965, Daniel Bell endeavored to explain the new interest in
futures studies. In his view the imminence of space travel constituted a compelling reminder that the future is also imminent. Contemporary transportation and communication are creating an increasingly interdependent national and international society. As a
consequence, business firms are increasingly devoting attention to
the preparation of projections into the future. Further, the heightened prestige of science and planning has also tended to focus
attention on the necessity for clarifying goals and evaluating trends.[36]

Thus, in Paris, the headquarters for the Council for the Future is
directed by political philosopher Bertrand de Jouvenel under the

[34] Meg Greenfield, "Science Goes to Washington," *The Reporter*, September 26,
1963, p. 24.
[35] For a thorough review of the movement, Henry Winthrop, "The Sociologist and
the Study of the Future," *The American Sociologist*, 3 (May 1968): 136–145.
[36] Daniel Bell, "The Study of the Future," *The Public Interest*, Fall, 1965.

sponsorship of the Ford Foundation. Its scores of reports are published in a series, *Futuribles*. In Holland, an international committee called "Mankind 2,000" develops mobile exhibits, films, and other materials indicating possible futures and stressing the importance of individual decisions in determining what the actual future will be. In Washington, D.C., there is a new organization called the World Future Society, under the leadership of Edward S. Cornish. At the RAND Corporation, the "Delphi Technique" of future forecasting has been developed. In essence, it involves the gathering of a consensus among groups of experts as to the nature and possible timetable for future developments in their respective fields. Another Ford Foundation-sponsored group is the Institute for the Future, with headquarters in Middletown, Connecticut. This group endeavors to work out computer methods for predicting the long-range social consequences of technological and economic change.

While science fiction writers enjoy free rein in the use of their imaginations about the future, others have undertaken somewhat more realistic projections. Some of the academic fields and book titles represented include: *L'Art de la Conjecture* by de Jouvenel; *The Future as History* by economist Robert Heilbroner; *The Future of Mankind* by German psychiatrist-philosopher Karl Jaspers; *Past and Future* by historian William H. McNeill; *The Next Million Years* by nuclear physicist Sir Charles Darwin; *The Year 2,000* by political analysts Herman Kahn and Anthony J. Wiener.

One of the most ambitious and provocative efforts along these lines has been a conference series sponsored by the California Institute of Technology, under the leadership of a geochemist (Harrison Brown), a biochemist (James Bonner), and a psychologist (John Weir). The 1957 conference produced a volume entitled *The Next Hundred Years;* a second in 1967 resulted in a set of proceedings entitled *The Next Ninety Years.* The Cal Tech group, for example, projected current world and national population trends to the year 2,057 and found that the present world population of over 3.3 billions is likely to approach 25 billions by the latter year. The 200 million Americans today are likely to be between 600 and 700 millions. What such population trends are likely to do to the earth's and the nation's natural and manufactured resources, including their psychological and cultural capacities, is vividly spelled out. Human technology and population growth promise to produce enough changes to assure the growth of the Futurist movement!

Practical Politicians

The much-maligned and much-neglected "Now Generation" of American politics is the practicing politician. Like practicing professionals in medicine, law, and the performing arts, the practicing politician is the human being whose *present* decisions necessarily tie the *future* to the *past*. His judgments are a blend of the artistry of politics and the science of politics. He is always where the action is. He is at once the architect and cement mixer of the political system.

A less flattering view of the practicing politician was taken by Moisei Ostrogorski, the Russian political analyst whose two-volume comparative study of British and American political parties, published in 1902, subsequently became a landmark in the political literature of both countries. Ostrogorski came to the American part of his studies during the 1880s and 1890s, a time of rampant corruption among political bosses and machines. Nevertheless, his data remains sound and his analyses perceptive by modern empirical standards, despite his exasperation with the failings of party politicians. In the manner of later structural-functionalists, Ostrogorski acknowledged that political machines exist because they meet the needs of society, even though parties are not a formal part of the political structure.[37]

Of the practicing politician, Ostrogorski wrote:

> The American politician, while constituting a separate class in American society, has not a distinct origin. He is recruited from all ranks of the community, as circumstances and personal taste happen to dictate, by a process of *natural selection*. The germ which produces the politician is the desire to obtain some public office or other . . . . To realize his ambition he begins to "study politics." It is not the "politics" of Aristotle, not even that of Columbia College, but it is none the less a science which demands great application and certain natural aptitudes. It consists of a technical part, which includes a knowledge of the machinery of the party organization, with all its wheels within wheels—the primaries, the committees, the various sets of conventions—and of the legal procedures in force for making the register and taking the vote. . . . The principal subject-matter of his "studies" is a sort of empirical psychology. He

---

[37] See the introduction by Seymour Martin Lipset, in his recent abridgment of M. Ostrogorski, *Democracy and the Organization of Political Parties* (Garden City, N.Y.: Doubleday Anchor Books, 1964), Vol. II on "The United States." The cited paragraph is from Chapter Six, Part Five, on "The Politicians and the Machine."

studies the men about him and their weak points, and by trading on the latter he tries to get as large a following as possible. He begins with his immediate neighbors. . . .

There is no sphere of public, political and economic activity into which the Machine does not penetrate, in which it does not wield an influence used solely for its own interests. A detailed analysis of the resources supplied by each of these spheres to the operations and the schemes of a Machine, in a large city or in a State, would present a really formidable whole, transcending in importance all that a legitimate government, however vast its powers, can aspire to. . . .

The imperturbable optimism, which is one of the essential traits of the American character, when confronted with the disorders caused by the Machine in political life, simply says, "It will right itself." It is not even shaken by the spectacle of the material ravages inflicted by the plundering politicians, but replies, "We can stand it; you cannot ruin *this* country. . . ." They declare that bossism is the inevitable outcome of all government, that without the boss there would be chaos. . . .

An earlier student of American politics took a more optimistic view. On the occasion of the adoption of the Constitution, Thomas Jefferson wrote his friend Hartley in 1787: "I have no fear, but that the result of our experiment will be, that men may be trusted to govern themselves without a master." In a very direct sense, Jefferson viewed self-government as requiring every man to be a "practicing politician." In 1790 he reiterated his belief:

Every man, and every body of men on earth, possess the right of self-government. They receive it with their being from the hand of nature. Individuals exercise it by their single will; collections of men by that of their majority; for the law of the *majority* is the natural law of every society of men.[38]

Thus, the concept of self-government makes every man a practitioner and an architect in political affairs. While some may spend only an occasional few moments in the voting booth, however, others devote a life-time of waking hours to "the practice." The quality of the practicing politician is nowhere better described than in a lecture on "Politics as a Vocation" delivered at Munich University in 1918 by the German sociologist Max Weber.

[38] Saul K. Padover, *Thomas Jefferson on Democracy* (New York: Penguin Books, 1946), pp. 15, 19.

Politics is a strong and slow boring of hard boards. It takes both passion and perspective. Certainly all historical experience confirms the truth—that man would not have attained the possible unless time and again he had reached out for the impossible. But, to do that a man must be a leader, and not only a leader but a hero as well, in a very sober sense of the word. And even those who are neither leaders nor heroes must arm themselves with that steadfastness of heart which can brave even the crumbling of all hopes. This is necessary right now, or else men will not be able to attain even that which is possible today. Only he has the calling for politics who is sure that he shall not crumble when the world, from his point of view, is too stupid or too base for what he wants to offer. Only he who in the face of all this can say "In spite of all!" has the calling for politics.[39]

A BEHAVIORAL APPROACH TO ARCHITECTURAL PROBLEMS?

There is a characteristic way in which a traditional student of politics would probably state the architectural needs of the American political system. With respect to the Presidency, for example, he might point to the need for strengthening the President's capacity to act responsibly in world affairs, coordinating his branch of the government or facilitating his relations with Congress. The traditionalist might view the legislative process as being in need of closer ties with the nation at-large and less with powerful organized interests. The future of the judiciary might be, in his view, primarily a problem of training and recruiting competent public-minded judges. The party system's greatest needs, he might suggest, are campaign finances and greater "responsibility." Pressure groups and lobbies need to be exposed to the public limelight in order to constrain their self-interested maneuvers. The electorate needs to be brought to the polls, he might say, in ever larger numbers. The mass media need to engage in more instructing and less inciting. In short, this approach to problems of American system architecture is ordinarily goal-oriented and institutional, usually dealing with executive, legislative, judicial, partisan, organized interest, electorate, and mass media as institutions.

While there is strictly no behavioral approach to system maintenance and architectural change, a behaviorist is likely to raise other

[39] Reprinted in Paul Tillett (ed.), *The Political Vocation* (New York: Basic Books, 1965), p. 61.

than institutional questions and problems. The difference has been illustrated in Bernard Berelson's discussion of the need to reexamine normative political theories about electoral behavior in the light of the findings of recent empirical studies of voters. According to Berelson,

> The normative theory of political democracy makes certain require-
> ments of the citizen and certain assumptions about his capacity to
> meet them. The tools of social research have made it possible for
> the first time, to determine with reasonable precision and objec-
> tivity the extent to which the practice of politics by the citizens of
> a democratic state conforms to the requirements and the assump-
> tions of the theory of democratic politics (in so far as it refers to
> decisions by the electorate).[40]

According to democratic philosophers, Berelson wrote, there are two behavioral preconditions for popular decision making. The first assumes that the average voter possesses a suitable *personality structure*. This personality, typically, can operate effectively, if not efficiently, in a free society. It has a capacity for involvement in situations remote from face-to-face experience, a capacity to accept moral responsibility for choices, a capacity to accept frustration in political affairs with equanimity, self-control and self-restraint as reins upon the gross operation of self-interest, a nice balance between submissiveness and assertiveness, a reasonable amount of freedom from anxiety so that political affairs can be attended to, a healthy and critical attitude toward authority, a capacity for fairly broad and comprehensive identifications, a fairly good measure of self esteem, and a sense of potency.

However, a great deal of recently produced behavioral knowledge challenges the validity of these assumptions. It has been found, for example, that social prejudice and restrictive political attitudes are associated with the authoritarian personality, which tends to be more evident among "the people" than among "the elite." Voters tend to have difficulty handling frustration, and a wide discrepancy between aspiration and political achievement leads some persons to overaggressive acts against the political environment and reduces their regard for political leaders. Comprehensiveness of group identification declines rapidly the lower one is on the socioeconomic

---

[40] "Democratic Theory and Public Opinion," *Public Opinion Quarterly*, 16 (Fall 1952): 313–314.

scale within the electorate. In a word, most American voters fall short of the "suitable" personality structure assumed for them in democratic political theories.

A second behavioral precondition assumed by democratic philosophers is a high degre of *interest and participation* on the part of the electorate. Political democracy requires a fairly strong and a fairly continuous level of interest from a minority, but also from the larger body of citizens, at least a moderate-to-mild interest, along with a readiness to respond in critical situations. Yet, empirical investigations reveal that less than one-third of the electorate is "really interested" in politics, and this portion is not evenly distributed among all parts of the electorate. The more interested people are more likely to affect others and thereby exercise a greater influence on the outcome of elections. Further, there has been a substantial decline in participation over the past half century; and, even where there is participation, it is more likely to be very poorly informed, contrary to the rationalist view of the voting decision.[41]

The variance between democratic fact and democratic ideal need hardly become the reason for discarding the democratic ideals. The normative preferences, which are noted in Chapter 11 as "Behavioral Patterns That Americans Prefer," remain precisely what they are— valued goals and ways of behaving. Among other things, scientific investigation provides a check against unrealistic assumptions that goals, that is, *future* states of affairs, *already exist*. Scientific investigation may help measure the temporal and organizational "distance" between present and preferred conditions. If investigations reveal that the American voter tends to be authoritarian, readily frustrated, poorly informed, and disinterested, it becomes clearer how much ground has to be covered before the democratic ideal is achieved.

Given such behavioral findings about this one subject of voting behavior, architectural questions may now be put more practically: What factors produce authoritarian tendencies, and how may they be minimized in the average voter personality? If it is not possible to remove voter frustration, how may it best be channeled as a creative force in American politics? If the voter is poorly informed, how may he be better educated and better informed? If he is disinterested, how may this alienation be minimized in the general interest?

[41] Berelson, *op. cit.*, passim.

These are obviously somewhat different questions from those put by traditionalists, although they deal with the same referents in the American political system and, almost invariably, they reflect the same value preferences. The American political system is inevitably the beneficiary of the two approaches, and would probably be advantaged by having still other approaches. The more a student knows about *both* traditional political theory and behavioral political theory, the more clearly he sees their complementary contributions to the problems of political systems architecture.[42]

---

[42] An impressive and authoritative set of examples may be found in the papers in Ithiel de Sola Pool (ed.), *Contemporary Political Science* (New York: McGraw-Hill, 1967) by Gabriel Almond, Robert Dahl, Karl Deutsch, Harry Eckstein, Heinz Eulau, Ithiel Pool, Lucius Pye, Edward Shils, and Herbert Simon.

Behavioral Interpretations of American Political Norms

Ideological and philosophical propositions about political life are usually stated as valuational *should's* or *ought's*, that is, as preferred ways of behaving. Many of these behavioral preferences have been articulated by particular philosophers who report their observations and evaluations of human experience, and then recommend what they conclude to be the best means to achieve what they consider to be the best ends. Such philosophers do not undertake to test their conclusions scientifically; however, this lack does not make the writings of such men as Locke, Bentham, or Jefferson less valuable or less influential. In fact, their views have become an integral part of the political value structure of a people; more political philosophy underlies American behavioral preferences than is ordinarily noticed. Contemporary behavioral science, utilizing its many concepts and theories, offers new ways of describing and analyzing many philosophical propositions and preferences found in American political philosophy. Some of these propositions are noted and restated in the following chapter. What kinds of political organizational behavior do Americans seem to prefer? What are their preferences in the area of communicative behavior? How may linguistic, transactional, decision, leadership, socialization, and conflict theories provide us with new views of American preferences in these aspects of political behavior? By attempting to translate the language of normative theory into some of the language of empirical behavior theory it may become possible to test scientifically the behavioral assumptions and recommendations of the philosophers.

11

Behavioral Patterns That Americans Prefer

The political culture of a people consists of customary ways of behaving and widely held attitudes on political subjects. When these are set down in philosophical tracts or repeated in political propaganda, such customs and attitudes are said to be that people's ideology (even though the average citizen might behave in contrary fashion or hold other attitudes). In other words, the community's ideology as articulated by its more educated members or its political leaders may be different from the empirically observed views of most of the people.

For example, one study, carried out in 1957–1958, asked questions of more than 3,000 political leaders drawn from among the delegates and alternates attending the national presidential nominating conventions of 1956. The same questions were put to a national sample of approximately 1,500 adults representative of the general population of the United States. Leaders (the convention delegates) and average Americans (the national opinion sample) were asked to agree or disagree with single sentence political statements, of which the following are examples:

The majority has the right to abolish minorities if it wants to.

Almost any unfairness or brutality may have to be justified when some great purpose is being carried out.

It is all right to get around the law if you don't actually break it.

People who hate our way of life should still have a chance to talk and be heard.

A man oughtn't be allowed to speak if he doesn't know what he's talking about.

A book that contains wrong political views cannot be a good book and does not deserve to be published.

Any person who hides behind the laws when he is questioned about his activities doesn't deserve much consideration.

Regardless of what some people say, there are certain races in the world that just won't mix with Americans.

The government ought to make sure that everyone has a good standard of living.

Both major parties in this country are controlled by the wealthy and are run for their benefit.

I feel that my political leaders hardly care what people like myself think or want.

The average Americans agreed with these particular statements to a significantly greater degree than did the political leaders or influentials. Interestingly, the reverse was true for the question: Most politicians can be trusted to do what they think is best for the country. On this many more political leaders than average Americans agreed.

In general, the American electorate tends to support the more abstract or general language of constitutional guarantees and democratic ideology. However, when particular guarantees or ideological propositions are related to specific and relatively familiar daily situations, the political leaders or activists are better able to see the relevance of linguistic abstractions to particular situations and applications. In the words of the director of this study:

American politics is widely thought to be innocent of ideology, but this opinion more appropriately describes the electorate than the active political minority. If American ideology is defined as that cluster of axioms, values and beliefs which have given form and substance to American democracy and the Constitution, the political influentials manifest by comparison with ordinary voters a more developed sense of ideology and a firmer grasp of its essentials. . . . The electorate displays a substantial measure of unity chiefly in its support of freedom *in the abstract;* on most other features of democratic belief and practice it is sharply divided. . . . The evidence suggests that it is the *articulate* classes rather than the public who serve as the major repositories of the public conscience and as the carriers of *the Creed.*[1]

This chapter is devoted to the author's impressions of how well-known propositions of American political ideology may be interpreted or restated from the perspectives of behavioral science concepts. These are the philosophical propositions or values that Americans—we decline to say whether these are the leaders or the average citizens—seem most to prefer. Every reader is invited to challenge the extent to which Americans prefer these patterns of political behavior Every reader is expected to have doubts about some, if not all, of the author's impressions. What is most important, however, is that every reader participate in the difficult intellectual and scientific tasks of learning how to differentiate between *preferred patterns* of behavior and actually *existing patterns,* that is, of discerning the differences and the relationships between political value and political fact.

ORGANIZATIONAL PREFERENCES

Behavioral scientists are aware that a people's traditional cultural preferences can promote or suppress different developmental patterns. A female prime minister, predictably, is a possibility in a nation that refers to itself as "Mother India" but less conceivable in one whose people speak of the "Fatherland." American valuations regarding groups and organizations may similarly be inferred from some of the nation's patterns of organizational history.

---

[1] Herbert McClosky, "Consensus and Ideology in American Politics," *American Political Science Review*, 58 (June 1964): 361–82.

Pluralism

Freedom of association is one of the most explicit behavioral preferences of the American people. It is an ideological doctrine written into the Bill of Rights of the Constitution. It is reiterated with the emergence and organization of every new minority group, since older organized groups often wish to deny the newcomers freedom of association on grounds of the latter's "deviancy," "subversiveness," "immorality," and so on. In so heterogeneous a society, with so many other freedoms operating, this wish to deny rarely sticks. Before long, the adversary groups are usually accommodating to each other and, in many respects, reinforcing each other's existence. Thus, the rise of unions activates the organization of manufacturers and business associations. Left-liberal groups such as Americans for Democratic Action spark the organization of rightist groups such as the John Birch Society, and vice versa. Paradoxically, even those who associate in order to deny freedom of association to others, as in the case of Fascist, Communist, and other authoritarian parties, successfully do so only if they themselves have had the freedom to associate.

New groups form easily in the United States as new purposes become visible. Old groups die reluctantly, but die they do, as old objectives are achieved. Few nations, relatively speaking, have as varied and complex a group structure. So accepted is the practice of organizing for political and other types of action that even officers of government are among the enthusiastic promoters of new organized interest groups. So cherished is the freedom of association that it often extends to protect organizations that in any other nation would be promptly classified and harassed as "subversive." Thus, in 1954, the Communist Control Act deprived the Communist Party of all legal "rights, privileges, and immunities" because of its activities as "the agency of a hostile foreign power" creating a "clear, present, and continuing danger to the security of the United States. Yet, in fact, the law—never comfortably received—has become a "dead letter" as a consequence of several Supreme Court decisions. On the one hand, the Court supported the Smith Act's definition of membership in the Communist Party as "a crime" (*Scales* v. *United States*, 1961). On the other hand, the Internal Security Act of 1950 continues to require all Communist and Communist-front organizations to register, which the Court held to be a form of self-incrimination, hence unenforceable (*United States* v. *Communist Party*, 1964).

Group Toleration

Few organizations in American life are so powerful or so dogmatic that they could not find an ally among other groups. The more experienced and skilled a group leader, the happier he is with the multiplicity of organized groups. He finds that having many adversaries, each on some different issue, often allows a flexibility of strategy that could not otherwise exist if there were only one major adversary. "Politics makes strange bedfellows" because the bed in a democracy is so big. Thus, too, legislative sessions and political party conventions are constantly the scene of negotiated agreements, first, among compatible allies and, then among adversaries. Even regulatory agencies such as the Interstate Commerce Commission tend to view as "clients" those very organizations they are established to watch and regulate.

Formalization

The American preference for a government of laws has predisposed the nation to rule making as a favorite procedure for specifying task expectations and circumscribing individual behavior. Popular respect for the Constitution and the laws of the land was born, historically, of fear of human caprice and malevolence, the behavior of individual men unbounded by clearly prescribed expectations. If an individual repeatedly violates a group's task expectations, the group must infer that he is either stupid or dangerous. For example, in the 1950s Senator Joseph McCarthy, in his investigations of communism and his attacks upon his senatorial colleagues, constantly violated the task expectations of the Senate. A majority of the Senators concluded that McCarthy was more dangerous than stupid and voted to censure him lest he undermine the Senate as an institution. The Jacksonian notion that all citizens are equally qualified to serve in public office is perhaps a by-product of the formalizing predilections of the American community: if the job is well described, any man can do it—any citizen may fill the job of President if he reads the Constitution carefully enough!

COMMUNICATION PREFERENCES

American concern for the communication process is clearly stated in the First Amendment, which has been referred to as not only the first of the freedoms, but also the freedom that antecedes all others. In it, all the known techniques of political communication are protected from government abridgment: speech, press, assembly, and petition. This simple roster has, of course, been liberally interpreted to include all the other techniques of communication developed by advancing technologies.

Free Speech

Communicative activity, whatever its form, is "good" in the view of most citizens of the most communicative nation in the world. England and France may be the birthplaces of the notion that most human conflicts can be resolved if men discuss and reason together; the United States, however, is the place where discussion (if not reasoning) is carried on most voluminously and noisily. In no other country, for example, is it as easy to elicit citizen responses for a public opinion poll. Further, in no other country are those with a vested interest in freedom of communication as quick and as powerful in preventing infringements upon this freedom; these vested interests include the press, the institutions of higher learning, and most political minorities.

While these influential protectors of freedom of communication could probably be sufficient unto themselves, they are nonetheless reinforced by a Supreme Court with a solid tradition in support of civil liberties and by a United States Senate whose rule for unlimited debate is among the political wonders of the world. Only a "clear and present danger" to the peace and integrity of the Nation is, according to the Supreme Court, sufficient grounds for placing constraints upon the communication process. Somewhat less clear are the constitutional constraints to be placed upon "obscene" and "lewd" matter. In other words, the content of what is communicated may be subject to occasional limitations on the grounds of national security and public morality, but never is the communication process itself subject to constitutional question.

How much communicative activity is worthwhile? Communicate

at all cost, seems the American response. Whatever the communication cost, the strain toward symmetry that accompanies it seems preferable to the alternatives: noncommunication, noncooperation, or incapacity to share information. An election campaign costing several million dollars is always preferable to one costing several million lives.

Yet, the cost of communication does receive attention from some of the most inventive minds in the country. Zip-code-reading computers will help keep postal rates down. One dollar pays for a telephone call across the continent. Millions of people, even children, have low-cost transistor radios. Most families, even the poorest, may be found seated at some time before a TV set. Technological advances and mass production continue to reduce the cost of transmission equipment. Advertising, which may inflate the cost of other economic goods, has clearly kept the cost of mass media communication close to zero for both the communicators and the audiences.[2]

Responsible Expertise

Americans are quick to recognize that different individuals in a community possess different kinds and amounts of information. Respect for specialized information is evidenced by the high prestige (albeit low salaries) enjoyed by the teaching and counseling professions. The advice of doctors, lawyers, and ministers is widely sought by people in this country. Government and business corporations are ready to pay lucrative consulting fees for the information possessed by a wide range of specialists. So prevalent is the esteem for the expert and the specialist that their endorsements are sought for goods ranging from beer and toothpaste on one hand to presidential nominees on the other.

In politics, recognition of expert knowledge also exists. It is assumed, for example, that special interest groups have more relevant information about matters of primary concern to them than do other groups; e.g., agricultural organizations are expected to know more about farm problems than, say, the United Steelworkers union. Government is organized in response to the need for specialized knowledge, and many agencies have as their primary function the production of such knowledge: the cost-of-living index of the Department

---

2 The merits of a well-informed citizenry—another valued feature of the American ideology—are discussed in the illustrative case study at the conclusion of Chapter 2.

of Labor, the international intelligence reports of the Defense Department, the State Department, and the Central Intelligence Agency,
and so forth.

This same respect for responsible expertise prevails among voters
who are usually willing to support the nominees of their party's
leaders or accept the opinion of a President regarding the best
policy course to take in world affairs. It is when the expert is demonstrably *irresponsible*, however, that he and the information he
brings to a situation are dismissed. Thus, it is common to observe
in American politics experts addressing themselves not so much to
the information at hand as to the veracity of the opposition as a
source.

"Show me. I'm from Missouri."

No phrase summarizes more succinctly the American attitude of general skepticism regarding the substance of information. Even the
most informed experts are called upon to justify their knowledge
claims with appropriate evidence. In politics, words must be matched
with deeds. Statements, in politics as in science, must have observable referents. As a consequence, American society has been characterized as empirical and pragmatic rather than mystical and
deterministic. Even among contemporary American churches, the
emphasis in religious activity tends to be upon "good works" in the
here-and-now.

Information is costly to acquire and rarely sufficient to produce
certainty. The amount that an individual will expend for information and the degree of uncertainty that he will tolerate are a function of the goal for which the information is needed. To be willing
to incur heavy information costs, the individual must be highly
interested in the purpose for it. The more salient the goal, the greater
the individual's demand that bias and error in the information be
reduced. In the United States, it is generally appreciated that the
individual is not likely to be able to afford *all* the information
needed to achieve an objective, nor is he likely to find complete
information even if he could afford it. As a consequence, Americans
give much attention to the principles by which information is produced and selected.

In the various constitutional and quasi-constitutional organizations, different principles of information selection prevail. The rules
of evidence in the courts is similar to that of the sciences, where the

rules of theory and evidence are perhaps the most explicit and demanding. The information-gathering responsibilities of the Federal bureaucracy are similarly demanding; a bomber that fails to fly or a fiscal policy that fails to forestall a depression are likely to have profound political consequences.

Congressional handling of information, on the other hand, tends to be more concerned with authoritative and politically significant opinion than well-confirmed data. Information is selected by the press primarily on the principle of audience interest. The political parties employ a similar principle to assure acceptance of information by the electorate. Organized groups, using the principle of self-interest, gather and organize information in whatever way is necessary to support the promotion of group goals.

Each of these distinct principles of information selection is generally considered respectable. Each principle is also usually subject to challenge. The press, for example, would never accept the standards of confirmation required by scientists or the courts, and vice versa.

"Watch your language."

In practice, the separation-of-power principle is as much a device for producing redundancy as it is for dispersing prerogatives among the branches of government. It has become a familiar part of the American political scene to see the statutory language produced by Congress modified and interpreted in the executive branch and further revised in the Supreme Court. This linguistic analysis is augmented by the challenges and defenses made by organized interests, the refinements or ambiguities invented by political parties, and the personal interpretations manifest in the behavior of each member of the general public.

With communication messages flowing throughout the community at relatively low cost, this linguistic review is basically an acknowledgement of the limitations of language as a carrier of information. Redundancy is a way of preventing erroneous decoding of the laws and public policies.

LINGUISTIC PREFERENCES

In describing purposes, enunciating public policies, and recording political practices, the American people rely heavily upon available linguistic tools. The definition conflicts carried on in the governing organizations may last for generations but with cumulative consequence. Political statements, whether fact, value, or description of a future state of affairs, are easily subjected to challenge, revision, and refinement. American reverence for The Word is pragmatic rather than authoritarian; "final" definitions and "perfect" statements seem neither necessary nor desirable. What *is* admired is the great utility of language in helping shape relationships among Americans vis à vis their agreements and disagreements.

Utilitarian View of Language

The "tool" emphasis in this and the previous chapter reflects an American predisposition about language. Americans prefer to think of language as a useful means rather than as an end. This general attitude toward language manifests itself when linguistic tools are employed as weapons, yardsticks, guideposts, or resources in political affairs.

Terms and statements are familiar elements in the conduct of political contests and negotiations. As a weapon, language is viewed, particularly among negotiating leaders, as expendable, but at a price. If a preferred term or statement is to be modified or "given up," the adversary, too, must give up something in the transaction. In doing so, each of the parties usually works to have the overt compromise satisfy his constituency that there has been no "sell-out." In this way, limited political objectives always seem feasible, at least linguistically. Further, parties to a contest may agree to retreat to verbal ambiguities either as a compromise or as a dilatory move to await a better time for battle.

Language may be used as a weapon not only to achieve compromises but also to incite conflict. The skillful politician who chooses the target for his verbal shots, particularly in anticipation of an election campaign, is limited only by personal inventiveness and taste in determining what words and statements he will use to inflame the adversary and arouse his followers to battle. Thus, for example, when the demagogic Senator Theodore G. Bilbo of Mississippi was charged with racial and religious intolerance by his opponents, he defended himself by declaring that he was for "every damn Jew from Jesus Christ down." The phrase confounded his opponents, but his supporters "understood" and loved him all the more for his deadly wit.

Americans also use language as a yardstick, that is, an instrument of measurement. For example, there is the recurrent reminder that deeds must measure up to words. Possibly one of the best known statements of this kind in recent years is the following from a Department of State bulletin of January 27, 1966: "We have said publicly and privately that we could stop the bombing of North Vietnam as a step toward peace although there has not been the slightest hint or suggestion from the other side as to what they would do if the bombing stopped." Finally the North Vietnamese agreed to "peace talks" if the bombing were halted. In 1968 the Americans halted the bombing, and negotiations were initiated in Paris. In time, the Americans came to realize that the North Vietnamese had only agreed to *talk about peace* and that talk did not necessarily mean *negotiate* a peace settlement. North Vietnamese words in Paris were, in the American view, entirely unsupported by the kinds of deeds customarily expected in a peace negotiation, e.g., bombing halt, freeze on troop movements, restraint in propaganda, prisoner exchanges, etc. Once American officials arrived at this conclusion about the Paris talks, their main task became one of demonstrating the futility of the talks to the rest of the world, demonstrating that is, that North Vietnamese deeds belied North Vietnamese words.

In their concern with language as a yardstick, American politicians tend to insist upon substantial evidence in support of empirical statements, at least where their adversaries are concerned. In an open, competitive politics, the result of this demand is the eventual flushing out of facts. The demand for evidence also moves key political concepts toward operational definition. When American politicians prepare themselves for decision and commitment on some public issue, the quantitative character of their inquiries about various alternatives is usually the best evidence that hard choices are about to be consummated. "How many dollars will it cost?" "How many of the people that I represent will it affect?" "How many votes will it gain or lose?" "How much closer to our long-run objectives will it take us, and on what evidence is such an estimate based?" In responding to questions such as these, the more operationally defined the terms and the better validated the replies, the greater is the confidence with which the politician proceeds to his decision.

To the extent that language may serve as a guidepost, Americans are willing to accept a certain amount of its susceptibility to error. Words are appreciated for the low-cost information they may provide rather than for any intrinsic merit. If a political term or a political statement can help orient an individual informationally or attitudinally, the linguistic guidepost is usually seen as worth the cost. It is on this basis, for example, that the Democratic and Republican party labels count so heavily in electoral politics. Straight-ticket voting is both a convenience and an assurance to most voters with partisan leanings. Candidate names below the top of the ticket are usually little known to most voters, if at all; the party label, however, prevents voting for an "enemy."

Language is also considered a resource. Sometimes a politician will "give" a particular segment of his constituency a favorite concept or phrase. A political campaigner may worry aloud about "Communists in government" or "left-wing professors on the campuses" without doing another thing about these matters; particular segments of his audience may simply be satisfied that the phrases were used. A significant use of language in this way occurred in Senator Goldwater's acceptance of the Republican presidential nomination in 1964. Having just defeated his opponents' attempts to incorporate an anti-extremism plank in the platform, Senator Goldwater used the term "extremism" as a verbal bouquet to certain of his supporters: "Extremism in the defense of liberty is no vice." (Although the bouquet was enthusiastically received by his immediate audience at the convention, Goldwater misjudged how costly the use of the term "extremism" would be in alienating moderate Republicans.)

Language is frequently used by Americans for maintaining the agenda of public discourse. Probably the most distinguished sources of key terms and statements for keeping alive fundamental issues are the Declaration of Independence and the Constitution. The American preference, seen in the behavior of major and minor party leaders, is somehow to relate—sometimes logically, sometimes not— a contemporary public issue to their party's traditional terminology. Thus, for example, in recent years both states' right advocates and individual rights supporters have articulated their respective positions within the definitional framework of the term "civil rights," always assured a high place on the agenda of American political discussion.

In the most elemental way, language is a political resource because it is a convenient tool for enumerating alternatives and measuring consensus. In a heterogeneous society in which information is distributed so widely and in such varied forms, even the most ungrammatical statement may make known points of view, feasible alternatives, and degrees of agreement. Such information has great utility for carrying the community toward an acceptable resolution of a public problem.

Principles

"Ideology" is a foreign-sounding term for most Americans, who view themselves as possessing "principles" rather than ideologies. Whichever the rubric, both principles and ideologies have as their building units political terms and political statements. One anthropologist, calling these "value-premises," reported the following basic set found in the American culture:

1. The universe is mechanistically conceived.
2. Man is its master.
3. Men are equal.
4. Man are perfectible.

These lead to at least three major preferences: (1) a preference for material well-being, which derives from the premise that man is master of a mechanistic universe; (2) an inclination toward conformity, which derives from the premise of man's equality; and (3) an optimism about the consequences of work and effort, that derives from the premise of man's perfectibility.[3]

One student of American electoral behavior offers the following comment about the place of political principles in American voting decisions. He notes that the electorate is generally assumed to possess a body of stable political principles or moral standards against which current issues are evaluated for decision. Two kinds of principles presumably prevail: those related to democratic procedures or rules of the political game and those having to do with the substantive content of democratic decisions.

With respect to the rules of the game, most Americans would presumably agree that rules have to be accepted in advance of controversy so that they will prevail even in the defeat of one or more sides. For most Americans, such principles read as follows, in statement form: Violence must not be involved in the making of electoral

[3] Cora du Bois, "The Dominant Value Profile of American Culture," *American Anthropologist*, 57 (1955): 1233–34.

decisions. The majority decision must be accepted as final in any particular instance, until appropriately appealed to a court, a legislative body, or the citizenry. The citizen must have proper respect for constituted authority. The citizen must, as a consequence of respect for other elements in the community, be prepared to make political compromises.

The substantive principles would probably include statements of the following type: America wishes to have peace with security. Democratic processes should lead to a better life for one's children. All citizens should share in a higher standard of living. Freedom must be protected for all Americans.

Yet, according to this observer, "the studies [of electoral behavior] show that a large portion of the party vote today is by this test unprincipled."[4] Yet the political principles of Americans are empirically ascertainable. In some studies they have been collected and listed in statement form. Often they are reiterated in the homilies of elementary civics classes. That they are a significant body of statements is perhaps best summarized in the phrase "respect for the law." The American devotion to the rule of law rests upon the assumption that somewhere an appropriate law has been or can be written.

Timing

"Remember that time is money." "Time runs out." These familiar observations, along with the simple fact that more timepieces are sold in the United States than any other nation in the world, suggests that Americans have a keen awareness of time.

To confirm this, we need only notice the volume of life insurance sales. Dozens of insurance companies currently have placed bets (face value of policies in force) in the amount of $700 billions on the lives of their millions of policyholders. Conversely, each policyholder is betting the insurance company that he is likely to die before his time. Very few cultures consider the lifetime of the individual as a unit to be managed from birth through childhood, adolescence, youth, middle age, retirement, to death. The time sensitivity of Americans is further underscored by their worldwide reputation for being "people in a hurry."

Within this attitudinal framework, it is not surprising to find that

[4] Bernard Berelson, "Democratic Theory and Public Opinion," *Public Opinion Quarterly*, 16 (Fall 1952): 313–30

time is also considered a valuable political resource, to be used with care and skill. Politicians in basic agreement with each other about a political goal and the means to implement it may find themselves at odds about moving "too fast" or "too slow" during implementation. In campaigns for election, one important concern of campaign managers is that their candidate may "peak" too soon or too late. A famous example of "peaking" on time was the upset election campaign of President Truman in 1948. Polls taken prior to the election revealed a "trend" in electoral support for him, which obviously culminated in his victory on Election Day. However, there is substantial evidence that, if the election had taken place either three weeks before or three weeks after Election Day, Truman would have been defeated.

As indicated above, Americans believe, by and large, in the perfectibility of man and in the progressive improvement of his institutions and affairs. This confidence in the long-run has permitted politicians to analyze and program policies for limited goals in the short run. The American preference is for accomplishing something in the short run while moving toward a long-run goal. This is often referred to as "American pragmatism."

TRANSACTIONAL PREFERENCES

Manifestly interested in negotiations and compromise, American politics has traditionally been candid about its trading and marketplace qualities.

The Political Deal

Theodore Roosevelt's "Square Deal," Franklin D. Roosevelt's "New Deal," and Harry S. Truman's "Fair Deal" have hardly been accidents of terminology. These highly political presidents were unabashed about giving the voters a sense of the transaction going on, in the meaning employed by Anthony Downs. The "deal" for the voter would presumably follow upon the election of these political leaders to office; implied was the exchange of a positional currency for a materiel one.

These appellations for particular national administrations were widely accepted. Their popularity rested perhaps mainly upon the modifying adjectives: "square," "new," and "fair." Even "deals" consummated in "smoke-filled rooms" seem to be accepted by most Americans *if* some measure of popular equity or morality accompanies the transaction. Americans generally view politicians as a necessary evil; political deals are similarly accepted.

The cultural underpinning for this attitude is substantial. The United States is largely a mercantile society in which the activities of business and trade are familiar to nearly all, and widely approved. Doing business, even among professionals and artists, is expected and respected. If an individual is particularly wrapped up in his work or his art, it is even deemed appropriate that he employ an agent to handle the business side of his affairs. Whatever the nature of the transaction and whatever the measure of equity on the part of the transactors, exchange is a central and deliberate part of American life.

Laissez Faire

If it is American to "work out a deal," it is just as American to let each man be his own judge of the fairness of the deal. Self-interest is a highly touted yardstick of equity in American society and political life. This view fits the prevalent free enterprise and individualistic ideology. Thus, for example, Lane and others found "that work life in an industrial society permits and even encourages social relations of a reciprocal team-oriented kind."[5]

This same sense of reciprocity pervades the political process as well. Individuals go into politics to get something out of it, that is, to improve their Effective Preference resources for some matter of public policy. The political parties and organized interests are essentially voluntaristic, and even the apparently intangible psychic rewards of participation must be counted as political currency for the party rank and file. Even voters go to the polls when they think it is "worth it"; proposals for compulsory voting have never been popular in this country.

Divide and Trade

The practice of dividing large denominations of political currency into smaller ones in order to spread the opportunities for trading

---

[5] Robert E. Lane, *Political Ideology* (Glencoe, Ill.: Free Press, 1962), reprinted in part in Joseph R. Fiszman, *The American Political Arena* (2nd ed.; Boston: Little, Brown, 1966), p. 75.

has been an unrecognized accomplishment of American politics. After all, what good is a million dollars if one man has it all and 999 have none. Even ten $100,000 bills held by ten individuals leaves 990 in a thousand with nothing. The typical American approach endeavors to convert the $1,000,000 into small denominations and then create conditions under which each of the thousand persons may gather as many dollars as he can. If some obtain only a few dollars and others hundreds of thousands, this reflects variances in trading skill rather than rigidities in currency denominations or marketplace conditions. This is perhaps another way of describing Sir Henry Maine's observation that "the Wire-Puller" in democracies is the leader who is skilled in cutting up political power [read: political currencies] into "petty fragments" and trading upon these fragments.

Skillful brokerage in American society is highly rewarded, whether in the "take" of the political boss, election to high office, high salaries for professional mediators, or other recognition. American history gives special plaudits to the "Great Compromisers." The currency units may be small and numerous, but it is precisely such size and quantity that give the marketplace its flexibility and capacity for accommodation.

PREFERENCES ABOUT INDIVIDUAL DECISION MAKING

The human individual—his person, his perfectibility, and his prerogatives—is a cherished "end" in American politics. Government is "of, by, and for the people," and "the people" is a numerous body of individuals. In his own way and to his own degree, each American is presumed to have an intrinsic capacity for the exercise of free will as well as a capacity to respond to appeals to reason. While the American community, it is believed, has a fundamental obligation to help shape the individual's character so that he may develop himself to his maximum potential as well as make reasonable decisions, Americans are also willing to nurture "characters" in the colloquial sense, who are different or unique as personality types.

Individualism and Individual Choice

While the great worth of the human individual is an ancient proposition in the Judeo-Christian tradition, it was not until the beginning of the seventeenth century that individualism was seriously dwelt upon as a political concept. The Dutch jurist Hugo Grotius explored the legal relations between individuals and their rulers, laying the ground work for Thomas Hobbes. It was Hobbes who looked very closely at the individual's psychological mechanism and at each man's "natural right" to do all he can to preserve himself. Benedict Spinoza went further, arguing that each man has a natural right to do all that he can do in any aspect of his behavior.

With the dawn of constitutionalism at about this same time, the notion of individual liberties in special aspects of personal behavior was added to the growing concern for the individual as a whole. Roger Williams made the argument for freedom of religious affiliation. John Milton wrote on behalf of the individual intellect as a seeker of the truth. The English Levellers made a political movement of the defense of the individual and his liberties. By the end of the eighteenth century, the Utilitarian philosophers—Jeremy Bentham, James Mill, and John Stuart Mill—had evolved an elaborate social and political philosophy that emphasized the centrality and dignity of the human individual, at the same time that it sought to summarize the good of all men in order to arrive at some measure of the "greatest happiness of the greatest number."

In the United States, individualism manifest itself in political arrangements to assure equality among men and also popular sovereignty. The frontier and the opportunities for individual escape to it reinforced the view that each man is as good as the next. The early solicitation of votes by political parties seeking control of the government through an election process also reinforced the regard given each individual—man by man, vote for vote.

In contemporary America, whether as an object of manipulation or as a popular sovereign, the individual is decidedly the target of large-scale, highly organized efforts to influence his choices. The advertising industry would hardly need to spend billions of dollars annually if the individual-in-the-mass were not such an elusive decision maker. Presumably, if most persons were conditioned-reflex machines that automatically responded in a given way to advertising stimuli, an advertiser would need to spend very little once he found the proper psychic trigger for most persons in his prospective audience. But because individuals *are* individuals, each more complex than the next, the best an advertiser can do is to try to get as many as possible to listen to him. The political propagandist has a similar problem, but often with more dramatic consequences;

votes by one or a few individuals can make an important difference in an election.

Despite the fact that the individual is the target for so much advertising, communication, propaganda, pressure, and organization, as many as two in every five adult Americans say that "I feel that my political leaders hardly care what people like myself think or want." The objective fact may be that leaders go to great lengths and expense to ascertain what the average citizen thinks or wants, but these particular average citizens—the two in every five—neither perceive nor believe this. What is more important, perhaps, is that those who wish to influence them believe otherwise.

Rationalism and Appeals to Reason

Eighteenth-century Enlightenment glorified knowledge and the rationality that could be derived from knowledge. The Founding Fathers were profoundly influenced by the Enlightenment and literally constructed a system of government that presupposed the reasonableness of a significant number if not all men. A major motivation for their accepting the fragmentation of national political power was to assure reasonable men the opportunity to debate effectively with each other various perceptions of reality and good. The "inevitable" consequence of such reasoned debate was supposed to be a democratic consensus on whatever issue was at hand. Emotionality and passion, they thought, should and would be abhorred in a society that gave free play to the rational faculties of men.

Few nations have had as persistent and respected an ideological tradition supportive of such rationalist assumptions about human nature. American religious and academic philosophers have emphasized the relationship between political institutions and the elevation of human nature and judgment. So have numerous political traditions which, on their face, may seem to be ritualistic or deceptive artifacts. For example, the politician who attempts to make a "public record" or "points to the record" responds to the assumption that, at least for some of his constituents, the "record" is a kind of evidence for arriving at judgments. (If there were not this ritual concern for the "record," the style of politics would presumably run *entirely* on appeals to the latest emotionality.) Similarly, the legislative and judicial processes in the United States rely heavily upon the rules of logic and evidence. That these exercises in rationality are not always, or even most of the time, successful is quite beside the point; the continued overwhelming commitment to them, along with the underlying assumption of human rationality, is what makes the American difference.

Character — Good and Rare

Perhaps one of the least disputed objectives of public education is the development of character. From kindergarten to university, in one formulation or another, the instructional program is, in part, intended to help the individual maximize the potentiality of his personal resources and to refine the attributes of his personality.

An overwhelming proportion of all this is straightforward role instruction: how to manage one's family life; how to get along with a great variety of types of people in a heterogeneous society; how to produce and consume knowledge; and so on. The role-informational inputs—most of it in some kind of linguistic propositional form— are, of course, guides to behavior presumed to be instrumental to particular goals. However, what constitutes "good behavior" or "good character" according to classroom precepts may run into substantial trouble under the test of events. Thus, is it "good citizenship" to stay home on Election Day? Most Americans would argue in favor of active exercise of one's freedom of choice at the polls, but others might argue that it is also an exercise of choice to reject the formally available alternatives. A similar difference appears with respect to other political decision making, for example, the decision to engage in riot or revolution. If it is *usually* not "nice" to engage in revolutionary violence, under what circumstances—including some historic ones—should one opt for revolution? In other words, there are indeed circumstances under which the best citizen might be the one who starts a revolution.

Perhaps the most important aspect of such role instruction as preparation for decision making is the commitment to formulate and communicate about the behavioral alternatives. If revolution is "unthinkable" in some societies and looked askance upon in contemporary American society, nonetheless the American approach is to leave the choice open and the unpleasant alternatives theoretically available.

Therefore, whether it be on such dramatic choices as revolution or war, or such less dramatic alternatives as voting or not voting, character building is a traditional part of the political and social enterprise of the United States. Even when revolutions, wars, and election days are not the immediate situations of choice, there may be much transfer of learning, and recommended behavior in one situation may be applied by analogy to others. For example, toleration learned in one's religious role often carries over into one's partisan or ethnic role behavior.

The "rare bird" is a "character" much condoned in American life. This is another aspect of American preferences regarding decision makers. If a person wants to be a "kook," it is his privilege, most Americans believe. And the choices that flow from his being a kook are also permissible if they do not infringe upon the rights of others. Respect and toleration of the unusual personality is substantially reinforced by many mechanisms in an entertainment-oriented culture. Movie personalities and political personalities are closely watched, particularly if what they decide to do in certain situations is entertaining or exciting. Entertainers set fashions in the decision making of individuals across the nation in matters from selection of hair styles to matrimonial morality. Politicians, too, are quite aware of their function as behavioral models; John and Robert Kennedy in recent years were particularly self-conscious in this regard.

Free Will, Within Limits

A contemporary version of an old libertarian proposition is that "everybody has a right to do his thing." Few characterizations of man are as deeply imbedded in American thought as the notion that each man has a capacity for the free exercise of his will. This is supported by the dogma of a predominantly Protestant religious culture. A strongly libertarian political ideology also assumes free will. And a free enterprise economic system adds another reinforcement.

In the extreme, various freethinker movements have emerged on the American scene as proponents of the *full* exercise of free will. In behavioral terms, this has often meant that whatever the individual decides to do in almost any situation is his and only his business. An individual may, according to this philosophy, think and say whatever he chooses. He may, in some public aspects of his behavior, also choose whatever courses of action he wishes. Free-will attitudes underlie individual decisions to engage in free love, drug consumption, nudism, use of obscenities, and other forms of activity which may be considered deviant by other people. For these others, free love seems to be promiscuity, drug consumption becomes addiction, colorful language becomes obscenities, and nudism is sinful. In such a context, the exercise of free will becomes social and political as devotees of the different points of view seek to establish limits for each other.

In the American case, the process of establishing limits in the exercise of free will is a cautious one. In the courts particularly, limitations upon individual prerogative are carefully spelled out, and always in terms of distinctions between individual and social consequences. If the individual choice and act has only individual consequences, the tendency is to refrain from obstructing personal choice. If the consequences are social and perceived by a majority as "undesirable," the tendency is to constrain the majority and defend the individual's prerogatives by insisting upon objective tests of those social consequences.

Thus, in contrast to most contemporary societies, the American is highly devoted and protective of the individual's activity as a decision maker. If many of these decision makers seem to act on the basis of emotionality rather than rationality, that may be more a problem of rationalist behavioral theory than of the individual's motivations. If the individual confuses his roles, that may be more a problem of the socializing instruction to which he has been exposed than any personal failing. If the reference groups that he takes into account as he decides seem unreal, that is because they may very well be unreal. The dynamics of human choice is likely to remain an intriguing area of inquiry for American behavioral scientists and for the political practitioners.

PREFERENCES ABOUT COLLECTIVE DECISION MAKING

Americans tend to give careful attention to the design of collective decision rules, and, once rules have been adopted, they give them up or change them only reluctantly. The overwhelming preference for the numerical type of decision rule is clearly evident, even in those situations where the numerical procedures are employed only rarely or perfunctorily. There is a decided American antipathy toward collective decision making in situations of crisis or threat. Further, particularly for the more important national choices, there is a willingness to create special decision rules or contingency rules to facilitate a choice under "special" circumstances.

Play by the Rules

The Anglo-Saxon "rule of law" tradition has had important consequences for American creation of and adherence to collective decision rules. Hamilton expressed this concern for orderly adherence to the rules in *Federalist* 68. Defending the Electoral College arrangement for electing a President, Hamilton argued that this device would "afford as little opportunity as possible to tumult and disorder." The Electoral College plan would also place "every practicable obstacle" to "cabal, intrigues, and corruption." We may assume that Hamilton reported the sense of the Founding Fathers in these words:

> The choice of *several*, to form an intermediate body of electors, will be much less apt to convulse the community, with any extraordinary or violent movements, than the choice of *one*, who was himself to be the final object of the public wishes. And as the electors, chosen in each state, are to assemble and vote in the state in which they are chosen, this detached and divided situation will expose them much less to heats and ferments, that might be communicated from them to the people, than if they were all to be convened at one time in one place.

Hamilton made a similar argument for the constitutional provision which authorizes the Congress to regulate the election of its own members. Although the Constitution leaves to the prescription of each state legislature the times, places, and manner of holding elections of senators and representatives, the Congress may, at any time, by law, make or alter such regulations, except as to places of choosing senators. Said Hamilton: "Every government ought to contain within itself the means of its own preservation." Election of members of Congress could have been left to the regulation of Congress only, the state legislatures entirely, or in part with the state legislatures and ultimately with the Congress. The third alternative, a divided collective decision rule, was the plan adopted. As Hamilton explains in *Federalist* 59, the dispersion of responsibility for rule making was expected to provide "security against an abuse of the trust" among those local, state, and national governing interests concerned with congressional elections.

It has, in fact, become an important part of the American collective decision-making experience that those who would destroy, set aside, or denigrate an established collective decision rule ought immediately to be suspect regarding their political motivation. This, for example, is the usual public response to the occasional major-party presidential elector who promises to vote for a third-party candidate; certain Southern Democratic electors announced their intention to vote for Thurmond rather than Truman in 1948, and a similar situation arose among Democratic electors supporting George Wallace in 1968. It is in fact within the constitutional rights of each elector to make such a "personal" choice except in those states where this is prohibited by state law. Yet, popular and press reaction to such announcements is invariably one of suspicion, since, according to the customary decision rule, the elector should cast his vote for the nominee of the party under whose name he was placed on the ballot.

In general, the American view is that most domestic collective decision rules are explicit, well tested, and equitable. Those who decline to go along with alternatives chosen according to these rules or who attack the rules without offering recommended modifications eventually come to be considered "spoilers" and "anti-system." The political team that plays vigorously and fairly within the established decision rules is, on the other hand, esteemed and feared by its adversaries.

By the Numbers

Military trainees are familiar with the phrase "by the numbers" which refers to the numbered steps according to which they must perform particular routines. "By the numbers" can also describe the overriding American preference for the numerical type of collective decision rule. The highest score in a game, the best measurable performance of some feat, and the largest number of votes in an election all seem to be part of a national predisposition toward quantification. In political collective decision making, these preferences are reflected in the widespread faith in majority rule. One or another formulation of majority rule appears as a basic decision rule within most branches of government as well as such extra-constitutional organizations as pressure groups and political parties.

The general preference for numerical decision rules, however, does not eliminate the verbal and violent types. Within the framework of many long-established numerical arrangements, the numerical may give way in practice to the verbal. Much congressional legislation is passed by unanimous consent only because proponents and opponents have already discussed and reconciled their differences in the knowledge that some ultimate numerical test was at hand and could be resorted to if necessary. Experienced politicians realize that severely contested collective decisions can be costly to all parties. The resort to verbal methods is thus a cost-reduction tactic, and, as such, a widely accepted decision procedure among the professionals.

On the other hand, the United States prides itself on having been born of revolution, on its willingness to resort to violence to defend certain political principles, and on its physical exuberance as a still-quite-young nation. Thus, the Civil War, as an exercise in violent decision making, is almost universally reported as a conflict among honorable men seeking to defend legitimate principles and resources. (Interestingly, whatever national shame is attached to that period by most historians tends to relate to the Reconstruction Era, during which there were severe aberrations of normal types of political organization and collective decision making.)

Nor is the necessity of dealing with rebellion or riot an unfamiliar part of American politics; recall President Washington putting down a Whiskey Rebellion, President Cleveland putting down a strike in Chicago, President Eisenhower using troops to enforce a school integration order in Little Rock, or mayors and governors calling for Federal troops to restore order in ghettos and on campuses. American devotees of Maoist "wars of national liberation" and Che Guevara guerrilla tactics as techniques of contemporary "confrontation politics" are deceived if they believe they are importing something new; they simply are unfamiliar with their predecessors in American history. Violent approaches to collective decision making are familiar American phenomena but, fortunately, almost always temporary in duration and employed with expressions of reluctance; e.g. President Eisenhower, commenting upon sending troops to Little Rock: "the sadness I feel in the action I was compelled today to take."

Anti-crisis

The British must conduct a parliamentary election whenever there is a vote of "no confidence" in the incumbent ministry. Many nations call for new elections whenever some national crisis is in progress. In the United States, most collective decision arrangements involve regular elections on fixed dates, thus assuring political decision making under noncrisis conditions most of the time. Even when a regular election does occur at a time of widely felt crisis, as during a world war or an economic depression, there is great reluctance on the part of political leaders to dwell in their speeches on the crisis difficulties. Nor do Americans readily "talk business" with an adversary who is threatening or actually engaging in violence; "restoration of peace" and "termination of duress" are characteristic phrases associated with typical American reluctance to make choices under crisis pressure.

Yet, the complaint is widely heard that we are also victims of "crisis politics." Mine safety regulations are given little attention until some great—and probably expected—tragedy in loss of lives occurs. Gun registration laws are passed only under the pressures generated by the needless assassination of great national leaders. Thus, a national antipathy for crisis decision making seems lost in a practical politics that moves from one crisis confrontation to another, or at least so it seems.

Special Rules for Special Circumstances

Rarely, if ever, can a general rule apply to all conceivable cases—at least, this is a fundamental assumption of the Anglo-Saxon political tradition. In jurisprudence, the case approach and the provision for equity law are examples of political responses to this assumption. What is acknowledged thereby is the impossibility of creating a perfect system of human self-management and collective decision making. Recognition of such fallibility makes it easier for all concerned to accept occasional failures and breakdowns of decision arrangements. It also leads the attention of political architects like the Founding Fathers to the need for contingency arrangements and special rules to meet unexpected or special situations.

Among the best known of such contingency arrangements are the numerous provisions for the election of a President. If the Electoral College fails to decide under its decision rule, the choice is to be made under another set of decision rules in the House of Representatives. If a decision in the House of Representatives is too long delayed, the action of the Senate with respect to the selection of a Vice President provides for an Acting President. If all these contingency decision arrangements prove inappropriate for special circumstances, something new may be and has been invented, as in the disputed Hayes-Tilden election of 1876.

In the latter instance, at issue was the legitimacy of the 1876 popular vote return in certain areas. If one set of returns had been accepted as official, Tilden would have been elected; if another set, Hayes would become President. Under the circumstances, Congress created a Special Electoral Commission of five Senators, five Representatives, and five Supreme Court Justices, equally divided between the political parties but with the fifth Justice chosen by the other four. As a consequence, although Tilden had the larger popular vote, the returns were judged in a manner that gave Hayes the Electoral College vote. Despite months of tension and uncertainty, the results held, undoubtedly because this special arrangement had been created by politicians who assured its legitimacy.

This flexibility and inventiveness in the creation of operable and acceptable special collective decision rules under special circumstances has been a little recognized resource of the American political system. A study of the rigidities of decision rules in other nations would undoubtedly confirm this observation.

PREFERENCES CONCERNING LEADERSHIP

Both leaders and followers in the United States seem to share a number of fundamental preferences about the place of leadership in the political community. There is, in the first place, the democratic, egalitarian inclination to accept every man as a potential leader. There is also a wide acceptance of "virtual representation," that is, the impression of representativeness because of some apparent similarity between leaders and followers. A strong preference for frequent evaluation of leaders is built into and reinforced by the practice of frequent elections, and more recently by the interest in leader popularity as measured by opinion polls. Finally, there is a widespread acceptance of what might be called "broken field running," in the processes by which individuals rise to positions of leadership.

Every Man a Leader

This may be another manifestation of the basic regard for the human individual in the American political culture. Even among the Founding Fathers, who by and large shared an elitist view of leadership, the political elite was to be essentially one of merit, skill, and achievement, rather than a "closed corporation" of divinely selected individuals. In other words, the Founding Fathers generally believed in an open elite into which new talent from the lower rungs of the social ladder could enter.

While the model of Horatio Alger may be a decreasingly interesting one to contemporary generations of young Americans, Horatio Algers in American politics still seem to be possibilities. The upper-class Franklin D. Roosevelts and the lower-class Al Smiths may be less the norms than the Harry S. Trumans, Hubert H. Humphreys, and Richard M. Nixons, whose modest beginnings and self-professionalization as politicians seem to demonstrate the still-substantial possibility that any fine American boy (soon, perhaps, also girl) may realistically aspire to become President.

Virtual Representation

If anything comes through as a solid finding of the inquiries into personal and social attributes of American political leaders, it is that most leaders share important similarities with their particular constituents. American political leaders are indeed better off, more educated, more skilled, and more of several other qualities than their followers. But in *some* dimension—race, nationality, religion, even appearance—the followers are able to identify readily with a leader. Thus, a citizen of Italian extraction, when he encounters an Italian-name candidate for public office, is likely to feel that such a candidate could best represent his own interests; his only measure of this may be the particular nationality similarity. Whichever attribute it may be, it nevertheless becomes the basis for identification, expectation of virtual representation, and support at the polls. The citizen prefers to "stick with his own."

It is also common for American followers to prefer that leaders be not only similar to themselves in some respect but "better" in that or some other characteristic. In the example of the Italian-name candidate above, the citizen may not expect the candidate to be a "better Italian" than himself, but might expect him to be "better" in terms of education or political skill.

Frequent Evaluation

If the Jacksonian tradition supports the view that every man may be a leader, it also establishes the practice of frequent election as a means for evaluating the performance of those holding office. The Founding Fathers, however, saw frequent elections as an opinion-sampling tool for the leadership rather than a performance-evaluating tool for the people. The Jacksonians emphasized the performance-evaluating aspect, with the willingness to "throwing the rascals out" if necessary.

In addition to frequent elections, recent generations of Americans have been provided with all kinds of opinion polling evidence about satisfaction with the performance of major political leaders. "How much do you like what the President is doing?" "Are you satisfied with President X's performance of his job lately?" Similar questions, with findings widely and frequently published, keep alive the popular leaders' concern with how their actions and images are "going over." No American politician is surprised by his constituent's question: "What have you done for me *lately?*" "Lately" is how often an American politician's performance is subject to popular evaluation. Under such conditions, it is difficult for political leaders to acquire the remoteness or sanctity of position so often found in other political cultures.

Variety in Investiture Processes

Investiture and divestiture pertain to the manner in which persons become incumbent in or are removed from particular public offices. The pattern of such incumbency conditions is here called "the investiture process." At the heart of this process is a collective decision situation during which, in one way or another, the members of the group approve or disapprove the incumbency of a particular individual. Associated with the investiture process are the various formal and informal avenues of ascent that individuals may follow to arrive at particular positions. There are also associated opportunities by which the members of the collectivity may learn about and evaluate the attributes of candidates for leadership.

In choosing their political leaders, Americans, as we have noted in a previous chapter, are particularly attentive to the collective decision rules that establish the legitimacy of incumbency. Party bosses, at the turn of the century, tended to work from behind the scenes, holding power *without* some legitimizing collective decision; this rather than the looting of the public treasury was perhaps the most serious complaint about the machine bosses. The American people have tolerated a substantial amount of corruption by some of those bosses, and have even exhibited a substantial amount of affection for them. However, what eventually drove the bosses out was undoubtedly public frustration with the inability to register a decision on whether or not a particular boss should be "in" or "out." Americans are accustomed not only to choosing their leaders but dismissing them as well.

The avenues of ascent to high public office are usually a matter of great informality and much variety in the United States. In some political communities, recruitment of top leadership may involve the elevation of particular individuals through succeeding steps in a clear political hierarchy. This was, in fact, the case in the early, more elitist days of the Republic. The man chosen to be Vice President was next in line to succeed to the Presidency, John Adams succeeding Washington, Jefferson succeeding Adams, etc. At a later date, the office of Secretary of State was the "build-up" position. Today, the roads to the Presidency are many, although a major-state governorship or a seat in the Senate often provides the fastest trip.

Schlesinger describes as the "political opportunity structure" the number of offices available, the frequency with which new men attain them, and the typical career paths men follow in order to advance in politics. In some states, for example, one rises to the governorship via local and state legislative offices; in others, the path is a mix of local executive and state legislative incumbencies.[6] Whichever paths are followed, they are never formally prescribed (except as in the case of a vice-presidential succession upon the death of a president) nor permanently fixed by custom. New generations of aspiring

[6] Joseph A. Schlesinger, *Ambition and Politics: Political Careers in the United States* (Chicago: Rand McNally, 1966).

leaders seem always to have the opportunity to create new ways of arriving at high office, and the American preference seems to encourage this kind of wide open opportunity structure.

Americans are also in favor of availing themselves of many opportunities for examining the traits and personalities of incumbent as well as prospective leaders. The opportunities for such evaluation usually come during election campaigns, and it is a clear expectation among Americans that such campaigns shall be conducted, even in one-party districts. The smug incumbent is held in low regard by American voters. The politician who acts as though he is safely "in" tends to offend, as Thomas E. Dewey so bitterly learned in 1948. Even the process of appointing high officials, such as Cabinet members and ambassadors, is taken quite seriously, despite every expectation that the nominee is likely to be confirmed by, say, the Senate or other agency involved in making the appointment. Awkward and often inadequate though it may be, public review of leader qualifications remains a significant preference in the United States.

PREFERENCES FOR POLITICAL SOCIALIZATION

In their politicization activities, Americans seem to be predisposed toward several patterns of action. Civic education, in its many forms and through its diverse agencies, is generally an approved even if indirect part of American life. Whether sincerely or not, American politicians, perhaps responding to public expectation, are inclined to present themselves as eager learners. With respect to politicizing attempts, group effort along educational-propaganda lines is considered as legitimate as free speech; on the other hand group demands for behavioral compliance is generally thought to have limits.

Civic Education

The difference between teaching "civics" and teaching "politics" is more than a splitting of hairs over terminology. The terms represent a difference in American popular opinion between approved and suspect political instruction. Civics, civic education, and citizenship training are the rubrics usually applied to time-honored, preprofessional curricula that presumably describe the student's civic duties and the general structure of his government. Such instruction is frequently found in the social studies offerings of elementary schools, the civics courses of secondary schools, the introductory American government courses at college, and the citizenship training part of adult education programs offered in many communities. Organizations such as the League of Women Voters and the Foreign Policy Association carry on civic training throughout the adult life of their members. These types of politicization ordinarily win general public approval, often on grounds that the public school and nonpartisan civic organizations provide the most objective information in a field —politics—that is filled with deception and controversy.

Political education, on the other hand, carries connotations that are troublesome and suspect, undoubtedly because politics is generally perceived as a troublesome and suspect activity. As one consequence, elementary and secondary teachers, an important segment of the citizenry, tend to avoid partisan involvement outside the classroom; in the classroom teachers are expected to offer impartial political comment or, preferably, refrain from political comment entirely. Until recently, off-campus partisan activity by college professors was frowned upon by most college administrations. The introduction of college students to practical politics through field work with political parties and interest groups is of very recent vintage and is carried on only experimentally at the secondary school level.

In the American scale of values, "practical politics" is ranked far below "civic involvement," and the notion persists that the two are different. The good-bad terminology extends to other aspects of civic education. Voter registration campaigns are laudatory, but party precinct work is self-seeking. American ambivalence on this subject is widely evident.

Teaching the Politicians

Even though the empirical evidence suggests that most Americans feel unqualified to advise their leaders, a basic tenet of American political philosophy is that every citizen is not only qualified but obligated to advise the leadership if he feels so moved. This has produced a significant ritual wherein the citizen is always welcome to make his views known to the politicians, and the politicians— whether in office or not, and whether they hear anything or not— are expected to listen attentively. From the point of view of socialization, the assumptions underlying this ritual are, first, that citizens have the capacity to teach something to politicians, and second, that politicians are eager and rapid learners.

The evidence suggests, however, that learning by politicians is best "facilitated" by the heterogeneity of groups in his constituency and the competitiveness of its politics. Very little politician learning goes on in one-party constituencies. The politician who has to campaign vigorously and build winning coalitions out of diverse elements is likely to be sensitive in his perceptions, eager for new information, flexible in his attitudes, cautious in his opinions, and adaptive in his self-socialization.

Legitimacy of Politicization

Even with the basic freedoms of speech, press, and petition, a nation may find objectionable those groups that too aggressively press their own points of view upon others. Constraints upon aggressive politicizing attempts hardly exist, particularly those by organized interests, political parties, and the mass media; the advertising culture further encourages strong political propaganda efforts.

But it is one thing to propagandize and another to achieve compliance. Without compliance, socialization is unsuccessful. Therefore American politicizing groups are constantly in search of methods for enforcing compliance. The American political culture, however, tends to put limits upon such compliance attempts. Party politicians, for example, are reluctant to exercise public disciplinary measures against disloyal fellow partisans; President Truman was even reluctant to see the Southern Dixiecrats thrown out of the Democratic party after their bolt of 1948. Public floggings for group disloyalty are certainly out of order, and even capital punishment as a mode of compelling compliance to the law has come under severe criticism. In effect, the sturdy concept of free choice and voluntarism are a major hurdle to successful socialization.

One consequence of these limits upon enforcement of compliance has been the tendency to invent social and psychological rather than physical modes of punitive action against recalcitrant group members. The cold shoulder has been refined as a substitute for the whipping post. Symbolic punishments have come to be employed as seriously as material ones. Member acceptance rather than group enforcement is becoming the principal technique by which politicizing groups endeavor to keep their members socialized.

CONFLICT PREFERENCES

American attitudes toward political conflict are perhaps better described by the term "acceptance" than "preference." Conflict is viewed as a relatively normal part of social and political life. Rules of the game as constraints upon conflict behavior are generally deemed desirable. Students of cross-cultural sports activity would undoubtedly discover interesting similarities in the recreational and political contests within different cultures; the two-sided team encounters, for example, in American baseball, football, and basketball provide an explicit cultural setting for the contests between political parties. There is also a propensity in American political life to "share the payoffs," that is, for devising imputations.

With respect to states of information found in American politics, there seems to be a perverse enjoyment of imperfect information, a special kind of excitement that comes with uncertainty about the outcomes of detective tales, spy thrillers, and general elections.

Perhaps the most ambivalent American attitude with respect to political conflict relates to war. Ideologically, in endless public declarations, Americans assert themselves to be a peace-loving people. Yet the evidence seems to demonstrate that it is a people easily roused to violence and ready to make war under certain circumstances. In this regard one source of confusion for most Americans is that modern warfare may be changing in character more rapidly than traditional American rationales for maintaining or employing arms.

The Normalcy of Conflict

Henry Adams complained bitterly that competition is "The Great American Idol." In many areas of American life he found competition valued as a laudatory form of social conduct—in business, in education, in politics, and even in relations between siblings and between spouses.

Another typical attitude toward conflict—moralistic in emphasis —may be read in the words of President Johnson on July 27, 1967, as he responded in a national address to the two weeks of ghetto rioting that had just occurred in Newark and Detroit.

The only genuine, long-range solution for what has happened lies in an attack—mounted at every level—upon the conditions that breed despair and violence. All of us know what those conditions are: ignorance, discrimination, slums, poverty, disease, not enough jobs. We should attack these conditions—not because we are frightened by conflict, but because we are fired by conscience.

The President's National Advisory Commission on Civil Disorders, decrying the fact that "discrimination and segregation have long permeated much of American life; they now threaten the future of every American," similarly observed in the introduction to its report:

> Violence cannot build a better society. Disruption and disorder nourish repression, not justice. They strike at the freedom of every citizen. The community cannot—it will not—tolerate coercion and mob rule.

> Violence and destruction must be ended—in the streets of the ghetto and in the lives of people.

In these statements neither President Johnson nor the Commission condemned conflict per se. What the President condemned was "the conditions that breed despair and violence." What the Commission disapproved was the notion that violence could be a technique for building a better society. Americans tend to be willing and ready to live with conflict, particularly if morally rationalized; they simply prefer forms of conflict less costly than violence.

The Utility of Rules

Americans are rule makers as well as rule breakers. Rules *for* as well as *of* the game are generally deemed desirable. Perhaps the principal utility of rules is in the breaking of them. The community that will not allocate resources to defend the constraints demanded in its own rules does *not*, by definition, have rules. The rules as written into law and regulation simply set forth in language the conditions under which the community may be expected to expend resources to defend its integrity. Breaches of rules are often tests of community willingness to expend resources. Such tests are themselves resources. To accept arson and riot as legitimate methods of protest, for example, is to acknowledge that the community provides no cheaper form of dissent. The breaking of a community's rules regarding arson and riot, therefore, is a way of testing the community's own evaluations on this matter. The poorly supported rule may not be considered a loss by the community, but it will certainly be interpreted as a gain by those who conducted the test.

Politics and Other Games

Baseball is the American game, emphasizing team coordination, short-run strategies, and showmanship. Americans tend to respond with most excitement to simplified, dichotomized confrontations. This may in part explain the unity of popular responses to Pearl Harbor and the Cuban missile crisis with their single easily recognized enemy as contrasted to the diffuse response to the Vietnam War with its vague enemy and uncertain objectives.

The game style of the Soviet Union, on the other hand, is of a different kind. The Russians are *aficionados* of chess, a contest between individual adversaries requiring long-run strategies, military-like maneuvers, and cool reason. Until recently, foreign policy making by the Soviet Union was also predominantly a one-man "game." Soviet strategies have been millennial, that is, more concerned with the long-run. With the exception of Khrushchev's personal showmanship, Soviet leadership has been remarkably impervious to audience and lacking in flair. Soviet public performance during conflict crises tends to be almost rote in style, repetitive in content, and often self-defeating in inflexibility. While entertainment and humor are an important aspect of American political competition, and often a relief from the intensity of that competition, these attributes are rarely found in the public comments of Soviet leaders.

While it may be easy to overdraw the relationship between American attitudes toward its political and other games, analogies and similarities do appear. If fun-and-games is a pervasive part of American life, including its politics, these preferences may also in part explain why the tension level among American politicians is lower than, say, that likely to be found in the Soviet Union.

Share the Payoff

"Total victory" is a suspect phrase among Americans. For example, President Roosevelt drew sharp criticism when he insisted upon the complete defeat of the Axis during World War II. Proponents of all-out victory in Vietnam, as another example, have attracted little support. Sports and commercial contests are characterized by second, third, and lesser prizes rather than by exclusive first prizes only. The popularity of share-the-wealth programs throughout American history may be another indication that Americans prefer non-zero-sum games.

This preference is a significant correlate of the political skills involved in producing compromises, creating coalitions, and "making everybody happy." Yet, it should be emphasized, that payoffs in the typical American political game do *not* usually give *equal shares* of the imputation to all members of the winning team. Instead, there is a ranking of prizes—president, vice-president, etc.—that makes it feasible to share unequally. With the existence of a first prize and the possibility of unequal sharing, a large degree of flexibility in negotiation and contest is possible. Of course capture of the first prize carries with it a zero-sum, winner-take-all quality that adds a certain sweetness and clarity of leadership to the winner's victory. It also facilitates the reduction of many choices to a manageable two. But the availability of second, third, and other prizes helps alleviate the bitterness of defeat and leaves open the possibility of further coalitioning for the next phase of the conflict. Above all, if there is something for nearly everybody in the game, the game is likely to endure long beyond its present players.

Information and Mystery

Americans often manifest boredom and hostility toward complete predictability. One sarcastic reaction to public opinion poll forecasts of election results, for example, is: "Why have the election at all?" Often enough, election upsets are a source of delight to the losers as well as the winners. There is an American inclination to enjoy mystery, that is, imperfect information. Suspense is a saleable condition, witness the overwhelming popularity of "whodunits" and spy thrillers.

Notice the difference in public reaction to a candidate who very early announces himself as available and to the one who for weeks and months hints that he is "thinking about it." Toward the first public attention rapidly dissipates; toward the second attention remains high and titillated. This same preference for suspense may affect the presentation of a program of government action in some field of public policy. The general program for American withdrawal from Vietnam, for example, was undoubtedly settled late in 1967 during the Johnson Administration. Despite the many contingent circumstances that were expected to surround each phase of the withdrawal, the main plan was well understood at that time. In the press, however, each phase is dealt with as a surprising new event.

War as Conflict

American attitudes toward international war are complex and ambivalent. This has been the case historically and in today's nuclear age. The American historical experience is, of course, filled with warfare of many kinds: revolutionary war, maritime war, civil war, frontier wars, territorial wars with neighbors (Mexico for example), territorial wars with distant nations (Spain), two world wars, and two "containment" wars (in Korea and Vietnam). Yet, the nation has always been a base for some of the world's most influential peace movements. Large segments of political leadership and citizenry have been devoted to the promotion of institutions of world government, such as the League of Nations and the United Nations. "Price tags," which the nation has been willing to pay, have been frequently placed by war-time leaders upon the unpleasant alternatives to war: a world unsafe for democracies (World War I); a world subservient to Axis tyranny (World War II); a world in which no small nation may be safe from an aggressive neighbor (Korean War); a war to prevent future wars (Vietnam).

American pacifism is also attested by the rapid demobilizations that have followed each of its military engagements until the end of World War II. The demobilization that was started at that time was quickly reversed in response to the behaviors of the Soviet Union. Since then such novelties as universal military service have become enduring and unpleasant aspects of American life.

Americans take special pride in having lost no wars and have consistently interpreted their involvements in international wars as moral and heroic enterprises. The Korean and Vietnamese conflicts, however, have produced widespread uneasiness about American military engagement. These two wars have been "untraditional" in their lack of clear confrontation with an explicit enemy our own size. The image of the greatest military power in the world fighting the small nations of North Korea and North Vietnam persists despite the clear involvement of the Chinese and Soviet Communists on the other side. Neither war has had the traditional declaration of war. Both wars have taken place at a time in history when all nations should presumably be deferring to the peace-keeping functions of a new world organization, the United Nations.

Thus, important American attitudes about war as conflict have, in contemporary situations, run into ambiguous circumstances creating national cognitive dissonance. Disturbing questions produce this dissonance. If the American people dislike war, why has this nation been a principal warrior in two costly "small wars"? If the United States is the protector of small nations, why has it sustained such heavy attacks against the small nations of North Korea and North Vietnam? If the United States so strongly supports world government, why has it interceded between the United Nations and the parties to "local" wars in the Far East and elsewhere?

Questions such as these ignore such elements in the case as the Soviet Union, Communist China, "wars of national liberation," the military incapacity of the United Nations, and similar difficulties. Nor are those who put these questions necessarily malevolent or unpatriotic. The questions simply reflect some of the grounds for contemporary American confusion in its attitudes toward war as a method of political conflict. Whether American political leadership can successfully introduce less violent methods of conflict into world affairs remains to be seen.

Name Index

Subject Index